A-3

Women in Comedy

Women in Comedy

by Linda Martin
and Kerry Segrave

Citadel Press   Secaucus, New Jersey

Published by Citadel Press
a division of Lyle Stuart Inc.
120 Enterprise Ave., Secaucus, N.J. 07094
In Canada: Musson Book Company
a division of General Publishing Co. Limited
Don Mills, Ontario

Manufactured in the United States of America

Library of Congress Cataloging-in-Publication Data

Martin, Linda, 1950–
   Women in comedy.

   Bibliography: p.
   1. Women comedians—United States—Biography.
2. Actresses—United States—Biography. I. Segrave,
Kerry, 1944–   . II. Title.
PN2285.M347   1986   792.2'3'0922   [B]   86-23206
ISBN 0-8065-1000-5

Contents

PREFACE   11

WOMEN AND HUMOR   13

1860 to 1919

INTRODUCTION   24

LOTTA CRABTREE   38

MAY IRWIN   42

MARIE DRESSLER   47

TRIXIE FRIGANZA   55

IRENE FRANKLIN   57

ELSIE JANIS   59

NORA BAYES   64

EVA TANGUAY   68

SOPHIE TUCKER   75

BEATRICE HERFORD   80

RUTH DRAPER   82

MABEL NORMAND   86

LOUISE FAZENDA   93

POLLY MORAN   97

The 1920's and 1930's

INTRODUCTION   100

FANNY BRICE   108

CHARLOTTE GREENWOOD   116

BEATRICE LILLIE   121

MOLLY PICON   128

GRACIE FIELDS 130
DUNCAN SISTERS 136
HELEN KANE 139
BELLE BARTH 141
GRACIE ALLEN 142
JANE ACE 153
GERTUDE BERG 159
MINERVA PIOUS 164
JUDY CANOVA 166
MAE WEST 173
THELMA TODD 191
ZASU PITTS 193
PATSY KELLY 198

The 1940's and 1950's

INTRODUCTION 203
CASS DALEY 206
MINNIE PEARL 210
ANNA RUSSELL 214
NANCY WALKER 219
CAROL CHANNING 225
JUDY HOLLIDAY 229
MARTHA RAYE 236
IMOGENE COCA 245
JOAN DAVIS 253
LUCILLE BALL 263
EVE ARDEN 277
MARIE WILSON 284
JACKIE "MOMS" MABLEY 288
JEAN CARROLL 293
KAYE BALLARD 296
PAT CARROLL 299
ELAINE MAY 301

The 1960's to the Present

INTRODUCTION 308
TOTIE FIELDS 320
ANNE MEARA 322
CAROL BURNETT 325
PHYLLIS DILLER 337

JOAN RIVERS 344

GOLDIE HAWN 356

RUTH BUZZI 363

LILY TOMLIN 366

GILDA RADNER 380

ANDREA MARTIN 386

BETTE MIDLER 389

MADELINE KAHN 398

SUZANNE RAND 400

MARILYN SOKOL 403

ZORA RASMUSSEN 406

ELAYNE BOOSLER 409

SANDRA BERNHARD 411

LIZ TORRES 413

MARSHA WARFIELD 415

WHOOPI GOLDBERG 416

ROBIN TYLER 419

SOURCES 424

PREFACE

This book presents profiles of superstars in the field of female comedy and covers the period from 1860 to the present. Our selection criterion was based on whether or not the women were known exclusively as comedians, or achieved their greatest fame in that field. We have excluded actresses who through the course of their careers may have played a number of comedy roles but who remained primarily actresses. The book is divided into four time periods and we have placed each woman in the era when she first reached comic stardom or enjoyed her greatest fame. Some of these women were famous over several decades.

Our list may not be complete enough for some people, but few, if any, of these women could be omitted from a list of famous female comics. Some had careers spanning over half a century, some only for a few years, but all have earned their place in the ranks of comic superstars. The only exception might be some of those who have emerged recently. More time will have to pass before their impact can be fully assessed. Some people draw a distinction between comic, comedian, and clown. Although we recognize these distinctions, for the purposes of this book we have used the terms interchangeably. The women profiled were ones who have made us laugh, which was our only consideration.

When one thinks about female comedians, the slogan "nobody chooses this job" comes to mind. Virtually none of the women in this book started out with the idea of being a comic. Many wanted to be actresses, preferably the pretty ingenue who landed the handsome leading man. It was considered unladylike for women to do physical humor, and unfeminine for them to do hard-edged verbal satire, because of its aggressive qualities. Women in the field of comedy have always been, and remain, a scarce commodity. This scarcity has also been due to the old myth that women have no sense of humor. This has made entry into the field of comedy harder for women.

11

The nature of comedy as a weapon sets it apart from other forms of entertainment such as dancing or singing, and has also made difficult the entry and acceptance of women as comic performers. Men have never taken kindly, and still don't, to the notion of being poked fun at by the sex which they traditionally considered inferior.

The images presented by these women over the years have waxed and waned, mirroring the conditions of women in society in general. When women were making gains towards equality, the female comedians expanded the range and depth of their material. During times when a retrenchment took place, when female gains were halted or rolled back, most women comedians were confined to negative images such as the "dumb" female.

The idea that women have no sense of humor has been around for a very long time and is still prevalent today. However, the women within the pages of this book all emphatically refute that old and lame canard.

Women and Humor

———◆◆———

Can women sing? Can women dance? Can women act? These are obviously silly questions, as well as being sexist. Such questions have never been seriously asked, nor should they be. A look at the entertainment business reveals that both sexes are fairly and evenly represented among singers, dancers, and actors. Women may or may not face other problems, such as a dearth of parts for females, or a lower salary than a man for an equivalent performance. But women do have equal opportunity in show business.

The field of comedy, however, is an entirely different matter. Female comics are, and have always been, a scarce commodity. The most popular explanation for this lack of representation is that women are just not funny. They don't laugh at jokes, nor do they create them. Raising the question: Can women be funny? or, Do women have a sense of humor? produces a debate that never arises in connection with a question like, Can women sing?

The subject of women and humor has gone back a long way, and has remained an issue. It was discussed in 1901, and is still a topic of interest today. For whatever reasons, society in general has thrown up a huge resistance to the idea that females can be comedians.

Traditionally women were not supposed to be funny; it wasn't ladylike behavior. The following opinion from a 1909 newspaper gave an indication of the relationship between humor and women. "Take women as a separate and distinct specie and you do not find much in her to arouse your sense of humor. . . . Measured by the ordinary standards of humor she is about as comical as a crutch. . . . A woman was made to be loved and fondled . . . she certainly was not made to be laughed at."

Writing in the January 12, 1901 issue of *Harper's Bazaar*, a man named Constant Coquelin felt a woman's sense of humor made her companionable but duty compelled her to conceal it. "For woman does not try to be funny. She leaves that to man." Coquelin decided that women didn't laugh at some jokes because their humor was both more sensitive and less broad than that found in the male. Regarding female humor Coquelin felt, "It encourages more often than it creates."

In the July 1902 issue of the same magazine another male writer came to a similar conclusion, arguing that a female's appreciation of comedy was more refined than man's. Females didn't laugh as much because their perception of the ridiculous was overpowered by their sympathy for the victim. The tears of sorrow overwhelmed the tears of laughter.

This idea of a gender division of humor was carried to an even further degree in *Atlantic* (December, 1922), this time by a woman, Elizabeth Trotter. She echoed her predecessors by claiming that females didn't respond to sarcastic humor or ridicule due to their sensitive nature. They couldn't, of course, create such humor either.

For Trotter the natural order of things divided humor along gender lines. "To men belong of right the more obvious sorts; the witty speech, full of ridicule, irony and satire; the rollicking joke; the jest which has become an institution — like the mother-in-law or the inter-city joke; and last, the funny story!" When you think about it that's about everything. To females she accorded the ability to embellish a narrative with imagination, sometimes the gift of mimicry, and most telling of all, "the ability to talk diverting nonsense."

Men were said to aspire openly and honorably to the title "Humorist" but not so for women. Regarding that title: "It is a fact that no woman covets it at its present value, or could have it bestowed upon her without being shamefaced about it."

A couple of years later (*New Republic,* November 26, 1924) Mary Austin informed her readers of the differences between the sexes. The proper forum for women's comedy on stage lay in imitation. Females were more humorless than males due to "the slower response of women to the humor of surprise." For Austin this distinction was "possibly biological" and was rooted in the fact that man, the ancient hunter, had always to be ready for the unexpected at every turn and thus had superior skill at this type of comedy. On the other hand, the female had "to keep still and hold steady," which supposedly explained the difference. According to Austin, this difference went back a long way, to "the age of grass-thatched huts."

The bawdy joke, noted Austin, has always been taboo for women, and would always remain so. Females didn't respond to such humor and were completely inhibited in its presence due to the "re-patterning of the neuroses of the woman by the double experience of mating and maternity."

While most of Austin's comments were considerably off the mark, she did hit on something with more than a little truth in it. And that was the idea that it was part of the code of life that man, with his pride, could not be laughed at by his women. Women did not laugh at such jokes, nor did they make them. It was the function of the mother/wife to afford a man a respite from the competition and stress of life and provide "the relief of uncritical response."

Although the writer felt a woman might get around this in certain narrow ways, such as making an individual man the butt of a joke in fiction writing, the general proscription held. Females could never offer a humorous critical treatment of, for example, politics or political figures, all male at the time, of course. This proscription of women making fun of men had the force of another "ancient taboo."

For the first quarter of the twentieth century, then, women were considered to be generally lacking in as keen a sense of humor as that found in the male. Remarkably, though, female comics of that period were proving just what women could do in comedy and were moving forward in a positive fashion to develop and expand their material. Unfortunately this was short-lived. The period from roughly 1930 to the early 1960's would see comediennes regressing to stereotypical roles. These submissive roles would be reflected in the answers to the ever-recurring question: "Do women have a sense of humor?"

During this second span of time the answers would be even less charitable than previously, as men sought to roll back any gains women had made, dominate the comedy field, and project women in a negative and demeaning fashion.

Margaretta Newell (*Outlook and Independent,* October 14, 1931) asked her readers: "What makes us duller than the dullest male." In part she felt it was the fact that it was cruel for a woman to laugh when a strong man suffered. Such laughter would show a lack of sympathy, and possibly endanger the material support provided by the male. She also believed that women's sense of humor was blunted by being so circumscribed. It was fine to laugh at men's jokes, in order to draw them out or boost their egos, but that was the only appropriate time for laughter.

Newell also considered the working women who were financially independent, and therefore not obliged to laugh at male humor. However, she found these women to be equally dour. "The women are as unequal to poking fun as the Dumb Doras of the home." She attributed this to the fact that they were engaged in a pioneering venture, working outside the home, and the associated stresses and strains compelled these people to be overly serious.

According to Newell, the issue went deeper, though, and revolved around the idea of courage. Men were prone to crack jokes during times calling for courage, and women lacked this trait. A female would not laugh at another woman's joke since she felt it would strengthen the hand of a potential rival for a man's attention, while laughing at a man's joke would enhance her own position.

The solution for Newell lay in developing courage, and since that depended on danger, women would have to welcome danger. Newell suggested that women should demand the right to join the Marines, and to have equal representation on the next polar expedition. Other absurd advice included; "A female fire-brigade, and an international sisterhood of broncobusters." Newell hoped that "it will come to pass in time that women will develop a sense of humor."

In 1951 writer Robert Allen (*Maclean's,* June 1, 1951) found himself confused by the issue. He discovered that females laughed either at the wrong time or failed to laugh at all. He had done extensive experimenting on his own wife and daughters, and assorted other females, using a variety of different types and styles of humor, and admitted to not understanding the female sense of humor.

This lack was attributed to the all-too-practical and realistic natures of women, and their mental images. These images were crucial to humor because they were limited to "mental pictures of new living-room drapes, wall paints, cute little spring suits." Jokes told by men did not focus on these concerns.

Allen apparently hadn't heard of, or didn't subscribe to, the theory that women always laughed at men's jokes to curry favor. In the end Allen decided to limit his joke-telling to all-male audiences, as he concluded that "Women have no sense of humor . . . wit and women just don't mix."

This article was considered important enough to be condensed in *Reader's Digest* magazine (April, 1964). Most interesting about that was the fact that it appeared in the *Digest* almost thirteen full years after it was first published. This was an exceedingly unusual practice for the magazine. Most of its articles appeared in the condensed version within a few months of the original publication, and a rare few over a year later. But not thirteen years later!

This illustrated perhaps the timelessness of the idea and the need to present it again in a different decade, to a new audience just at a period when the image of the female comic was beginning to be liberated. This condensed article was one of the last-ditch efforts to hold back that tide.

Writing at the same time as Allen, humorist James Thurber (*Maclean's,* June 1, 1951) outlined some of his problems in dealing with unsolicited material sent to him by would-be female humorists. Addressing himself to an anonymous Miss G.H., but presumably meant for all aspiring women, Thurber concluded, "Why don't you become a bacteriologist, or a Red-Cross nurse, or a Wave, like all the other girls."

One of the harsher judgments on the issue was rendered by Sarel Eimerl (*Mademoiselle,* November, 1962) who drew an analogy with the posh Plaza Hotel's being open equally to the rich and the poor, stating that, "a woman who really makes one laugh is about as easy to find as a pauper taking his Sunday brunch in the Edwardian Room." She claimed there were no standup comics of the likes of Benny or Hope, no female story tellers, mimics or clowns to match the men, and that the idea of a "Marx Sisters" was ludicrous.

Eimerl named six female clowns, Channing, Coca, Burnett, Walker, Ballard and Diller, and felt they worked desperately hard for a laugh by torturing their bodies and distorting their faces. She felt they were obviously uneasy in the field of comedy and were overcompensating. While they put up a terrific physical struggle for each laugh, Eimerl concluded, these six women combined "came out about even with the sum total of laughs Jackie Gleason or Jack Benny can draw without moving a muscle."

The current crop of comediennes were, said Eimerl, "at best, unglamorous; at worst, fairly gruesome . . . or generally ugly." Being a woman and a comic were incompatible, and the comediennes knew it. Since the accepted idea of a sexy woman was the shy ingenue type, it followed that most women connected being kooky with being unattractive, and that the only thing that would compel a female to trade off whatever sexuality she possessed for kookiness was a "sense of desperation." Such despair stemmed from being physically unattractive. Eimerl did concede that a few women could combine sex appeal and comedy, citing Judy Holliday and Lucille Ball as examples, but they were few and far between. She failed to mention that both of those performers were firmly entrenched in the "scatterbrain" mold.

Eimerl quoted a female writer on the Perry Como television variety show, Selma Diamond, as arguing that women would have a better chance in comedy if the system were not stacked in favor of men. However, Eimerl then marshalled evidence to try and show that this was not, in fact, the case. According to the man in charge of talent at NBC, Dave Tebert, women had the same chance as men. The problem was that female standup comics were not aggressive enough or forceful enough to deal with the drunks and hecklers often found in the audience.

Lest someone should argue that females could be as funny as men, in private and away from the professional arena with its associated pressures, Eimerl had evidence to the contrary. She used the example of the Jack Paar late-night television talk show, forerunner of Johnny Carson. According the Eimerl, the Paar show was hospitable to all types of comedians and very informal, just like a home living-room. Despite this, Eimerl had no trouble concluding how the battle fared—the men "are funnier."

The talent coordinator on the Paar show was Bob Shanks, who was said to have been conscious of the need for female comics on the show. Apparently he searched New York City in an effort to find comediennes. When a potential candidate was found, she was invited to have a very informal interview with Shanks. There were no lights, audience, or cameras to generate any type of pressure situation and thus purportedly provided the best of all possible environments for these aspiring comedians. But still there were "almost no 'amusing' women." In the space of three years, Shanks interviewed about 500 women but passed only twenty of them.

By Shank's account "the wit was missing." While allowing that the females were often intelligent and pleasant, he found them not to be good story-tellers, unable to make the most of their experiences in their comedy, and lacking in "quickness of response." Shanks conceded that social conditioning was such that if a girl was funny she was advised to drop that particular attribute and repress her humorous talents.

Eimerl was all for this repression, noting that school girls who were funny may have dazzled the boys but would shake their confidence as well. Comedy was performance arising from skill and wit, and performance was a male role. Funny girls would not be asked out on dates. Since going to the junior prom was more important than being witty, comedy should be submerged.

"The creation of comedy, wit, and humor involves highly complex thought processes," concluded Eimerl. But women with real savvy repressed their comedy skills. Those who didn't, didn't know what was good for them. They would lose out with men and would be labeled "odd women."

John Fisher, in a 1973 book on English music halls, devoted a chapter to the eternal question, "Are Women Funny?" Noting the lack of comediennes, he commented, "Jokes as such hang uneasily on feminine lips, while knockabout is even more unbecoming." He considered Gracie Fields as basically a singer who "happened to lapse into comedy," while he couldn't imagine Gracie Allen being funny alone, without George Burns.

Fisher's perspective in the 1970's was much like his predecessors, but generally there was a change in that decade, coinciding with a trend to more aggressive female comics in the business. Writers began to concentrate on the socializing processes which inhibited comedy in females. It was ultimately the aggressive, manipulative, and sociopolitical aspects of humor that set it apart from singing or dancing.

Both Naomi Weisstein (*Ms.*, May, 1974) and Anne Beatts, writer for the television comedy show "Saturday Night Live" (*Mademoiselle*, November, 1975), agreed that the myth about women having no sense of humor was still strong. Both stressed the idea that a young girl or teenager was subjected by role pressures to laugh at a boy's jokes. Being popular and getting dates meant you didn't hog the conversation, you got the boy to talk about himself, and you laughed at his jokes, in the same way you let him beat you at sports.

The only funny girls Beatts remembered from her school days were not "real" girls. They were overweight, or handicapped in some way. Real girls didn't have an active sense of humor. They displayed only passive humor, by laughing at the jokes of boys. The boys were the football players while the girls became cheerleaders. It was the males who performed while the females stood on the sidelines and applauded. Beatts's experience was that if she was funny she couldn't be a girl, and if she was a girl she couldn't be funny.

Comedy is aggressive and hard. Women are not supposed to be hard. They are supposed to be nice to men, children, and animals. Being pervasively nice is not conducive to comedy which requires satire and ridicule. Women who do break through into comedy are branded with all sorts of unpleasant labels, such as strident, dyke, or frustrated. Men who skillfully poke fun at women are called insightful, great comics. Women who poke fun at men are ball-busters or man-haters. Women are not even safe poking fun at other women. They are considered anti-female or catty as in the case of Joan Rivers. When women are funny, men become scared. As Beatts commented, it's because "knowing that humor is the best of weapons, they're reluctant to put it into our hands. Maybe they think we'll be funnier than they are."

Samuel Janus, a New York psychologist, who has been studying comics for years, noted that "Humor, effectively used, is a most potent source of power; it is especially needed and adopted by those who have no other 'recognizable' form of power. Minority groups have long seized upon comedy as the expression of their will and power. The ability to make a person laugh with them, not at them, is a vital one."

Discussing the low number of female comics in the 1980's, Janus concluded: "The fact that women in comedy account for, at most, 12 percent of the field, whereas in all the other areas of show business they represent at least 50 percent of the population, attests to their lack of credibility as a power figure."

One of the functions of humor is political comment. It can be used by the overclass to maintain inequalities of race, class, or sex. It is ridicule of the powerless. "It serves to put whoever it is in their place by showing that they can't be taken seriously, that they're too stupid or dumb or ugly or childlike or smelly or mean to count as human."

Jokes, however, can also be used by the underclass as a means of survival in which the group adopts a rebellious humor to share their common misery and poke fun at their oppressors. Examples are Jewish humor and black humor. Lenny Bruce once had a routine about Jews and blacks being natural comics because it was valuable to them as a survival tactic. If you entertained your oppressor you might not have to work as hard.

Ridicule has become acceptable in the context that it was all right to attack a group as long as you were a member of that group. Richard Pryor does a lot of jokes about blacks, while Mel Brooks does a lot of jokes about Jews. Female comics naturally have done a lot of jokes about women. Consider the storm of protest that would erupt if Brooks did Pryor's material or Pryor did Brooks's stuff. Yet men have always been able to ridicule women and get away with it.

As Weisstein has noted, there was no such tradition of rebellious female humor. While it is true that women did jokes about their own gender, it was self-deprecating, not insurrectionary. The development of rebellious humor required individuals of the group to come together, to recognize their victimization and move on from there. Women in groups had not traditionally been productive in that sense. It was often assumed that if a group of women were socializing together, it was not what they really wanted to be doing. They were together almost by default. Either they couldn't attract a man, were waiting for a man, or their men wanted to be away from them at that particular time. Women were socialized to believe that their lives should revolve around men. They were also trained to regard other women not as sisters, but as potential rivals. Women were expected to be charming, which meant "being beautiful, passive, accepting, and mute." Being funny would not get you a man.

Weisstein also noted that women have been often defined as "ridiculous persons." This image does not lend itself to rebellious humor. In other words, women have frequently been the object or butt of jokes.

The development of a rebellious humor also depended on members of the oppressed group having a knowledge of a common oppressor. This helped individuals realize their own harsh circumstances were not due to personal inferiority or character defects but inflicted on all members of the group. For women though, there has been little of that knowledge.

As a result many of the jokes told by female comics have been self-disparaging. In an experiment reported by Joan B. Levine (*Journal of Communication,* 1976), it was found that "females indulge in self-deprecatory humor to a greater extent than do males." The recordings of four male and four female comics were studied for self-disparagement. These comics included Totie Fields, Moms Mabley, Phyllis Diller, Lily Tomlin, George Carlin, Robert Klein, Bill Cosby and David Steinberg. "The data showed women deprecated themselves 63 percent of the time; males railed against their own individual shortcomings in a total of 12 percent of their cuts. The men may make more jibes against their gender, but not at their own expense . . . Unless more research reveals a different etiology for the genesis of self-deprecatory humor, it can be surmised that comediennes are echoing the values of their social milieu in order to attract and keep a mass audience."

In 1976 Joanne Cantor, a professor of communications at the University of Wisconsin, found that both men and women thought jokes ridiculing women were funnier than those ridiculing men. Women, moreover, showed no loyalty to their sex. In fact, they enjoyed these kind of jokes more than men did.

Researchers Dolf Zillman and S. Holly Stocking (*Journal of Communication,* 1976) offered an explanation for this preference. "Because of its apparently negative consequences for 'machismo,' self-disparagement holds little promise for the male. Even when presented in a humorous fashion, it gives little cause to rejoice, for the blow to the male ego may be too serious a matter to warrant laughter. For the female, on the other hand, humorous self-disparagement, as a clever form of submission which apparently pleases others, may hold considerable appeal."

Zillman and Stocking speculated that men found self-disparagement by females less funny than women did because "the traditional role of the female has been to serve as a convenient target for disparaging assaults, and that, as she disparages herself, she takes the fun out of the game she is supposed to play. It seems not good enough to witness the female being put down. The fun, apparently lies in seeing someone else give it to her."

Losco and Epstein, researchers at the University of Wisconsin, in 1975 published results of a study testing 100 subjects for their reactions to certain cartoons. "Both sexes," they reported "preferred cartoons in which the butt of the joke was a female. Male subjects failed to see the humor in a cartoon which depicted an officious male receiving his comeuppance from a female, but rated as very funny a similar cartoon in which the sexes were reversed. Female subjects showed no such bias."

Ugly and dumb had become the standard images for female comics. While it may have been true that some comediennes were fat or plain, many were attractive if not downright beautiful. Appearance was irrelevant in any case. Fat comics like Dom DeLuise or plain comics like Don Rickles were not continually harping on their looks.

As for the dumbbell stereotype, Samuel Janus has found comics of both sexes to be in the bright-average to genius-level of intelligence.

There is nothing wrong with self-disparaging gags. In humor everything is a target. Even the grossest handicapped joke can be funny. What is disturbing is when self-disparagement of females becomes a norm, and the stereotype of dumb and ugly becomes so pervasive that it is believed to be true.

Women in comedy are becoming more conscious of self put-downs. Many have been analyzing their material and trying to move towards a "woman's humor." The phrase is used cautiously. Female comics don't want to be ghetto-ized. If their work is judged separately from that of men's, the implication would be that they can't compete on the same level, and that their output is inferior.

Yet female comics and their audiences appreciate a shared feminine experience. As writer Kathleen Fury has commented, this type of material "provides the laughter of recognition: 'Oh yes, I've been there. I know about that.'" This humor in no way excludes men. Males can identify with the jokes by relating them to their own wives, girlfriends, mothers, and sisters. Or they can be angered by a joke if they find themselves the target.

A major goal of feminism is to end discrimination. Females have a difficult struggle ahead of them to achieve equal representation in comedy. Their low numbers attest to the deeply entrenched prejudices which society has shown towards women comics.

One consolation is that psychologists like Seymour and Rhoda Fisher and Waleed Salameh, who have intensively interviewed comedians, have found no differences between the sexes. Commenting about the female standup comics he studied, Salameh concluded that they "had the same personality profile, aspirations, self-image, creative outlook and ability as the men."

1860 to 1919

INTRODUCTION

The entry of both women and men into comedy in particular, and the entertainment field in general, was dependent on the development of the mass entertainment business. This development took place during the middle part of the 1800's, roughly from the period 1830 to 1860. Prior to that time the self-contained act which toured independently was all but nonexistent, due, for one reason, to a sparse population divided up into small cities.

More important was the transportation problem prior to about 1840. Roads were few and far between and macadamized streets were only a few decades old. The railroad did not then exist and travel was long, difficult, and dangerous. It was hardly fit for man or woman. Entertainment was provided largely by local or resident companies. Touring was generally out of the question, although showboats had toured with some variety entertainment as early as the 1830's.

The period from 1830 to 1860 brought a number of important changes to America which facilitated the development of the self-contained, independent act, as well as mass entertainment as a whole. One was the transportation revolution wrought by the train, which made travel much faster and safer and made trips possible to previously inaccessible places. In this period the population of the United States doubled and larger cities began to spring up.

This led to a demand for more entertainment as urban people found themselves with a certain amount of leisure time. In earlier times, this leisure would have been spent in pursuits more common to country spaces and small hamlets, such as walks in the woods, quilting bees, or games in open areas. The new cities made these activities more difficult, and the populace was ready to turn to other leisure pursuits as variety shows got off to a tentative start.

The composition of the population determined the type of entertainment—and humor—that took place on the stage. Much of the increase in population came from immigration from various European countries. Cities also absorbed many people from the rural areas of America. In 1850 some 17 percent of the population was illiterate.

While this diverse group did have some leisure time, they didn't have much money. The variety entertainment that sprang up thus had to meet several needs if it was to be successful. It had to first of all be cheap, and due to the high rate of illiteracy and the immigrant's confusion with the English language it had to be simple; it had to appeal to the lowest common denominator. And it had to appeal to men, since they made up virtually the entire audience.

Women were expected to be submissive homemakers, motherly and retiring, while actors were seen as immoral, vulgar and exhibitionist. Thus entertainment was not a fit career choice for women, nor did they venture out to become part of the audience. One of the reasons men went out was to escape the Victorian domestic life.

The first variety-type entertainment to develop was the minstrel show in 1842 in New York City, performed by whites in blackface. By the 1850's the concert saloon had emerged in various cities and offered entertainment along with the booze, largely to increase alcohol sales. These saloons quickly came to dominate the entertainment scene. The atmosphere was an all-masculine one, and rowdy. Customers drank, smoked, swore, talked obscenely, chewed tobacco and spat. They were quick to show their displeasure with what was taking place on stage by stomping their feet, booing and hissing. Customers apparently were drawn from all walks and social stations of life.

In these concerts saloons women were a fixture, but as the drink servers. Their job was to drink and flirt with the men, and hustle drinks, since they were paid a percentage of what they managed to sell. These women were often as big a draw as the stage entertainment. Not all of them were prostitutes but most were, and the resultant association of the concert saloon with prostitution further lowered the reputation of these places, along with variety entertainment and performers in general. There were said to be "no virtuous girls in the concert saloon."

The result was a public outcry against such establishments in the 1860's. Astute operators began to distance themselves from the situation by dropping the name "concert saloon" and substituting "variety theatre" or "variety hall." They still served drinks and catered to an all-male trade but eliminated the other undesirable features which had brought the saloons into such disrepute.

Tony Pastor, the famous vaudeville impresario, was associated with one such New York hall, the "444," as early as 1861. It was described as "low and vulgar" but apparently represented a step upward. The entertainment featured at that time included minstrel numbers, straight and comic songs, dances, acrobatics, banjo playing, and farces as afterpieces. The comedy was often "indelicate."

Women weren't doing any comedy, but they were on stage from the end of the 1850's onward, as most establishments featured a chorus line with up to a dozen members. They performed various dances in scanty outfits and did the famous can-can. The first chorus lines were recruited from an obvious source, the saloon waitresses. Many of the dances they performed were considered risqué and indecent, but to the all-male crowd their sex appeal was enjoyable.

Their initial popularity and drawing power caused their numbers to swell dramatically as other establishments set up their own chorus lines. In the early 1860's the legislature of the state of New York outlawed waitresses in concert saloons, due to the public outcry. This gave a marked boost to women, since they now had to make their living on the stage, and not as waitresses who hustled drinks.

In those days variety performers, both men and women, were all general utility performers and expected to fill in when and where needed. The specialty act, where the performer came out and just did "his thing," had yet to come to the fore. Thus by the last half of the 1860's female entertainers had become established on the stage. They all had to serve in the chorus line and the afterpiece, but the more talented among them got to perform their own specialty as well, and that was always a song or dance.

Women were not doing any comedy as solo acts, or as a member of a team. They were involved, though, in the farcical afterpieces. The latter part of the 1860's also saw the development of the male two-person act. Till then entertainers had performed either solo or in larger structured pieces such as the afterpiece, the minstrel show, or the chorus line. The two-man act caught on and became the rage by the end of that decade and into the 1870's.

The chorus line continued to be more and more popular and continued to exploit female sexuality with scantier and scantier costumes. Mark Twain, who witnessed one such chorus line, remarked that the brevity of their outfits "would make a parasol blush." The popularity of females in the chorus and the male two-person teams led somebody to do the obvious and establish a male/female team. Such teams existed by 1870, but were few in number. Such a team had the advantage of female sex appeal and of being novel.

Outside of the chorus line, women were still seen relatively infrequently on stage but were well received by the male audiences, often regardless of talent. In the time of the minstrel show's beginnings, not only did the white play the part of blacks but males also did the female roles.

The number of such male/female teams was only a handful and virtually all were husband and wife. Some of the large houses in New York City would not feature even one such pair during the course of a season in the early 1870's. Being paired with a male performer was beneficial to women, however. It provided a measure of safety from the raunchy male audience, as female entertainers were still expected to fraternize with the drinkers and "The women were looked upon as legitimate prey for anyone."

The teams did minstrel routines, songs and dances, pantomimes and immigrant dialect routines, the latter being extremely popular as a result of the wave of immigration then sweeping America. The male half of the team did the comedy; the woman entertained by dancing and/or singing, in some cases "just looking pretty." Women had no experience with comedy skills, having entered variety solely from the chorus line. Men, on the other hand, had comedy experiences and traditions and were schooled in the comedy of the tambo and bones routines which dated from the early minstrel shows.

Nor did the mixed teams deal with any domestic situations in their routines or any of the tensions between the sexes in their humor. Consideration was given only to the concerns of men, which was understandable, given the makeup of the audiences. It was said of the female halves of these few teams that they "played the role of sex object and/or assisted male performers in treating the asexual concerns of men."

Tony Pastor had made his first attempt to clean up variety as early as 1865 when in the summer of that year he established a "Family Circle" at his theater. It was to be a place where men could bring their wives and children and see respectable entertainment in a clean atmosphere. He also offered Saturday matinees and advertised them as shows that women and children could attend in safety without bringing an escort. A few women came, but not many, and those that did were described as being "rough" and of the servant class.

By the mid 1870's Pastor was admitting women free to Saturday matinees, but his idea of a mixed family audience remained just a dream. Variety continued to be unappealing to women and they mainly stayed away. Throughout the 1870's it remained virtually an all-male preserve. Respectable women of any class wouldn't attend what amounted to stag entertainment, and the performers wouldn't change their brand of humor just for the sake of a handful of women who might happen to be in the crowd.

Pastor kept working on attracting the family audience anyway, and during the last half of the 1870's began to make headway. He offered a variety of gifts and inducements to lure more women into the audience. He gave away turkeys to women, and on other designated nights held prize draws for women in the crowd; hams on Monday evenings, barrels of flour on Wednesdays, dress patterns on Fridays, and ten tons of coal on Saturday nights.

By the beginning of the 1880's Pastor had moved his theater a few times. He finally settled in a fashionable area and had established a reputation for respectability for his hall. His example led to other theaters copying his successful marketing techniques.

Pastor imposed a no-drinking and no-smoking policy. He also promised women that any masher who approached them in the audience would be thrown out. Mashers at that time received a lot of media attention and they were said to be everywhere, in parks, on buses, on the streets and "especially in theatres." Newspapers warned that if a female let down her guard for a minute she could find herself seduced or drugged and would wake up in a brothel, or on a boat bound for some white slave market in a distant country. Most women, it was said, carried hatpins for protection.

Pastor's giving away gifts and the resultant attraction of female patronage was called, "The most important moment in the development of the theatre." Disrespectable places still abounded, to be sure. The concert saloon dive survived and was still haunted by prostitutes and raunchy entertainment. Women didn't attend these, but they started, in the 1880's, to make up a sizeable portion of the audience at places like Pastor's and those of others who followed his methods. As more and more halls became respectable, female attendance soared.

The American urban population expanded greatly between 1880 and 1890, increasing by 61 percent that decade, and variety theater proliferated. Pastor, and other entrepreneurs who followed, also imposed rigid standards on the kind of material performers could use on stage. All "blue" material was strictly out of bounds. Pastor didn't enforce his rules rigorously, but others did. The raunchy low life saloon was rapidly turning into the respectable, clean, urban, middle-class vaudeville house it would remain until its demise some decades later. Booze was also disappearing from such places.

The number of female performers increased as the content of acts changed to keep pace with an audience becoming increasingly more feminine. Women still did very little on their own in comedy. The more talented and obviously comically inclined were limited to expressing humor through song, or in comedy plays on the legitimate stage, or in the afterpiece of a variety bill.

Males continued to control the humor and jokes through the two-man teams and solo acts. The humor was often broad, frantic, and slapstick and performed by men wearing loud and silly clothes, and with lots of silly props. About this time a man named Charlie Case pioneered the monologue. He came on stage dressed normally and with no props except a piece of string that he twiddled with. He told jokes and funny stories to the audience. It was an unusual style for the time, even for men.

In the mixed teams the style changed somewhat. There were more of them, though not many in absolute terms, and in many cases the female still supplied only window dressing, duded up in the stylish fashions of the day, which supposedly drew more women into the theaters. The two factors soon worked together and became equally cause and effect. More women in the audi-

ence led to more women on stage, and more female performers
put more women into the audience.

The content of the mixed act changed as well. The male still
did the comedy, but more and more attention was devoted to
domestic humor, such as the foibles of married life and the problem of lovers, and so on. And with this, women began to take on
a more important role in the mixed act.

Prior to the 1890's, the mixed act had the male doing comedy
along with dancing, acrobatics and perhaps even some juggling
while the female did a song and dance, played straight, and
displayed her good looks. As the 1890's came in, comedy was still
the man's preserve in the teams. There were no lone female comics except those who sang comic songs.

As the last decade of the nineteenth century unfolded, vaudeville, as variety then came to be called, saw a further increase in
the number of theaters and the number of mixed teams. Benjamin F. Keith was the first to popularize the word vaudeville when
he applied it to his New York Variety show in the mid 1880's. The
term is thought to have derived from Val de Vire, the river valley
in France where they had a tradition of singing bawdy songs.

The female half of the team was beginning to be picked less for
her looks and ability to wear clothes and more for her talents as a
comic foil. Economic reasons had a hand in this increase and dictated that most of these teams were married couples. Unlike the
two-man act, the married couple didn't have to split salaries and
they could thus play at a cut rate compared to the all-male
teams. A non-performing wife traveling with her husband on tour
was considered "excess baggage." There was an incentive for the
man to use his wife in his act, since two could in fact live almost
as cheaply as one. The husband would only have to go after a
slight salary raise over what he got as a solo act. The price was
right for the bookers, who got the two almost for the price of one
and were eager to cash in on the vogue for two-person teams, particularly mixed ones.

By the turn of the century such mixed teams had increased sub-
stantially. The men still wanted to handle the comedy, but that
changed slightly after the turn of the century. With more in the
field competing for jobs, a mixed team wasn't assured of work just
because of the presence of a woman. The novelty factor was
wearing off.

Thus if a woman showed talent, the man might let her get a
few laughs the first season, and maybe let her get half of them the

next year. It was just good business to maximize the effect of your act. In these years the funny women wore outlandish makeup and clothes.

In a very few cases, if the woman was exceptionally talented, the man might let her get all the laughs, as happened with Burns and Allen. But it was not an easy thing for a man to do, and was inevitably a big blow to his pride. He would be kidded mercilessly for it on the circuit by his friends. Still, the number of mixed teams where the female played straight foil vastly outnumbered the other type of mixed act. Of all the women in mixed teams that evolved out of vaudeville, only Gracie Allen attained any kind of national stature and following. The others did not outlive their times and were consigned to obscurity.

B.F. Keith and partner E.F. Albee rose to prominence with their chain of vaudeville theaters by 1900 and onward. They continued Pastor's trend to cleaning up vaudeville as the audience became more educated and middle-class. Pastor may have been slack in enforcing his rules, but Keith and Albee went at it with a vengeance. Besides imposing rigid standards on his performers and their material, Keith expected the same from his audiences. He once lectured an audience, at the intermission of one of his shows, on how to behave. Hats had to be removed, and there was to be no stomping, whistling, smoking, spitting on the floor, or crunching of peanuts. Bouncers were employed to make sure that everybody in the crowed toed the line.

Keith and others like him brought decorum and refinement to vaudeville as they catered more and more to middle-class tastes and sensibilities. Fast disappearing was the rough and tumble knockabout comedy which was truly "kick in the gut" style and appealed to the lower classes. This humor was being replaced by a more sophisticated drawing-room style with more verbal banter. This de-emphasis on crude comedy made it easier for women to participate, since role expectations did not include roughhousing. All of this was partly in response to the growing family trade in the audience. Thanks to labor-saving devices and decreasing family size, women also had more time to attend spectacles such as vaudeville.

By the first decade of this century, women were an accepted and normal part of the audience, and female performers, such as Eva Tanguay and May Irwin, stressed clothes, jewelry and cosmetics to appeal to women in the audience. While it was then considered all right for a woman to attend those spectacles, there was much more resistance to a woman becoming a performer. Evangelist Billy Sunday said, around 1910, "Young women should shun the stage as they would the bubonic plague. The conditions behind the footlights, especially for chorus girls and show girls, is something horrible."

Sketches for mixed teams were usually written by men, which further added to women's difficulties in establishing a reasonable image as creatures equal to men. One prolific writer named Will Cressy had 33 of his sketches being performed simultaneously in 1901 by various teams. All of his material reinforced the status quo: "male characters were either nobler, more sensible, or less materialistic than the women characters, who were either sillier, more designing, more helpless, or somehow had less 'character.'" These sketches must have been very reassuring to men, since the women, in effect, promised to love, honor, and obey.

The coon song had originated with the few blacks who performed on the white circuits, with roots from the minstrel era. They were treated with condescension and allowed very narrow roles. The coon song singers lampooned their own race with lyrics containing the stereotypes of the day; blacks were lazy, unreliable, general no-accounts, and so on. They had little choice but to perform these songs if they wanted to make a living on the white stage. The coon songs became so popular that whites took them over, notably May Irwin in 1895 and later Sophie Tucker and Marie Dressler. These tunes represented a backlash against blacks as the effects of their fairly new freedom were being felt, in much the same way that Irish dialect humor was rampant during the influx of the Irish. The coon songs would remain popular well into the twentieth century.

Just before the turn of the century, the "kid" character became popular with comics. It was successful because it appealed to almost anyone who liked kids, and more importantly it "offended no one." Female comics, over the decades, have continued to essay the child character more often than males, probably due to its non-threatening aspects.

This whole period of time saw a marked change in the condition of women. The old Victorian style woman was giving way to a newer, more liberated woman. The main driving focus of feminism then was suffrage. When the United States passed the 19th amendment to the Constitution in 1920, giving women the right to vote, some states had already granted that right, but most had not. Women were having fewer children and the advent of some labor-saving devices gave them more leisure time to do other things. Living in large cities, they could avail themselves of educational and cultural activities the rural farm wife of a previous decade had never dreamed about. With city public transit systems, women could come and go more easily on their own without a man. Women wanted more access to the professions, divorces were no longer unheard of, they were seeking and getting more general education, and more held jobs.

The dearth of men for the labor force during World War I gave many women a chance to work. They enjoyed having their own money, and became exposed to freer and less cumbersome clothing and hair styles. Much of the factory work women took up during the war couldn't be done in standard women's fashions and so many adopted pants and shorter hair.

It was during this period, from 1860 to 1920, against this backdrop of growing feminist consciousness, that female comedians of national repute emerged. The first female comedian was Lotta Crabtree who got her start shortly before 1860 in the far west, where, if anything, the variety halls were even raunchier than in the east. She sang, danced, did physical bits and essayed a kid character. She was in fact a kid when she started, and she stuck with the kid characterization throughout her career. She combined the innocence of childhood with a certain amount of discreet sexuality, often showing her knees on stage, which was fairly hot stuff back then.

Four more, Dressler, Irwin, Trixie Friganza, and Irene Franklin, would hit stardom before the century ended. Dressler made it in musical variety and vaudeville with impersonations, comic songs, coon songs, and a few self-deprecating shots about her weight. She turned to comedy because she felt she was too homely for anything else. She went on to a second phase of success in films around 1930. Irwin divided her time between musical plays on the legitimate stage and vaudeville, where she scored with comic songs and coon songs as well as doing fat jokes about herself. She was the first woman to do a lot of jokes on stage alone, without music.

Friganza appeared in musical comedies and vaudeville with comic songs, dances, and playing of instruments. She used a great many self-deprecating fat jokes and she also threw in the earliest image of a man chaser, although she refused to do such material after she married. Franklin did character sketches, kid routines, and comic songs in vaudeville. Doing impersonations was common enough then, but usually it was one star doing another. Franklin was one of the few who mimicked ordinary working people.

Shortly after the new century dawned, four more women emerged as superstars: Elsie Janis, Nora Bayes, Eva Tanguay, and Sophie Tucker. Janis wrote all of her own material and was a renowned mimic. She was also dominated by her mother. Bayes succeeded in vaudeville and musical comedy and along with Tanguay and Janis established the "difficult" female comic image. Tanguay was one of vaudeville's biggest stars and her electric and brazen performances on stage were events. One of the first stars to effectively use PR techniques to hype her career, she also introduced sexually suggestive material into her act. Critics loathed her, perhaps because in her aggressive and sexual performances she epitomized the American female. Tucker graduated from coon songs into comic sexual songs full of double meanings. She eventually found nightclubs to be her best medium. She also kidded herself about her weight.

Of this group of women, all except Crabtree and Janis were overweight. Being heavy though was the fashion of the times and thinness was not then worshipped as it is today. Having overweight women onstage was said to make it easier for the equally overweight matrons in the audience to identify with them. Fully half of these women used self-deprecation about their weight, even though it was stylish. This trend was more pronounced before 1900.

Some of these women began to break down barriers, writing their own material, managing their own careers, and demanding and getting other professional concessions. Salaries were truly enormous, with some getting $3,000 a week or more. Prior to World War I an average workingman worked ten hours a day for about $2. The sexual image conveyed by those like Tanguay and Tucker was of the free-spirited type, not satisfied with only one man. In their personal lives some of these women were far ahead of their times in regard to sex. They took men where they found them and dropped them as soon as they got bored, without a qualm.

By the turn of the century there were few women established as "comic talkers." This lack was due to the fact that "the male-dominated nature of early variety had created a bias that inhibited the development of female comic ability." In fact only two solo standup female comics had emerged, Herford and Draper, both true pioneers.

Draper preferred to operate as a self-contained act, doing her own bookings and appearing not as a part of a vaudeville bill but as a concert performer giving an entire show herself.

Herford, the first woman standup, did not draw praise for her accomplishments but instead received criticism from women about her material. Too demeaning to females they said. This showed the high degree of feminist consciousness at the turn of the century. Her material was much less demeaning for women than that of later comics, but it would be the 1960's before any female comics would draw the kind of feminist ire that was directed at Herford.

In style Herford and Draper were very similar. Both used few if any props and both wrote their own material. They delivered monologues in which they spoke to imaginary stage characters rather than directly to the audience. That required a lengthy buildup to a funny ending, as opposed to rapid fire one-line jokes. Generally, jokes were more popular material among standup male comics than monologues and those who did do monologues usually addressed the audience directly, as most modern monologuists do today.

This difference can be attributed to a softening effect that talking to a stage character has. It allowed audiences to be more like eavesdroppers, overhearing a conversation. This distanced the audience from the performer, so that manipulation was less overt. This technique used by Herford and Draper allowed them to use the monologue style without directly threatening the audience in an aggressive manner.

The material these two women used was quite similar in content. Largely it was a gossipy, over-the-back-fence kind of humor, very much in the so-called "feminine" tradition. Considering the kinds of social barriers Draper and Herford must have faced, their success in the traditionally all-male preserve of standup comedy was all the more remarkable. Herford's accomplishments were such that feminist criticism of her was wholly uncalled for. By their endeavors Herford and Draper made it easier for every female standup comic who came after them, and were the true ancestors of that group.

By the middle of the 1910's a new medium had become a force to be reckoned with, and that was the motion picture industry. Initially vaudeville theaters might show a film between acts, but later the process would reverse itself as theater owners found there was more money in showing films than in booking vaudeville acts.

The film industry would eventually kill vaudeville.

Early movie comedy was crude slapstick. Films ran only one or two reels in length, ten to twenty minutes, and of course were silent. This left little time or method for plot or character development. What you usually got was one slapstick sight gag stretched out to fill the film's length. In those beginning years, movies appealed to the lower classes, with upper-class people generally avoiding them entirely. Just as early vaudeville slapstick appealed to its initially lower-class audiences, so the pattern repeated with film. Thus the status of a woman doing comedy in this medium was especially low, partly due as well to the very physical nature of slapstick comedy.

It was said of film comic Mabel Normand that she was "doubly vulgar because she was not only a comedian, she was a comedy girl. By the double standards of the time, a girl's vulgarity was measured by what she did in public." By role definition, doing physical stuff like pratfalls was not ladylike, it was vulgar. Normand was the epitome of slapstick, and that was vulgar. Actress Gloria Swanson, who once had a brief association with Keystone studios, quit immediately after Mack Sennett told her he felt he could make another Normand out of her. Said Swanson, "I felt about it the way my mother felt about motion pictures in general—it was somehow not respectable."

Motion pictures were a fertile ground for comics in the last half of the 1910's. Five women would emerge as stars; Normand, Louise Fazenda, Polly Moran, Alice Howell, and Billie Rhodes. Four of them spent all or part of their careers with Sennett's Keystone company. His own attitude toward women certainly was chauvinistic. The biggest use of women in his films was for their decorative effect—witness his bathing beauties. Nevertheless, females benefitted. Never had so many female comedians emerged from the same common ground in so short a space of time. It would happen only once more in the future, and that would be from television's "Laugh In" of the late 1960's. Coincidentally or not, both of those periods featured a high level of feminist activity and consciousness.

All five comics had in common the roughhouse, do-anything-for-a-laugh brand of slapstick humor, Rhodes less so than the others. She was the only one who offered any resistance to roles she regarded as second class and, not surprisingly, her career was the shortest lived of the five. None of them achieved the kind of fame and acclaim accorded to the male comics of the period such as

Keaton, Chaplin, or Lloyd. And that wasn't due to lack of talent but more to lacklustre vehicles and an absence of the star buildup accorded to the men. After all, there was a certain amount of shame connected with being a woman in comedy.

Normand came closest of all to the peak, and was perhaps the most talented. Her career went down for good when a witchhunt decided her moral conduct wasn't appropriate to that of a lady. Of these five, only Fazenda and Moran were able to continue their careers into the talking picture era, although both of them were reduced to character and supporting parts. They were no longer stars. The sound film moved away from broad physical humor and diminished the appeal of slapstick artists. Fazenda made herself up grotesquely for her films and thus became one of the first to create the "ugly" image. Howell's career ended with the silents, but before she was through she had laid the rudimentary groundwork for the "dumb woman" in film and elsewhere.

Women had not done slapstick to any large degree prior to the late 1910's, mainly because it was simply something women didn't do. Active and physical movements were traits not displayed by "proper" women. Films opened up that avenue to women, since by that time a general change in role expectations had occurred. Feminists pushed for equal rights and women did some of the physical work during WWI which had previously been barred to them. This change at first only affected the lower classes, but films needed women to play against the men and be the objects of rescue from buzzsaws and railroad tracks.

With these films having little character or plot development, nothing was left but broad comic burlesque. The early film women never got to rescue men, but they participated equally with them in other respects. If one of them was hit in the face with a pie she would throw one back. Or she would equally kick a man in the pants, and be kicked herself. All these women doing physical humor led, in turn, to a greater acceptance of slapstick by women.

By the time 1920 came, women could be said to have made major advances since Crabtree had first surfaced in 1860. After a spate of self-deprecation, which had mostly passed, the prevailing image of these women was one of good times and frivolity. Their sexuality rivalled that of men and they projected a sense of independence. Active physical humor with men was on a give-and-take basis. Only one woman of this entire group used a little bit of the man-chasing image. Only one felt the need to make

herself look ugly. And only one female used anything like the
"dumb woman" image, and that was mild compared to what
would come in later periods. Also, two women were operating as
solo standup comics.

Generally speaking, it can be said that making oneself up to be
deliberately ugly and the use of self-deprecation was at a
minimum. This period then had been good to women. Inroads
and gains had been made and the future for female comics
looked promising.

LOTTA CRABTREE

Enormously popular in her time, Lotta Crabtree was perhaps the
highest paid actress of the day. At the height of her career, in the
year 1890-91, she made over $86,000. President Harrison came to
see her twice in that one season. She was so well known that she
was easily recognized from the single name "Lotta." She began as
a child entertainer in mining camps of the west, driven by her
mother's determination for her success, and soon conquered the
rest of the United States and England. Now long forgotten, she
entertained for over thirty years. Her peak years were the 1870's
and 1880's. She retired almost one hundred years ago in 1891.
She was the first female entertainer to achieve a national, lasting
fame who could truly be called a comedian.

Lotta's full name was Charlotte Mignon Crabtree and she was
born in November, 1847, in New York City where her father John
ran a bookstore and her mother Mary Ann (Livesay) worked in
her family's upholstery business. John Crabtree came down with
gold fever, a common affliction in those years, and went to California in 1851 to make his fortune. Like so many others, he never
did strike it rich.

Lotta and her mother followed in 1853 and found themselves
living in a mining community known as Grass Valley, where Mary
Ann ran a boardinghouse. It was here that the family met Lola
Montez, a famous actress of the time. Mary Ann had by then
enrolled her daughter for dancing and singing lessons. Montez
was interested in taking the child on tour with her, child stars
then being in vogue, but Mary Ann refused. Lotta's mother was
by then determined that her daughter would be a star, and that
she herself would guide Lotta's career.

At the age of eight, in 1855, Lotta's chance came. A theatre owner in the community—they were then living in the town of Rabbit Creek, later called La Porte—was looking for a child actress because one of his rivals was using a daughter with a great deal of success. Pushed by her mother, Lotta made her debut in that small saloon theater. Decked out in an Irish costume, she did an Irish jig and reel and other dance steps as well as singing some ballads. Irish dances were popular since half of California's immigrant population at that time was Irish. The audience loved her and showered the stage with coins and gold nuggets, one worth $50. This shower of money frightened Lotta, but Mary Ann rushed out on stage and gathered it all up. Henceforth, until her death in 1905, Mary Ann would manage not only her daughter's career but her finances as well.

The tavern owner was Mart Taylor, and Lotta and her mother formed a theatrical troupe with him and set off to entertain at mining camps. Travel by horseback over dangerous trails was hazardous. Lotta sang, and danced, and did pantomime, sometimes in blackface. She had also added banjo playing to her list of talents. Mary Ann played a triangle on stage. In 1856 the Crabtrees moved to San Francisco and Lotta performed frequently in that city as well as continuing to make forays to perform at the camps. By 1859 she was known as "Miss Lotta, the San Francisco Favorite." From the age of ten on, her earnings supported the whole family.

In San Francisco most of Lotta's performances were held in raucous little theaters called melodeons, usually located in close proximity to a bar, and where the clientele was all male. They were places "no decent woman would enter." Somehow the young Lotta was able to establish a quiet decorum in such settings while she performed.

In her performances she did parts in skits and plays, and performed solo pieces. She sang songs like "The Captain with His Whiskers Gave a Sly Wink at Me," and in a soldier's uniform sang "Rally Round the Flag, Boys." She used a great many physical routines throughout her career. She winked, she contorted her features and used plenty of high kicks. One critic referred to her comic methods as "anatomical."

By 1864 Lotta had left the goldfields behind and was touring the east. She appeared in New York City in a variety program at Niblo's Saloon but made little impression at that time, doing better in Chicago and the Midwest. During this tour she played Topsy, the impish black character from *Uncle Tom's Cabin,* and did a parody of singer Jenny Lind called "Jenny Leatherlungs." In 1867 she achieved her breakthrough to national fame by starring in a play called *Little Nell and the Marchioness.* It was adapted especially for her from Dickens's *The Old Curiosity Shop* and featured Lotta playing both title roles, one of pathos, the other of comedy. From that moment on she "took a distinct and high rank as a star in eccentric comedy." Her popularity equalled that bestowed on rock stars a century later. All over the country people were dancing to the "Lotta Polka" and the "Lotta Gallop." Police sometimes had to escort her out of the theater, and early groupies sometimes beset her hotels.

For the rest of her career she would tour the country in a series of different plays, performing before full houses everywhere and to multiple encores. She even played successfully in London. The plays themselves were little more than vaudeville routines worked into play format with plenty of opportunity for Lotta to sing, dance and "riot" around the stage.

Some of the plays were used year after year for decades, some for only a few seasons, but in any given year Lotta usually worked from a repertoire of at least a dozen. In all of her plays she was always improvising. She would add new dances, alter her lines, and invent new business in general, a practice that was hard on the supporting cast.

Her main reason for improvising was due to her being what is known in show business as a "slow study," someone who has difficulty memorizing lines. With all the plays in her repertoire, improvising was the only way she could cope. The traveling company consisted of a dozen or so people, males and females, all rigorously screened by Mary Ann for moral character. Lotta directed all of her own plays, although any formal direction would have to be said to be minimal.

In one of her vehicles, *The Pet of the Petticoats,* she played six parts. In another, *Family Jars,* critics said she kept "the audience shrieking with laughter." She also appeared in *Hearts Ease,* a gold rush farce, was a lighthousekeeper's daughter in *Zip,* and a gypsy girl in *Musette.* In *Firefly* Lotta did a solo on a snare drum and in *The Little Detective* she did a comedy dance and a "hoopty-dooden-doo," or Swiss yodeling song.

All of her vehicles were tailored especially to her talents, and from 1870 onward she toured with her own company instead of picking up supporting players from local stock companies along the way, as was then the custom. It was generally agreed by critics that Lotta was not a particularly good actress, nor were her vehicles high dramatic art. It was her comic abilities that critics and audiences loved and that allowed her to amass a fortune greater than any entertainer had ever managed to put together until that time.

Near the end of the 1890-91 season Lotta took an unexpected pratfall on stage and limped off in pain. The diagnosis was a broken vertebra and, though she took a long recuperation, she never fully recovered. She tried a brief comeback in late 1892 but had to cancel the tour after a few weeks, as the pain was too much. She then retired.

Still youthful looking at forty-five Lotta had been playing child parts up to the end of her career. She often wore boy's clothes on stage and was as likely to play male child parts as female ones. A type of child character she often portrayed was the homeless waif, orphan, or gamin, roles which were very popular with audiences.

Lotta was still on top when she retired, but signs of slippage had started to show. By the mid-1880's critics were seeing, and pointing out, the incongruity of a woman in her late thirties romping about in children's clothes and using a high-pitched voice that was more and more "breaking." Theater owners sometimes found themselves apologizing for her "hoarseness."

She never performed again after 1892, although she did appear in San Francisco in 1915 when the Panama-Pacific Exposition held a "Lotta Crabtree Day," with the ceremonies held at "Lotta's Fountain" a 30-foot, $10,000 structure she had given the city in 1875 to provide water for the horses, and which, with additions, remained a city landmark, at least into the early 1970's. She also appeared briefly at a few soldiers' benefits during World War I, but became increasingly reclusive after her mother's death, devoting herself to painting and philanthropic endeavors. Lotta Crabtree died in 1924 and left an estate of $4 million, all to charity.

As early as the 1860's she smoked cigarillos and showed her legs in public, which was considered daring at the time, yet still retained an air of innocence. During her act she often pulled up her clothes to reveal her knees, and rolled off couches in a flurry of raised petticoats. It was this innocence which was said to have been a key to her success, at a time when many entertainers, and audiences, had reputations of a dubious nature. Her childlike appearance and infectious personality all helped to reinforce that image.

She never married, and one theory for this was that Mary Ann had made short work of any suitors; but a second theory was that she would never have been acceptable to the public in that state since she played so many child parts, which meant Lotta had put her career ahead of marriage.

While she could be saucy or "sweetly risqué," she mainly provided wholesome entertainment, not that easy to come by during the time of her career. She was popular because she appeared in bright parts, "not dissolute parts, not parts suggestive of vice or misery, but parts of laughter and gayety and smartness."

Her attraction was universal. She appealed to children because they saw her as one of them, to men because she teased and flirted and flashed an ankle or a knee, and to women because they knew that no matter how she behaved on the stage "her private life was utterly moral." Some idea can be obtained, however, of the social status of a comedian in those days from Lotta's attempts in 1893 to join Sorosis, an exclusive New York women's club dedicated to literary and charity work. Lotta would have been the most famous and wealthiest of the members but was refused admission, apparently due to the low esteem members of the theatrical profession were held in "by women of refinement."

Lotta was incapable of doing straight drama and whenever confronted by such scenes as "stage love" she would find it ridiculous and immediately set out to mock it with a wink or a kick. Of her comic career it was said that she was the "cause of more merriment than almost any other entertainer of her time."

MAY IRWIN

May Irwin enjoyed her greatest popularity from the 1880's through the first decade of the present century. She was often known as "Madame Laughter" and was described by *Theatre Magazine* as "the funniest stage woman in America." She performed professionally for over 45 years but when she retired she was only fifty-nine years of age. It is instructive to note how society viewed women and aging in the early 1920's, for *The New York Times* referred to her as "the grand old lady of comedy, the Mark Twain of the American boards."

Irwin had the distinction, dubious now, of introducing and popularizing the phenomenon of "coon shouting." She specially tailored vehicles for herself, a daring and unusual step for a woman at that time. In the late 1800's she branched out to form

her own company, foregoing a male manager. She was warned, of
course, that she wouldn't be able to manage the other female performers in her company.

She was born Ada Campbell in June of 1862 in the village of
Whitby, Ontario, Canada. She and her older sister Georgia
demonstrated singing talents at an early age and the pair performed at various church and school affairs. When their father
died, the family found itself almost penniless and Mrs. Campbell
decided to try and capitalize on her daughters' talents. The family
moved to Buffalo, New York, in 1875. The manager of that city's
Adelphi Theater, Daniel Shelby, got them a booking at a Roches-
ter variety hall where the sisters made their professional debut in
1875. They sang duets such as "Sweet Genevieve," dressed in pink
stockings and pantalettes, and earned $30 a week.

They were successful enough that Shelby hired them for his
own theater, and he was credited with rechristening them May
and Flo Irwin. From there they went on to entertaining in variety
houses, touring mostly in the Midwest until January, 1877, when
they became members of Tony Pastor's company and appeared in
New York vaudeville for the first time.

They stayed with Pastor's company for seven years, performing
as a singing sister act and in burlesques or comic sketches such as
"Pirates of Penn Yan," a takeoff on the Gilbert and Sullivan
Pirates of Penzance. Many of the skits done were basically improvisation, with virtually no rehearsal, and Irwin played everything
from old, decrepit women to infants. Pastor had initially billed
the sisters as "Infantile Actresses, Vocalists and Character
Artistes." Over those seven years their salary went from $60 to $80
a week.

In 1883 the sister act broke up when May accepted an offer to
join the Augustin Daly stock company where she stayed for four
years. Daly had spotted her while she was with Pastor. As a
member of the Daly group she played mostly supporting comedy
roles, and it was here that she honed her skill as a "legitimate
comedienne." Of her stint with Daly it was said that she became
"the most striking and vivacious soubrette of his theatre." She
appeared in such productions as *The Magistrate, A Night Off,*
and *The Recruiting Officer.* The group toured the country and
made two separate trips abroad. In 1887 Irwin left the Daly
company, confessing that she "was never at ease in the confining
form of legitimate comedy; she preferred the freedom to improvise which the music hall gave her."

She joined the Howard Athenaeum Company of Boston and, perhaps more to the point, received three times the salary she had gotten from Daly. Over the next decade she appeared with a number of different groups and managers, usually in farces, which were full-length entertainments with music, often designed specifically for Irwin's talents. Many of them were written by John J. McNally. Some of the vehicles were *A Country Sport (1896)*, in which she introduced the song "A Hot Time in the Old Town," and *The Poet and the Puppet*, which was a takeoff on Oscar Wilde's *Lady Windermere's Fan*, where she popularized the song "After the Ball." This last was one of the few sentimental songs that she did.

The vehicle that brought her the most fame then was the 1895 McNally farce *The Widow Jones*. A reviewer wrote of her in that farce; "Her fund of personal humor is prodigious." She had a strong and a loud voice, and in that vehicle she sang a song called "I'm Looking for de Bully," with music done in ragtime, a form developed by blacks and just then coming into vogue. The verses themselves were done in "Negro dialect." This type of loud singing using comical exaggerated black speech patterns and ragtime music, was no more than racist stereotyping of the razor-toting, shooting-dice-for-"sebens" Negro. Known as "coon shouting," it became popular around the turn of the century.

Many performers adopted this style, including Sophie Tucker, but it was Irwin who introduced and popularized it. She used no makeup but later followers of this genre often used blackface, Tucker among them. When "May Irwin's Bully Song" was published in 1896, the vogue took off. Others of this type done by Irwin included "Hear Dem Bells," "Crappy Dan," and one she wrote herself, "Mamie, Come Kiss Your Honey Boy." During the performance of her "Bully Song," "she made great sport by bringing a little colored boy on the stage with her."

Curiously, May gave a couple of different versions as to how she came to learn this type of material. She claimed to have picked up the music one summer when she overheard a group of black servants singing at a hotel. She then tried to imitate them, but failed repeatedly to capture their style. She finally invited the blacks to perform for her until she was able to duplicate their mannerisms. Another time she denied studying blacks and declared that "any success that I may have with these songs is the result of intuition."

The Widow Jones brought her fame in another way as well. One scene from the play featured a somewhat prolonged kiss between Irwin and co-star John Rice. In 1896 Thomas A. Edison filmed the scene for "Vitascope" and released the fifty-foot-long, close-up film as *The Kiss*. It was one of the earliest commercially released films and earned May a place in screen history. This first screen kiss, torrid lovemaking by the standards of the time, aroused the moral indignation of the clergy, and brought forth demands for "censorship of those new-fangled, soul-destroying living pictures." Irwin appeared in only one other film, *Mrs. Black Is Back* (1914).

Near the end of the last century she was hailed as "a famous fun maker; of jolly, rotund figure, and with a face that reflects the gaiety of nations, she is the personification of humor and careless mirth." In 1897 *The New York Times* described her as having "the grace of Columbine, the eyes of Innocence, the mouth of a comedian, and the chin of a Roman Emperor."

In 1897 she began to appear in plays under her own management, a remarkable step for a woman to take in those days. When she formed her own company she was warned that she "would never get along handling a lot of women." The warning was groundless, as Irwin continued her success, splitting her time between musical comedy plays on the legitimate stage and vaudeville performances.

Some of her legitimate stage vehicles were *The Swell Mrs. Fitzwell* (1897), *Kate Kip, Buyer* (1898), *Sister Mary* (1899), *Madge Smith, Attorney* (1900), *Mrs. Black Is Back* (1904), *Getting a Polish* (1910), *Widow by Proxy* (1913), *No. 33 Washington Square* (1915) and *On the Hiring Line* (1920), which was her last appearance on the legitimate stage.

Sister Mary was a well-mixed bag, as it contained "considerable rhyme, in the shape of coon songs, a Robert Louis Stevenson cradle refrain . . . a Japanese ditty . . . a remarkably realistic game of whist, a cake walk, a duel . . . and several other items." In 1900 *Munsey's Magazine* praised Irwin's performance, concluding that it was a vehicle "that rests the tired brain, induces healthful laughter."

During the run of *No. 33 Washington Square* Irwin had written to President Woodrow Wilson suggesting he form a department of laughter in his government. This was during the dark days of World War I. Actually it was a press agent's scheme. The result was that Irwin took her entire troupe to Washington, where they put on a performance of the comedy before Wilson, all of his cabinet members, and 600 members of the National Press Club. After this "command" performance, Wilson had Irwin over to the White House the next day and named her "Secretary of Laughter."

One of her best-known pieces was *Mrs. Peckham's Carouse,* a one-act play written especially for her by George Ade. First performed in 1906, it was a satire on the reform moralism of the day, with Irwin playing Mrs. Peckham, who through innocence and totally at odds with her principles, becomes drunker and drunker. In playing this part Irwin never moved out of a chair, but her comic effect was "devastating to the vaudeville audiences." She used the play for several seasons on the stage and then used it in vaudeville.

In 1899 Irwin was compared to "a female Falstaff . . . whose sixteenth-century grossness and ribaldry has been refined and recast in a nineteenth-century mould." She had been slim when she started her career but had put on weight over the years, a fact that *Variety* had not failed to notice in 1907 when it commented that "at her entrance she looked like a sister team."

She began her vaudeville act that day "by describing the pathos of becoming fat and bemoaning the fact that she no longer had a visible waistline." Fat jokes about herself continued to be a staple part of her act until she retired. In 1915 she closed her act by joking that her "waistline will never be what it uster."

A typical Irwin vaudeville performance consisted of a mixture of songs and jokes. One of her bits involved using a newspaper on stage, a current one, and making some of the stories in them humorous. It was a technique used sixty-odd years later by comedian Sandra Bernhard who spoofed ads in current magazines. Some of May's better known comic songs included "Don't Argify," "Mr. Johnson, Turn Me Loose," "Frog Song," "I Needn't Come Around." She prided herself on never having offended her audience "with salacious song or speech."

Irwin was not considered to have been an overt feminist, but by taking charge of her own career she achieved a degree of professional independence. As a backlash to this, a good deal of media attention was devoted to Irwin as cook and housewife, possibly to denigrate her achievements. In December of 1897 *The New York Times* published a lengthy article on Irwin the "accomplished housewife." In the course of this article the following quote was elicited from May; "I'm a thorough home woman; I never was intended for the stage." In view of her career of some 45 years, this statement was utter nonsense.

In fact, by 1912 Irwin was coming out with more overtly feminist statements although still divorcing herself from the suffragette movement. She wrote of her anger upon hearing people talk about a "woman's sphere," meaning the home. "Woman's sphere," she insisted, "is the same as a man's, and that is the world."

For the woman sometimes referred to as "Madam Laughter" or the "Dean of Comediennes," humor was an unfathomable and almost genetic trait. "Humor is spontaneous. It is born with one or it is not. It cannot be acquired and it cannot be forced. . . . To me humor is unanalyzable. It comes or it does not. It is as mysterious as and less controllable than electricity." Irwin felt comedy was more difficult to play than tragedy because the latter was more in keeping with life in general. "It is easier to make people cry than to make them laugh, and it would not be hard to work yourself up into a state of mind for tragedy, but if you don't feel funny, you can't be." She once said, "An onion could make people cry, but nobody had ever succeeded in raising a vegetable to make them laugh."

May retired from show business in 1920 and died in October, 1938, at the age of seventy-six. Remembered more for her vaudeville work than for her appearances on the legitimate stage, she was one of the most beloved comic characters of her time.

MARIE DRESSLER

She considered herself to be so homely that she titled her autobiography *The Life Story of an Ugly Duckling.* Convinced as a child that she would never make it on looks alone Marie Dressler turned to comedy and became one of the superstars of vaudeville and the stage as a physical, knockabout comic. She made a few silent movies at the height of her fame, only to find her career go into a ten-year eclipse. Considering herself washed up as she was approaching sixty, Marie was rescued and revived in the movies. Playing a different type of comedy, one combining her broad humor with pathos, she found the second phase of her career to be even more successful than the first. For the last four years of her life she reached new heights of popularity and was one of Hollywood's biggest box-office attractions.

Marie Dressler was born Leila Marie Koerber in 1869 in Cobourg, Ontario, Canada, the daughter of Alexander and Annie (Henderson). Alexander was a would-be piano teacher but a man with a temper and very little tact. These traits caused him to lose pupils almost as soon as he got them. The family found itself moving continuously from one small town to another, both in Canada and the United States, as the father exhausted the supply of pupils in each place.

Dressler made her stage debut at the age of four in a church pageant in which she played Cupid. Poised on a pedestal with bow and arrow, she was not supposed to move. As might be expected, she did move, and toppled right off the pedestal, drawing lots of laughs in the process. It was her first stage fall, but many more would follow. Dressler claimed that even at that early age she was aware of her shortcomings in the looks department and was deliberately doing pratfalls to get attention. Nobody ever said, "Isn't she a beautiful child," but they often said, "Isn't she funny." She took the offensive since she preferred to be laughed at rather than pitied. It was a way of getting people to like her.

At the age of fourteen she left home, with no formal education, determined to succeed in show business. It was at this point that she took the stage name of Marie Dressler, borrowing it from an aunt whom she had never met. This change seemed to have been instigated by her mother, who didn't want her Irish relations embarrassed by having a relative on the stage. Being an entertainer in those days was something that people, especially females, didn't go into. It was a low-status occupation with a poor reputation.

Marie answered a newspaper ad and joined a barnstorming stock group managed by Robert Wallace. Troupes came and went frequently in those days and Dressler was a member of a number of such traveling troupes. She received $8 a week from the second troupe she was a member of, and performed in everything from grand opera to comic opera, often as a member of the chorus. She was considered "too big for a soubrette [a pretty, frivolous, female character] and not beautiful enough for a prima donna," and did character parts in productions such as *Under Two Flags* and *The Mikado*.

One company she did stay with for several years, in the early 1890's, was the Bennett-Moulton Opera Company. Marie considered this particular experience her most valuable and toughest training. The company learned a new comic opera each week while, at the same time, rehearsing another, and performing a third. By the end of a year Marie had a repertoire of forty comic operas. She entertained in such vehicles as *Bohemian Girl* and *The Black Hussars*. One role called for her to knock a baseball into the audience every night. She made her debut in New York City in 1892 playing a brigand in the comic opera *The Robber of the Rhine*, written by Maurice Barrymore, father of the famous clan.

That piece wasn't too successful, so to earn extra money (she was supporting several family members) she resorted to singing two songs nightly at a Bowery beer hall for $10, and also singing on Sunday nights at Bial's Music Hall. She continued to play in a variety of musical revues, with different companies and performers, including Eddie Foy. In 1896 she opened in New York in *The Lady Slavey*, which proved a big hit and gave Marie her first taste of real stardom.

She played a music hall singer named Flo Honeydew. She was called "the gem of the performance" and the play ran for four years, including an extensive road tour. Some critics found her humor "coarse," but the majority felt she essayed the role of Flo "with the agility of a circus performer and the physical elasticity of a professional contortionist."

It was Barrymore and Foy who helped her get fully into comedy. Barrymore once told her she had picked the wrong trade. "You're a born female clown" he said. It was this encouragement which helped lead her into comedy. At first, clowning didn't come easily. Foy advised her to establish the comedy angle from the beginning, with her opening entrance, by stumbling down a flight of stairs. She did so with good results, and "ever since then I've been bumping into scenery to amuse the customers."

Over the next decade Dressler appeared in a variety of musicals on Broadway, and in vaudeville, working with the likes of Anna Held and Weber and Fields. In *The King's Carnival* (1901) she did a bit as the Queen of Spain rocking the Infanta, played by an adult, in a gigantic crib. She also did a comic dance with two males in which the three danced backwards onto three chairs and then fell head over heels backwards. Dressler suggested the routine but the men objected. When she offered to do the fall part by herself, the men refused to let her show them up and grudgingly they did the fall as well. In vaudeville at the turn of the century she became a favorite doing imitations and coon singing. Some of her famous songs from that period included: "Every Race Has a Flag but the Coon," "All Coons Look Alike to Me," and "I Never Liked a Nigger with a Beard."

She first played with Joe Weber in his revue *Higgledy-Piggledy* in 1904. Weber and Fields had separated at that point and Dressler later played with them both after they had reunited professionally. With Weber she appeared as Philopena Schnitz, heiress to a pickle fortune, and she wore a huge diamond pickle on her breast. One of her most popular appearances was in the 1906 production *Twiddle-Twaddle* in which she did a sketch of two then popular melodramas. She appeared in a burlesque called "Tess of the Vaudevilles," and one of her bits, in which she was satirizing current singers, had her carrying a basket of vegetables which she commenced, nightly, to throw at the audience.

In 1907 she made a successful appearance in London, and was received just as warmly as on this side of the Atlantic. She sang songs like "A Great Big Girl Like Me," and was called "a 200-lb. entertainer of the first magnitude . . . able to set you laughing at one moment and the next to bring the hard lump of pathos to your throat."

In 1910 Dressler achieved her greatest success on the stage when she starred in the musical comedy *Tillie's Nightmare*. She played a boardinghouse drudge named Tillie Blobbs in a plot that was a variation of the Cinderella theme. Tillie was the drudge with a beautiful and idle sister. Unlike Cinderella, Tillie remained a drudge at the end, left with only her dreams. In this production Marie popularized the song, "Heaven will Protect the Working Girl." She played in this vehicle off and on for a few years. One critic termed her performance "a bit crude, perhaps, but spontaneous, real, and thoroughly good-natured." Another writer, commenting on the broad, slapstick nature of her comedy, wrote, "Irony is too fragile a tool for her to use . . . she employs the open palm of the hand."

She continued to appear in other revues, not all of which were successful. A production of her own in 1913, "Marie Dressler's All Star Gambol," lasted only eight performances. Nevertheless, by 1914 she was a top headliner of both vaudeville and Broadway shows and was commanding in the neighborhood of $1,500 a week.

That same year she began her movie career. Mack Sennett with his Keystone gang was then famous as a producer of one- or two-reel slapstick comedy shorts. Sennett decided he wanted to make a full length, six-reel, feature comedy after hearing a rumor that D.W. Griffith was set to make a full length drama. That drama turned out to be *Birth of a Nation.* The idea of making feature-length films was novel at the time. Exhibitors were wary of how the public would accept them. Movies had picked up the nickname "the flicks" from the tendency of early films to do just that, flick over the screen, and for a time there was a serious debate as to whether or not watching movies would damage the eyes.

Sennett's backers wouldn't go for the idea of a full-length comedy until Sennett mentioned Dressler's name as the star. Mack had seen and admired her work in vaudeville and thought she was a big-enough name to carry the film. The backers agreed and they set to work adapting *Tillie's Nightmare* for the screen. The result was *Tillie's Punctured Romance,* said to be the first full-length comedy film, and a huge hit.

Dressler got top billing ahead of two supporting players soon to become noteworthy in their own right, Mabel Normand and Charlie Chaplin. In her autobiography Dressler claimed she picked out both Normand and Chaplin for the film. They were both then relatively unknown members of the Keystone company and it was more likely that Sennett picked them out of his company for their supporting roles.

The casting of these three together proved to be inspired. The plot had a mercenary Charlie pursuing both the pretty Mabel Normand and his ex-girlfriend Dressler, who, in the meantime, had become suddenly wealthy. The trio was backed up by the entire boisterous and energetic Sennett company. The humor was not subtle or soft, it was broad physical slapstick at its best. While courting Marie, Chaplin playfully tossed a brick at her head. When girlfriend Normand first spotted Dressler and Chaplin together while they were dodging traffic in the middle of the street, she remarked, "What's this he's got—one of Ringling's elephants?"

As a farm girl lured to the city by Charlie the cad, Dressler got drunk in a restaurant and careened and staggered about in a series of crazed dances. Later, after she thought she had inherited a fortune, she threw a party in her new mansion and went wild,

throwing a cake, shooting off a gun, and producing general pan-
demonium. In a chase scene at the film's end, Marie was standing
near the edge of a pier when a Keystone Kops patrol wagon
pulled up. As might be expected, the wagon slammed into her
behind, knocking her into the water. Efforts to pull her out of the
water resulted in her being dunked four more times. The comedy
may have been "pants-kicking" humor, but audiences loved it,
and today the film is still shown occasionally.

Dressler didn't intend to give up her stage career, and she continued to work in that medium until World War I. Her first film
was so successful, though, that two sequels were made, *Tillie's
Tomato Surprise* (1915) and *Tillie Wakes Up* (1917). In the latter,
Dressler played a neglected wife who had a one-day fling at Coney
Island with a neglected husband. During the film they jumped
into an ice wagon to avoid being seen together, froze into the ice
and had to be chopped out. Dressler also got to portray pathos,
having her heart broken by a cruel husband. This sadness con-
trasted with her usual flamboyant comedy and was a successful
formula she often used in the future. These two films, however,
lacking the strong supporting cast of the first, were not successful.

Dressler appeared in a few short comedies in 1917 and 1918 but
she essentially put her career on hold during the war years. She
devoted most of her time to entertaining troops and making
appearances to sell war bonds. At war's end she helped found the
Chorus Equity Association, and was president of that organization
in 1919 during the actor's strike of that year. By 1920 Dressler
found herself pretty well washed up. She received no film work at
all, save for a couple of shorts done in Europe. She appeared on
the stage in a couple of revues, but only sporadically.

For most of that decade she was largely without work. During
this period she spent a couple of years working as a hostess at New
York's Ritz Supper Club. Some attributed her decline to a changing public taste for more youth, beauty, and love. Homely and
overweight Marie, then in her fifties, did not fit any of these
categories. Perhaps a more cogent reason for her lack of work had
to do with her role in the strike, after which "she was persona non
grata with most important managements."

In 1927 Marie got a small part in a film, *The Joy Girl*. It was
only one day's work but she got good notices which came to the
attention of an MGM scriptwriter named Frances Marion, who
came to Dressler's rescue. Marion had scripted *Tillie Wakes Up*,
and before that Dressler had befriended her as a cub reporter

when Frances was seeking an interview with her. Marion fashioned a script for her. *The Callahans and the Murphys* (1927), which Marion and producer Irving Thalberg sold to MGM. The rescue was timely because Dressler was reported to have been considering taking a job as a housekeeper on Long Island.

Marie was cast as Ma Callahan, with Polly Moran co-starring. The two women played hard-drinking heads of raucous Irish families who were constantly fighting and arguing with each other. At one point the pair got progressively drunker as they toasted an upcoming marriage and ended up pouring beer down each other's blouses. The picture got good notices, but immediately drew a storm of protest from Irish-Americans who didn't like the stereotypes presented. They picketed the film throughout the United States, and an embarrassed MGM studio withdrew the film shortly after it had gone into circulation.

Despite this setback, Marie continued to get more parts. She appeared in eight more films by 1930, as a supporting comic player. In 1928 she and Moran appeared in *Bringing Up Father*, described as "rolling pin humor." Also that year she appeared in *The Patsy*, another raucous physical comedy co-starring Marion Davies, in which "it seemed Dressler might actually flatten Miss Davies in the commotion."

In 1930 Frances Marion was instrumental in getting Marie a part in *Anna Christie* which she was adapting for the screen from Eugene O'Neill's play. It was the first talking picture for Greta Garbo. Marie played a serious role, that of Marthy, a waterfront hag. Her performance was impressive enough for MGM to put her under contract, and from then on her roles were designed especially for her.

She and Polly Moran co-starred in four more comedy films together, mostly in the same vein as before, that of constantly arguing and bickering friends. In one, *Caught Short,* she played a boardinghouse "dragon." MGM had their doubts about the film's prospects because there was no love interest in it, but it was fairly successful. In that film Dressler tried out a Murphy bed and the bed folded up into the wall with Marie stuck in it. In this group of films Moran usually got the pair into trouble or caused Marie to look bad in the eyes of her family. Marie would then come up with some way to provide a happy ending, while Moran got hers—something like a dunk in a mud bath or a cake in the face. Dressler also appeared in a few straight dramatic roles.

From 1930 until her death from cancer in 1934, she was one of Hollywood's biggest box office stars. Several magazine and newspaper polls cited her as the top box-office draw in 1932 or 1933. She was then earning $5,000 a week. Two films from that period stand out. In these Dressler was able to fully combine low comedy and sentiment to best advantage. The first was *Min and Bill* (1930), in which she was teamed with Wallace Beery. They played a pair of older sweethearts, with Marie being the keeper of a rundown waterfront hotel.

On how she prepared for roles Marie once said, "I had to first get my teeth in it, so to speak, and then sort of roll it over and put gravy on it before it was really mine." Another time she stated her ambition was "to go into every picture you can and upset the plot at least twice."

Dressler did have her own standards in comedy. She felt she had never been coarse or vulgar, although she admitted to being rough on occasion: "I may have stood on my head and knocked my co-stars around as if they were ninepins, still I always did it with refinement." Or as she put it another way, "A lady may stand on her head in a perfectly decent self-respecting way." Dressler won the Oscar for Best Actress for her role in *Min and Bill*.

Her other major film paired her again with Beery in the 1933 release *Tugboat Annie*, the role she is probably best remembered for, along with Tillie. As Annie Brennan she again combined comedy with pathos. This time the pair played irascible but lovable waterfront rats. In the film Marie had to deal with her heavy-drinking husband and, through various plot complications, save her son's aground passenger ship and retrieve her beloved tugboat, the *Narcissus*, which had been sold to pay damages caused when her husband was drunk.

Dressler was a master of slapstick, farce, improvisation, and sentiment. Realizing from an early age that she was homely, she was determined to succeed anyway. She refused to let her looks be a disadvantage, and turned to comedy for expression. Although some of her early humor was generated by "crude reference to her girth," she did by and large avoid self-deprecating humor.

Some time around the end of World War I she was present at the Newspaper Women's Club of New York annual ball when Will Rogers called her over. He told Marie he was chairman of a committee to pick the most beautiful woman in the room, but there were so many of them in the room he was afraid to pick one for fear of offending the others. He asked Marie if he could pick her, because the "crowd would kinder laugh it off and nobody'd get mad." Marie agreed and took the whole episode good-naturedly.

She even claimed to feel sorry for beautiful women, since she didn't have to spend hours everyday over makeup and beauty care. Her career had its ups and downs and in the early 1930's, when she was sixty, she came back from the oblivion of the 1920's to entertain a whole new generation. Dressler became a bigger draw than stars like Garbo, despite being "an aging, ugly and bulky lady."

Summing up her career Marie Dressler said, "I was born homely. . . . and for fifty years it has been my lot to make my living on the stage where the first requisite for a woman's success is supposed to be a face that's easy on the eyes. I was born serious and I have earned my bread by making other people laugh. . . . when everything else fails I get my voice down to the audience and make a face."

TRIXIE FRIGANZA

She started her career as a svelte chorus girl but quickly put on weight and turned her size into the chief source of her humor. Her comedy was mainly self-deprecatory and, like Sophie Tucker, she was one of the early queens of the fat jokes. She weighed about 190 pounds and was termed a "rollicking butterball who sang and danced with skill and zest." She was very popular at home and abroad in both musical comedies and vaudeville.

Trixie Friganza was born in November, 1870, in Grenola, Kansas. Her birth name was Brigid O'Callaghan and she later took her mother's maiden name for stage purposes. Growing up in Cincinnati, she found herself, at eighteen, working in a dead-end job as a salesgirl for $3 a week. Running off with a touring musical, *The Pearl of Pekin* she upped her salary to $18 a week as a chorus girl. Her mother went to the city police for help in getting her daughter to return home. After the chief of police talked to Trixie, he convinced her mother the girl's morals would be no more endangered as a chorus girl than they would be as a salesclerk.

By the mid 1890's Friganza had established herself as a musical comedy star and appeared in numerous vehicles such as *A Christmas Night* (1894) and *The Belle of Bohemia* (1901), in which she made her successful London debut. Some of her other stage hits were *The Girl from Paris* (1901), *Sally in Our Alley* (1902), *Twiddle Twaddle* (1906) and *The Passing Show of 1912.* She appeared in vaudeville for the first time in 1906, where she did an impersonation of Marie Dressler. It was 1912 before she turned to vaudeville in earnest and was termed a "riotous hit," often head-lining at the Palace Theatre in New York. She billed her act as "My Little Bag o' Trix."

In vaudeville her added weight was said to have increased "the lightness of her comedy and the gaiety of her spirit." She sang and danced and did comic turns on instruments such as the bass violin. She also presented one of the early images of the man chaser, always on the lookout for a suitor, singing about her "gar-bage man" or lamenting, "Won't Someone Kindly Stake Me to a Man."

One song she introduced early in her career was "No Wedding Bells for Me." It remained popular with audiences for years, but Trixie finally refused to sing it any more after she herself got mar-ried. Another of her popular numbers was "I'm Not Having Birthdays Any More."

On the vaudeville stage she soon became known as the "cham-pagne girl" and it was there that she excelled at "fat jokes." She accentuated her own weight by wearing numerous costumes, one on top of the other, and then discarded them one by one throughout the course of her act. Of her girth she remarked, "When I started in show business I was so thin that you could blow me through a keyhole. Now you have to take down the whole door to get me through. . . . By putting on one-third more weight I doubled my salary." She described her figure as a "per-fect forty-six" and her favorite stone as a brick. She told her audi-ences that "the way for a fat woman to do the shimmy is to walk fast and stop short."

She was popular with audiences as a comic, but not as any sort of militant. In 1908 Trixie and other early suffragettes tried to see the Mayor of New York. However, "she won from the crowd the only jeers she ever had heard."

Trixie continued to appear in vaudeville and in musical comedies on the legitimate stage. In the early 1920's she began to appear in films as a character actress, making her last appearance in the 1940 release *If I Had My Way.* Her roles were minor and she almost always appeared as a member of an all-star cast. Her movie parts were usually comic, and she was described as the

"Beefy, gray-haired old gal who played society dames." In 1931 *The Billboard* called her "the Perpetual Flapper."

In 1939 she sold her house and all of her possessions and donated the resulting fortune to the Sacred Heart Academy in Flintridge, California, near Pasadena. Trixie Friganza retired and moved to that convent the same year. Some convent officials were reluctant to admit her, possibly because of her background as an entertainer. However, she lived there without incident until February, 1955 when she died at the age eighty-four.

IRENE FRANKLIN

In 1908 a contest was held to find the "Most Popular Woman Vaudeville Artist." The winner was Irene Franklin, now almost totally forgotten, compared with contemporaries like Marie Dressler and Eva Tanguay. Franklin specialized in comic songs and impersonations. At the time of her death she was compared to the then highly popular Beatrice Lillie, although Franklin was said to have been not quite as subtle. She delivered all of her comedy through song, did many kid impersonations and wrote her own material.

Irene was born in St. Louis in June, 1876, the daughter of stock company players. She made her first stage appearance when she was just six months old, carried on stage by her parents in the performance of a melodrama. She was back at age three and a half doing her own number, a song and dance, "Peek-a-boo, and Dardanella." She continued to appear on stage, sporadically, as a child, including some appearances in Australia and London when she traveled there with her parents.

In 1895 Franklin was nineteen and back in the United States. Both of her parents were then dead and Irene launched her career in American vaudeville. Initially she had a difficult time and could get little work. Tony Pastor used her in his theater in New York, but only when he needed a last-minute substitute act. Franklin knew something was lacking in her act, a problem solved when she was introduced to Burt Green by Pastor.

Green had formerly been the house pianist at Pastor's theater and he told Franklin that she needed a special arrangement of her material to suit her style, something the current pianist wasn't providing. Green did some arrangements for Irene to which the audience responded enthusiastically. The pair eventually married and remained a team, with Franklin writing the material and Green supplying the music, until Burt's death in 1922. Franklin's career took off after her alliance with Green and she always credited her husband with guiding her to stardom. Burt claimed he was "just part of the scenery of Irene Franklin's act." The truth lay somewhere in between.

At not much past the age of twenty, Irene was an established star of vaudeville. She did a lot of kid songs, written by herself and Green, such as "I Don't Care What Happens to Me," "I'm Nobody's Baby Now," and "Somebody Ought to Put the Old Man Wise." The latter she sang as a little girl, dressed in rompers or a short dress. She did satires on topics such as feminism with "The Woman Policeman," or the trials and tribulations of an unmarried woman with "If I Don't Lock My Family Up, It's the Old Maid's Home for Me." During Prohibition she did a number called, "What Have You Got on Your Hip? You Don't Seem to Bulge Where a Gentleman Ought to," a song risqué for its day.

She portrayed a wide variety of characters on stage, and besides the "resentful little girls" she did characters such as a hotel maid, a Childs Restaurant waitress, an old farm woman, and a flirtatious school teacher. A hotel chain once complained about her portrayal of the maid, and Childs Restaurant complained that she depicted their waitress as too haughty. Franklin also once raised the ire of early feminists when an interviewer asked her if a woman's hardest job was getting a man. She replied, "No, holding him!"

Franklin often worked without doing costume changes, relying instead on her flaming waist-length red hair. She did all sorts of different business and arrangements with it on stage, to portray various characters. A reviewer wrote of her act, "She injects so much humor . . . that she is irresistible. Her 'kid' songs are unforgettable, and her slangy dissertation of a chorus girl invading the Great White Way was a little masterpiece of characterization."

In 1907 she did a song, "Expression," in which she "illustrated all the human emotions by facial expressions." In 1908 Irene introduced the song "The Red Head" in which she was a little girl who told of the agony of being called names such as "bricktop" and "firehead" by other children. This became Irene's identification song for the rest of her career. She remained exclusively on the vaudeville stage until 1907, when she first appeared on the legitimate stage. Thereafter she was seen in a number of musical comedies and revues such as *Hands Up* (1915) and *The Passing Show of 1917*. However, vaudeville continued to provide her with most of her work. During the war she entertained the troops in France and then returned to vaudeville, with more occasional appearances in musical comedy plays.

As vaudeville died out, Franklin turned to film work in the early 1930's and appeared in over twenty, with her last appearance in 1939. Her roles were undistinguished and were all bit parts. In June 1941, three days after she turned sixty-five, Franklin died in poverty at the Actors Fund Home in New Jersey, largely forgotten. Her talents had been uniquely suited to vaudeville and her enormous popularity had rapidly faded after the demise of that institution; also, there was the difficulty of playing child characters as one got older.

During her career it was common for entertainers to do impersonations, but usually they did each other. That was a tradition that Franklin had moved away from, for she did impersonations of ordinary working women and children. These were typical members of her audience and their identification with her characters accounted for much of her popularity. In more recent times it has been said of Franklin that "her comic style is most closely approximated by that of Lily Tomlin."

ELSIE JANIS

As with most female comedians of her day, comic songs were a mainstay in the routines of Elsie Janis. But it was her talent as an outstanding mimic that Janis was best remembered for. She gave comic imitations of dozens of stars of the time, female and male, and she always did them without benefit of makeup, or props or disguises of any kind. She owed her success and her career to her mother, who guided and dominated Elsie in every way. Elsie's mother was indeed the ultimate stage mother, though it was something Elsie never complained about, or rebelled against.

She was born Elsie Bierbower in Columbus, Ohio, on March 16, 1889. Early in her career she took the stage name of Janis, which had been suggested by a theatrical photographer. Her father was a railway brakeman and her mother had her own profitable real estate business. After Elsie's birth, Mrs. Bierbower concentrated all her energies on preparing Elsie for a career on the stage, something Mrs. Bierbower felt she had missed out on by "being such a fool as to marry Johnny Bierbower." Elsie proved to be an apt pupil and by the age of three she was playing around with scenes from *Romeo and Juliet* and was already doing imitations. As Elsie later remarked, "I can't remember the time when I wasn't imitating somebody." Even at that early age she did everything from "animals to railroad trains."

She debuted at the age of five at a local church function, stealing the show with songs, dances, and imitations, of Anna Held, for example. She then astonished everyone, including her mother, by mimicking a pompous speech delivered just a couple of hours previous by a Sunday School superintendent.

She quickly became known as "Little Elsie" and appeared at other amateur entertainments around town. When she was about seven years old she performed at the White House before President McKinley. (Elsie's mother had been acquainted with the McKinleys from the time he had been Governor of Ohio.) At the White House Elsie did her imitations for the President, who was duly impressed and prophesized a career on the stage for her. If Mrs. Bierbower needed any encouragement, this was more than enough. She immediately pawned her jewelry and sold the household furniture to raise money to take Elsie to New York in an effort to further her career.

Elsie made her professional stage debut at about eight years of age when she appeared with James (father of Eugene) O'Neill's company. At about ten Elsie was appearing in vaudeville where she did imitations of such popular stars of the day as May Irwin, Pauline Hall, and Dan Daly. It was unlikely that Janis had ever actually seen these performers, but somehow she was able to offer well-received imitations.

Due to her tender years, Elsie and her mother ran afoul of the New York Gerry Society, a group which attempted to regulate the abuses of child labor. Mrs. Bierbower was able to obtain a special dispensation for her daughter to go on stage. It wouldn't be the last battle staged and won by Mrs. Bierbower over some aspect of her daughter's career.

In her New York vaudeville appearance of 1900, Janis did imitations of Fay Templeton, Lillian Russell, and Weber and Fields.

She spent the next few years with stock companies in various cities where she played a variety of child roles, including Little Lord Fauntleroy. Between acts she did her own specialities, and became the best-loved child performer in the country.

She was back in New York in 1905 where she appeared in a revue called *When We Were 41*. The only high spot of the show was Janis's impersonations of stage stars. As a result of this success, she became a Broadway star the next year, as the lead in *The Vanderbilt Cup* which ran for two years, until 1908. Again her impressions were a hit. It was this vehicle that lifted her into the ranks of superstars. Elsie was only sixteen when the show opened, the youngest Broadway star in a long time.

Some of her musical comedy vehicles were *The Fair Co-ed* (1908), *The Slim Princess* (1910), *The Lady of the Slipper* (1912), *The Passing Show* (1914), *Miss Information* (1915), *The Century Girl* (1917) and *Puzzles of 1925*. In these shows she introduced many popular songs such as "Florrie Was a Flapper." She wrote lyrics for some of the shows and by 1917 had written more than two dozen songs, four motion picture scripts, in which she had acted in the mid 1910's, as well as numerous newspaper and magazine articles. These musical comedies were little more than a vaudeville show tied together with a weak semblance of a plot, and Elsie got to do her imitations throughout. It was with her impressions in vaudeville that Janis made her greatest impact. She also toured abroad and was a big hit in both London and Paris.

In vaudeville she became known as the "Lady of a Million Laughs," and while her routine remained relatively constant, including light patter with the audience, comic songs and dances, and impressions, those whom she mimicked did change. She impersonated people such as Eddie Foy, Eva Tanguay, the Barrymores, Irene Franklin, Harry Lauder, George M. Cohan, Sarah Bernhardt, Bert Williams, Fanny Brice, Beatrice Lillie, Ethel Barrymore as Fanny Brice, and Will Rogers. In 1916 the *New York Dramatic Mirror* reported that, "Miss Janis offers little caricatures, vividly drawn with a keen and intelligent sense of humor and deftly exaggerating just a few of a player's peculiarities of style and personality."

She might do an impression of Sarah Bernhardt singing "Swanee," Harry Lauder as a Scotch Romeo, or singing "You Take the High Road," George M. Cohan singing and talking out of the side of his mouth, Eddie Foy prancing about with his Irish clog dance, or how the song "Yes, We Have No Bananas" would be sung by different people such as Ethel Barrymore, George M. Cohan, Fanny Brice, and Will Rogers.

Elsie wrote all of her own material, and as a mimic it was said that "Miss Janis is unexcelled. She does not merely suggest the person she imitates, she is that person . . . a consummately skillful mimic." Elsie's own favorite imitation was Eddie Foy, and she found that her audiences were never content until she did her impressions. She stuck to her mimicry throughout her career, never tiring of doing it, and never wishing to venture into serious drama: "I know that I amuse folks, so I intend to hew close to that line."

When Janis decided to imitate somebody she would go to a show that person was appearing in, sit out front and observe closely. She never had to do this more than twice to be able to do an imitation. She regarded her work as "somewhat like that of a newspaper cartoonist, who purposely exaggerates certain characteristics in order to give a more striking air of reality to the finished picture." She felt that most people she imitated objected, at least deep down, and that they would always contend that Janis's portrait of them was never a good likeness. Her targets were always entertainers. She never used famous people from other fields, such as politics, "because I don't believe the general public is particularly interested in this sort of thing," she said.

Over the years Elsie's vaudeville salary had climbed from virtually nothing to as high as $3,500 a week before World War I broke out. She was at the height of her career and earning power in 1917 when she left it all and paid her own expenses to France, where she threw herself wholeheartedly into entertaining the American troops. During 1917-18 she gave hundreds of shows, at times as many as nine a day, often within the sound of cannon fire, and became known as "The Sweetheart of the A.E.F." (American Expeditionary Force).

She was back on the stage in 1920 with her own revue, *Elsie Janis and Her Gang,* which was a revue without scenery and composed exclusively of soldiers, amateurs back from the war, whom Elsie had taught to sing and dance. Such revues were in vogue in the early part of the 1920's and Elsie played them for several years, touring across the country.

She continued her career throughout the 1920's, but some of the snap and pep had left her act. It didn't have the same meaning to her then, nor did it match her war effort in terms of its perceived importance in her mind. In 1929 she was off work for awhile with a serious illness, and then in the summer of 1930 her mother, and constant companion, died. A couple of months later Elsie announced her retirement from the stage after close to three decades. She was then forty-one years old and said she could never quit as long as her mother was alive, because Mrs. Bierbower "loved the theatre so much."

It was the mother who had dominated and controlled Elsie's career. From the beginning right up until her death, Mrs. Bierbower made war on anybody who got in the way of her daughter's career. It was she who fought for top billing for her daughter, for the big numbers in a show, for the star's dressing room, and so on. While Elsie was on stage her mother was in the wings rooting, cheering, and praying. She went everywhere with Elsie, including France during World War I.

The control was as complete when Elsie was grownup as when she was a child. Mrs. Bierbower "supervised her meals, woke her up in the morning, dictated her schedule, coached her, chose her wardrobe and material, told her when to go to bed. She even went along on Elsie's dates." Not surprisingly, Janis had few dates, all discouraged by her mother. Not long after her mother's death Elsie jokingly suggested her own epitaph could read, "Here lies Elsie Janis, still sleeping alone." Soon thereafter she did finally marry; she was forty-two, he was twenty-six. But the couple soon separated.

Of the mother-daughter relationship, Mrs. Bierbower once remarked: "There are Elsie Janises born every day, but not mothers to give up their whole lives to them." Elsie concurred and called her mother her greatest comfort. "She gave up her whole life for me. Her only thought was furthering my career." Elsie added that, "I was a strange little puppet. . . . She turned me off and on at will, like a music box."

With the death of her mother Elsie's career on stage largely ended. She returned to film work, this time, though, behind the scenes, where she worked as a scriptwriter and lyricist on several feature films. She continued her writing career as well, with more articles and a couple of books. She made her last public appearance in the 1940 film *Women in War*.

In 1935 she became noteworthy by being hired by NBC as one of their radio announcers. The network then had 26 announcers, and Janis was its first female announcer. Announcers then had various duties such as doing commercials, cuing programs and reading news bulletins. The network's head of announcers, Pat Kelly, tried Janis at reading news bulletins but then vowed she would do no more, since "Listeners complained that a woman's voice was inappropriate." Janis's career with NBC was short lived.

In 1939 she attempted a vaudeville-style comeback in New York with a series of Sunday concerts featuring the same sort of act she had always done. Critics enjoyed her as much as ever: "Her inimitable mimicry—a mere twitch of a facial muscle often brings an uncanny likeness of the target for her spoofing." Audiences, however, failed to materialize, and the show folded after just four performances.

Janis died in 1956, a few weeks short of her sixty-seventh birthday. A versatile and outstanding mimic, as well as an all-round revue performer, she had no equal in her field. As she once commented about herself, "I've always been considered a bit odd."

NORA BAYES

Nora Bayes's self-proclaimed ambition was to be known as "the best entertainer in America." While she didn't realize that particular objective, she did become one of the top few women stars of the first quarter of this century, gaining her fame on the Broadway stage in musical comedies, and in vaudeville. She was a singer of both comic and straight material, was married five times, possessed a large ego, and had a reputation for being difficult and temperamental.

She was born Dora Goldberg in 1880 in an unconfirmed location, variously reported as Los Angeles, Milwaukee, Chicago, or Joliet, Illinois. Her parents were devout Orthodox Jews and they regarded the theater as a place of evil. Nora was allowed to take singing lessons as a young teenager but only after she had convinced her parents that she wanted only to sing at religious services. Her first teachers encouraged her to study for the opera, but Nora had other plans. Whenever there was an amateur night at the local vaudeville theater, she would sneak away from home to perform.

At seventeen she was living in Joliet and ran away to Chicago, where she married the first of her husbands and got her start in vaudeville. By getting married she had freed herself from parental wrath. She knew her parents would never have let her seek a career on stage, since to them "the theater and all its works represented the lowest damnation and mortal sin." Her first professional job was as a singer at the Chicago Opera House, which put on melodramas with vaudeville entertainment between the acts. The manager refused to give her a chance until Nora said she'd work for nothing if she wasn't better than anybody else in the show. She got the job and the $25 a week in salary.

She spent a season in San Francisco with the Fischer Stock Company before returning to the New York vaudeville scene in 1902. That year she made a big hit with a comic drinking song, "Down Where the Wurzburger Flows," and had little trouble getting work after that. She used a number of stage names in her early career, including her real one, before finally settling on Nora Bayes. From about 1904 to 1907 she toured in Europe and enjoyed particular success in London.

Back in the United States, Flo Ziegfeld spotted her and in 1907 put her in the first edition of his *Follies*. She played a soubrette, a flighty, frivolous female named Topsy, and became a big star. She was back as a star of the 1908 *Follies,* this time with her second husband, song and dance man Jack Norworth. Working as a team they were a sensation, and introduced a song, "Shine on Harvest Moon," written by Norworth.

Bayes had first met Norworth when she heard him humming that tune one day while passing his dressing room. She liked the song and offered to help work with him on it. When the song was published the credits read, "Words and Music by Nora Bayes and Jack Norworth."

She had once billed herself as "Empress of Vaudeville," and while she teamed with Norworth they were billed as "The Happiest Married Couple of the Stage." Offstage was a different matter. Nora's salary in the Follies had risen from $75 to $450 a week and she made twice what Jack did. She ordered him around "almost as though he were a servant," made him walk her dog and wouldn't let him smoke in the house. She was also very jealous, and one day in 1909 when she caught him kissing a girl backstage, she decided to get even by changing their billing. Henceforth it would be,"Nora Bayes, Assisted and Admired by Jack Norworth."

Jack walked out of the *Follies* of that year in a huff over his treatment at Nora's hands, and shortly after Bayes left as well, to pursue Jack. Ziegfeld got an injunction preventing them from appearing in the United States. However, the couple got around this by going to England and performing successfully there.

The lawsuit by Ziegfeld dragged on for a while before it was finally resolved and the couple resumed their American careers. At one point Nora claimed she quit the show only after Ziegfeld insisted she wear tights and ride an elephant, both of which she considered beneath her dignity. The effect of all this publicity was to send the salary of the pair up to $2,500 a week.

In 1913 the couple divorced, but Nora remained a strong believer in the institution of marriage: "Marriage is the only state to be in. I believe a woman should have as many love affairs as she likes, but only one at a time." The life story of the pair was filmed in 1944 under the title *Shine on Harvest Moon*. Bayes was played by Ann Sheridan.

Besides vaudeville, Nora appeared in numerous musical comedy Broadway shows such as *The Jolly Bachelors* (1910), *Little Miss Fix-it* (1911), *Maid in America* (1915), and *The Cohen Revue of 1918,* in which she did a lampoon of the then current knitting craze. Bayes worked tirelessly on knitting a sweater for a soldier, oblivious to first the burglary of her home and then its destruction by fire.

Her penchant for taking undeserved credit showed up again in the 1918 production of *Ladies First*. Famed writer Ring Lardner sent her a song he had written for the show, thinking she might like to use it. She did, and when it was published the credit read: "By Nora Bayes and Ring Lardner." Ring was peeved and noted glumly that she'd only "changed two words in the lyrics."

After her divorce from Norworth, Bayes continued in vaudeville as a solo, In 1915 she was billing herself as "The Greatest Single Woman Singing Comedienne in the World." A typical song from her act was "I Work Eight Hours a Day, I Sleep Eight Hours a Day, That Leaves Eight Hours for Lovin'." A critic for *Variety* wrote: "Miss Bayes had an extensive repertoire of songs which ranged from semi-classical to the comedy types. She had the exceptional knack of putting over a song which continually brought her countless copyists." She introduced or made popular many songs which are still well known today, including "Has Anybody Here Seen Kelly?," "Take Me Out to the Ball Game," and George M. Cohan's familiar World War I tune, "Over There." At the end of 1918 she received the ultimate tribute of having a Broadway theater renamed "The Nora Bayes Theatre" in her honor.

In 1917 she was having some sort of trouble with her booking office, so she put together her own revue and toured with it. She was onstage herself for the better part of two hours and drew her songs from a repertoire of 144 she had committed to memory. She was termed "a whole cabaret show in herself." An example of her demanding nature occurred when she walked out on a $1,500 a week, thirty-week deal when she was refused an extra $75 she demanded after signing the contract.

She continued doing revues and appearing in vaudeville into the 1920's; her salary increased to $3,500 a week and then to $5,000 a week. Her health began to deteriorate that decade and she became increasingly temperamental, often more interested in telling audiences about her children than in giving them comedy and songs. At one point E.F. Albee refused to let her play his circuit anymore. Other stories surfaced about tantrums backstage and broken contracts.

In April of 1926 Nora was headlining the vaudeville bill at New York's Palace Theater during a week in which guest stars appeared on each program. One day Sophie Tucker arrived to be the guest and was slated to go on as soon as she arrived, just before Bayes. Nora, however, refused to relinquish her spot, and when management ruled in Tucker's favor Bayes stormed out of the theater. She was suspended for the rest of her week's run and word went out that she should never appear in a big-time theater again.

A couple of years later, in March of 1928, she approached the man in charge of booking at the Palace and asked him to place a billboard in the lobby announcing she would appear the next week. The man, Eddie Darling, refused, saying he felt Mr. Albee would fire him. After some persuasion he reluctantly agreed, and the next day Bayes drove by the theater to see the billboard. A few days later she was dead from cancer.

Though she had earned as much as $100,000 a year at her peak, she was virtually insolvent at the time of her death, a consequence of high living and a generous nature. She had often given freely of her time, entertaining troops during the war and sometimes singing at Bowery missions.

Bayes had a gift for imitation and burlesque and the type of low and husky voice that was popular at the time. She loved her audience and her "forte is a rough laughing common sense — something of the bad boy in it, something of the dangerous woman, something of the natural girl." She felt the most effective comedy songs were those with a "pathetic and sentimental theme" and she selected her songs accordingly. She refused to do certain kinds of material, such as "mother songs" and "flag songs," which she thought were overworked. She may not have been the best, but for twenty years Nora Bayes was one of the biggest names in the entertainment world, her only peers being Elsie Janis and Eva Tanguay.

EVA TANGUAY

In vaudeville Eva Tanguay always played to capacity houses who had come to see this unique entertainer with "her songs, her madcap humor, her freakish costumes and her crop of tousled hair." She billed herself, among other things, as a "Cyclonic Comedienne." She was aggressive, frivolous, raucous, and had a devil-may-care attitude. She was brazen and electric, doing provocative dances and singing sexually suggestive songs. Her dresses were deliberately outrageous, and she was a master of publicity stunts and public relations gimmicks when those arts were still in their infancy. Some called her beautiful, others called her ugly. Some thought she was talented, others judged her devoid of talent.

One thing for certain was that audiences adored her while the critics hated her. These critics, all male, felt very much threatened by the bold female they saw on the stage. She was the single biggest star in vaudeville's history, male or female. Her sexually suggestive material was a forerunner of the type used by Sophie Tucker and Mae West, who were obviously influenced by her. She projected a boisterous and extravagant image, the complete opposite of the decorous, repressed housewife, and ideal woman of the time. She symbolized the growing restlessness of women emerging from Victorian darkness and was very much a forerunner of, and influence on, the liberated 1920's flapper.

Eva Tanguay was born in Marbleton, Quebec, Canada, in August of 1878, the daughter of Octave and Adele Tanguay. When she was about five the family moved to Holyoke, Massachusetts. However, Mr. Tanguay died soon after their arrival and the family was left destitute. At age six or seven Eva made her first appearance on stage at an amateur night at a Holyoke variety house, and won first prize.

She continued to make frequent local appearances, until one day a traveling group of entertainers, the Francesca Redding Company, was playing Holyoke when its juvenile lead fell ill. One of the troupe's owners, Francesca Redding, saw Eva on the street and was impressed enough by her to convince Mrs. Tanguay to let her troupe take Eva on the road with them. Her formal education was forgotten and most of her salary of $8 a week was sent home to help her destitute family. Eva was then eight years old. She toured with that company for five years and played all the child parts, including a long stint as Little Lord Fauntleroy.

During her teen years Tanguay worked on the stage as an acrobat and chorus girl. As an acrobat she developed muscles she would put to good use later on as a brawler. When she was a chorus girl in the late 1890's, she had begun to carve out her own unique style. During a number in one musical, "Hoo-Doo," she momentarily broke away from the other chorines and did her own ad lib dance routine of shimmys and shakes. The audience enjoyed it, but another chorus girl named Tessie took exception and offered criticism, whereupon Eva suddenly grabbed Tessie by the throat and proceeded to choke her. Stagehands had to drag her away, and Eva later boasted that Tessie had been unconscious for three hours.

She appeared with various musical comedy companies and made her debut in New York in the 1901 production *My Lady,* which starred Eddie Foy. Tanguay had one number to sing for which she stepped out of the chorus line and took center stage. During a performance early in the run, one of the girls in the chorus line threw a bun to her boyfriend in the audience. The boyfriend threw it back and the laughter increased. All this while Tanguay sang her number. At its conclusion she rejoined the chorus and the line danced off. Once backstage Eva grabbed the girl and commenced to bang her head against a brick wall. Once again stagehands had to come to the rescue.

A great deal of publicity was generated. The incident even made the front pages of newspapers, indicating the appeal of entertainers of the day and/or the frivolity of the times, as well as revealing the whole science of publicity and PR work, then just coming into its own. After that incident Eva was given a larger, rewritten part and a bigger salary, and the theater was full every night. She had left behind forever the anonymity of the chorus line, and certainly must have learned that erratic and impetuous behavior could be handsomely rewarded.

By 1903 she was being called the youngest star on the American
stage and was headlining in the "Eva Tanguay Comedy Company"
as well as starring in two other musical comedies that year. One
was *The Chaperones* in which she introduced a song called "I
Don't Care" about a woman who was independent enough not to
care what anybody thought about her. It was a song that became
her trademark, and she soon became famous as the "I Don't Care
Girl."

Her next stage appearance was in the 1904 musical comedy *The
Blonde in Black* in which she played a character who was
exuberant, energetic, pleasure-seeking and who freely boasted of
her charms. So popular was Tanguay in that part that her role
was enlarged and the comedy was renamed *The Sambo Girl.* This
vehicle crystallized Eva's image, and for the rest of her career she
would be this type of character, both on and off the stage, in the
same sense that Mae West was Diamond Lil was Mae West. Audiences were attracted to both the character and to Eva, while critics and censors reacted with alarm.

In 1906 she left the legitimate stage and moved to the relatively
freer arena of vaudeville. Over the next quarter of a century she
would rarely stray from her new home. For many people, "Eva
Tanguay was American vaudeville." By 1908 she was making $500
a week, and she decided to introduce the story of Salome, or the
Dance of the Seven Veils, to her audience. The Strauss opera
Salome was first presented in Germany in 1906 and featured the
dance in which Salome fondled the severed head of John the Baptist, killed after rejecting Salome's advances. During the dance
Salome discarded her veils one by one.

The New York Metropolitan produced the opera, but only for
one performance after luminaries such as J. Pierpoint Morgan and
W.K. Vanderbilt demanded it be stopped as "revolting and disgusting." All this was enough to make the dance a fad of the
decade, with many comics doing burlesques of it. This led to
further outrage on the part of reformers, and several cities and
states, including Ohio and Pennsylvania, banned the dance
outright.

According to Tanguay, she did the dance wearing only "two
pearls." Her costume was scanty, but not quite that drastic, and
consisted of some beads and a bit of jewelry, besides the veils. She
did the dance and discarded the veils one by one. Her sister was
in the audience and fainted, fearing that Eva would be arrested
for indecent exposure. The audience loved it, but the Mayor of

New York City threatened to close the show if she didn't don more clothes. In describing her performance Eva reflected, "I was no classical dancer. . . . so I mixed in some Highland Fling and Sailor's Hornpipe and everything else I knew." As always happened with Eva, the controversy served only to enhance her career.

The team of Nora Bayes and Jack Norworth had just walked out on Florenz Ziegfeld and his *Follies* and Flo quickly grabbed Tanguay. Due to the Salome publicity she was able to demand top billing and a salary of $1,200 a week. A couple of years later she was commanding a salary of $3,500 a week, the highest in vaudeville. It was not uncommon for her to run afoul of the authorities. Around 1916 officials in Syracuse banned a theater where she was playing from showing photos of her in action. The theater was deluged with requests from people wanting these posters for souvenirs.

She was one of the first entertainers to go in for outrageous and outlandish costumes. Her gowns normally hung from her shoulders to her hips and sparkled, shone, and gleamed; they often were covered with feathers and furs. She once had a dress fashioned from one, five, ten and fifty dollar bills that she had sewn together. Another time she created a costume out of Lincoln pennies. One costume was trimmed with sugar and coal, items perhaps harder to come by than dollars during World War I. Another dress was covered with pencils and memo pads.

While spending a fortune on her wardrobe, Tanguay also spent more on personal publicity and advertising than any other big star. She employed as many as four press agents at the same time. Among the various nicknames and slogans created for her by her own staff or the trade papers were the following: "The Electrifying Hoyden," "Mother Eve's Merriest Daughter," "The Genius of Mirth and Song," "Our Own Eva, America's Idol," and "Vaudeville's Greatest Drawing Card."

For one publicity stunt, around 1908, she sold newspapers on a street corner accompanied by a trained elephant. In 1910 she appeared at an amateur night under the alias of Lillian Doom and was a great hit. (Other stars of the era had tried the same but failed, including Bert Williams. Gloria Swanson, appearing in disguise, failed a screen test at the peak of her career.) Tanguay's entrance on stage was always heralded by a blare of trombones. Publicity photos deliberately showed her at her most outlandish "with bosoms bursting out of bras and thighs rippling with fat."

Throughout her career her hot temper continued to come to the fore. She once pushed a stagehand down the stairs in Louisville, Kentucky, because he was in her way. That outburst led to a $50 fine in court and a civil suit which was settled for $1,000. Tanguay, who liked to carry $1,000 bills around with her, simply peeled one off her roll and handed it to the stagehand. In Evansville, Indiana, she slept through a matinee, for which the house manager fined her $100. Enraged, she took a knife and slashed the theater's house curtain to shreds.

When she was playing in Sharon, Pennsylvania, she asked the manager to install a large mirror in her dressing room, in place of the existing smaller one. When the man refused, Eva complained to her audience. Receiving no sympathy from them, she then harangued them, calling them "a lot of small town saps." None of this did anything except to enhance her career, which undoubtedly helped to contribute to her combative nature. Audiences liked nothing better than something unexpected, or not usually on the bill. When they went to see the mercurial Eva Tanguay, they never knew just what might happen.

Sexual indiscretion could ruin a female star's career quite easily and quickly, and on very flimsy evidence, as with Mabel Normand. But Tanguay got away with things other women couldn't, a similarity she had with Mae West. Eva had become too big and too popular a star, and again like Mae West, her stage and real persona had shaded into one personality. People expected her to behave offstage in a certain way, and when she did, it was more readily accepted.

She was once traveling through the Midwest on a train with her current lover—just one of many over the years—when the pair got into a fistfight with the conductor over an open window. Eva and friend were put off the train at Des Moines and arrested. The next day the judge released them after remarking he had been a Tanguay fan for years. She was once caught in bed with one of her press agents by private detectives and the agent's wife. While living in New York, police were called to her apartment to break up a fistfight between Eva and her latest lover. She would often announce engagements of marriage to the press when the men named knew nothing at all about it. Until the end of her career she battled management and constantly walked out on engagements over slights, real or imagined.

On stage she clowned with a passion, danced, showed her legs, and ridiculed herself. She sang risqué and suggestive songs over the objections of bluenoses and vaudeville bosses. Vaudeville was very much a clean family type of entertainment and vaudeville tycoons such as E.F. Albee had very strict and puritanical codes about what could and could not be done on stage. Tanguay ignored such dictates and performed songs, besides "I Don't Care," with titles such as "It's All Been Done Before But Never the Way I Do It," "Go As Far As You Like," "That's Why They Call Me Tabasco," "I Can't Help It," "Egotistical Eva," "Give an Imitation of Eva," "I've Got to Be Crazy," "I Want Someone to Go Wild With Me," "Tune In on Eva," and "I May Be a Nut, But I'm Not a Crossword Fan."

While she sang her songs, "Tanguay ran wildly across the stage and seemed to carom from one corner of the set to another, wriggling her breasts, kicking her legs wildly, and shaking that thing. Often she appeared to be having an orgasm." The critics disliked her as much as the audience loved her. Her singing and dancing were denounced from coast to coast as vulgar and amateurish. She was called "overweight and ugly" and said to have no talent.

Writing in the *Chicago Tribune*, Percy Hammond stated that he "could think of no entertainer who entertained him less." He likened her singing to "the wail of the prehistoric diplodocus." Another reviewer said her "stage costumes ranged from the weird to the grotesque." Her dancing was called "the very doggerel of motion."

During World War I she appeared wrapped in French flags and sang "The Marseillaise." Distinguished critic Heywood Broun reviewed this performance, and summed up his overall impression of Tanguay in the *New York Tribune:* "There should be some moral force, or physical if need be, to keep her away from the 'Marseillaise.' She should not be allowed to sing it even on her knees, and it is monstrous . . . as a climax to a vulgar act by a bouncing singer in a grotesque costume begirt with little flags. . . . The only cheerful song in her repertory yesterday was one in which she hinted that some day she would retire. . . . She is the parsnip of performers."

Tanguay promptly took out an ad in *Variety* in which she attacked the Broun review and included the following thought: "Have you ever noticed when a woman succeeds how they attack her until her character bleeds? They snap at her heels, like mongrels unfed, just because she had escaped being dropped into FAILURE'S big web." It was an attitude faced by many women over the years.

During the first quarter of this century women such as Tanguay, Tucker and West had begun to present a new image of women, one that was aggressive, uninhibited, and overtly sexual. It was an image the male critics were not used to, not comfortable with, and not prepared to accept. It was this image that the critics attacked, not the talent, or lack thereof, that these women possessed.

Tanguay continued to perform in vaudeville into the 1920's and remained a superstar. In 1924 *Variety* said that "What Ruth is to baseball, Dempsey to pugilism and Chaplin to pictures, Tanguay is to vaudeville." Her appearances were then limited due to her declining health and the beginnings of the demise of vaudeville itself, although she was back in vaudeville in 1930 after a three-year absence. One of the numbers she did then was a comedy song, "Mae West, Texas and Me," about the mob having christened her, West and Texas Guinan as the "Unholy Three." After that she grew more and more reclusive during the last twenty years of her life.

Because of the extravagant spending, her generosity to others, unlucky real estate speculation and the stock market crash, she lost all of her fortune, estimated to be as high as $2 million. In 1933 she went blind, and it was Sophie Tucker who paid for the cataract operation which restored her sight. In 1937 arthritis made her an almost permanent invalid for her last decade of life.

On the occasion of her sixty-eighth birthday in 1946 she granted an interview to a reporter. It was conducted through the screen of her bedroom window while the interviewer stood outside. She had hopes then of a film of her life being done. Eva Tanguay died, less than six months after the interview, in January, 1947. She left no will and had assets of $500. In 1953 a film was released starring Mitzi Gaynor. Called *The I Don't Care Girl*, the movie was dismally received.

Tanguay enjoyed writing doggerel throughout her career and often talked in that fashion. When asked how she became famous she would reply, "When I put on tights, my name went up in lights." It was a style emulated decades later by boxer Muhammad Ali. The key to her success lay in her personality, something she exploited to the fullest She admitted "that her success relied in part on the fact that she did behave in a crazy fashion, and because she was a terrible and crazy actress, who acted like an insane person, audiences flocked to see her." Tanguay claimed her entire success was due solely to the exploitation of her personality through publicity stunts and the media attention to all her scraps. She said, "As a matter of fact, I am not beautiful, I can't sing, I do not know how to dance. I am not even graceful."

She, and a few others, symbolized a new aggressiveness in female comics. It was a move towards independence which would soon be quashed by a male-dominated society. The groundwork for the aggressive and uninhibited woman comedian was laid early in this century by those like Tanguay but would never be fully realized until the late 1970's.

Usually Tanguay was oblivious to her critics and detractors, but occasionally she did display some resentment about being considered a "harum-scarum don't care creature." In her retort to Broun she expressed the frustration of a woman attempting to succeed in the pressured world of show business, and trying to overcome the difficulties of playing a "man's game," saying, "I have beaten your game, and it's a hard game to beat."

SOPHIE TUCKER

Sophie Abuza made her debut singing in her parent's Hartford, Connecticut, restaurant. Between waiting on tables she would entertain the customers with popular songs. The 145-pound teenager was a hit with the clientele, many of whom were actors or performers themselves.

Sophie also entertained in local amateur shows. At concerts she would hear calls for the "fat girl," but, as she explained, this would only encourage her: "I would jump up from the piano stool, forgetting all about my size, and work to get all the laughs I could get."

Sophie and her parents had emigrated from Russia a few months after she was born in 1884. Although the restaurant provided the family with an income, profits were meager. Sophie detested the long hours of hard work. When she was sixteen, she eloped with Louis Tuck, the driver of a beer wagon. They soon had a son Bert. When they ran into financial trouble, the Tucks moved in with Sophie's parents, and shortly after the marriage fell apart.

Back working in the restaurant, Sophie was determined to become an entertainer. She saved up some money and ran away to

New York, telling her mother in a letter that she would send
money home every week for her son. It took a great deal of
courage for a girl in her teens, coming from an Orthodox Jewish
family in which the ideas of divorce and show business were repel-
lant, to embark on such a career.

At first Sophie had difficulty making a go of it. She found some
work singing in modest restaurants as she had at home, but this
brought in little money. She had fantasies of turning to prostitution, but fortunately she was befriended by a Jewish family who let
her live with them until she got a steady job.

In 1906 Sophie changed her surname to Tucker, and that year
she was hired to sing at the German Village for $15 a week. She
sang up to one hundred songs per night. A month later she was
accepted in an amateur show at the 116th Street Music Hall.
There was one condition, however. The manager felt that since
Tucker was so "big and ugly" (she was then 165 pounds), she
would have to appear in blackface. Sophie accepted the offer,
even though she hated the ordeal of putting on blackface. She
knew she would never be the kind of woman to perform in "pink
tights or G-string."

Tucker began to tour the vaudeville circuit billed as a "World-
Renowned Coon Shouter," and soon built up a following. This in
turn led to a contract to play the burlesque theaters. One day her
trunk with costumes and makeup failed to show up in time for her
performances. For the first time Sophie performed without blackface, and proved she could appeal to audiences without any disguise. In fact she became known for her blond hair, gold sequined
gowns, furs, and jewelry.

In 1909 Tucker was offered a part in the *Ziegfeld Follies*. Nora
Bayes was the star of the show. According to Sophie, she stole the
show from Bayes on opening night, so Tucker's routine was cut
back to one song. When Eva Tanguay replaced Bayes in the New
York run of the *Follies*, she wanted Tucker's song, so Sophie was
fired. Because of the anxiety of being without work, Tucker temporarily lost her voice.

It wasn't long, however, before Sophie signed on with the William Morris agency and was back on vaudeville. Her material consisted of "hot songs" filled with double entendres. Tucker felt
the songs were meant to be humorous rather than shocking. She
insisted that there was "a belly laugh in every line." Nevertheless,
some of these songs got her into trouble with the censors. In Chicago she was banned from singing "Angle Worm Wiggle," and

Atlantic City forbade "Who Paid the Rent for Mrs. Rip Van Winkle, When Rip Van Winkle Was Away?"

Tucker's act became so successful that she was soon headlining and making recordings. In 1911 the black composer Shelton Brooks offered Sophie his song "Some of These Days." It became her signature. Other songs that she sang were "Nobody Loves a Fat Girl, But Oh How a Fat Girl Can Love," "I May be Getting Older Everyday (But Getting Younger Every Night)," and "My Yiddishe Momma." She was the first to introduce Irving Berlin's "Blue Skies." Sophie made a point of getting to know the young songwriters in Tin Pan Alley, and they often wrote songs for her.

The year 1914 was an important one for Tucker. She played the Palace Theater in New York, earning $1,000 for her performances and winning praise from critics and audiences. She also got married to Frank Westphal, a comedian and musician. They did an act together for several seasons, but Westphal was frustrated because Sophie made more money than he did, and she had star status. He left the stage, and Sophie set him up as a mechanic. The final straw came when Westphal saw the sign over the building: Sophie Tucker's Garage. The marriage eventually ended in divorce.

In her autobiography, *Some of These Days* (1945),Sophie commented on the problems of being a highly successful female performer. She explained that it was lonely on the road, and that men did not ask her out: "Once you start carrying your own suitcases, paying your own bills, running your own show," she said, "you've done something to yourself that makes you one of those women men may like and call a 'pal' and a 'good sport,' the kind of woman they tell their troubles to. But you've cut yourself off from the orchids and the diamond bracelets, except those you buy yourself."

Tucker did marry a third time, however. Her husband Al Lackey (could there be a more appropriate name!) became Sophie's manager, but Sophie got tired of supporting him and they divorced in 1934. This last marriage prompted the lyrics for a song Tucker liked to sing: "There is not going to be a fourth Mr. Ex. I'm darned if I'll pay any more alimony checks. I'm living alone and I like it."

In 1916 Tucker began changing her routine. She hired five jazz musicians, as this music was coming in vogue, and billed the act as "Sophie Tucker, the Queen of Jazz and her Five Kings of Syncopation." They played Reisenweber's, a famous restaurant in those days, and the Winter Garden Theater. Tucker's voice sounded so much like a black singer's that people who had never seen her perform but had heard her recordings assumed she was black. The act was very popular, but after five years her musicians were demanding more money, and Sophie thought they were forgetting that she was the sole star.

The act disbanded, and Tucker hired a pianist, Ted Shapiro, to accompany her. She kept him on for the rest of her career, no doubt because he respectfully called her "Miss Tucker" at all times. The hiring of Shapiro heralded a new era in Tucker's life. In 1922 she began a tour of English music halls. Well received by British audiences, Sophie played the Palladium and Rivoli, among other theaters. One British critic called her "a big fat blonde genius" (Sophie was up to 194 pounds). Another praised her act, saying: "She pours a bucketful of Tuckerisms over our delighted heads. She is not young, nor slinky; she will admit to the deficiency of both with a disarming frankness. But she tells us, and the whole gamut of stark satire is uncovered in the saying, that she has a kiss like a hungry mosquito. Whatever she says, the assembled world roars with delight at the sound of her voice."

From that time onward, Tucker was to divide her time between America and Britain. She even appeared with Beatrice Lillie in *Charlot's Revue.*

In 1928 Sophie first sang "I'm the Last of the Red Hot Mommas," written for her by Frank Yellen. It became her trademark. Her fame was such that by 1932 she was paid $7,500 a week at Loew's.

Tucker also branched out into films, and made seven features between 1929 and 1944. Vaudeville was on its way out as a result of competition from movies and radio, and Sophie had to follow the trends. But she never cared for film-making. The roles she was given didn't suit her style, and some of her best scenes were cut.

Radio was also unappealing to Tucker because, as she once told an interviewer: "You can't do this, you can't do that. I couldn't even say 'hell or damn,' and nothing, honey, is more expressive than the way I say 'hell or damn.'"

In 1938 she starred in the popular Cole Porter Broadway musical comedy *Leave It to Me.* But her 1941 Broadway role in George Jessel's *High Kickers* was panned by reviewers. Tucker continued to work successfully in clubs, though. In 1944 she starred in a revue at the Copacabana, and a critic for the New York *Sun* noted that: "Sophie Tucker isn't cooling off any, and for that matter neither is her doting audience."

During the 1950's Sophie was seen in nightclubs and on television. She was working on a new act with George Jessel and Ted Lewis when she died in 1966 at the age of seventy-nine.

Tucker's style of comedy had been similar in some respects to that of Mae West's. Because of her size, Sophie couldn't play the meek little blonde who needed protection. Instead, she was the bold brassy hunk of woman, flaunting her sexuality through bawdy songs like "But He Only Stays Till Sunday" or "I Just Couldn't Make Ma Feelin's Behave." Her comedy was energetic. The implications of her lyrics were that it took a lot of man (or men) to satisfy her needs. In tunes like "You've Got to See Your Mama Ev'ry Night" or "You Can't Deep Freeze a Red Hot Mama" Tucker made it clear that she expected the man to perform or else. The aggressiveness in her act was no doubt a way of avoiding being victimized as a fat girl. It was tempered by her comic delivery and playful manner.

When Tucker became famous, she refused to allow any theater manager to censor her work. She felt that as long as audiences liked her material, she would use it. Sophie had always been outspoken about performer's rights. In 1938 she had been elected the first female president of the American Federation of Actors union. Her term of office was not an easy one, as there were charges against certain members for misusing funds.

Unlike Mae West, Tucker included self-mockery in her routine, often making fun of her weight. She also focused on the disappointments that women suffered in love. Men were unfaithful, lacking in responsibility, and difficult. But Tucker was never self-pitying. She made it clear that she could make it on her own. She asserted her independence in songs such as "I Ain't Takin' Orders From No One," "Never Let the Same Dog Bite You Twice," or "No One Man Is Every Going to Worry Me."

Nor did age slow her down. Like West, Tucker refused to dwell on being an old lady. On the contrary, she maintained her sense of humor and her sensual style. When she sang "I Am Having More Fun Since I Am Sixty," she meant it.

BEATRICE HERFORD

Beatrice Herford was one of the first female monologists to appear on the vaudeville stage. Her example paved the way for famed monologist Ruth Draper, who in turn influenced Lily Tomlin.

Herford was born in Manchester, England, in 1868. Her father was a Unitarian minister and her upbringing was genteel. Yet she and her brother Oliver both showed a talent for comic invention and irony. Her brother eventually took up satiric writing and drawing, while Beatrice went on the stage.

Herford gave expression to her talent from an early age. She was always pretending to be someone else, and one of her favorite characters was a "rich, sought-after woman of the world." She also did impersonations of family and friends. These were so well received that Beatrice began performing in other people's homes. Friends persuaded her to take up a career as an actress and by her early twenties she was appearing in provincial theaters in England.

In 1895, at the age of twenty-seven, Herford made her debut as a monologist in London. Among audience members were George Bernard Shaw, Ellen Terry, and Henry James. Her excellent performance established her reputation for humor. After marrying a wealthy American, Sydney Hayward, Beatrice moved with him to the United States.

Her first stage appearance there was at the old 39th Street Theater where she acted in the comedy *She Stoops to Conquer*. Beatrice then resumed writing monologues and began to give solo performances in vaudeville theaters. This was considered quite a risk for someone of Herford's class and education. Critics wondered if mass audiences would understand Herford's subtle irony, but of course they not only understood what she was saying, they laughed heartily at her comedy.

Herford performed with few sets or props, often only a chair. Her dress was conservative, her appearance understated. Although Beatrice acted only one role, she evoked many other characters. Her monologues were slices of life, peopled by ordinary female characters—a young reciter, a bored shop-girl, a sociable seamstress, a harassed mother, a ticket buyer. She often made use of accents to define a character.

In one piece, Herford played a young girl visiting the National Gallery in London: "What I like to do is to watch those people copying the pictures. I think their copies are often lots prettier than originals," the young lady naively confessed.

In another monologue, "A Professional Boarder," Herford conversed with her fellow boarders (all imaginary) at breakfast: "Oh, going to have your picture taken; is that so? Where do you go, Mrs. Watson? Oh, no, I don't care for his pictures at all. I had mine taken there, and I wanted to burn them all up, but they cost so much, so I gave them all away to my relations."

Quoting a line or two doesn't do justice to Herford's monologues, since they did not really depend on one-line gags. They were more in the style of personality portraits. The caricature in her material was very gentle and her viewpoint was upper-class. Much of the subject matter is dated today, but several of the published monologues still raise a smile, and this without benefit of Herford's acting to bring them alive.

As well as playing the Keith vaudeville circuit, Beatrice was also seen in Broadway revues and plays. She continued to perform only into the 1930's, although she lived until 1952.

Fantasy was central to Herford's life. In her Massachusetts home, Beatrice had her own 125-seat theater which she named after Rosina Vokes, a famous nineteenth-century English actress. She and visitors like Ellen Terry would perform there.

Herford claimed to do all her monologue writing outdoors during the months of September, October and November. To stay warm she would "bundle up and chase the sun around the house."

In a May, 1906, article in *Ladies Home Journal* Beatrice commented about her inspiration: "I never consciously study types with a view to making copy of them; but when I start in on a monologue I find that my memory has stored up innumerable little characteristics, expressions and motions and inflections of the type I've chosen."

Beatrice's work had always been admired by critics. In 1924 Alexander Woollcott noted that "all the monologues are studies with a minuteness of discrimination that is truly wonderful, they fairly bristle with wit."

Dorothy Parker, writing in the March, 1921, issue of *Everybody's Magazine,* had this to say about Herford: "You have all that you can do to restrain your whoops of laughter, not so much because they might annoy your neighbors as because they might prevent your hearing some of Miss Herford's succeeding remarks."

Audiences sometimes exercised restraint for other reasons, however. Herford remembered appearing in a small town where
nobody laughed or even smiled at her monologues. She thought
her performance a failure. Afterward a gentleman came backstage to shake her hand. As Beatrice told it, "He said he knew it
wasn't polite to laugh at a lady, but that he'd had a hard struggle
that evening, and that a 'dozen times' he thought he'd 'have to
bust right out laughin'."

Yet Herford felt that, on the whole, men were openly responsive
to her humor. In a May, 1906, interview in *Ladies Home Journal,*
she remarked, perhaps without realizing the irony of her comment: "The American man does love to laugh at his women folk.
Every time he recognizes one of his wife's peculiarities in a sketch
of mine he's as pleased as a boy with a new top."

As for women, Beatrice thought they had varying responses to
being satirized, however good-natured the tone. Some didn't
recognize themselves as the targets, others appreciated the joke on
themselves, while some were offended.

There were politically-minded women in Herford's day who felt
that her material demeaned females, or held them up to ridicule.
Beatrice took a rather patronizing view of these critics: "Life is a
long, serious matter to the suffragist, isn't it? Now I'm particularly
fond of women, but if they were not absurd at times they wouldn't
be so delightful."

This would not be the only time that a comedienne was accused
of being a traitor to her sex. The conflict between art and politics
would reappear continually throughout the history of female
comedy.

RUTH DRAPER

Ruth Draper always appeared alone, but the stage came alive with
dozens of her characters whenever she performed. Over the span
of her career she created 39 monologues portraying 58 individuals,
and evoking hundreds more through her imaginative conversations.

Using a few shawls, some hats, an overcoat, and perhaps a couple of chairs or tables, Draper was able to convey the personality

of an old woman or a young girl. Without the aid of elaborate props, costumes or supporting actors, Ruth presented complete characters and settings.

Many, though not all, of her monologues were humorous, with the audience laughing throughout her performance. Because of this, and due to her influence on future comedians like Lily Tomlin, Draper played a part in the development of women in comedy.

Ruth Draper was born in New York City in 1884. Her parents were Dr. William Henry Draper and Ruth Dana, daughter of Charles A. Dana, editor of the New York *Sun*. Due to Dana's eminent position, the family often entertained prominent guests. Draper was the second youngest of six children. Her genius developed early, and she spent hours amusing her family by imitating relatives, servants, and guests. One of her first fans was the pianist Paderewski, a family friend. He urged her to go on the stage, even though this was still considered radical for a proper young lady.

Ruth had not been comfortable with traditional schooling and the major part of her education was supervised by a governess. With no interest in furthering her formal education, Draper found the idea of becoming a performer intriguing. She began to entertain for charities in 1903 and built a fine reputation and loyal following. Between 1910 and 1913 she performed 35 times in the New York area. One of her first sketches was based on the woman who sewed for her family: "Its could be fixed," she would say.

Draper was inspired to continue her work when she saw the comic monologues of Beatrice Herford. She was also influenced by a Chinese play, *The Yellow Jacket,* which had very little scenery: "I understood," she said, "the extraordinary illusion that can be created with nothing."

In 1913 Ruth traveled to London where she gave charity performances hosted by the British aristocracy, including King George V and Queen Mary. Henry James became one of her admirers and encouraged her by saying, "You have woven your own very beautiful little Persian carpet. Stand on it!" John Singer Sargent painted her portrait in character.

Draper's success led her to the decision to appear professionally. In 1916 she accepted a small part as a lady's maid in the play *A Lady's Name*. It ran for only six weeks in Atlantic City, Montreal, and New York. In 1917 she made another try in theater. She performed in an interpretation of a Strindberg play and one of her own sketches, "The Actress," at the Comedy Theater in New York. Her own work was the piece praised by the critics. This convinced Ruth that in the future she would always work solo and appear only in sketches that she herself had created. She never appeared as part of a vaudeville bill, but booked engagements and halls herself where she gave a one-person concert, unusual at that time for man or woman.

During World War I Draper entertained enlisted men in the U.S. and overseas. During her travels, she picked up several accents and dialects which she would later incorporate in her act. Her wartime journeys gave her material for some thirty sketches. Broadened by these experiences, Ruth was once again ready to try the professional stage. In 1920 she was booked into London's Aeolian Hall, and was a success.

The Times critic on January 30th, 1920, raved: "For two hours yesterday afternoon Miss Ruth Draper kept a large audience at the Aeolian Hall smiling and laughing, now and then feeling a little lump in the throat. . . . Her observation is almost wickedly keen, her expression of it is pointed and polished till it is as clear and bright as a diamond."

Said *The Observer*: "Miss Draper sees intensely, understands piercingly, and can express cleanly. . . . At the bottom of it all lies sympathy. She can jest because she understands."

Draper's London success was the stepping-stone to more European engagements. She performed in Paris and Germany and continued to return to Europe during the next thirty years of her career. Her fame grew to such an extent that she toured Latin America, Africa, and Asia. In 1928 her audiences were so large that she had a nineteen week run at the Comedy Theater.

Draper had several suitors during her lifetime, but she never married. She did, however, have a major romance with a young Italian poet, scientist and classical scholar, Lauro de Bosis. Ruth was forty-three at the time, de Bosis twenty-six. There was talk of marriage and children between them, but the relationship ended in tragedy. In 1931 de Bosis was killed after flying solo over Rome distributing anti-fascist pamphlets.

Fortunately for Draper, her work provided, as it always had, the fulfillment she required. In her letters she had once written: "I must work, for I see it is the only way to make me realize that I have something worth living for."

Ruth's monologues ranged between five and fifty minutes. Her two-hour program, usually containing seven sketches, was performed about one hundred times a year. In one of her comic monologues, "Doctors and Diets," Ruth portrayed a woman taking three other ladies to lunch, only to find they were all on diets. After a meal of turnip, raw carrots, and lemon juice, three chocolate eclairs were ordered.

In another humorous sketch Draper portrayed a woman at an art exhibit making ridiculous comments about the paintings. Reviewed in the *Literary Digest* of February 9, 1929, this monologue spurred the critic to write: "Miss Draper's restraint in not going to the limit of the farcical possibilities of the situation is remarkable. It is an extremely comic character sketch, but Miss Draper doesn't try to make it funny just for the sake of being funny. She sticks to her character, she hints at all sorts of things about her which are not funny, and when she goes off the stage we feel we have made the acquaintance of a real person."

Draper's sketch "In a Church in Italy" was also in the comic vein. She portrayed six characters and evoked twenty. The central character, an American tourist, read out of Baedeker and then tried to spot the sights mentioned in the guide. The peripheral characters were a beggar, a young girl, an English artist, a German tourist, and an old peasant woman.

Also reviewed in the *Literary Digest* of February 9, 1929, this sketch was noted as being "very funny but at the same time it is hardly exaggerated, or exaggerated only so much as keen, friendly observation will exaggerate any human act. Far from laughing at the tourist in a superior way, and setting her down as one of the ridiculous travelers who make us ashamed of our country while abroad, we feel that every one of us sounds a good deal like that."

The sketch entitled "The Italian Lesson" was one that particularly amused audiences. Ruth portrayed a society woman in her boudoir whose teacher has come to read Dante with her. Distracted by dogs and children ("Pat him on his head, sweetheart — that's his tail"), a lover ("I picked up a charming young Englishman last week, Sir Basil Something — I put him on a scrap of paper in the blotter"), servants, husband, and friends, the lady manages to translate exactly one sentence of Italian.

Some of Draper's other well-known monologues were "Opening a Bazaar," "At an English House Party," and "The Debutante." Not only was Ruth able to bring characters to life but she could also create entire locales with the minimal props. Thornton

Delehanty of the New York *World* marvelled that with only a few
pieces of furniture she was able to convey a hospital, an English
drawing room, or an Irish hut.

Francis Bellamy writing in the March 20, 1929, issue of *Outlook
and Independent* was similarly impressed by the scope of Ruth's
ability. "Perhaps," he wrote, "a combination of the talkies and the
movies and the theater might possibly include all these abilities,
but even then in our own judgment, there would be something
lacking. In fact, here is the human comedy."

And Richard Skinner critic for *The Commonweal* in January,
1930, praised Draper for her "uncanny power of observation, both
as to details of gestures and speech," and her "acute sense of
comedy situation and of the humor of incongruous remarks."

Draper prepared for her work in front of a mirror in order to
perfect certain facial movements. She had superb ability as a
mimist, but she tried to personify an individual, never mimic or
impersonate anyone. In the early part of her career she did not
work from a script but had all her sketches memorized. As a result
few of her performances were the same. Later in her life, she
wrote down her monologues, and recorded the high points of
some of her pieces in 1950.

Ruth's fame had peaked during her concert days, but she continued to work until her death in 1956. She had been pleased to
see that a new generation of young people were making up her
audiences. As she had wished, her coffin was draped with the
shawls she had used to create her wonderful array of characters.

As a woman of the upper classes Ruth had been hesitant to
become a professional entertainer. It had taken her many years to
accept money for her talent. When she did she was highly successful. Her self-reliance allowed her to use her intelligence to the
full, and she created female roles that showed depth and imagination.

MABEL NORMAND

Mabel Normand was the first female comedian superstar of the
movies. On more than one occasion she was called a "female
Chaplin" although she never attained those heights; her career
was too brief and her vehicles were too substandard. She never

got a chance to display what she might have been capable of, since her fame was cut short by a couple of scandals which effectively ended her career. Her reign as queen of the silent films lasted only about a dozen years until she fell victim to the sexual double standard. She will forever be immortal, however, as the originator of the custard pie in the face in films.

It was Normand who was instrumental in getting Chaplin started in films. It was Normand who taught him in the beginning and it was Normand who directed Chaplin in a number of his early films. In return, Chaplin sexually propositioned her at least once, and refused to be directed by her any longer, not because she was incompetent, but because she was a female. Mabel directed over a dozen early films, but today she has been largely ignored and forgotten as a director, a victim of male revisionist history.

As time went by she became more and more difficult to work with, partly due to the star system then coming into its own, which coddled and pampered those who were "hot," and partly due to a long, stormy, and ultimately unsatisfactory relationship with Mack Sennett. She was also the victim of unwanted sexual advances from Sam Goldwyn. In those days, men like Goldwyn and Chaplin hit on everything that moved, without drawing any adverse comment. Women were ostracized and banished for much less. Normand died at 37 of tuberculosis, exiled from the film industry.

She was born in November of 1892 in Staten Island, New York, the daughter of Mary and Claude Normand. Her father was a piano player who traveled the New England coast playing in theaters, but he never advanced beyond nickel and dime status. Little is known about her childhood, and her formal education was thought to be very brief or even non-existent. She got her first job at about the age of fourteen, working in Manhattan in the pattern-making department of the Butterick Company. From there she moved on to become an artist's model and regularly posed for two leading artists of the day, James Montgomery Flagg and Charles Dana Gibson, of "Gibson Girl" fame.

A model friend suggested Mabel try her luck in films. At Vitagraph studio she was given a few roles. Her first film was the 1910 release, *Over the Garden Wall*, made at the company's Brooklyn studios. Normand had no theatrical experience, but breaking into films in those days was a much simpler process, since nobody had very much experience in the new medium. After a few roles at

Vitagraph, Mabel moved over to the Biograph studio in Manhattan, which was then run by D.W. Griffith. It was there that she met Mack Sennett, a Biograph director and actor. She appeared in two dozen Biograph shorts, as all films were in those days, mostly directed by Griffith or Sennett.

In *A Dash Through the Clouds* (1912) she was filmed in a biplane taking pistol shots at bandits below. It was said to have been the first time a woman was filmed in flight. In the 1911 release *The Diving Girl*, Normand appeared in full-length black tights, daring then, and was a forerunner of the bathing beauties Sennett would later popularize.

In 1912 Sennett left Biograph to form the Keystone Film Company and took Mabel with him, A third member of the group was Ford Sterling, who shortly left Keystone. Legend has it that Mabel and Mack one evening were attending a performance by English comedians, and Mabel, impressed by one of their number, recommended Sennett give him a chance to replace the departed Sterling. That comedian was Charlie Chaplin.

Within a few months of his arrival at Keystone Chaplin had begun to direct himself, a task he would never relinquish again to anybody else. He did learn much of his basic knowledge of film technique through Normand's guidance and she did direct him in six films, something he soon refused to continue. Chaplin claimed in his autobiography, where he also admitted making an unsuccessful pass at her, that it was because their personalities clashed. Perhaps a more cogent reason was "that he resented Mabel because she was a woman."

She was impulsive and given to practical jokes. In June 1913 in the film *A Noise From the Deep* she ad libbed and threw the first custard pie into the face of the first film recipient, Fatty Arbuckle.

Sennett's style of comedy became an immediate hit with audiences and Normand became famous almost overnight as "Keystone Mabel." She was just five feet tall and never weighed more than one hundred pounds, but she had no trouble fitting into the rough and ready, very physical style of Sennett slapstick comedy. She threw herself with abandon into any physical gag, and Marie Dressler remarked about her, "she was the first great comedienne of the screen. Always willing to risk life and limb to give the fans a thrill, she used to spend half of her time laid up in hospital for repairs."

Even as a superstar she would never let a double do any of the leaps, falls, or spills. When a doctor advised her not to take chances with her safety, she replied, "What in hell's the difference, if it makes a lot of people laugh?" When Sennett spoke of his comics, he said that "Mabel Normand could do everything Chaplin could do. . . . To me, she was the greatest comedian that ever lived."

In those days filmmaking was very informal, which may explain why Normand got to direct any films. The Sennett group would often wait until they heard of some interesting public event and then rush there to film it. One day Keystone heard that the city of Los Angeles planned to drain a small lake in Echo Park. When city workmen arrived to pull the plug a camera crew was waiting and so were Mabel and her screen boyfriend sitting in a rowboat in the lake. The film was built around that premise. Another time Mabel was given a rag doll and rushed out into a passing civic parade to harass a marching fireman. Scripts were often not used at all, or only written after filming was complete, for the benefit of the film cutter. Films were one- or two-reelers, and ran ten to twenty minutes.

Normand was willing to do anything, from being hit in the face with a pie to being dragged through a riverbed. In *Mabel's Awful Mistake* (1913) she was the beautiful and trusting country girl lured to the city by a promise of marriage. When she learned the man was already married, she decided to return home, but the man wouldn't let her. The villain tied her to a planing table in a sawmill and turned on a buzzsaw. Her boyfriend from the country arrived in the nick of time to save her. In *Barney Oldfield's Race for a Life* (1913) the villain, whose advances Mabel had spurned, tied her to a railroad track and bore down on her in his locomotive. Again she was saved in the nick of time by a host of rescuers, including a handcar full of Keystone Kops.

Chaplin and Normand appeared together in eleven films, such as *Mabel's Strange Predicament* in which Chaplin's tramp character first appeared, *Mabel's Busy Day*, and *Mabel's Married Life*, all 1914 releases. Their pairing culminated in the 1914 release *Tillie's Punctured Romance*, in which the pair shared second billing behind Marie Dressler. This film was six reels long and was the first feature-length comedy film.

When Chaplin left Keystone to go on to bigger and better things, Mabel was regularly paired on the screen with Roscoe "Fatty" Arbuckle and the team was a big money-maker. In the 1915 release *Fatty and Mabel's Married Life*, Fatty stepped out for the evening, over Mabel's protests. Mabel, home alone, soon became unnerved by funny movements behind a curtain and had to call for help. The rescuers were the Keystone Kops. In another release of that year, *That Little Band of Gold,* Mabel and Fatty portrayed first a married couple, then divorcées, lovers, and finally husband and wife again, all in the span of two reels.

From about 1913 to 1926 Mabel was the undisputed queen of film comedy; her versatility and popularity with audiences were unsurpassed. "She had an impish quality and a gift for mimicry, pantomime, and inventiveness that soon made her an international favorite . . . with her broad yet skillful portrayals of working class gamines she became probably the outstanding comedienne produced by the silent screen."

During her time at Keystone she had received offers to go to other studios, but she stuck with Sennett. From the beginning the two had engaged in an on-again-off-again love affair during which engagements and wedding dates were set and then broken on more than one occasion. They never did marry, and one reason was said to be Sennett's habit of running around with other women. Another reason was that Sennett was said to have wanted Mabel to settle down after marriage, devote herself to the role of wife and mother, and retire completely from the screen. It was a request that Normand flatly rejected. Although the couple appeared to carry torches for each other they ultimately let themselves drift apart. This affair would leave its mark on Normand and eventually contribute to the decline of her health.

Mabel quickly began to tire of the repetitive nature of the slapstick comedies. She found them too short and too fast and physical in action to challenge her abilities. She knew her talents were greater than the demands placed on her and wanted to do feature roles. After a lover's quarrel with Sennett he finally agreed and established the Mabel Normand Feature Film Company for her in 1916. She was allowed to pick her own director and costars and the resultant six reel feature length film *Mickey* took a then unheard of eight months to film in 1916-1917.

She played a woman from the West who moved to New York, inherited a fortune, and was pursued by a villian who lost out in the end. Some typical Sennett action vignettes were included, such as Mabel disguising herself as a jockey to win an important horse race. In general, though, the film and the comedy were gentler, more subtle, and more subdued. Advance publicity for the film claimed that Normand had said "farewell to squash pie comedy to do something more genteel."

This proved a kiss of death for the film and Sennett couldn't find any theater owner willing to book it. It languished on the shelf for over a year until 1918 when, according to legend, it was shown on Long Island because the theater owner needed a last-minute replacement for a cancelled film. From there, business built on word of mouth and the film became a popular financial success.

By that time Mabel had left Keystone for a five-year contract with Sam Goldwyn. She was permanently estranged from Sennett and still looking for vehicles to fully display her talents. Her contract with Goldwyn called for a salary of $1,000 a week the first year, rising to $5,000 in the fifth year. She made about sixteen features for Goldwyn over three years, including *The Venus Model* (1918), *Peck's Bad Girl* (1918), *Sis Hopkins* (1919), and *The Slim Princess* (1920). Her roles were mostly those of working girl Cinderellas with equal parts of drama and comedy. The films made money but the vehicles and direction were poor and Normand was less successful than with her shorts at Keystone.

It was while she was at Goldwyn studios that her reputation for being difficult to work with came to the fore. She, like many other stars, was extravagant with money. She would think nothing of spending $6,000 a day on clothes, or tipping a sales clerk $100. Pining over Sennett, she entered the Hollywood party scene and had taken up cocaine, an addiction she would retain until her death.

Mabel began to show up late for work repeatedly, or disappear for days at a time, causing production delays and expenses to mount up. One of Goldwyn's other actresses had three violinists on the set playing background music to help her with her work. When Normand heard about this, not to be outdone, she approached Sam and asked for, and got, a seventeen-piece jazz band.

In 1921 Sennett wanted Mabel to return. Since she'd left Keystone, *Mickey* had become a big hit, but the studio was foundering financially. He wanted Normand back to bail out the studio. Goldwyn was growing weary of her demands and behavior and agreed to tear up the remainder of her contract. That year she made *Molly O'*, but disaster struck before it was released.

In February, 1922, William Desmond Taylor, a prominent director, was found shot to death. He was married and carrying on affairs with at least two women, an actress named Mary Miles Minter, and Mabel Normand. It turned out that Normand was the last person to see Taylor alive, having left his place shortly before the murder. The case was never solved. While nothing ever implicated Normand in the murder in any way, much of the pub-

lic rose against her in righteous indignation, Civic groups and
women's clubs boycotted her films and called for them to be
banned. Mary Minter's career was also finished after the murder.

This episode came on the heels of the Fatty Arbuckle scandal
the previous year, wherein Roscoe was tried on rape and murder
charges which were later proved to be fabricated. This incident
caused the film industry to appoint Will Hays as a czar to super-
vise the morals of the film colony. A decade later another female
comedian, Mae West, would again shake the puritans out of their
trees and force Hays to adopt a rigid censorship of films, the remnants of which are with us today.

When *Molly O'* was eventually released it proved to be a box-
office success. To his credit Sennett stuck by Normand and she
made two more features. The last one was *The Extra Girl* (1923),
a comedy about a small town woman trying to make good in Hollywood. That film had just been released when tragedy struck
Mabel again.

On January 1, 1924, Normand's chauffeur shot a wealthy oil
heir with Mabel's pistol after the two had had a jealous argument
over her. Upon investigation the chauffeur also turned out to be
an escaped convict. Once again Normand's innocence was never
questioned, but while her career had seemed to have been recov-
ering from one scandal, it couldn't survive two. Outraged groups
again demanded the banning of her films and within days of the
shooting states such as Michigan, Kansas, and Ohio had indeed
banned her work from their jurisdictions. This time Sennett didn't
stand by her. He dropped her contract by telling her the Hays
office had placed a ban on her films. They hadn't, officially; the
public had done it for them. It was Mack's way of washing his
hands of Normand. Mabel never made another feature film.

In 1925 she made her debut on the stage in a short lived and
unsuccessful play. By 1926 she was back where she started, making five short films for Hal Roach that year and the next. The
silent era was fast closing and Roach was recycling some of the
stars of that era in shorts that were pale imitations of the originals. And Normand no longer had public support.

Arbuckle was also finished as a film actor after his scandal,
though he was completely innocent of any wrongdoing. He did
continue to work, however, as a director, under an assumed
name. In Hollywood though, it was an open secret that it was
really Arbuckle.

Mabel fared less well perhaps because she was a woman, and
was exiled. Sexual promiscuity was treated more harshly in women

than in men. By this time Mabel was in rapidly failing health and was in and out of sanatoriums with tuberculosis, the disease that killed her in February, 1930. In 1974 Broadway belatedly paid tribute to her in the comedy *Mack and Mabel,* based on the lives of Normand and Sennett.

During her career she made 23 features and 167 comedy shorts. She did her own stunts, took pratfalls, threw pies, ran wild, and kicked men back. As she said, "I wasn't satisfied with merely being kicked." Chaplin recalled how films were made in the Keystone days. "We used to go into the park with a stepladder, a bucket of whitewash and Mabel Normand and make a picture."

LOUISE FAZENDA

Louise Fazenda was one of silent film's most popular comics. She never quite attained the heights of Mabel Normand, but along with Normand and Polly Moran she was one of the leading female motion picture comedians of the early film years. All three spent at least part of their career with Mack Sennett and his Keystone company. Louise's style was broad and physical, with lots of roughhousing thrown in and little in the way of real screen romance. Her career lasted until the end of the 1930's, although her peak years in terms of popularity were from 1915 to the end of the 1920's. The sound era rapidly hastened her decline in popularity. Her best remembered screen characterization was that of a farmer's tomboy daughter, an oft-repeated type for her to portray. Her rube from the sticks character was a forerunner of that done later by Judy Canova.

Louise was born on June 17, 1895, in Lafayette, Indiana, but moved to Los Angeles with her family when she was only two or three. Her father opened up a grocery store and Louise often helped out after school. She later used some of the customers she remembered as models for characters she played in films. Of her childhood, Fazenda recalled that, "I grew into a homely sort of kid and I knew it. . . . At school I stood around waiting to be chosen for an angel in a school play. I never was."

As a youngster she had no ambition to be an actress. She had her heart set on being a teacher, or a writer, or both. After attending Los Angeles High School, she was preparing to go to college when her father's business failed, making her plans financially impossible. She then held a series of jobs, including working for a dentist and a tax collector and clerking in a candy store.

Once when she was at home between jobs she complained to the woman who lived upstairs about her lack of employment. This woman suggested that Louise do the same type of work she was then doing — appearing as an extra in films. So, about 1913, Louise approached Universal and began her film career. One of her first parts was an Indian squaw in *A Romance of the Utah Pioneers,* for which she was paid $2.50 a day. She also played a maid, in black-face, in *A House Divided.*

Fazenda kept hounding the casting people at Universal and sometimes she got work as an extra, sometimes not. If no parts came her way she offered to do stunt work, which she learned as she went, even mastering a three-story jump without the benefit of a net.

When she first started in pictures Fazenda had hoped to do straight drama and become what she termed "a sob artist." She did get a chance early on to try for a serious part, but when she attempted to make the dramatic entrance called for she accidentally tripped and did a pratfall. The director told her to do it again, which Louise did, without admitting it had originally been an accident. Her comedy career was launched. She then began to appear regularly in one of the more successful early comedy series, *The Joker,* by Universal. She played a variety of roles including Western cowgirl, harassed wife, flirting cashier, or country rube.

In 1915 she was recruited for the Sennett company after answering in the affirmative the questions, "Can you shoot a gun?" and "Can you take a fall?" She started at a salary of $5 a day and quickly became one of the group's leading comics. By 1919 she was called "the stellar feminine funmaker at the Sennett Comedy Shop."

She was thrown off cliffs, had honey smeared on her back so a bear would chase her, and was bounced in the air on the stream of water from a fire hose while suspended by wires. She was chased by lions, threw pies, was hit by pies, had raw eggs dropped down her neck, and was kicked off the top of a house into a pond. In those days pictures were rarely scripted. The group would gather with their equipment, a gag, and let nature take its course.

In *The Great Vacuum Robbery* (1915) Louise was one of a pair of bank robbers who tried to rob a bank by crawling down an air pipe and sucking up the bills from the vault with a vacuum cleaner. In *A Versatile Villain* (1915) she was again a bandit. This time she was trapped and blown up inside a dynamite storeroom. She had her first starring role for Sennett that same year in *A Gay Old Knight*. Her screen appearance was typically described as "grotesque makeup, with an antiquated dress and skinned-back hair." Fazenda had to buy all her own screen costumes, as everyone did in those days, and she did her own costume selection.

In 1918 she was seen in *The Kitchen Lady,* marking her first appearance for Sennett as the country bumpkin. In that film she had a love scene in which she and her partner were leaning against a water heater which, naturally, burst and showered them with water. Dressed in a gingham dress, pigtails and long pantalettes, this image quickly became her trademark and she was thereafter rarely seen except in calico, men's workshoes, unattractive pigtails, and a homemade curl that was stuck down in the middle of her forehead and was particularly unappealing. She had created one of the first stage "ugly duckling" caricatures. It would be oft-repeated in the future by other women. Fazenda had cast "aside the proverbial beauty aids of Hollywood for the homely garb and makeup of the low-comedy farce comedienne."

She often portrayed the underdog struggling against some hostile situation, with the audiences rooting for her to overcome the obstacle, although she rarely did. She might be trying to remain loyal to a father, or stoically facing the affections of some boob who seemed to offer her her only avenue of escape from life on the farm. She brought a touch of sadness and Chaplinesque pathos to her parts which tended to moderate what otherwise would have been completely burlesque comedy. *Down on the Farm* (1920) was her first feature-length film.

As Sennett's style matured Fazenda got to play parts with a little more sophistication, but most never advanced beyond the coarse physical humor of the time. After five years with Sennett she branched out on her own and worked at almost all the Hollywood studios over the next couple of decades. She briefly turned to vaudeville in 1921, but quickly came back to Hollywood the next year. For the rest of her film career she appeared mostly in supporting comedy roles that were often caricatures, such as a cantankerous old maid. She did a straight dramatic role once in a while, and even, on occasion, sang in a film.

In 1928 Fazenda appeared in *Tillie's Punctured Romance,* a remake of the 1914 Marie Dressler film. It bore no relation to the first, save for the title. Shortly before the filming of that picture she had made a few changes in her own life. She shortened her hair to a bob, eliminating the pigtails which Sennett had once insured for $10,000 as a publicity stunt. She had also married producer Hal Wallis. At that point Fazenda considered retirement but changed her mind.

All of her later pictures weren't rural, but many were. In 1939 she appeared in a remake of *Down on the Farm*. The previous year she had been featured in *Swing Your Lady* in which she played a backwoods woman from the Ozarks who was both a blacksmith and a wrestler. Her last film was the 1939 release *The Old Maid* in which she played a straight role. She then retired and devoted herself to charitable works until her death in April 1962 at the age of 66.

With the advent of talkies the broad physical style of comedy began to wane and Fazenda, though she appeared in some 40 films in the 1930's, didn't enjoy the same popularity that she did in the 1915 to 1928 period. Her later films gave her a chance at times to do more character than caricature, but she never shook the roughhouse image, "a reputation as a quality bruiser — with just enough mild character roles in between to hold her franchise as a lady . . . a cross between Mother Hubbard and Strangler Lewis."

Fazenda had once said that she preferred drama over comedy, but felt she would never get away from comedy since she did it so well. When asked her feelings about her brand of physical humor, she said, "Of course I don't enjoy being thrown about like a bag of meal — who does? . . . Unless there is romance at the end. But, alas, there never was for me."

She wasn't an unattractive woman, but like so many other of the female comics her physical appearance was downplayed. She was termed "a plain-looking woman" and "not classed as a beauty."

It was pointed out that although Louise wasn't beautiful, she wanted to be. Described as not measuring "up to the accepted standards of beauty," she was advised that she could take heart from the fact that she had succeeded in spite of this handicap.

At the height of her slapstick fame with Sennett, she said, "There aren't many women doing 'nut' stuff are there? . . . I think one reason must be that all women like attractive surroundings and pretty clothes and hate to be laughed at." Louise herself didn't want relatives or friends watching her work at making films, under any circumstances. But she was quite happy to let them laugh at her on the screen. As one of the top silent film comedians she mugged her way through some 300 films. Moreover, she did it with "the gift of grimace and a true sense of pantomime."

POLLY MORAN

She was described as a "raucous, buck-toothed comic star and character comedienne." Her name was Polly Moran and she abandoned a vaudeville career to enter films in the mid 1910's. She quickly became one of Sennett's great comics during the latter part of that decade, second only to Louise Fazenda, to whom she was sometimes uncharitably compared: "Louise managed to avoid the buxom roughness of Polly Moran, whose coarse humor contained none of the sensitive aspects which Miss Fazenda's personality and acting brought to the screen."

Nevertheless Moran was one of the handful of early female film comic stars. Her popularity peak was from 1915 until the early 1930's. During the last five of those years she was paired with Marie Dressler in half a dozen movies that had good success. It was for those films that Polly was most remembered.

She was born Pauline Theresa Moran on June 28, 1883, in Chicago, the daughter of a contractor. In school she was noted more for her sense of humor than for her attention to academic work, and at the age of fifteen she abruptly quit school and went on the road with a touring opera company, with whom she sang and acted. She moved on to parts in musical comedies on the stage and then to vaudeville, where she did a single act of singing and comedy. As a trouper she toured the United States, England, the European continent, and South Africa. *Variety* described her vaudeville routine as "her semi-nut impromptu way of performing."

She was doing well enough in vaudeville, but one day, in between bookings, she decided on the spur of the moment to go to Hollywood and try her luck there. She appeared in one film, *The Janitor,* which attracted the attention of Mack Sennett. Mack signed her up with Keystone and she began to appear in his films in 1915. With the odd exception, such as an occasional nightclub tour, the rest of her career would be in films.

Over the next few years she appeared in over two dozen comic shorts, including *Her Fame and Shame, His Naughty Thought, Cactus Nell,* and *Sheriff Nell's Tussle.* Her comedy style was the broad and physical slapstick of the time and she was always ready for a plunge in the mud. Within a year of joining Keystone she was a comic favorite and "pretty much the whole of North America has giggled and galed with laughter at her comedy work . . . she is irresistable." During her Sennett days one critic commented that "Miss Moran in character parts is distinctively sleazy, and never lazy." This was a compliment. She had few equals at broad burlesque humor, "particularly when a grinning husband-hunter—which she was often."

After 1918 she briefly returned to the stage but was back in films by 1921, this time in features. She was relatively inactive for a few years until the 1927 release *The Callahans and the Murphys,* which first paired her with Marie Dressler and led to a renewed surge of interest in her work. In that film Moran and Dressler played a heavy drinking and boisterous pair of Irish friends who headed large clans and were forever fighting with each other. "Somehow their relationship survives the rockiest disruptions, usually caused by selfish, status-seeking Polly. Sentiment and slapstick are the main ingredients of this film." The Irish community objected to the picture due to the Irish image it presented, and lobbied, picketed, and militantly protested the film, causing MGM to withdraw it from circulation not long after it had been released.

Polly appeared in a couple dozen feature films over the next five years or so, but the ones with Dressler were the most memorable: *Bringing Up Father* (1928), which was described as "rolling-pin humor," *Dangerous Females* (1929), *Caught Short* (1930), *Reducing* (1931), *Politics* (1931), and *Prosperity* (1932). In *Caught Short* Moran had a tussle with a Murphy bed, and lost. MGM wasn't sure about a film with two women as the leads, since "the studio had doubts because of the lack of love-interest, but it was a big success." In *Reducing* Moran tangled with weight reducing machines, and again lost.

MGM paired Moran and Dressler in "lightweight formula comedies." Moran was usually stubborn and would do something to throw the both of them into a dilemma or make Dressler look bad. It was then Dressler's responsibility to come up with a solution to the dilemma, to produce a happy ending. "Meanwhile, Polly's comeuppance would be in the form of slapstick indignities—a cake in the face, a plunge in a mud bath, and so on. She supplied the low laughs, while Marie provided the heart in such films." Dressler felt the films did justice to neither one of them, and once said that, while she respected Moran's abilities as a comedienne, that didn't prevent her "from believing that each of us plays better without the other. I am pretty sure Polly feels the same way."

The pairing ended in the early 1930's with Marie's illness and death. Polly continued to appear in films over the next decade, mostly in character comic roles in a much smaller number of pictures. She retired in 1941 after *Petticoat Politics,* but returned in 1949-1950 for small parts in two films, one of which was *Adam's Rib.* She died, age 68, in January of 1952.

She'd been as much of a clown offstage as well as on. After *Adam's Rib* she said, "I worked in that picture two days before I got a real look at myself. After that I never went back." She once showed up somewhere with two black eyes and explained she "got 'em skipping rope without a bra." She once figured out that if the sounds of all the comic falls she had taken were combined into one noise, "it would make a volcanic eruption sound like a day in the library." She was happy as a comic and never aspired to glamorous or serious roles. She once compared her appearance to that of "an old, beaded bag." Rough and coarse she may have been, but the audiences loved her just the way she was.

The 1920's and 1930's

◆•◆

INTRODUCTION

Two distinct trends developed for female comics who reached stardom during the twenties and thirties. One was a continuation of the liberalizing images which flowed from the pre-1920's, best exemplified by Belle Barth and Mae West. The second, and dominant, trend was a backlash against social gains which thrust women comics into much more limiting and derogatory stereotypes, such as the man chaser or "dumb" woman, as done by the likes of Jane Ace, Gracie Allen and Judy Canova.

This rollback had started in a modest way before 1920, increased during the twenties and then escalated dramatically during the 1930's, fueled by the Depression. The dumb woman image bolstered the male's need to see himself as breadwinner, protector, and decision-maker in the family at a time when these roles were increasingly stripped away from him by the harsh economic realities of the day. The images of woman as dumb, man chaser, and physically unattractive, even when they weren't, would dominate the nature of female comedy for three decades, with no loosening up until the end of the 1950's, and no real change until the late 1960's.

It was a period which was very much opposed to any kind of comedy which showed women in assertive, aggressive, or indepen-

100

dent roles. The few exceptions were women who had already established themselves or managed to rebel, like Mae West.

During the 1920's vaudeville continued to be the dominant entertainment forum and enjoyed perhaps its finest and most lucrative decade, providing a respectable environment for its audiences and dispensing clean and non-offensive material to the mass of spectators. Already the motion picture industry was making deep inroads into that audience, and with the rapid rise of radio from about 1930 onward vaudeville was doomed. The end of vaudeville can be dated at about 1930. It did continue for a couple of decades after that but in a very sporadic fashion.

Fanny Brice began in burlesque and vaudeville, where she did comic songs, Jewish dialect, parodies and impersonations. For the last decade she played Baby Snooks, the kid character, a role that threatened to overpower her. She popularized the image of sticking with your man no matter what, even when he mistreated and abused you. She conveyed this image on stage and in her real life, and was a far cry from the likes of Tanguay or Bayes, who changed men like hats.

Charlotte Greenwood was famous in the 1920's and beyond, first in vaudeville musical comedies and later in films, with comic songs and her trademark of awkward physical humor. The media depicted her as very ugly and as tall as a building. She was neither. Beatrice Lillie, Molly Picon, and Gracie Fields enjoyed their greatest popularity during this era, although they would remain active for much longer periods. All appeared in musical revues, vaudeville, and comedy plays, doing comic songs, skits and impersonations. They were free of negative images, although Fields, the most physical of the three, was usually tagged as being unattractive.

The Duncan Sisters were essentially one-hit wonders from a musical comedy smash in the early 1920's, but they made that hit work for them for decades. As a female comedy team they were a rarity, a matchup that is still seen infrequently. They always appeared onstage as children, and talked in a childish way.

Helen Kane enjoyed half a dozen years of fame, all on the strength of a single phrase. Onstage she had the dress and hair style of the 1920's and was quickly adopted as the symbolic flapper. Flappers were considered more liberated and independent, freer in dress, action and morals. Yet Kane only looked the part of a flapper. Her onstage characteristics included a vacant stare, and she did her stuff in baby talk. It was 1930 and the assertive image of the flapper was already being downgraded.

Only one stand-up comic developed during this period and that was Belle Barth. She was the first to go in for quick jokes, as opposed to monologues. Her material was mostly blue, being openly sexual and direct. As such she was effectively banned from appearing on any of the mass media, which were all very clean. Instead she was confined to the nightclub and hotel circuit, which she successfully played for decades. A forerunner of the likes of Lenny Bruce, she made it easier for women to use such explicit material in later years, if they wished.

Radio began to compete with vaudeville as a family-oriented entertainment medium, and virtually every home had at least one set by the early 1930's. Any remaining remnants of the goofy looks brand of humor disappeared with radio, as the verbal element came to the fore. A comic appearing on radio couldn't hold up a region to ridicule the way he had done in vaudeville, since the radio audience was now larger and scattered everywhere. Women were fair game, however, as objects of ridicule, and radio produced some of the most negative stereotypical female comics of all the media.

Leading the way was the dumb woman. This stereotype had been introduced around 1914 in vaudeville. The responsibility for that fell at the feet of the now long-forgotten team of Ben Ryan and Harriette Lee. A married couple, they had started in vaudeville in 1911 but didn't do very well. Ryan had done all the comedy to start with but Lee turned out to be the more talented comic, so she took over. By 1914 Ryan had become the smart feeder while Lee was the dumb woman.

During one bit with a dictionary, Lee tried to look up the word for an animal that was eaten for breakfast. She turned to the word canteloupe before Ryan figured out she meant antelope. Another time Lee told the story of a man who stole "$10,000 and two bugs." After much verbal repartee, Ryan finally dragged out of her that she was referring to a bank clerk who stole "$10,000 and flees." Reviewers referred to Lee's "inimitable dumb talk."

Performing at the same time was another mixed team, William Montgomery and Florence Moore. In this pair the man was also the feeder, but they differed in that Montgomery served as the butt of Moore's aggressive insults. One sketch had Montgomery complain about his car, saying that the machine had hit him in the nose. Moore shrilly replied, "Good! It saved me the trouble."

Her patter was wisecracks and rapid-fire insults, although Montgomery usually managed to get the last word in.

At that time, Florence Moore mirrored the emergence of a new style of woman. Neither Lee nor Moore used grotesque makeup or clothes, or outlandish props. The Moore team spawned no imitators. The Lee team produced many. Both Lee and Moore were attractive women. Lee didn't try to hide that fact, but Moore did and claimed in fact that she had to. Moore had spent a year on stage trying to be funny but without success, because "I maintained a certain standard of decent looks." Finally at a matinee where she was doing poorly, she began to make grotesque faces, and this drew laughs. She made more faces and that drew more laughs. The result was that "after that the managers refused me work unless I obliterated every possible claim to looks while on stage."

The message from these two teams was clear. If an attractive woman was doing aggressive comedy, she had to mask her looks. However, if she did the dumb role, then she could retain her looks, although a dumb woman comic didn't have to be attractive. This generalization remains basically true today. Presumably it was, and is, less disconcerting if a pretty woman played dumb.

By the 1920's the dumb woman stereotype was gaining momentum. In 1921 the comic strip "Tillie the Toiler," featuring a woman long on looks but short on brains, was born. It was so successful that soon thereafter King Features assigned cartoonist Chic Young to create a clone. The result was Dora Bell, from whence came the phrase "Dumb Dora." Young then created the original "Blondie" cartoon character, described as a "bird-brain."

Female dumbness was quickly becoming almost a criteria for entry into comedy. It was big in vaudeville during the last years of the 1920's, and both Jack Benny and Bob Hope incorporated a Dumb Dora into their act during that time. The Dumb Dora character offered women a forum for their comic talents which offended neither their audiences nor the male halves of their team. The whole notion of men being the stronger, more important, and superior sex compared to the weak and inferior females became even more entrenched and widespread during the 1930's. A Gallup poll in 1937 indicated that 82 percent of Americans agreed with the idea that females should not be competing for, or holding, jobs with men who had families. Two-thirds of Americans, and 60 percent of females, indicated they wouldn't vote for a woman running for president, regardless of ability. Three out of four American cities barred married women from teaching posts, while the federal government ruled that it wouldn't hire married women, which led to mass dismissals of females from jobs.

The Depression changed the battle of the sexes from a cold war back to a hot one. Women's independence was a luxury of the good years and there was no longer a place for it. More and more females found themselves relegated to the hearthside in supporting roles. Bobbed hair was out, as was all "mannish" behavior. The Dumb Dora creation was a silly and harmless creature obviously not capable of competing in the real world and posing no threat to males in any sphere. She provided a soothing picture to traditionalists. Up until the crash of 1929 the new woman had been breaking down barriers and unnerving the natural order by acting in unexpected ways. These women had gone against type and threatened to be equal with men. All that was finished by 1930. Efforts then went into placing women back into the home and shoring up the hurting male ego.

The Dumb Dora enjoyed enormous popularity. "It seems more than coincidental that a society threatened by the triumph of female suffrage and by the brazen sex-role transgressions of young women in the twenties so enjoyed the stage stereotype of the dumbbell." The most popular of all the Dumb Dora types was Gracie Allen. She, and all the others, played on the belief that females were weaker and less intelligent than males. It was a belief held by women and not just men. Females loved Allen's humor, and much of her fan mail came from her own sex. Women could observe one of Allen's silly schemes and say to their husband, "Now that dumb I'm not." That said more about feminine self-image than it did about Allen herself. It was apparent that "Gracie was the epitome of what men wished all women to be."

With the medium of radio the projection of the dumb woman image developed in a slightly different fashion from that of film and vaudeville. Being non-visual it couldn't present a dumb woman just by having her look dumb. Radio got around this by having women comics mangle the English language. Their misuse of words and confused diction made them convey stupidity. Of the six comics who emerged from radio as stars during the 1930's, four demolished the language. These were Jane Ace, Gertrude

Berg, Gracie Allen, and Minerva Pious. Only Marian Jordan and Judy Canova could apparently put a correct sentence together.

Playwright Richard Sheridan's creation in 1775 of Mrs. Malaprop, a talkative woman who left a trail of shredded phrases behind her, set the standard for humorous speech. Her name came from the French "mal a propos" which meant inappropriate or unsuitable. A word that is similar in spelling to the correct one but "ludicrously different in meaning" is a malapropism.

Malapropisms were just one aspect of language butchering, and Jane Ace was tops in that area. She found that people who met her in real life were disappointed that she wasn't as dumb as her radio character. Gracie Allen was another comic whose stage persona was confused with her actual personality. Reporters were astonished to discover her intelligence, so entrenched was her onstage image of a feather-brain. There was a great deal of creativity behind Allen's illogical ramblings. She had a true sense of the absurd, and at least rescued her dialogue from insipidness.

Marian Jordan managed to escape the dumb stereotype, and she could even speak English correctly. Her character was that of the eternally patient, understanding, and long suffering wife. Married to a character that was a pompous blowhard, Jordan delivered a clear message to women—stay with your man and put up with whatever he does.

Berg continued the language-bashing tendencies but projected a more intelligent image. She was the all-knowing mother, dispensing wisdom to her clan and neighbors. Although her show bordered on gossipy soap opera, Berg came out looking better than her radio peers, probably because she wrote her own scripts. As a dialect comedian, Minerva Pious gained her greatest fame on Fred Allen's program, where she systematically destroyed the English language every week. All of these radio women were married on their respective shows, except Canova. Canova could also talk straight and only had traces of the airhead swirling about her hillbilly characterization. Being single, though, she fell firmly into the grasp of another favorite stereotype. Canova played a man-hungry woman, always chasing but never catching.

Motion pictures became firmly established as an entertainment medium during this period and would continue to increase their audience size for some time to come. There was no longer any class distinctions in the spectators; everybody went to the movies. With the advent of sound, screen humor moved more to drawing room comedy with verbal banter establishing the humor. Short features continued to be produced but they played a smaller and smaller role as the industry moved increasingly to the feature-length format. The image of the dumb woman was obvious in the women who emerged as film comedy stars, but was not as pervasive as on radio.

These comics could talk properly, as motion pictures relied of course on visual elements. They gave the appearance of being dumb through gestures, facial expressions and so on. Pitts and her handwaving were a prime example. Movie comics presented a wider range of images, however, than found in their radio counterparts. Mae West, in particular, established herself firmly as a woman who took no guff from any man.

West started her career in the early 1910's in vaudeville, and later the legitimate stage, where she had already formed her comic persona. It was films, though, that made her famous. The rigid censorship of the Hays office tried to harness her, and her response was to turn more to comedy, to lighten the impact of her rebelliousness. Thus by a strange twist of fate we had the dour, rigid, and puritanical male establishment, through its agent Will Hays, giving America its steamiest, sexiest, and most irreverent female comedian. West was a supreme comic caricature, a parody of a woman who used sex to obtain her goals. Dressed in sequins and tight gowns, with tons of makeup, she exploited the sex object role to the hilt. She used and manipulated men and knew what she wanted, and how to get it. She was definitely no man's woman.

Dorothy Devore began the switch away from slapstick to a more romantic type of humor. Her films were a transition from the short subject to the later feature-length films of the 1930's which depended on situation comedy generated from boy/girl relationships, and which sprang from verbal banter as the sound film made full use of its voice.

Thelma Todd, Patsy Kelly, and ZaSu Pitts all had separate careers, but in the early 1930's they were paired first as Todd/Pitts and then Todd/Kelly in a series of slapstick shorts. These pairings were unique in that they were among the very few female comedy teams in film history. Modeled after Laurel and Hardy, the female teams were never as popular as their male counterparts. The public was only willing to accept females in slapstick under certain conditions. Men had to be around as co-stars or rescuers. Audiences were not prepared to accept a female team doing slapstick as independent, albeit zany, characters. Women could not be self-sufficient, they had to be dependent on men.

Prior to being teamed, Todd was one of the few women given credit for both beauty and comic skills. She avoided the dumb image but was a foil for most of the big-name male comics of the day. Pitts was branded as ugly and confined to comedy from early on in her career. She became a successful comic with her fluttery, hand waving, scatterbrained antics. Kelly continued on in her career as a wisecracker in dozens of films, where she was comic relief and a supporting player to the famous Hollywood stars. Playing the friend of a beautiful woman was often her lot.

Billie Burke's career had two phases. The first, in which she became known for her beauty and for playing in light musical comedy plays, ended about 1920 when she was professionally inactive as the wife of Flo Ziegfeld. Back into films in the 1930's and 1940's, she achieved her greatest fame portraying giddy and ineffectual females, the basic dunderhead.

By the end of the 1930's the image of female comics had changed markedly, becoming more demeaning to women. Feminism had waned through the 1920's as the main focus of its drive and energy, suffrage, had been attained. The progressive image of the flapper had also faltered after the crash of 1929. Hard times became the economic rule. Men, threatened economically and in fear of losing their traditional masculine roles, turned women into scapegoats. They forced them into inferior or submissive roles.

The result was that female comics did more kid characters, and were frequently labeled unattractive. They were portrayed as man chasers and, above all, as flighty airheads. Verbal self-deprecatory material was not much in evidence, but then it wasn't necessary, since it came out of the mouths of dumb females "naturally." The idea of separating physical beauty and sharp comedy was then in evidence. These traits would become virtually mutually exclusive. If a woman was attractive she would have to play the "dumb" role. Too many positive attributes in a female were threatening. Self-confident role models for females were unacceptable. Female comics were no longer sharing their humor with audiences, they were being laughed at.

FANNY BRICE

Today Fanny Brice is probably remembered more as the subject of the stage and film biographies *Funny Girl* than for her own achievements in the field of comedy. These productions dealt more with the events of her personal life and gave little sense of her comic talents, concentrating on the difficulties of her private life to the exclusion of her own considerable accomplishments. Fanny encouraged this by using part of her act to parade her private misery in front of her public.

A natural and untrained talent she carved out a career first as a musical comedy star, most notably in the *Ziegfeld Follies*. As vaudeville and live stage shows waned, she switched to radio and enjoyed another long and successful run as one of America's best known and most loved child characters, the devilish Baby Snooks, a character so dominant it threatened to engulf Fanny herself. She held sway for forty years as one of America's foremost women comics.

She was born Fannie Borach, October 29, 1891, on Manhattan's lower east side, the daughter of Rose (Stern) and Charles Borach, a gambler known as "Pinochle Charlie." Fanny was a natural entertainer from an early age. As a youngster she put on one-cent admission shows in a backyard shed where she impersonated a hungry and poor old woman. When she went to Coney Island she approached strangers and tearfully asked directions on how to walk home to Brooklyn. This ruse usually produced carfare from the stranger which Fanny then promptly spent on food and rides at the park. From her neighborhood she also picked up a variety of European accents which, years later, she would use to good advantage in doing dialect comedy.

Her mother was an immigrant from Hungary who could neither read nor write, although the family eventually owned seven saloons. While her mother ran the business, Fanny's father encouraged her to stand on the tables and the bar-tops and sing. She and some neighborhood newsboys also sang in poolhalls and backyards for pennies or whatever they could get. It was those newsboys who encouraged Fanny to enter an amateur night contest at a local theater.

In the summer of 1905, this thin and gawky fourteen-year-old emerged from the Keeney Theater in Brooklyn with the $10 first prize. She had won for singing something called "When You Know You're Not Forgotten by the Girl You Can't Forget." She also picked up $3 in change which the audience had tossed on the stage for her.

This bit of success was enough to encourage Fanny to move directly into show business. She had never liked school and had only attended haphazardly, running away whenever she could. After her win she quit school permanently and began to enter every amateur night contest she could find in the area, often winning. Some weeks she was able to make as much as $30. In between she held a few odd jobs. She was once a singer of illustrated songs at a stereoptican parlor, and was a sweeper and ticket-taker at a Manhattan nickelodeon.

At fifteen she won a spot in a George M. Cohan musical production. By then she had changed her last name to Brice, borrowing it from a family friend named John Brice. She was tired of having her real name made fun of by friends who called her "More-Ache" and "Bore-Ache." Several decades later she would alter her first name slightly, dropping the "ie" in favor of a "y." Her job with Cohan was over almost as soon as it started. The part called for her to sing and dance. She had no trouble with the singing but she wasn't much of a dancer and once Cohan saw her lack of talent at the first rehearsal he fired her immediately.

She did manage to land work on the less fussy burlesque circuit, clean entertainment in those days, where she sang and danced in the back row of the chorus. Fanny was determined to improve her dancing and enlisted the aid of good dancers, those in the front row, to teach her. She had no money to pay so she cleaned out her mother's apartment of all feminine underwear and paid for her lessons with one piece of underwear per week.

Brice continued to work the burlesque circuit for a few years without notable success until 1910 when she met a struggling young songwriter named Irving Berlin who gave her a song to perform titled "Sadie Salome," suggesting she do it in dialect. Fanny performed it at the Columbia Burlesque house in New York in a Jewish dialect as a parody of the Salome dance. She wore a sailor suit and threw in a liberal supply of facial grimaces. The audience loved it and from then on she built her act around physical humor, parodies, and the Jewish dialect.

The move to comedy was a wise one for Brice, since she was a tall and thin woman who had been trying to become a chorus girl in an age when short and stocky chorines were in vogue. Working

at the Columbia House had earned her $25 a week. Florenz Zieg-
feld came to the show one night and signed her up for his famous
Ziegfeld Follies, at $75 a week. *The Follies* was the most presti-
gious production in show business, the goal of every entertainer
and Fanny remained a headliner with the *Follies,* appearing in all
editions except one, for the next thirteen years.

She also played vaudeville and appeared in other musical
variety productions during those years.

Her career with the *Follies* almost turned out to be as short as
her sojourn with Cohan. For her debut with Ziegfeld she sang a
song called "Lovey Joe," a "coon" song in black dialect. During
rehearsal she delivered one of the lines as "I jest hollers for mo'"
which was how she felt it should be done. The man in charge of
that particular number told Fanny to change it to "more," but
Brice refused on artistic grounds, whereupon she was promptly
fired. Ziegfeld came along though and personally smoothed things
out. In her debut in the *Ziegfeld Follies of 1910* Brice sang it her
way and she was a smash. The audience called her back for
twelve encores.

The Ziegfeld girls were renowned for their beauty and it was
pointed out that in this respect Fanny was "by no means a Ziegfeld girl." Eddie Cantor, with whom she worked, described her as
"Fanny with her funny face. . . . Fanny the kind of girl who was a
man's best pal." In a somewhat contradictory manner he also
remarked on her beautiful clothes and that "she had the figure to
wear them." Another critic remarked about her funny face and
her "mouth which when she grinned broadly seemed to be an ugly
gash in her features."

Due to her work in the *Follies* and other stage productions she
quickly became one of Broadway's best loved musical comics. Her
charismatic personality combined with her Jewish characterizations and humorous parodies kept her audience in hysterics. She
portrayed a fan dancer who had trouble with her fans, or a
clumsy ballet dancer who teetered her way through "The Dying
Swan." She did send ups of Hollywood beauties, she satirized
Camille, and she did an impersonation of a vamping Theda Bara.
She lampooned modern dance and did takeoffs of famous histori-
cal figures such as Madame Pompadour. As Mme. DuBarry she
would come on stage and say, with a thick Jewish accent, "I'm a
bad voman, but I'm dem good company." Eddie Cantor called
her a "great comic artist . . . the best comedienne of her time."

Much of her work in those early years was basically improvisation. "She never worked out her stiff-jointed, bucking routines until she faced the audience." She relied on them to tell her what they wanted. "What the audiences seemed to want were her slapstick grimaces, crossed eyes, awkward stances, and shrill voice." In a typical vaudeville act in the mid 1910's she opened with a comic song, "Becky's Back in the Ballet," wearing a ballet skirt, did impressions of a salesgirl in a shop, played a Jewish mother bragging about her daughter's intelligence, and ended her act with a song, dressed as a man.

She mixed in some serious material as well. In 1921 she introduced a song, at Ziegfeld's suggestion, called "My Man," which was a melodramatic and maudlin torch song about a woman's devotion to a worthless and disloyal male. Fanny took to the song, since it paralleled her personal life so well, and delivered it with such emotion that it soon became her trademark. As soap-operish as the song was, the audience embraced Brice's sentiments in it. Brice accepted, with a fatalistic shrug, all the crap her man could dump on her. Anti-feminist sentiments to be sure, but in keeping with the accepted female role of the day. It was the idea of the vulnerable, subservient female. Brice, obviously a dedicated career woman, was very much a conservative traditionalist when she talked about the role of women in society. About being a comedian in general, Brice remarked, "If you're a comic you have to be nice. And the audience has to like you. You have to have a softness about you, because if you do comedy and you are harsh, there is something offensive about it." This statement really only applied to women, and not to men. Being inoffensive and nice, after all, was what women were all about, or so they were conditioned to believe.

The first phase of Brice's career peaked during the 1920's when she appeared in big-time vaudeville and Broadway stage productions in addition to the *Follies*. She was also seen in six movies, starting with *My Man* in 1928 and ending with *The Great Ziegfeld* in 1936, as well as a small part in the film *Ziegfeld Follies* in 1946. Her first film was based on the song of the same name and featured Brice as a woman maltreated by her man. In real life she had spent fifteen years with confidence man Nick Arnstein, who had treated her poorly. She stuck by him through two prison sentences and a federal trial, and gave him countless thousands of dollars over the years, which he wasted. He was unfaithful to her constantly and it was over this that the couple finally divorced in 1927, although she carried a torch for him for the rest of her life.

Virtually everything she appeared in was a hit, except a 1926 serious stage production, *Fanny*. She had just finished a vaudeville tour and wanted to try something dramatic. In preparation for this she went so far as to have her nose straightened by plastic surgery. She had always thought of it as being funny looking. The play itself went over terribly. Audiences stayed away, critics hated it, and Fanny herself said, "Oh, it was just terrible." The world was not ready for a serious Fanny Brice.

In 1929 she had married Broadway showman Billy Rose, who wasn't too well known at that time. No better example could be found of a marriage doomed to failure by the macho attitude of a man who could not contend with the success of a woman. It was a problem that has plagued other female comics but nowhere so obviously as in the case of Brice and Rose. Billy couldn't bear to be swallowed up by his wife's fame. He became a man obsessed with surpassing Brice's fame. Some time after they had married he opened up a cabaret and had his name installed in huge neon lights outside. While admiring this display, he overheard two passersby. One said, referring to the sign, "Who's that." The second replied that it was Fanny Brice's husband.

Rose himself said, "A couple of years after I married Fanny . . . I was violently unhappy about being known as her husband." His obsession with besting his wife was carried to such an extreme that he regarded the following as a victory: When the movie *The Great Ziegfeld* played in Boston the name Fanny Brice was changed in the local billing to Mrs. Billy Rose. The couple split up in 1938, due mainly to Rose's infidelity. When the press asked Fanny for a comment on Billy's latest girlfriend, Eleanor Holme, Fanny replied, with admirable style, "I can do anything she can do better, except swim." Said Rose at the time of the breakup, "Miss Brice is one of the brightest and cleverest stars the stage or screen has ever had, but it's no fun being married to an electric light."

In the mid 1930's Brice played in two more editions of *The Ziegfeld Follies*. Flo was dead by then and the revivals were staged by the Shuberts. Her comic talents were as well honed as ever: "The skilled and subtle one, with an evil talent for sly dissection of all that is fake and preposterous." Nevertheless, her career was definitely on the wane at this time. The glory days of vaudeville and the *Follies* were long past, and Fanny was forty-five years old.

She was then to begin the second phase of her career, one that would win her wider fame and larger audiences than ever, the Baby Snooks phase.

A preview of Snooks took place in 1912 in vaudeville when Fanny first introduced a baby routine into her act. Such routines were fairly common at the time, but Brice was concentrating on other aspects of her career and material, and the baby routine was not used again. She felt she didn't need it. Fanny Brice has always been described as a blunt and forceful woman who has insisted on controlling her own material.

A closer approximation to Snooks was unveiled at a party in 1921. Fanny was asked to entertain and she did a parody of a burlesque song "Poor Pauline," singing it as a six-year-old. One of the guests nicknamed the character Babykins and suggested that Brice use it in her routine. Brice did, but not until the 1930 Broadway production *Sweet and Low*. Babykins was dropped from the revue after a couple of weeks. Fanny was then making about $3,000 a week. For the 1934 *Ziegfeld Follies* the character returned, now named Baby Snooks and dressed in a bib and baby's dress. In the *Follies* of 1936 the brat was back again, now starting to be mentioned in reviews. For a time Baby Snooks's mother was played by Eve Arden.

Fanny had appeared on radio in 1932 on a short-lived series, but only as a straight singer. In a 1936 radio version of the *Follies* she introduced Snooks to the entire nation. That series was also short lived but she was back in 1937 with NBC on a program called "Good News of 1938." From then on Snooks would be on the air continuously until Fanny died, and very quickly Baby Snooks became the only part she played as an entertainer. This new character gave Fanny material for the new medium and rescued her from her own advancing age, something she regarded as an enemy which always had to be fought.

The "Good News" program continued through 1939 and then became known as the "Maxwell House Coffee Time," a thirty-minute weekly show split into two fifteen minute halves. Monologist Frank Morgan had one of the completely separate parts while Fanny Brice as Baby Snooks had the other. This format continued until 1944 when she got her own half-hour "Baby Snooks Show," which ran until Fanny's death in 1951. By the latter part of the 1940's Brice was earning $6,000 a week for the Snooks show. She regarded that as stealing money, since she was able to do Snooks blind. "I don't have to work at it. It's part of me."

Another reason that Fanny turned to, and felt so comfortable with, Snooks was that there was less trouble with censorship when things were said through the mouth of a child. As Brice once remarked about an adult character sketch she was doing, "We'd be ready to rehearse, and they'd say: 'You can't do this, you can't do that. This will offend, and that will not sound nice.' And I knew this couldn't happen with a baby. Because what can you write about a child that has to be censored."

The Snooks show was a family situation comedy; Snooks had a mother, father and brother on the show. This cunning and mischievous six-year-old Snooks was a clever tyrant, all too ready and willing to throw a tantrum to have her way. One of the show's trademarks became the lengthy and loud cry "Waaah" at the end of each show. Another remembered phrase was when she asked her father, "Why-y-y, Daddy?" Snooks was a rather typical radio child, incorrigible and irreverent, particularly towards adult institutions, in the same vein as Red Skelton's "Junior."

On the show the parents played a perpetually feuding couple, with Baby Snooks especially adept at playing one against the other. When father came home with lipstick on his collar, Snooks would find a way to bring it to her mother's attention. She would leave the shirt "accidentally" where her mother would find it, even after she had accepted a 25¢ bribe from her father to hide the shirt in the wash and say nothing.

The parents were a typical American couple, in a typical American home, dominated by a small demon. Her father tried to be the calm and reasonable parent as he dealt with his child's endless schemes. On various episodes Snooks put a bee's nest under the tea cozy at her mother's club meeting, she cut her father's fishing line into foot-long pieces, and she put marbles into her father's piano. A more ambitious project had Snooks cutting the fur off her mother's mink coat, gluing it all over her baby brother Robespierre and then selling him to a neighborhood kid as a pet monkey. Many of these episodes ended with a spanking, hence the cry "Waaah" at the program's end.

Brice identified so closely with her Baby Snooks character that she often stayed in character for as long as an hour after the broadcast was over. The voice returned to normal but the Snooks temperament, actions and thinking were said to remain. Fanny said, "I love Snooks, and when I play her I do it as seriously as if she were real. . . . I am Snooks. For twenty minutes or so, Fanny Brice ceases to exist." In interviews she was less and less out of character, often abandoning her natural voice. Radio listeners were often surprised that Snooks was played by a middle-aged woman and not a real child. Fanny became more and more absorbed by Snooks, almost to the point of subjugation.

Brice was able to escape the usual stereotypical pits that female comics were assigned to, that of a dummy or a man chaser, but she could only do it by becoming a child character. She was no longer an adult, and thus provided no threat to male dominance. The child character, as used by male comedians such as Red Skelton, provided alter egos for the men. For Brice, though, Baby Snooks was all. She also found that she wasn't taken seriously by the public. "They don't expect it and they won't take it from you. You are not entitled to be serious. You are a clown."

She once remarked that she didn't want her daughter to have a career. "Because if a woman has a career, she misses an awful lot. And I knew it then, that if you have a career, then the career is your life." This bitterness was at least partly due to the troubles she had had with men in her own life over the years. As she said, "Everything else in my life I ever wanted, if I tried for it, I got it. But with men, the harder I tried, the harder I flopped." It was this aspect of her life that was played to the hilt in her film biography. This was done not because it was the most dramatic or interesting or entertaining aspect of her life. It wasn't. It was played that way to be an object lesson to all women, an example of what success can do to a woman. And to point out that perhaps it wasn't worth it.

It has been remarked that Brice proved females could be successful comedians without making fools of themselves or other women, or without exploiting her sexuality. Fanny, it was said, didn't do jokes about domestic chores. This was true only because Brice had abandoned both her sex and her adulthood. As Baby Snooks she had become an asexual child.

The problems of playing a child as she grew older increased. Age held a great terror for her. She became more worried about her appearance, would study the mirror and remark, "I'm getting wrinkled. I'm through." She regarded television as her enemy. While Baby Snooks was convincing as a character on radio, Brice felt it would never work on television, that she looked too old.

In May 1951 Fanny was almost sixty years old. Her radio program was doing well, but radio was just about down for the count in terms of anything except music and news. She died that month of a stroke, on a day she was scheduled to do her show. As movie director George Cukor said, "Fanny was one of the great, great clowns of all time."

CHARLOTTE GREENWOOD

Charlotte Greenwood specialized in low and broad comedy, attaining stardom on stage, in vaudeville, and then in movies. She was best remembered for her tall, thin, angular body, her awkward movements, her acrobatics, a general lack of "grace" and, in particular, her high kicks. She used to claim, "I'm the only woman in the world who can kick a giraffe in the face." Her height was much commented on and was given skyscraper status. It was once reported that she "looks like a human Woolworth Building when she is on stage." (It was once the tallest building in the world.) Actually she wasn't that tall, but as often happens with "negative" physical characteristics found in females, they were exaggerated out of all proportion. She was five feet nine, or perhaps ten, in height.

Charlotte was born in Philadelphia in June of 1893 and had reached almost her full adult height by the time she was twelve years old. School was a miserable, uncomfortable and unhappy time for her. She was always the tallest kid in class and she was indeed gangly, forever stumbling and tripping and falling. She didn't consider herself funny at the time, nor apparently did her classmates. She was just plain awkward. The only part of school she liked was singing, which she did often, and well. At about age fourteen she gladly left school permanently, being mortified and ashamed of being tall, thin, and awkward. She felt her only assets were her voice, and the fact that she could dance a little. About 1906 she had a job in the chorus line of a musical comedy, *The White Cat,* since, "There didn't seem to be anything else I could do."

While with that production she met another member of the company, Eunice Burnham, with whom she became good friends. One day Burnham suggested the two of them form their own vaudeville act with Eunice playing the piano and Charlotte singing. They set off on their own in 1908, billing themselves as "Two Girls and a Piano" and earned $25 a week each, playing the "small time" circuits. They spent two years constantly working on their routine, trying to improve it enough to crack the big time circuits. They finally got such a booking in Chicago, where the theater manager previewed the acts before they went on. After watching them he commented that he liked the two of them, but didn't care for their act, and asked to see something else. Not having anything else to show, it was back to the small-time for another stretch, this time over a year.

They continued to try and improve the act and it was during this period that Greenwood developed the comic trademarks she would retain for the bulk of her career. One story, likely apocryphal, had it that the pair once followed a dog act on a bill in which the dog had left a deposit on stage. Charlotte didn't notice it and did an unexpected and ungainly pratfall. Thus was born the awkward Greenwood. A more mundane, but probably accurate, story had it that after a performance one night Burnham mentioned to Charlotte that she had done a little twist which the audience regarded as funny and perhaps Charlotte should embellish this the next time out. Until that time Greenwood had been deadly serious about her work and she took pains never to make any of those awkward, yet natural for her, gestures which had embarrassed her so much in the past. Regarding her stage presence in those days she commented, "I was so afraid of showing what I considered my awkwardness that I hardly dared to move."

The night after Burnham's suggestion Charlotte did her twist again and got laughs. Following that she experimented more and more with gestures that had mortified her as a youth and got more and more laughs. By 1912 the act was making $500 a week, Greenwood was more and more getting top billing and their act was "the highest paid 'girl act' in vaudeville." The gawky and gangly Greenwood character was now almost fully developed. She had become known "for her ability to kick one leg over her head." In the act Charlotte did comic songs and dances such as "I may not be so pretty,/And I don't dress like a queen./I may not be so witty;/I am over sweet sixteen./My face is not my fortune/ (It looks like the morning after),/But I still maintain/That I retain/(Bing! Bing!)/My girlish laughter!"

She was not an unattractive woman but she was into self-deprecation, aided by reviewers. One wrote that "Her face is nearly as ugly as that of Polaire." The latter was popular in vaudeville then and began her career as a freak act with a 15-inch waist. Polaire was regularly billed, unfairly, as the "Ugliest Woman in the World."

Others paid tribute to Charlotte's comic abilities. "Miss Greenwood is undiluted joy. She is funny all over. Her face is a comic mirror for every laugh." Another remarked that "Miss Greenwood is the tall, awkward girl whose limbs seemed to take involuntary excursions to all portions of the stage, and who is described as being loose jointed as the latest toy from the toy factory."

In 1912 she left the team and moved on to appear on the stage, in featured roles, in a number of musical revues, including *The Passing Show of 1912, The Passing Show of 1913*, and *Town Topics*. In between she continued to do vaudeville and in 1915 she was noticed by producer Oliver Morosco, while performing with a partner named Sydney Grant. Grant was five feet two and the pair used the height difference for much of their laughs, the development of the last of Greenwood's major comic traits.

Morosco was impressed enough that he had a straight play, *Your Neighbor's Wife*, rewritten into a musical, *So Long Letty* (1915) for Charlotte, and both she and the play were enormous hits. It ran for four years and marked Greenwood's rise to superstardom. "That started her career as Letty Pepper, who was funny largely because she was taller than anyone else and could kick higher." Earl Carroll provided the title tune and Charlotte and Letty became permanently identified together. She sang, kicked, and danced her way, as Letty, through a number of sequels: *Linger Longer Letty* (1919), *Let 'Er Go Letty* (1921), *Letty Pepper* (1922), and *Leaning on Letty* (1935). She played in this last vehicle for five years, touring off and on around the country. The character of Letty was that of an "eccentric spinster," and "she was given to comic capers as broad as she is long."

During the 1920's and 1930's she appeared in a number of other stage musicals and revues, including *The Music Box Revue* (1922), *Hazzard Short's Ritz Revue* (1924), *LeMaire's Affairs* (1927), and *Wild Violets* (1932), which marked her debut in London. She also continued to make solo appearances in vaudeville during the 1920's, when she reached her greatest successes, heading the Palace in New York City. Her vaudeville act consisted of two parts. Sketches for the first part included "Her Morning Bath," "Movieland," in which she played "one of the lesser cinema queens in the rough-and-tumble skit," and a spoof investigation of why men preferred blondes. While a *New York Times* critic considered the content of the last skit out of date even in 1927, he liked it because it provoked "considerable amusement, due largely to the antics of the star." The second part of Greenwood's act was made up of comic songs delivered with all the awkward mannerisms for which she had become renowned.

For the woman sometimes called "Lady Longlegs," her most famous and best remembered skit was "Her Morning Bath." This routine was said to have "killed them in vaudeville." It concerned an unemployed woman who got up one morning and took a bath to prepare for a job interview that day. While in the tub the phone rang, the meter reader arrived, and the iceman delivered a large block of ice, leaving it on the floor for the woman to put away into the icebox herself. Emerging from the bath with a towel held firmly around herself the woman tried to accomplish this, which she did "by placing one foot against the top of the icebox door to keep it open, holding her towel with one hand, and bending down and lifting the cake of ice into the box with the other." While so occupied a burglar leaped through the window and yelled, "Stick em up." Blackout, and end of skit.

With the demise of vaudeville, beginning around 1930, Greenwood moved easily into films and embarked on a long career there. She had actually appeared in a couple of silent films, her first being *Jane* (1915), but her major film work took place in the 1930's and 1940's, including a film version of *So Long Letty* (1930). Some of her other films included; *Palmy Days* (1931), *Down Argentine Way* (1940), *The Gang's All Here* (1943), and *Oklahoma* (1955). The role of Aunt Eller in the last had actually been written especially for her by Oscar Hammerstein II but prior commitments had prevented her appearing in the Broadway stage play. In films, she played the lead in some low budget comedies but mainly appeared as a supporting player in musicals and comedies. "Tall, energetic, and quite kooky, she added gaiety and spice to some Fox musical comedies of the 40's." Altogether she made a number of short comedies and forty feature films, with her last film appearance being in the 1956 release *The Opposite Sex*.

She briefly had two radio comedy shows, "Life With Charlotte" and "The Charlotte Greenwood Show." Both aired in 1944 over NBC. Her stage career continued into the 1950's and she appeared on Broadway in 1950 in Cole Porter's *Out of This World*, in which she played the goddess Juno. The show wasn't particularly well received but Charlotte drew praise: "The lanky, long-legged Letty is still able to give a special glint and warmth and stop the show." Retiring in the late 1950's, she died in January 1978.

Back in 1909, when still teamed with Burnham, Greenwood had been billed as "The Laughing Hit of the Season," a description that would be appropriate over the following forty years. She did have a few dramatic roles, but throughout her career she remained firmly entrenched in the public's mind as the woman who could "kick high over a man's head or step over a dining room table without breaking it or her stride."

Not all reviewers considered her ugly. One said she was "that rare combination, a woman comedian who is not only funny but at the same time a pleasure to the eyes." That quote was penned in 1923 and illustrated the idea that beauty and comedy were almost regarded as mutually exclusive traits in females, a sentiment that has remained strong and still is with us, to some extent, over sixty years later.

Much of Greenwood's humor, in whatever media, came from that familiar old stereotype, the homely woman trying to catch a man, as typified by the following exchange between a restaurant customer and Charlotte the waitress.

CUSTOMER: Stop winking at me.

CHARLOTTE: Can't a girl get a hair in her eye?

CUSTOMER: You must be man-crazy.

CHARLOTTE: Well, a girl can't go through life with a tray of food on her arm. Say, haven't I seen you around?

CUSTOMER: No, I usually eat in good restaurants.

CHARLOTTE: I'm glad you came in here. I'm looking for a man.

CUSTOMER: I doubt you'll find one here.

CHARLOTTE: I guess you're right, now that I see you better. Look, you're a guy and I'm a girl. Doesn't that suggest something to you?

CUSTOMER: Yeah, I want my check so I can get out of here.

Greenwood not only overcame her sensitivity to her height but turned it to her own advantage. Toward the end of her career she commented that she "capitalized . . . on the gawky movements of my long legs and made a success on the stage. That cured my sensitivity." Once she concentrated on doing what was natural for her, her fortunes improved dramatically.

Greenwood may have been happy with her awkward and klutzy image when young, but she had a different picture regarding the future. When she was about 30 years old she remarked, "Being a skinny young woman who does queer things with her hands and feet is all right. But to be a skinny old woman, haunting the managers' offices in search of a job and hanging around the stage doors, hoping somebody will lend me enough to pay my week's board . . . it would be what Sherman said war was." She was well aware of the extra hazards and difficulties that women faced in retaining their comic identities and images into old age. With that fear in mind, Charlotte Greenwood had resolved to be a big hit when she was young in order to have a safe and comfortable old age. She was successful on both counts.

BEATRICE LILLIE

Mrs. Lucie Lillie, a concert singer of Irish descent, gave birth in Toronto, Canada, in 1898 to her second daughter, Beatrice. Mrs. Lillie was determined that both her daughters would be musical. Muriel, the oldest, showed a definite talent for the piano, and Beatrice was given singing lessons.

Beatrice was not very fond of either the lessons or the sentimental ballads she was expected to sing. The elaborate facial and hand gestures she was trained to make to convey objects or emotions during a song would become the basis of her miming skill, a talent essential to a comedian. When Beatrice was growing up, however, she hadn't the slightest idea that her future would lie in comedy. Not that she didn't have a sense of humor. She was dismissed from her church choir at the age of eight for making faces at the congregation.

Beatrice joined her mother and sister in the Lillie Trio and the family appeared at local theaters. Mrs. Lillie was ambitious for herself and her daughters and decided to move to England in search of fame and fortune. Her husband, John, remained behind in Toronto.

Beatrice, then sixteen, was billed as a child soprano, and she appeared for a week at the Chatham Music Hall. She also obtained a part in a play at the London Pavilion. Her break into comedy came soon after. Andre Charlot, a producer famous for his vaudeville revues, auditioned Beatrice as a singer. Seeing that he was getting bored by her romantic ballads, Beatrice decided to get his attention by burlesquing the song "We're Drifting Apart, So You're Breaking My Heart." She also sang the comic song "The Next Horse I Ride On, I'm Going to Be Tied On."

Amused by her clowning, Charlot gave her a three-year contract. Lillie was primarily a singer, but Charlot began to recognize her ability as a comic and he kept her in his revues, writing funny material especially for her. In one of her early sketches, Beatrice was dressed in a green satin evening gown. A long-stemmed chrysanthemum protruded from her bosom. She sang in a piercing soprano with the music propped against the flower.

During World War I, Beatrice often took on male parts, since most of the available actors had been drafted. Reviewers noted that she made "quite a nice boy," and one critic called her "one of the most dapper and accomplished of contemporary male impersonators." Lillie added to this androgynous impression by getting her hair cut very short. She was to wear it in that masculine style throughout her life.

She usually wore fez-shaped caps matching her outfits, and these caps along with her short hair became one of her trademarks. A six-foot-long string of pearls which she twirled vigorously while onstage also became a regular feature of her costume. And the phrase, "Get Me," became her standard way of taunting audiences.

In 1920 Beatrice married Robert Peel. She eventually became Lady Peel when Robert inherited the Baronetcy. They had a son, Bobbie, one year later. The marriage was not a happy one. Most of the Peel fortune had been squandered and Robert drifted from one job to another trying to establish a career for himself.

Beatrice did not intend to give up the stage, and she continued to travel and work throughout the marriage. Beatrice was determined to leave her "Lady Peel' title behind her when she was working, but at least one critic was class conscious. Writing in 1931, Harrison Dowd remarked: "Breeding is always apparent in her. . . . Her refinement is positively sensational, considering she is primarily a grotesque. Perhaps it is the combination of these opposites that creates the sensation. . . . It is like entering a drawing room and beholding a duchess performing like a crazy downstairs maid."

Lillie herself downplayed her high society connections. In her autobiography she commented: "I think it's important to be able to laugh at yourself before you can laugh at anybody else, and to detect and deflate pomposity or bad manners, anywhere up or down the social scale."

She recalled that a dowager at a party once tried to impress Lillie with her jewelry: "You know," the dowager gushed, "I clean my diamonds with ammonia, my rubies with Bordeaux, my emeralds with Danzig brandy and my sapphires with fresh milk. And you, Miss Lillie?" she asked. Replied Beatrice, "Oh, I don't bother cleaning mine. When they gets dirty, I simply throws them away."

Although they never divorced, the Peels lived apart. When Robert died of peritonitis at the age of thirty-six, he was living with someone else. Beatrice too had found a new partner, John Philip, an actor. He remained her lifelong companion, but they never wed. Lillie's son was tragically killed in the Second World War.

A year after her marriage to Peel, Beatrice appeared in several more Charlot revues. They were so successful that Charlot took his company to New York. Lillie made her American debut in 1924 at the Times Square Theater. Co-starring with her was Gertrude Lawrence. The New York critics were enthusiastic about her performance, calling her "enormously funny." Alexander Woollcott could "think of no clown more comical than Beatrice Lillie."

Lillie spoofed Fanny Brice while Gertrude Lawrence mimicked Sophie Tucker. Both were dressed as twins in baby carriages and played ukeleles. They called themselves the Apple Sisters, Cora and Seedy.

After Charlot's revues closed in 1926, Lillie accepted a role in the Hollywood silent film *Exit Smiling*. She played Violet, an understudy and maid of all work for an acting troupe. So lowly was the character that Violet played "Nothing" in *Much Ado About Nothing*. Critics liked the film and Beatrice was to appear in five other films during her career, the best known being *Around the World in Eighty Days,* which was released in 1956.

But Lillie was not fond of movie-making. In her autobiography she remarked that "Endless retakes weren't for me. I needed an audience to coax into its first laugh. Once I had that, I could build it into further laughter, and the louder it grew, the more blithely I could improvise the next bit of comedy."

It was thus the stage that provided Lillie with the majority of her work. She appeared in numerous musical comedies like Rodgers and Hart's *She's My Baby* (1926) and Noel Coward's *This Year of Grace* (1928). Coward was to become a close friend, though he was not above complaining about Beatrice. He felt her real genius was as a solo performer because she could make immediate con-

tact with the audience. According to Coward, she tended to ad
lib too much and play to the audience, which threw other actors
off.

Nevertheless, Beatrice continued to appear in Coward's plays.
When she appeared in his *Set to Music* in 1939, George Jean
Nathan wrote in *Newsweek* that Beatrice took Coward's somewhat
"feeble" lines and "with her own genius for healthy low comedy
converts them into gay and bouncing sport. . . . She is, it seems,
one of the few persons in the entertainment world who doesn't
need material with which to work. She can apparently make it up
as she goes along. With one dart of her eye she can spare a skit
writer a dozen lines."

Lillie herself admitted to her preference for improvising: "Too
many rehearsals are bad for me. I begin to get bored and lose
that spontaneity so essential in comedy. That's why I like to build
up my parts during a play's run, introducing new lines and business on the spur of the moment."

Coward wrote a musical spoof for Beatrice called *After Dinner
Music,* which she performed on vaudeville's Orpheum Circuit.
Playing an aging prima donna who is asked to sing before her
guests, Lillie wore a bright red wig, green velour gown, and carried a mangy feathered fan. During the course of the prima
donna's impromptu concert, her fan lost its feathers, her gown
knocked the china plates to the floor, and her attempt at high
"C" caused a lamp to lose its shade and the light bulb to explode.
She sang about an "old-fashioned girl in an old-fashioned garden,
wearing an old-fashioned gown, with her old-fashioned stockings
about to fall down." She then launched into that sad ballad "The
Roses Have Made Me Remember What Any Nice Girl Should
Forget."

In 1935 Lillie appeared on Broadway and in Chicago in *At
Home and Abroad.* She introduced several humorous skits,
including one in which she played Mrs. Blogden Blagg who tried
to order "two dozen double damask dinner napkins." A reviewer
for *Literary Digest* in November 1935 noted that she was "a little
of everything. She is a Russian ballet dancer with such vehemence
and deliberately wicked burlesque that serious Russian ballet-
dancers must blush for themselves. She is a cockney barmaid, a
Montmartre night-club singer, a jester in bold sketches, her personality blanketing the proceedings. . . . She is at her best when
the show built around her is flip, impudent and brash."

That year Beatrice was also heard on radio in a program sponsored by the Borden Milk Company. She felt that "no cows, not even the sponsor's herd, should be sacred, and he didn't object to my unburdening myself of such lines as 'Let's pour a can of milk over Junior and see if he will evaporate too.'"

Beatrice Lillie was now well established as a comedian. She was making between $6,000 and $8,000 a week in vaudeville. Dubbed "Queen Bea" and "a mistress of sophisticated slapstick" her pantomime and satire were compared to that of Chaplin's. In 1944 S.J. Woolf of *The New York Times Magazine* commented that "Her humor is a form of caricature, distinctly personal. In lesser artists it would degenerate into low comedy. She always holds it on a high plane. . . . She succeeds in doing this not only with exaggerated gesture but also with vocal vagaries as well as costumes (she designs them herself) in which colors shriek at each other."

During WW II Beatrice entertained in London, and also toured army bases in the Mediterranean, Africa, the Middle East, France and Germany. She received several service medals for her contribution.

After the war Lillie continued to appear in revues in both the United States and Britain, such as *Seven Lively Arts* at the Ziegfeld and *Better Late* at the Garrick. She sang comic songs with lyrics like "Maude you're full of maggots, and you know it," and made up gags about Florence a housemaid who bragged about an imaginary trip to Africa: "We shot a lot of elephants, tigers, lions, cantaloupe and rats."

In 1952 she was seen on American television. That year she also performed in *An Evening with Beatrice Lillie,* which ran for a year at the Booth Theater in New York. The Broadway box office took in three quarters of a million dollars and won Lillie a Tony for her performance. She then took the show on tour in the U.S., Canada, and England until 1955. A recording of the revue was released in 1956.

In one sketch in the show Beatrice was dressed as a schoolboy whose father (played by Reginald Gardiner) was trying to explain the facts of life in a most inarticulate manner. Confronted by the puzzling explanation the schoolboy asked, "Does mother know?" Lillie also sang several comic songs including "Wind Round My Heart, We Should Never Have Dined A La Carte" and "There are Fairies at the Bottom of My Garden." As a lovesick lady she practically strangled herself with a scarf as she sang "Please Be Kind" — "If you leave me, dear, my heart will lose its mind."

Beatrice was a master at the double entendre. Many of her lines had sexual or indecent allusions but the dignified Lady Peel could carry them off without offending.

Critics and audiences were very enthusiastic about the show. Margaret Marshall, writing in *Nation* in October 1952, said of Lillie: "She has all the essential and formal requisites of her calling — skill, experience, sophistication, a sense of timing; yet she uses them in such a way as to create the effect of spontaneous, artless, improvised fooling meant only for friends and relations. . . . For all her seeming abandon she exercises such restraint that every movement counts, and a gesture in her economy is worth more than many another's whole bag of tricks."

John Mason Brown describing Lillie's technique in *Saturday Review* in October 1952 said that she disassociated "herself from any solemn or sentimental material. . . . For a perilous moment or two she may seem to be playing a number straight. Her manner on entering can be earnest, her face frozen. In no time, however, the mischief breaks through. It can express itself in a gesture, a tone, or a twist of the body that is slightly, though unmistakably, exaggerated. . . . Nonsense takes over, and everything becomes gloriously and giddily goofy."

In 1954 Lillie visited Japan and was fascinated by the Kabuki Theater. She immediately thought of how she could spoof the highly stylized Japanese drama and she created a sketch for her show called "Kabuki Lil." Dressed as a geisha with a knitting needle through her wig, Beatrice sat cross-legged on a pile of cushions. Speaking in gibberish she went through a tea ceremony spiking her drink liberally with Gordon's Gin, and banging loudly on a gong from time to time.

Lillie continued to work in revues throughout the late 1950's and early sixties. Not all of her material was first-rate, but Lillie's gift for ad-libbing often saved feeble lines. As Kenneth Tynan noted in *Holiday* in September 1956, "The traditional comic formula is: Tell them what you're going to do; do it; then tell them you've done it. Miss Lillie's is: Tell them what you might do; do something else; then deny having done it."

One of Lillie's last major vehicles was the 1964 Broadway comedy *High Spirits,* a musical version of Noel Coward's play *Blithe Spirit.* The play ran for a year at the Alvin Theater and, true to form, Beatrice, in her role as Madame Arcati, ad-libbed her way through every performance.

Her penchant for improvising was one of the things that co-stars remembered best about Beatrice. Bert Lahr recalled a revue he was in with her called *The Show Is On*. Lillie played a ticket seller at the box office and Lahr played a customer. He was supposed to step up to the window and exchange gags with her. "Well, one night when I stepped up," he said, "she slammed the window in my face. Then she shouted 'So sorry. Box office closed for the night.'"

Lillie's willingness to experiment was only one of her talents. As Kenneth Tynan noted in *Holiday* in September 1956: "Her gift is to reproduce on stage the grievous idiocy with which people behave when they are on their own: humming and mumbling, grimacing at the looking glass, perhaps even singing into it, hopping, skipping, fiddling with their dress, starting and stopping a hundred trivial tasks—looking, in fact, definably batty. . . . To carry it off as she does requires a vast amount of sheer nerve and more than a whiff of genius, which is really another word for creative self-sufficiency."

Tynan also felt that Lillie was different from other North American comedians of her time: "Almost without exception, American comediennes get their laughs by pretending to be pop-eyed man-hunting spinsters. Miss Lillie is as far removed from these as a butterfly is from a guided missile." Perhaps her early experiences playing male roles gave Beatrice a taste for something besides the flighty dimwit so prevalent among female comics.

Beatrice herself did not elaborate on what it was like to be a female comic, but she did note in her autobiography that "I've found that men as a rule resist laughing at women. The explanation can probably be found buried deep down in the general subject of s-e-x."

She felt that her own ability to elicit laughs came from an inborn feeling for comedy and fun. "Sure, comedians have worries and tragedies like other people," she said, "but if you can't see the lighter side of life, your humor won't come across."

In 1979 DRG reissued a recording of some of Lillie's greatest performances. Enthused reviewer Peter Reilly in *Stereo Review* in September 1979: "In a way, Beatrice Lillie originated the 'send-up' as we know it in modern entertainment—taking material that is in itself perhaps not meant to be funny and, by a subtle change of perspective, making it hilarious. . . . No one, except perhaps Lily Tomlin has ever been able to tread the fine line between tasteless (and quickly) boring 'camp' and genuinely effortless parody as gracefully, elegantly, and hilariously as Beatrice Gladys Lillie."

Sixty-five years after Beatrice first appeared in Charlot's revue, her humor was still coming across.

MOLLY PICON

It was said her eyes resembled those of Eddie Cantor and her stage manner was a cross between Harpo Marx and Fanny Brice. She attained stardom in New York City's Yiddish theaters in the 1920's with songs and humorous character studies. She appeared in musical comedies and was responsible for a whole trend away from the heavy opera singer to the physically lighter musical comedy star. As her fame grew she made appearances all over the United States and the rest of the world, as well as in vaudeville where she was a headliner. In the end she always returned to her first love, the Jewish theater of New York.

Molly Picon was born in a New York City tenement on June 1, 1898, the daughter of Lewis and Clara (Ostrow) Picon. The family moved several times before settling in Philadelphia when Molly was three. Mrs. Picon worked as a seamstress for actresses in that city's Yiddish stock company. Mr. Picon also worked in the needle trades. At the age of five, Molly tried out at a children's amateur night contest in a local vaudeville theater where she won the first prize — a five-dollar gold piece — with a comic song.

She continued to perform at local amateur events in the city, and at the age of six her mother was able to get her a place in the Jewish stock company. With that company she played kid roles for 50 cents a night, three or four times a week. By the age of nine she worked at a nickelodeon where, between films, she sang ballads illustrated by slides, and made $15 a week. After three years of high school, she dropped out to devote herself full-time to the theater.

At that time she used to introduce herself to theater owners and booking agents by saying, "I sing, dance, play the piano and ukelele, and do somersaults." She spent a couple years with an

English-language stock company in Philadelphia and left them to tour the vaudeville circuit coast to coast in 1918-19. She was then with a singing and dancing act called "The Four Seasons." Molly appeared as "Winter," apparently because she was the only one who could do a Russian dance. The group found themselves stranded in Boston without funds and had to split up. Molly turned for help to a local Yiddish theater run by Jacob Kalich who, as it happened, had just had a soubrette come down with the flu. He hired Picon, who quickly grew to be popular.

Within a year Kalich and Picon married and in 1921 he took her to Europe to familiarize herself with Jewish theater at its source and to perfect her Yiddish. On the boat trip over, Kalich wrote the first starring vehicle for Picon, a musical comedy called *Yankele,* the Yiddish equivalent of Peter Pan. Picon's part was that of a small boy. An extended tour of Europe with that and other vehicles was highly successful and her good notices preceded her back to the United States when she returned in 1923. She opened that year at New York's famous Yiddish Second Avenue Theatre with *Yankele,* which had sold out before she arrived. At that time Yiddish theater in Europe and the United States was into serious and ponderous operas, starring females who weighed at least 150 pounds. Picon weighed only 100 pounds, which was one of the reasons Kalich cast her as a small boy in some of her early vehicles. Over the coming decades Kalich would write most of Picon's material. He concentrated on the light musical comedies which suited her talents and transformed the Yiddish theater.

Molly spent the remainder of the 1920's playing at the Second Avenue Theatre in vehicles such as *Shmendrik* (1924), in which she played a Simple Simon type, *Hello Molly* (1929) and *Comedienne* (1930). By the end of that decade a larger audience beckoned and she headlined at the Palace for $2,500 a week. She did songs translated into English from Yiddish, character studies and impersonations, such as a depiction of people at a wedding, and a monologue about a street girl. She did songs such as "The Immigrant Boy," and an interview with "Mister Ziegenfeld." During the 1930's she made $3,000 a week heading vaudeville bills at the Palace. She continued to perform at the Yiddish theater, where she became known as the "Sweetheart of Second Avenue." She also toured across the country in vaudeville, doing sketches such as "Making Love in Four Nationalities" and "The Jewish Wedding," singing, and imitating Charlie Chaplin.

She toured the world extensively in the 1930's, performing all over Europe, in Russia, South America, and South Africa. While Kalich wrote the musical comedy vehicles for her, Molly wrote all her own songs as well as all of her "comedy business." In 1942 she appeared in *Oh, What a Life* at Second Avenue, based on her own life, and a reviewer wrote that "She sings generously, dances gaily, and . . . shows what a gifted comic she is." Picon was one of the first entertainers to go to post-war Europe, where she helped to revive the spirits of the surviving Jews. Back at Second Avenue at the end of the 1940's, she celebrated her 25th anniversary there in *So Long as You're Healthy,* of which *New York Times* critic Brooks Atkinson wrote: "Miss Picon is just as ingratiating with her ingenious comedy and sentimental ballad singing." The following year she appeared in *Mazel Tov Molly,* the 30th vehicle written for her by Kalich, in which she was described as displaying "puckish wit and delightfully outlandish manners."

Over the years she had also found time to appear frequently on radio and to make some film and television appearances. She has continued to perform up to the present, and while her activity has declined in recent decades, she has continued to entertain Jewish and Gentile audiences with her own style of humor, right into the 1980's.

One of the reasons she held her audiences over so many decades was her penchant for doing something new and different in every show, "walking a tightrope, tap dancing, doing a sleight-of-hand act, entering on a horse, playing a new musical instrument." As a comedian she was a superb mime and made excellent use of her hands, face, and voice. It was said that she had the "gift which made Charlie Chaplin a universal favorite without speaking a word."

GRACIE FIELDS

Born in a poor mill town in England, Gracie Fields rose to become that country's favorite female comic. Her love of entertaining and obvious sincerity propelled her to the top, eventually making her the highest paid female entertainer in the world. As with most female comics performing live in that era, she was a singing comic. The same talents which had captured British audiences were used by her to conquer American fans as well, and she became famous on both sides of the Atlantic. She enjoyed her greatest popularity from about 1920 to 1950.

She was born Grace Stansfield in 1898 in the cotton mill town of Rochdale in Lancashire. Her parents were poor working people and Grace was born over a fish-and-chip shop. Her father, Fred, was a handyman and mechanic. Her mother, Jenny, was deeply stage struck and held a variety of jobs, including doing laundry for theatrical troupers. The Stansfields lived across the road from a boarding house where actors often stayed. Jenny was determined that her daughter go on the stage.

Gracie's education was limited to primary school. She never had any formal instruction in theatrical arts, although her mother taught all of her children to sing at an early age.

In school she was very shy and reserved, but at the age of seven she won an amateur singing contest and determined to make the stage her career. After that she sang in local concerts and in local theaters. At ten she became a member of a children's troupe known as "Haley's Garden of Girls." She next began to work half-time at the local mill as a cotton winder and spent half-time at school. Her stay at the plant was short-lived, as she sang for her co-workers and gave comic imitations of the foreman, which eventually resulted in her being fired when she was caught. She briefly held a couple of other town jobs, including one at a paper bag factory.

Gracie felt she had a natural singing voice and bought records of current recording stars to study and teach herself as best she could. Her mother also sang and encouraged her, while Gracie credited her father with being a "born comic."

A short time later she joined another troupe "Nine Dainty Dots." With this troupe she sang, clowned and did cartwheels, which remained a part of her act for decades. She also did impressions of stars, one being George Formby, senior. By the time she was thirteen she was unemployed and in danger of returning to the mill if she couldn't find work on the stage. Fortunately the following year she caught on with yet another troupe, "Charburn's Young Stars." She stayed with that group for two years and it was at this point that she changed her name to Gracie Fields.

The theatrical manager told her that Stansfield was too long and her mother came up with several ideas before finally settling on Gracie Fields. With the Charburn group, Gracie sang, danced and acted in comedy skits. She was paid four shillings a week to start. Fields credited Fred Hutchins with developing her comic talents at that time. When she was on stage with him she had to ab lib until he gave her the signal to stop.

Her next job was with a revue called *Yes, I Think So*. She celebrated her sixteenth birthday with this show and toured for eighteen months. The comedian with that revue was Archie Pitt, who mounted another revue called *It's a Bargain* and signed Gracie up as second lead. In that show she imitated the likes of Charlie Chaplin. The revue ran for two and a half years and toured all over the country.

When that show ended Pitt staged yet another revue in 1918 called *Mr. Tower of London*. This one starred Gracie, making her famous. It enjoyed enormous success, and ran for nine years with an estimated seven million people taking it in. In that show Fields did songs, acrobatics, and took part in skits. She played over 4,000 performances and was the acknowledged draw of the show. She played in a number of other revues until 1931, after which she performed her own solo act.

During the 1930's Fields played virtually every theater in the country, always as the top of the bill. She opened theaters, movie houses and shops, and people came out in droves to see her. At such events her fans expected her to play the fool and Gracie would always oblige, believing that, "You can't disappoint the customers." In 1928 the Duncan Sisters had taken the musical story of Uncle Tom's Cabin, *Topsy and Eva*, on tour to England. When Rosetta Duncan became ill Gracie stepped in and learned the part in 24 hours. She performed without pay as the black-faced Topsy until Rosetta recovered.

During the middle 1930's while Gracie was separated from her first husband she and painter John Flanagan fell in love. Ultimately the relationship broke up because Flanagan "could not accept her fame." Her reputation was so great during the 1930's that both a 400-ton paddle steamer and a hybrid tea rose were named "Gracie Fields." In 1978 a large new theater was opened in Gracie's home town of Rochdale and named after her.

She had become such a big star by 1930 that she received a two-week booking in America at New York City's Palace, the most prestigious vaudeville house in the country. It was her first American performance and got off to a poor start. Fields later analyzed her failure by saying, "I was tryin' to be a bloomin' American instead of bein' myself." She was able to recover from her nervousness and finish the engagement on a successful note, living up to the billing the Palace had given her, "Gracie Fields—The Funniest Woman In The World."

Gracie remained a superstar in England, where she appeared at theaters like the Palladium, making up to $5,000 per week. She released her first record in 1928 and by 1933 was able to celebrate the pressing of record number four million. At that time it was said that no singer in the world had sold as many records with the possible exception of Caruso. She continued to make records into the 1970's, for a total of over 300 recordings.

Her act consisted of songs, some serious and some funny, mixed with stories and facial mugging and physical humor thrown in for good measure. Part of her grimacing routine included, "Raised eyebrows, bulging teeth and pursed lips." She was also prone to break up a song by turning a cartwheel in the middle of it.

Although one writer did grudgingly admit she was handsome, and said that "People who expect to see a rude horse-faced buffoon are surprised," most critics considered her unattractive. Fields went along with it and often said to her audience, "I have teeth that were made by a mechanic. I wear glasses. And my legs-eh, lad, I'm glad I earn my money with my throat."

Her best known song was "The Biggest Aspidistra in the World." She also did patriotic songs such as "There'll Always Be an England" and "God Bless America." Her comic songs were about such subjects as betrayed maidens, with titles like, "Walter Walter, Lead me to the Altar." Her humor was described as salty, sometimes vulgar, and even bordering on the bawdy.

Throughout her career she retained her Lancashire accent and her factory girl personality. A typical act might have Fields punctuate her songs with a high kick, groan audibly after telling a corny joke and do a ribald imitation of a soprano. Mimicking was another of her strong comic suits. Not all of her comic songs were screechers, but most were loud. The songs involved gentle satirical comedy, the plain comedy of everyday life. On stage she usually worked completely without props.

Her style has been described as "large friendliness, cheerful common sense and persistent joy in what is ridiculous." It has also been termed "sheer animal vulgarity, including flea-scratching and grimaces." Fields made her first film in England in 1931, *Sally in Our Alley,* which was a big success. She was the biggest box office draw in Britain during that decade. The song "Sally" became Gracie's signature song.

A number of her films were shown in America, enhancing her reputation on this side of the ocean. She was called the "most refreshing comedy personality to hit the American screen in many a year."

The majority of her early films were directed by Basil Dean, who "saw her less as a heroine than as a clown, and she was normally lovelorn, only to lose the man to an ingenue in the end. Most of the humor was broad caricature." The films themselves were not particularly good, being "flimsy and unreal." It didn't matter, though, because the audience went to see and hear Gracie.

Hollywood watched Gracie's career with interest, but MGM decided to pass. Their British boss considered her a great comedian but felt her humor was too national. Darryl Zanuck of 20th Century did bring Fields to Hollywood in 1938 for a four-picture contract. She spent about eight months in Hollywood but didn't like it and asked if her first film could be shot in England, to which Zanuck agreed. She didn't want to work in Hollywood because she was afraid "they'd make me half an' half, sort of, and they mightn't use the right halves either."

Even though the film was shot in England, *We're Goin' to Be Rich* (1938) proved her worries were well-founded. The studio gave her the glamour treatment and Fields wasn't happy with the result. "I thought we were going to get something fancier like, so that we could show American audiences what I can do. This film won't do it." When she moved to California after the outbreak of the war, she did make several movies there. She made her fifteenth, and last, film in 1945, *Paris Underground*.

Fields was at her best in live performances and by the late 1930's she made an estimated $1 million a year from her films, records, and stage appearances. She was so popular that when she infrequently was heard on the radio most of Britain stayed home to listen. "Parliament was once adjourned because she was about to broadcast." When she was ill in 1939, legions of fans gathered outside the hospital to wish her a speedy recovery.

All of this changed in 1940 after the war broke out. Her husband, Monty Banks who was born in Italy but had lived most of his adult life in the United States, was declared an alien and fled to the U.S. to avoid prison. Gracie went with him and was denounced in the press as a traitor and a deserter. Innuendos were raised that she had taken all of her assets out of the country. That accusation was even raised in Parliament.

She spent much of the next several years entertaining Commonwealth troops in every corner of the globe, as well as war workers on both sides of the Atlantic, all for free. At first, whenever she sang in Britain she was usually met with hostility, but soon won over the audience. Her war effort went mostly unreported by the British press. It was 1947 before she fully regained her former status, when she did her first radio series for the BBC. It was titled "Our Gracie," the nickname by which she was known world-wide. Her fan mail reached almost 4,000 letters per week. She also continued to tour, using the same "low but clean" blend of comedy and song. Only the cartwheels had gone, a concession to age.

In the United States she got her first network show in October 1942. It was a nightly show, only five minutes long, usually consisting of one song and one story. In a typical program she sang "The Biggest Aspidistra in the World" and told the story of cockney Bill who was blown through a window by a bomb. "Crikey! I got outa there just in time." For this show she received $2,500 per week. Audiences demanded more and the show was expanded to fifteen minutes in 1943 and then to a weekly half hour in 1944. She reappeared again briefly on American radio with a show in 1951.

By the mid 1950's she was starting to slow down a bit and wasn't touring quite as much. She made a few forays into straight dramatic roles on American television. By the mid 1960's she was in semi-retirement and had a number of final, farewell concerts. She gave a Royal Command performance at the age of 80 and was still receiving offers of work at that time.

Over the years the theater had always been her favorite medium in which to perform. She didn't mind radio and television if there was an audience in the studio. Film making she actively disliked, at least in the beginning. For her the magic of theater lay in its live audience. Her real and sincere affection for her fans played a large role in her success with them. She felt television was cruel to performers who were getting older, and she said, "I'd rather be with an audience than have a man pointing a black box at me." For her services to the British entertainment industry she was made a Dame of the British Empire in 1979. She died later that year at the age of 81.

DUNCAN SISTERS

Female comedy teams have always been a very scarce commodity and it was the Duncan Sisters who were by far the most popular and well known of that group. They struggled for a number of years before making it big in vaudeville in the musical comedy *Topsy and Eva*. From then on they were essentially one-hit wonders, touring in that vehicle for decades.

Rosetta Duncan was born in Los Angeles in November 1900; her sister Vivian followed in June 1902. Their mother died in childbirth and their father, Samuel Duncan, was in the real estate business. The sisters had the beginnings of their musical training at the hands of their father, who could play a number of instruments. He encouraged his daughters to sing and taught Vivian to play the piano. The Duncan sisters made their debut as small children entertaining at church functions. From the beginning they worked as a team. Rosetta, dressed up as a little Dutch girl, would sing and yodel. Vivian played the piano and sang.

From the start Rosetta was the acknowledged leader of the two and was also considered a "natural-born" comedian. In school she was the class cut-up, always dreaming up ways to make the other kids laugh, and often being sent home as punishment for disrupting the class. At that early age Rosetta knew what she wanted: to be on the stage and make people laugh. Both girls took singing lessons for several years, starting at about age eleven. When Vivian was twelve she was making six dollars a week by playing the piano in a nearby movie theater at night. The only piece she knew was "Aloha," which she varied in tempo to suit the movie: soft for love scenes, fast for exciting parts. When the management caught on to her limited repertoire, she was fired.

The sisters continued to perform and sing at church concerts and anywhere else they had the chance. They often sang and did little comic acts at vaudeville amateur nights. By about 1915 they had made their professional debut in vaudeville and toured the west coast in the *Kiddies Revue,* a production by Gus Edwards. Their older sister had recently moved to New York and wrote to Rosetta and Vivian urging them to try their luck there. The sisters set out for that city but got only as far as Chicago when their money ran out. Stranded, they took up an offer to tour on one of the cheaper vaudeville circuits playing small towns in the area, splitting $25 a week between them.

Eventually they did manage to arrive in New York, and in May of 1917 they made their debut at the Fifth Avenue Theatre with a 12-minute act, which consisted largely of their singing. They were not particularly impressive and were termed a "stereotyped sister-act." A reviewer for *Variety* said, "The Duncan Sisters are not ripe as yet for the big time." Despite the review, they continued to get work, appearing in a number of musical revues, both in the United States and in London, England. The sisters wrote all of their own material and they "always appear as children, in short frocks and half-length hose; and we talk in a childish voice."

By the early 1920's the Duncans had achieved a measure of success because, the sisters felt, their act was original and had grown out of the things they had done as children. Their routine by now contained comic sketches as well as songs. Moreover, the supreme accolade of imitation was being awarded them. Dozens of sister pairs were making the rounds of vaudeville managers, claiming to do the same things as the Duncan sisters. The Duncans sang straight songs as well as comic ditties such as "I Gotta Code in By Dose" and "The Prune Song." They finished one of their numbers, "She Fell Down on Her Cadenza," by "hurling an assortment of vegetables, including celery, beets, carrots and even a cabbage at the audience."

Early in 1923 the sisters were in California and were approached by a man who was interested in putting them in motion pictures. The three of them talked the idea over but none of them could come up with any concrete proposals. Finally the man said, "I guess we'll have to black you up," a reference to the then common practice of whites appearing in blackface on stage or screen. This gave the Duncans the idea of doing a version of Uncle Tom's Cabin, with Eva and Topsy being the main characters. Rosetta and Vivian quickly came up with a musical comedy version titled *Topsy and Eva.* They wrote the music and the lyrics, jazzed up the story, added lots of comedy, and did an outline of the story. The book was written by Catherine Cutting.

The sisters had decided to do it on the stage instead of on film, and the production opened in San Francisco in July of 1923 with Vivian playing Eva, the sweet and innocent heroine, and Rosetta playing Topsy, in blackface of course, and clowning brilliantly. Both characters were children. The show was a smash hit everywhere that it played and the Duncan sisters enjoyed long runs in cities such as Chicago and New York. In 1924 Rosetta and Vivian had a gross income of $179,000. By 1928 they were worth over $1 million. Yet in 1931 they filed for bankruptcy, the victims of poor investment choices and the stock market crash.

After their New York run they took the show on the road to England, France, Germany, South Africa and South America, always playing the roles in the language of the host country. They were wined and dined by royalty in several of the countries they toured. While touring in London in 1928, Rosetta was ill and unable to perform for about a week. The last-minute replacement, blackface and all, was Gracie Fields, who acquitted herself well in the part.

They toured *Topsy and Eva* off and on for twenty years until 1942, the year of their last tour. The play itself had been revised a number of times in those intervening years. In addition the sisters sometimes appeared in other variety productions such as *Clowns in Clover* in London in 1928, and the road version in 1934 of *New Faces*. The bulk of their work, though, was *Topsy and Eva*.

They made a film version of the comedy in 1927 but it was a failure. As a silent film it just couldn't capture the verbal aspects of the play which were so important to its humor and success. The movie had three directors, one of whom was D.W. Griffith, who called Rosetta "The Female Charlie Chaplin of the Screen." They made only two other films, both undistinguished. The last was *It's a Great Life,* (1929) their only talking film. They were occasionally heard on radio and Walter Winchell reportedly once paid them one thousand dollars a minute to sing on his radio show.

In 1942 they announced their retirement, but in 1952 they started performing again. They appeared chiefly in clubs and on television doing material from *Topsy and Eva,* songs such as "Rememb'ring" and "I Never Had a Mammy" which had become famous in their own right. They also did other songs from the 1920's which they had helped popularize, such as "Bye, Bye, Blackbird" and "Side by Side." In 1959 Rosetta was killed in a car accident after a club date in the Midwest. Charlotte Greenwood described her as "the greatest clown on the American stage." Vivian continued to perform for a time as a solo act.

Topsy and Eva has not stood up over time primarily because the material was blatantly racist, although the Duncans themselves were not. It was written at a time when such material was common and not questioned with regard to stereotyping. Rosetta's temperament as the impudent Topsy was, "I'se mean an' ornery, I is, mean an' ornery. I hate everybody in the world, and I only wish there were more people in the world so I could hate them too." In *Topsy and Eva* they poked fun in a mild way at the foibles of the day. The dim-witted Topsy functioned as a perfect foil for the straight man Eva.

As comedians their strong suit was said to be the excellent rapport between them and their sense of timing. They also suggested wholesomeness, partly no doubt, due to their childish parts and clothes.

They "had a good deal of tart commentary on hypocrisy and pretension, much of which was no less effective for being implicit rather than explicit."

HELEN KANE

Helen Kane enjoyed half a dozen years of heady fame from 1929 until 1935, all based on a bit of gibberish which she accidentally added on to a song. Even half a century after the fact, there are probably few people who aren't familiar with the nonsense phrase, "boop-boop-a-doop."

She was born Helen Schroeder in 1904 in the Bronx, and used the name of her first husband on the stage. In the mid 1920's she was an obscure singer without a whole lot of talent when she got a small part in the comic production, *I'll Say She Is,* a Marx Brothers revue. In 1927 she was back on the stage on Broadway with another small part in *A Night in Spain,* but this vehicle closed after only 22 performances.

At that point in her career she had made little impression on anyone. It was said that she had by then "developed a peculiar style of singing." This was a reference to the squeaky and babyish voice which she affected. One Chicago critic acidly remarked about the producer who had brought Kane to that city, that he "should be forced to spend seven hours listening to her sing." Kane persisted in her career, however, and in 1928 she landed a booking at the Paramount vaudeville theater in New York City.

She was backstage rehearsing her song, "That's My Weakness Now." When she came to the end she felt that something was needed, a sort of an interlude. On the spur of the moment she ad libbed the phrase "boop-boop-a-doop." Backstage people thought it intriguing and Kane kept it in. The next year she appeared in the revue *Good Boy* and introduced the song "I Wanna Be Loved By You," adding her squeaky phrase onto it, of course. She added "boop-boop-a-doop" to other songs as well but perhaps the only other song closely identified with it was "Button Up Your Overcoat." When she did this number in vaudeville, Helen would tear the buttons off the coat of her accompanist.

Kane was now a full-fledged superstar. In 1929 she was headlining at the prestigious Palace Theater in New York, the mecca of vaudeville, where she became the "baby-talk prima donna" with the vacant stare and pout. Her material was considered to be "not unamusing." She conquered the audience with endless rounds of "boop-boop-a-doop" tacked on to most of her songs, and as *The New York Times* called her in November 1929, she was "the insinuating queen of the baby-talk singers."

She enjoyed enormous fame and became a symbol of the flapper of the 1920's. The feminine public adopted her "bee-sting lips and short Italian bob" completely. She was wiggly and giggly and pert and saucy, with a turned up nose. Over the next few years the public couldn't get enough of her, and she appeared on radio, in nightclubs, made recordings, as well as making nine Hollywood films. "There were Helen Kane games and contests and there were 'boop-boop-a-doop' toys." She made as much as $8,000 a week and once received $5,000 for going to a high society party and singing five choruses of "Button Up Your Overcoat." A cartoon strip emerged, "Betty Boop," which was modeled after her, as was an animated "Betty Boop" in the movies. Created by Max Fleischer, the animated Betty Boop continues to enjoy a cult following.

In 1935, still at her peak, Kane said she was tired and worn out, quit show business, and disappeared from public view. In 1950 Debbie Reynolds appeared in the musical film *Three Little Words* and did the song, "I Wanna Be Loved By You." Reynolds lip-synced it on film, for Helen Kane had been called out of retirement to dub the lyrics for Reynolds. From then on Kane made a comeback of sorts and appeared occasionally on radio, television, and in person until shortly before her death in September of 1966 at the age of 62. But the craze was, of course, long past and interest in Kane was marginal.

She had parlayed a phrase, a baby voice, and puckered-up lips into a national craze. Such phrases were more common in that era. Jimmy Durante had his "cha-cha-cha," Bing Crosby his "vodo-de-o." Kane's success, based on what it was, was certainly hard to fathom. Part of it was certainly due to the infantile image Kane presented, a form of innocence latched onto in the face of the evils of the Depression and the start of the rise of Hitler. It was a non-threatening image of the tractable and ready-to-please female. It was a role that couldn't really be filled by a man. Men could and did do child characters, but they were always rough and tough brats. Kane lulled her audience into a remembrance of their childhoods, almost always perceived as calm and safe. Some evidence for this came from the performer America adopted to fill the void left by Kane's sudden and unexpected retirement. It was another female baby, but a real one this time—Shirley Temple. Helen Kane's contribution to American female comedy is indeed a strange story.

BELLE BARTH

Belle Barth was not as well known as some of the other female comics but her contribution was important nonetheless. More significantly, she was only the third female stand-up comedian. And she was the first to use the format of short jokes, as opposed to the monologues of Herford and Draper. While the comedy of the latter two was a gentle "feminine" type, Barth dealt with the sexually explicit. *Time* magazine called her "the brass-voiced entertainer and doyenne of dirty ditties."

She was born Belle Salzman in New York City in 1911 and later took her first husband's name for stage purposes. She left high school before graduation and began a vaudeville career in the latter part of the 1920's. In those days her material consisted mostly of impressions of stars such as Sophie Tucker, Al Jolson, and George Jessel. She later added lampoons of strippers Lili St. Cyr and Gypsy Rose Lee, which were described as "devastatingly funny take-offs."

As she turned more and more to bawdy songs and ribald jokes, she found her only venue to be nightclubs and hotels which she played from about the 1930's onward, right up to her death. She also made a number of records, termed of the "party type" with titles such as "My Next Story Is a Little Risque" and "If I Embarrass You, Tell Your Friends."

Her jokes included the following:

When the world war broke out, I joined the WACS. Right away, they sent me to the worst spot, Guadalcanal. The doctor who gave me the physical took one look and said, "What a canal." So then I figured, what the hell, at least I'll see a lot of action, and I felt as happy as the girl who got raped on Essex Street and thought it was Grand. But I had my disappointments in the service; I discovered that a 21-inch Admiral was only a television set.

Barth once said that she loved music and children but she couldn't read music and therefore couldn't teach kids, so she decided, "I'd teach grown-ups a thing or two." She frequently played clubs in Las Vegas and Miami and was playing Caesars Palace in Las Vegas when she was taken ill in 1970. She died the next year at age 59. She once boasted that she had been "thirteen years on the beach without an arrest." Actually her repeated use of taboo words had kept her in and out of courts on charges of obscenity, but this never diminished her popularity. Her records sold in the millions and she earned the nickname "the female Lenny Bruce," although she had preceded him.

While contemporaries such as Tucker and West used sexual material in an indirect manner, Barth delivered her material in a graphic and straightforward way and was one of the first entertainers to use blatantly x-rated material. As such she was effectively blocked from appearing in the mass forms of the media such as vaudeville, or radio and television, which were all very "clean" and family oriented.

Barth was limited to plying her trade on the club circuit, since a woman delivering her type of material was unacceptable anywhere else. The current crop of new stand-up women comics can regularly use crude humor if they wish, while a comic like Belle Barth was truly pioneering in this style.

GRACIE ALLEN

She was perhaps the dizziest of all the dizzy dames, the dumbest of all the dumb Doras. She was the prototype of all the scatterbrains to come, the mistress of illogical logic. She was Gracie Allen. Together with her husband and partner, George Burns, she performed for thirty-five years, most of those years as a national favorite. Burns and Allen achieved success in four different mediums, vaudeville, radio, film, and television, with their peak popularity being in radio.

Over all those years Gracie's character remained consistent, across all four media. While she may have been queen of the airheads she did get away from the broad physical slapstick and funny clothes which marked so many of the early comics. She dressed in regular street clothes, relying solely on verbal humor and the interplay between herself and Burns. This image of a senseless woman with lightweight mental abilities was one which the American public never seemed to tire of.

She was born Grace Ethel Cecile Rosalie Allen in San Francisco in 1895 to Margaret (Darragh) and George Allen. Her father toured the vaudeville circuit as a song and dance man, and at about the age of three or four she appeared in his act dressed in a top hat and suit. She later attended school in San Francisco until the age of fourteen, when she teamed up with her older sisters in vaudeville as a dancer.

A few years later she joined the Larry Reilly Company, another vaudeville act, doing dances and jigs, and playing Irish colleens. She toured with that group for several years and worked her way up to one of the star attractions. She then left that group after a dispute with Reilly. Allen felt she deserved better billing than the "and company." Reilly disagreed, however. She then briefly teamed up with a man named Boylan Brazil in an act featuring Boylan as a fast-talking jewelry salesman and Gracie as a simple country girl named Sally Simpkins. They only managed to obtain poor bookings and Gracie left the act in disgust.

She settled in New York City in 1922, hoping to land some acting work. She had trouble getting parts and so enrolled in secretarial school, staying for three months. One night that year Allen attended the theater at Union Hall, New Jersey, where her roommate was appearing on a vaudeville bill. Backstage after the show she was introduced to George Burns, who was appearing on the same bill. Burns was then performing a song and dance and verbal patter act with a man named Billy Lorraine. Their act was billed as Burns and Lorraine—Two Broadway Thieves, because part of the act was made up of imitations of stars such as Eddie Cantor and Al Jolson. This team was in the process of breaking up at that point. Burns was immediately struck by Allen and felt she would be a perfect foil for him in his act. He quickly persuaded her to join him and they debuted as a team in 1923 at the Hill Street Theater in Newark, New Jersey, receiving $15 for three days' work.

In the beginning it was Gracie who played the straight role while Burns delivered the jokes, which was how Burns had operated in the past. This time though it wasn't working. Gracie was getting more laughs delivering the straight lines than Burns was for the jokes. From the audience response Burns recognized Allen as a "natural comedienne," and in the space of a couple of months the roles were reversed, with Gracie as the scatterbrained comic while George took on the role of a cigar-chomping straight man, feeding lines to his ditsy partner. These roles would remain permanent. Burns has claimed theirs was the first mixed act to get laughs without resorting to funny clothes, although in the first few months when Burns was trying to be the comic he wore "a flashy gold jacket, large red bow tie, baggy pants, and turned-up hat." When the roles were reversed, Burns went to an everyday, nondescript suit.

When Burns saw the act wasn't working the way it was originally set up, he admitted, "Finally I saw the light. . . . I started playing the serious, exasperated male, leading up to Gracie's nitwit gags." Thus Gracie the dumbbell was born. According to George it was the audience that forced the image on Gracie. He analyzed the jokes Gracie used and found that some fell flat. The audience, he believed, "didn't want sarcasm from Gracie. The audience didn't want her to be smart." Burns then began to collect Dumb Dora jokes. When he switched the act around and became the straight man, he said "It broke my heart." Apparently he took a lot of kidding from his vaudeville pals for giving Allen the jokes. Perhaps the only consolation was that Gracie was a "dumb comic."

Initially Burns and Allen didn't get much work, and what they did get were bookings on the circuits playing small towns. They were known in the trade as a "disappointment act," one that filled in at the last minute for ill performers. They got their break when they substituted at a leading vaudeville house and were a success. Soon they were booked into the better theaters. They toured with Loew's circuit for nineteen weeks at $400 a week with a routine called "Dizzy," based of course of Gracie's character. In 1926 the couple married and also that year were signed by the Keith circuit for a reported $750 a week. The contract was for five years, the longest ever signed up to that time.

The routine that got them the Keith contract was called "Lamb Chops," about a young man who spent all his money taking his girl friend out to eat at restaurants. The routine had a lot of jokes about eating, then a rage in vaudeville.

George: Do you like to love?
Gracie: No.
George: Do you like to kiss?
Gracie: No.
George: What do you like?
Gracie: Lamb chops.
George: A little girl your size, can you eat two big lamb chops alone?
Gracie: No, but with potatoes I could.

In the act they played boyfriend and girlfriend who exchanged verbal repartee about themselves and Gracie's mythical family. Burns's reaction was that of exasperation. It would be decades later before they would play a married couple and before Burns would adopt his more familiar sardonic attitude towards Gracie. Allen played a "nonsensical young girl who made ludicrous statements that she believed to be true."

One of her greatest talents lay in her ability to give the impression that she wasn't telling jokes at all but merely reciting facts, and to make people believe her wildest lines were true. Gracie was the airhead ingenue and Burns her long suffering boyfriend.

Gracie: All great singers have their trials; look at Caruso. Thirty years on a desert island with all those cannibals.
George: You've got the wrong man.
Gracie: No, you're the man for me.
George: But they say I'm through as a singer. I'm extinct.
Gracie: You do not.

Gracie's relatives were a constant source of humor.

Gracie: Did you know my brother was held up by two men last night?
George: For how much?
Gracie: Oh, all the way home!

"My uncle eats concrete. Mother asked him to stay to dinner, but she said he was going to eat up the street."

Critics loved them as much as the audience. Reporting on one of their vaudeville performances, *Variety* stated that, "Miss Allen is an adorable 'dizzy' with an ingratiating prattle. . . . A tip-top comedy interlude for the best vaudeville."

Some have tried to argue that Allen represented a different type of dumbbell, that in her own fashion she was articulate, full of ideas and could think logically, if her original absurd premises were accepted. Therefore, she was as *Billboard* described her, "the sophisticated Dumb Dora." There is little substance to this argument, though, as Allen was naive about the world, didn't know the meaning of words and involved herself in endless silly schemes, particularly during the TV run. The character was a regular, garden variety type of Dumb Dora.

During their vaudeville days the couple toured Europe. In England, where they were billed as "The Famous American Comedy Couple," one critic wrote about Allen, "Excepting Beatrice Lillie, she is perhaps the most adroit female laugh-getter in vaudeville." In London in the summer of 1929 they made their radio debut when the BBC asked them to do a show. It was so popular that it was held over for twenty weeks.

Back in the United States in 1930 they appeared on a star-studded bill at New York's Palace Theater with, among others, Eddie Cantor. The Palace was then getting ready to phase out vaudeville. Cantor was impressed and booked Gracie on his radio program, without Burns. Soon they were booked together on other programs and on February 15, 1932, their own show, "The Adventures of Gracie," premiered on CBS radio, where it would be heard continuously for eighteen years. Allen had some trouble adapting to radio, succumbing to mike fright which plagued stage performers switching to radio. She had also experienced stage fright when she first started working with Burns. After their first radio program, they always insisted on having a live studio audience. By 1940 the pair were making a reported $9,000 a week.

Their program started out resembling their vaudeville act, with a boy/girl routine at the beginning and a skit at the end of each show. It would be a decade before the show switched to a domestic comedy format. Much of the humor was based on language jokes. Jane Ace was the queen of malapropisms, but Gracie had her own way of mangling the language.

George: You're absolutely brilliant. I'm beginning to think you are a wizard.

Gracie: I'm a wizard?

George: Yes. You know what a wizard is.

Gracie: Yes, a snowstorm.

George: Well, if that's a snowstorm, then what's a blizzard?

Gracie: A blizzard is the inside of a chicken. Anybody knows that.

George: Then if that's a blizzard, what's a lizard?

Gracie: A lizard is a man that's smart. . . . A genius.

George: Did something happen to you when you were a baby?

Gracie: When I was born I was so surprised I couldn't talk for a year and a half.

George: Did you hear silence is golden?

Gracie: No, what station are they on?

George: It's an adage, you know what an adage is.

Gracie: Oh sure, that's where you keep your old trunks.

Gracie also kidded George and used comic comebacks to go one-up on her partner. "You ought to live in the home for the feeble-minded," said George. "Oh, I'd love to be your house guest sometime," replied Gracie. "Gracie, all I have to do is hear you talk and the blood rushes to my head." "That's because it's empty," retorted Gracie. Allen often mentioned her latest screen heartthrob and always got a reaction. Charles Boyer in particular caused George to do a slow burn. After one of Burns's criticisms, Allen would often take it as a compliment and say, "Oh, George, I'll bet you tell that to all the girls." George would sometimes crack a joke to which Allen would reply, after an appropriate pause, "I don't get it." These two phrases quickly became national catchphrases, and "Gracie Allen" became an affectionate nickname for any female nitwit.

Gracie's mythical relatives were a well used source of humor on their radio series: "These relatives . . . are either nitwits, convicts, or a blend of the two." They resided at addresses such as Alcatraz, Sing Sing, and San Quentin. One of the biggest running gags on the program began in January 1933 when Gracie set off in search of her supposedly missing brother. Allen chased this brother all over the airwaves, turning up unexpectedly on various programs on all the networks; not just nighttime variety shows, but mysteries, soaps, and daytime serials. Soon other media joined in, with newspapers publicizing Allen's quest, and magazines featuring pictures of her looking in various places, such as Coney Island and at the top of the Empire State Building.

Her real brother was an accountant in San Francisco, and once the press found him he was hounded so much that he went into hiding for a few months until the publicity blew over. This stunt had been dreamed up by a CBS publicity man, had lasted a few months and had the desired effect of boosting the program's ratings. Jokes about "Gracie Allen's brother" were as common then as elephant jokes would become decades later.

Another well-remembered stunt occurred in 1940, an election year, when Gracie entered the political fray as a presidential candidate for the Surprise Party. Once again she appeared unannounced on various other programs to give her political views. When asked what party she was affiliated with she would respond, "Same old party—George Burns." An article under her byline on why a woman should be president was published in *Liberty* magazine and she published a booklet, "How to Become President" through the "Gracie Allen Self-Delusion Institute." This stunt went so far as to schedule a three-day convention in Omaha. The campaign slogan was, "Down with common sense, vote for Gracie." When the real election was held, Gracie Allen garnered a few hundred write-in votes. That wasn't her first experience in politics, however. Some time previous, to boost the ratings, Allen had run for Governess of the State of Coma.

The shows, radio and later TV were written by a team of three or more male writers. Burns participated actively in contributing material, overseeing the writing, story conferences, and editing. Gracie played only a minimal role in the development of her character. She received scripts only on the day of the show at which time she excised any double entendre lines, "smartalecky" lines, or anything else she felt was not in keeping with her character. Generally she "entrusted all of her career decisions" to Burns. Her delivery on the show was rapid fire in a high pitched voice, with a total unawareness of the studio audience. The voice was not her real voice.

During the 1930's the program was usually among the top five shows but started to decline towards the end of the decade, reaching a low point in 1941. The boy/girl routine had grown stale, as well as Gracie's flirtatious interludes with the show's announcer. Moreover, the couple were in their early forties and the characters were no longer believable due to that. Gracie remarked at the time to Burns, "I can't continue to play this character. . . . I'm thirty-five! [She used a birthdate about ten years younger than she really was] . . . When you are thirty-five you tell jokes about cooking, about roast beef in the oven."

So in 1942 the format of the show changed to a domestic situation comedy format, with the pair playing a married couple. Their character types remained the same. Gracie was the scatterbrained housewife constantly getting herself and George into problems. Burns was the long suffering and frustrated husband driven to the brink by his wife's lunacy. The style of the program was similar to "Easy Aces." This change was successful and it was the format carried over to television when the pair made a successful transition to the tube in October of 1950, after eighteen years on radio.

The couple branched out into films beginning in 1930, and made numerous shorts as well as close to twenty features. Their first full-length feature film was *The Big Broadcast of 1932*. Allen played in only three films without her husband. In one of them she had the distinction of being the first actress to have a movie named after her, *The Gracie Allen Murder Case* (1939). Her last film was the 1944 feature *Two Girls and a Sailor*, after which she declined further film work in order to spend more time with her children.

Compared to her radio and television success, her film career was minor. Most of the films featured Burns & Allen in excerpts from their vaudeville routines or in segments of anthology films. Often they appeared as "names" to shore up an otherwise mediocre vehicle. They remained in character in their films. In the 1934 release, *Six of a Kind* they were passengers on a long-distance auto trip, irritating the couple who were driving, Mary Boland and Charles Ruggles. In exasperation, Boland said that you couldn't hurt Allen's feelings. Ruggles suggested they could try, but Boland retorted it wasn't worth the effort, since she would only drag out her strange relatives such as the niece with three feet. At that point George asked how this was possible and Allen responded that her brother had written to say that Gracie wouldn't recognize her niece since the last visit, as "she's grown another foot."

As might be expected, magazines brought up the question of what Allen was like in real life. Was she as dumb as her character? In its October 1947 issue, *Independent Woman* stated, "Gracie isn't so dumb off the air," as if the reverse had been expected. The female writer admitted she knew Allen didn't have an off-the-air reputation as a dummy but wondered, in her article, whether or not playing a dummy for so long might not have left its mark. The writer concluded Allen was content to professionally play the "dumb dame" and loved to laugh, even at herself. The author conveyed the news that Gracie had said she bungled things in real life the same as she did on the air, and that off the air she never argued with Burns, since "he always seems to end up in the right."

Allen's popularity continued strong through the 1940's. She had a newspaper column, ghostwritten, which was carried by as many as 125 papers, and her fan mail was enormous, much of it from women. Gracie attributed her popularity with females to the fact that she was too dumb for them to be jealous of her. "A woman can't be jealous of me when her husband either affectionately or unflatteringly terms her just like Gracie Allen."

Back in its July 1940 issue, *Independent Woman* asked the question, "how Gracie Allen gets that way." The answer was provided in an article under the byline of George Burns, who analyzed Allen's appeal.

His paternalistic and sexist attitudes toward females reflected those of society in general. It was this attitude that stereotyped the female comic as dumb: "Gracie is an exaggerated caricature of a familiar and amusing type of scatterbrained woman that all of us have encountered now and then. . . . Gracie gets her laughs—we hope—because we often think the way Gracie talks, but we pride ourselves that we never talk the way Gracie thinks. . . . I'm sure everyone has seen and heard couples all over America who carry on conversations at least a bit in our vein. Everyone has heard wives pick out autos on account of the color of the seat covers or ask their husbands why we don't pay the neutrality bill. . . . Gracie's remarks on the radio are very similar to those of a charming, goodnatured child."

Allen had been reluctant to appear on television and told George it was "one thing I will not be pushed into." Nevertheless, Burns was eager to move to the new medium and convinced her. The half-hour program was seen biweekly for the first two years and weekly from the fall of 1952 onward. A strong ensemble supporting cast had been established on the radio program and some of them made the move with Burns and Allen, notably Bea Benaderet as neighbor Blanche Morton. Larry Keating was added a couple of years later as her husband, Harry, after considerable turnover in that role the first couple of years. It fell to neighbor Harry to play the role of the exasperated male. George had dropped this posture and now played the befuddled husband in a clearly sardonic style. Gracie, of course, was the same old Gracie.

The action of each episode took place in the Burnses' home or the Morton residence, basically a replica of the structure of the radio program. Burns also functioned as an on-screen narrator with his own all seeing television set. He would speculate just where Gracie might be at that moment and what she might be up to. Burns would then retire to his den and turn on his set. Lo and behold, there would be Gracie just where he thought she might be and the audience would then follow the action with him. George was watching "The George Burns and Gracie Allen Show" right along with the audience. The show never made the top ten, but it did draw as many as 30 million viewers per week.

The show's format consisted of an opening monologue by Burns, in the early years, followed by a sketch and then a closing bit by the pair. The skit part always involved one character or another with a problem which Gracie got a hold of and ran wild with, usually involving the Mortons in some improbable scheme. A sample plot line was: "Gracie thinks Harry Morton is in love with her. Gracie, convinced of neighbor Harry's passion, cools his ardor by giving him a sandwich spiced with chopped shoelaces."

In one episode she tried to prevent a student from failing college and becoming a cattle inspector. In another she dressed up the show's announcer, Harry Von Zell, as an African witch doctor in order to chase away unwanted guests. One of the shows sponsors was Carnation Milk and Gracie often wondered how they were able to get milk from carnations. She once made iced coffee by putting the can in the refrigerator. She read a recipe once which said that frankfurters shouldn't be cooked long for best results, "So she chopped them up short." She sewed buttons on George's shirttails so nobody would know if he lost them, and trimmed the hedge with Burns's electric razor.

The most popular part of the show was the end piece in which the two came out onto a bare stage for a few minutes of comic banter, much as they had been doing for over thirty years. Gracie's relatives were still the butt of many jokes, and Allen's brand of illogical logic was much in evidence.

> George: Gracie what do you think of television?
> Gracie: I think its wonderful—I hardly ever watch radio anymore.

> Gracie: I'll never forget the night I had to call the doctor for my cousin Marie . . . she got up in the middle of the night and gave the biggest scream you ever heard.
> George: What happened?
> Gracie: We looked down and her feet had turned black.
> George: What did you do?
> Gracie: We sent for the doctor.
> George: What did the doctor do?
> Gracie: He took off her stockings and we all went back to sleep again.

Such exchanges were not limited to George.

> Gracie: Blanche, I heard some gossip about you from a woman.
> Blanche: Oh-what was it?
> Gracie: I don't remember—I forgot it the minute I told it to her.

Another of television's best known catchphrases occurred at the end of the patter bit when George, tolerant and bemused as ever but totally unable to understand her, turned to her and said, "Say goodnight, Gracie." The couple taped their last program in June 1958 and went off the air, after eight years, not due to declining popularity but on doctor's orders due to Gracie's ill health. It marked the end of a character to whom for "millions of husbands she was the exasperating essence of all wives." Burns summed up the screen Gracie by saying she wasn't really crazy, but made sense in an illogical way. "She's off center. Not quite right, but nearly right."

Burns came back the next year with "The George Burns Show" and most of the same cast. Allen didn't appear in the program, but was frequently mentioned. The show wasn't successful and lasted only one season. He later tried another situation comedy and a couple of replacements for Gracie, but it didn't work. Burns had to wait until nearly the end of the 1970's when he again achieved huge fame as a solo, wisecracking octogenarian.

Gracie Allen died of a heart attack in August 1964 and the entertainment industry had lost an unparalleled comic artist who had gotten the majority of laughs for America's longest-playing comedy team. She had claimed that she had never enjoyed show business and the strain took its toll. The idea that the real Gracie was not like the stage Gracie was an idea that was not easily believed or accepted; "people naturally assumed that Gracie was . . . Gracie."

During the last couple of years of their TV show Allen had begun to grow withdrawn and tense and to suffer from migraine headaches, the health problems for which she would soon retire. Burns felt these ailments were brought on by "the chronic strain of making like someone she isn't."

JANE ACE

In a 1775 play titled *The Rivals,* British playwright Richard Brinsley Sheridan introduced a character called Mrs. Malaprop. She got laughs through her ridiculous misuse of words, her confusion resulting from the resemblance in sound of the appropriate word to the inappropriate one, which triggered the laughs. The character proved to be so popular that the term "malapropism" became part of our everyday language and denoted any such misuse of a word.

An example of a malapropism is the "chickens come home to roast." This one was uttered not by Mrs. Malaprop but by Jane Ace, one of radio's great scatterbrains from the 1930's and 1940's. Sheridan may have created Mrs. Malaprop, but it took the radio and television industry to turn out malapropisms at almost assembly line speed. As a mangler of the language, as a mistress of misspeak, and as an all around "dumb woman" Jane Ace had few rivals. In the narrower and more specific field of malapropisms, it was no contest. Jane won hands down. So prolific was she with them that one critic began labelling her output as Janeaceisms. Another paid her the tribute of calling her funnier than the original.

Together with her real-life husband Goodman Ace, she starred in the long-running domestic radio comedy series, *Easy Aces.* Like one of her contemporaries, Gracie Allen, Jane portrayed the dizzy dame, dumb woman, or scatterbrain. The humor was largely character comedy zeroing in on the silly and foolish personalities of the females and the ridiculous situations they entangled themselves and usually their husbands in.

The couple were both born in Kansas City, Missouri (Jane in October, 1905). Goodman had always wanted to be a writer and spent about ten years working as a reporter for the Kansas City *Journal-Post*. By 1928 he had his own column in which he did film and drama reviews. That year he married Jane Sherman who was the daughter of a Kansas City clothing salesman. The couple had met at a dancing school. Virtually nothing has ever been written about Jane's early life up until her marriage. She was described as having a talent for acting and a sense of humor, but there was no indication she ever had a desire to enter show business.

In 1928 Ace approached the manager of radio station KMBC, the CBS affiliate in Kansas City, and convinced him to give Ace two fifteen-minute programs a week on the air. Goodman was interested in supplementing his income. One program was aired Sunday mornings, during which he read the comics to children. The second program was on Friday nights and consisted of movie reviews and assorted Hollywood gossip. Ace received $10 per week for each of these shows. One night, either in 1928 or 1929, Ace was just finishing his movie program when he got a frantic signal that, due to some error, the station had nothing to put on the air for the upcoming fifteen minutes right after Ace's show. The signal was for Goodman to somehow fill in the time. Jane happened to be in the studio that evening and Goodman called her over. The pair then ab libbed humorously on a bridge game they had played the previous night and about a recent local murder.

This accidental program drew a large listener response and the couple found themselves with a regular twice-weekly program, *Easy Aces,* for which they were paid $30 a week. Ace reportedly gave Jane $10 a week. After several months Ace went after a raise of $20 a week. The sponsor refused and he promptly quit. This announcement led to another large listener response and a different sponsor quickly stepped forward the very next day to continue the show.

A Chicago advertising agency man happened to hear the show and offered the couple a thirteen-week spot on the full CBS network at a salary of $500 per week. Out of this salary, "Jane took what she needed." The show debuted in October 1931 from Chicago and after eleven weeks it wasn't clear whether the option would be picked up or not. The network suggested that the Aces test listener interest by appealing to their audience to write in and save the show. This the Aces did, generating quite a bit of fan support, variously reported as 20,000 or 100,000 letters.

After two seasons the program couldn't find a sponsor and moved to New York where a new one was found. The show was then heard four times a week during the day for two seasons. In the fall of 1935 the program switched to NBC, sponsored by Anacin, who would stay with them till the end. It was heard three times a week for fifteen minutes each evening. In November 1943 it moved to CBS and ran one-half hour per week, finally going off the air in January of 1945, after a run of over 14 years and more than 2,400 broadcasts.

From the beginning Goodman Ace wrote, produced, and directed every program alone, as well as playing the male lead. During the first nine years of their three-times-a-week format they broadcast a full 52 weeks a year with no vacation. After that Ace wrote himself and his wife out of the script for four weeks every winter. By 1942 their salary was said to be $3,500 a week. Ace could write a script in as little as an hour and a half, and rehearsals were generally informal, just once over quickly.

During the show itself the performers sat around a table and talked into a concealed mike. It was concealed in order to prevent any "microphone fright." Most radio shows began with no audience, but almost all quickly changed to doing their shows before a live audience, since the big-name entertainers switching from vaudeville to radio wanted and needed some sort of live audience feedback. *Easy Aces* was never performed before an audience, had no laugh track, and only sparse sound effects.

For a short while the show centered around the game of bridge, about which the Aces were fiends in real life. On the way home one night Ace chastised Jane for her play. It seems that the Aces had lost something like $8.40 that night. He continued to upbraid Jane the next morning at which point she got mad and informed her husband she wouldn't appear on the show anymore. Goodman pleaded with her and she finally relented just before air time that night. She did give up playing bridge, though. In any event, the show quickly moved into the broader sphere of the standard domestic comedy series. Despite its long run it never placed all that high in the ratings. One reason was that for most of its run it was pitted against *Amos 'n' Andy,* which was near the top of the ratings. Still there were enough loyal fans to keep the series on the air.

On the show itself the plot always seemed to play second fiddle to the lines themselves. The characters portrayed by the Aces were certainly better off financially than most of their listeners. The Aces played a well-to-do couple who lived in a prosperous Manhattan neighborhood. Ace was a successful advertising executive in the city, and Jane played a housewife with worries about such things as how to find her friend a husband, how to trick her husband into buying her a mink coat, how to keep her maid happy, or how to get her friends into the country club. No social issues, serious or otherwise, were ever raised on this program. The series aimed not for belly laughs or broad humor, but character foibles and verbal wit.

The comedy radiated from the amiable Jane, a hopeless dimwit. The structure of each episode was basically the same, with Jane getting herself involved foolishly in some kind of problem and somehow managing to get out by the program's conclusion. Against the nonsense of Jane stood Goodman, often dragged into the problem himself. He was a voice of logic and sanity, driven to exasperation by Jane. When confronted by some of Jane's foolishness, he would often moan, in despair, "Isn't that awful." This rigidly stereotypical view of females was of course very demeaning to women, but this scatterbrained caricature has been all too common in show business and was never really called into question, at least until the 1960's.

On one of the episodes the maid refused to work because Jane's mother was coming to visit and the maid didn't want to clean up after an extra person. The whole situation was resolved after a series of manipulations in which Goodman ended up sleeping on the couch. Another typical show featured Jane on jury duty. She managed to arrive late, disappear during the trial, get a substitute for herself without permission, and generally cause so much disruption that the judge had to declare a mistrial, stating she should never do jury duty again. A third show had Jane spending the entire program trying to get her husband to buy her a mink coat.

Jane was also pictured as very dense. Someone would say to her, "Hello Jane, I haven't seen you for weeks. Where have you been?" To which her reply would be, "Just fine," in a dreamy fashion. Her character's overall intelligence can be gauged from the following radio dialogue about mirrors: "They don't make mirrors like they used to. I can remember when I used to look in a mirror and I looked almost like a schoolgirl. Those were the days when they knew how to make mirrors."

But what she was most famous for and most remembered for where here endless string of malapropisms. "He's a ragged individualist. . . . Time wounds all heels. . . . We're insufferable friends. . . . Familiarity breeds attempt. . . . Words of one cylinder. . . . Congress is still in season. . . . Fly in the oatmeal. . . . I've been working my head to the bone. . . . We're all cremated equal. . . . Thumbnose description" and others "too humorous to mention." All of these were delivered by Jane in a dry nasal Midwestern twang.

The show did have supporting players, with the two best known being a Mrs. Benton and Jane's best friend, Madge, who was single and had an asinine giggle. Jane was much distressed at her friend's lack of a husband and naturally many misadventures revolved around Jane's attempts to end Madge's spinsterhood.

In spite of the content of the show, the program was largely hailed by the critics, and fans, not just as a humorous program, but praised as an "urbane comedy," as "literate" and as having attained a "high standard of quality." One critic for *The New York Times* said "there is no other program . . . even remotely like it." A *Newsweek* reviewer said, "It was adult comedy that was funny." These words of praise may have had more to do with how bad the other programs were instead of how good *Easy Aces* was.

The program ended and went off the air, not in the usual fashion, but on a rather bizarre note. Ace didn't believe in having any kind of personal relationship with his sponsor, feeling that it would destroy the working relationship. As a result Goodman had not bothered his sponsor at all over the years, nor had the sponsor ever interfered with Ace, at least until the end of 1944. At that time Anacin, sponsor since 1935, sent a note to Ace complaining about a new musical interlude he was using on the show. Goodman became furious and sent a note to Anacin complaining that he didn't like the way Anacin was packaged either. He upbraided the company for packing its products in cardboard boxes instead of tin and said that the public was being gypped. This being wartime, no tin was available for such uses and Anacin became even more furious and cancelled the show as of January 1945. This time no groundswell of fan support materialized to resurrect the program.

Goodman went on to other writing work and Jane went into retirement. One day while cleaning house she came across a pile of old *Easy Aces* scripts, which the pair edited and, through an agent, sold to over a hundred local radio stations, earning about $75,000 a year for a couple of years. They also earned the distinction of being heard over more stations that way than when they were broadcasting live.

In February 1948 they debuted over CBS in a new weekly half-hour series called *mr. ace & Jane*. Goodman played an advertising executive who lived next door to a radio announcer. Generally, though, the format was the same. His wife continued to constantly get into trouble. Jane remained Jane. Critics again praised the show as "one of radio's sharpest and wittiest excursions into satire." CBS insisted the show be done with an orchestra and an audience and, grudgingly, Ace agreed. He did refuse, though, to ham it up in a raucous style and the program never really adapted itself to the audience format. This time around the show was unsuccessful and it went off the air in 1949. In 1950 *Easy Aces* was resurrected as a TV series on the now long defunct DuMont network. The show aired for fifteen minutes each week and was a video version of the radio show. It lasted for only six weeks.

Throughout her radio career Jane found herself "forced to live in public almost the same sort of life" as she played on the radio. With close friends she could be herself but with others she found that "when I met people they were disappointed when I wasn't as dumb as Goodie made me appear in the script." People weren't particularly anxious to meet her at all when they were told she was a normal, intelligent woman. Jane decided that "If they will like me better if I'm dumb, I'll be dumb." Jane claimed that by adopting this pose in real life, the Aces were invited out more and "Jane was the life of the party."

Interviewers felt compelled to raise the question of whether or not Jane was as dumb off the air as on. One reporter concluded that she wasn't really as addlepated as she acted, and a second interviewer decided that "Basically Jane's brain is O.K. No Einstein, she, but she knows plenty." A third writer, in an attempt to say something about her, could only manage to come up with the lame description that "she likes to shop for clothes, prefers only a minimum of jewelry." For his part Goodman Ace kept up the fiction of his wife's low intelligence, in a tongue in cheek fashion. When asked about Jane he was likely to reply, "Oh, she's all right if you like Jane," or "Well . . . she's kind of stupid."

Jane Ace kept very much in the background, but it was in keeping with her own philosophy about a woman's place. "I always do whatever Goodie thinks is best. . . . I've figured this out about marriage: Whether husband and wife have careers or are just average couples, the man wants to feel superior, and the marriage will break up if the wife tries to take charge. The more important the husband is in the family life, the more successful the marriage will be. If the wife isn't the mental inferior, she should act that way."

Some of the malapropisms from *Easy Aces* remain witty even today, but the program itself was a long way from being sophisticated or urbane. It was just one of many programs that portrayed women in a demeaning manner and relied on getting laughs from the stereotyped presentation of the dumb woman.

When their show left the air in 1950, Goodman Ace went on to become one of television's best known and most sought-after comedy writers. Jane Ace retired from show business and died in November of 1974.

GERTRUDE BERG

Many comics have a supply of "Jewish Mother" jokes. One comedienne took the "Yiddishe Mamma" gag to its extreme and embodied the archetype. Gertrude Berg, a short plump woman better known as her radio and TV character, Molly Goldberg, created a Jewish mother that audiences not only laughed at but admired. Her character, based on her own mother and grandmother, became such an entrenched part of the U.S. entertainment world that the Girls Club of America honored her as the Radio and TV Mother of the Year in 1950.

Berg was born in New York City in 1899. Her father, Jacob Edelstein, ran a resort in the Catskill Mountains, and Gertrude wrote and performed skits and monologues for the guests. In 1918 Gertrude wed Lewis Berg, a mechanical engineer. The union would last a lifetime. Their two children, a son, Cherney, and a daughter, Harriet, were born in 1922 and 1926.

Gertrude enrolled in writing courses at Columbia University. The Jewish Art Theater was the only outlet for her work initially. She had a difficult time getting pieces accepted by magazines and most of her writing was rejected.

In 1929 her husband's career was faltering. A friend suggested that Gertrude bring in some extra money by trying to sell some of her skits to radio. She had written a dialogue between two sales-girls that her friend thought was "a riot." Berg offered the script, called "Effie and Laura," to CBS, and a manager there liked it enough to offer her four half-hour episodes. Berg played one of the characters.

The show flopped after one broadcast. Gertrude recalled, "I was in 77th heaven until after that first broadcast. I thought everything went off beautifully, but apparently nobody else did."

After hearing one of Milt Gross's dialect stories on the radio, Berg tried again. She wrote a script called "The Rise of the Gold-bergs" and sold it to NBC. She purposely wrote the script in an illegible handwriting so that at the audition she could read it her-self with the proper Yiddish accent. The director was so impressed with her acting that he hired her for the part. The program was first broadcast in 1929. Gertrude playing Molly Goldberg always opened the show by called up an air shaft to her neighbor, "Yoo hoo, Mrs. Bloom." The Goldbergs were an immigrant Jewish family in the Bronx. Molly's husband, Jake, was played by James R. Waters. Roslyn Siber played the daughter, Rosalie, and their son Sammy was played by Alfred Ryder and then Everett Sloane.

Like all Jewish families, this one consisted of plenty of relatives, friends and neighbors. Some of the regular characters were Uncle David, Seymour Fingerhood, Mr. Fowler, the handyman, and Uncle Carlo. The fifteen-minute radio show outlined the financial and cultural rise of the Goldbergs from immigrants to well-established New Yorkers.

Berg received $75 for the weekly series, but part of this money went for the payroll of the cast. By 1931 the program had caught on and was increased to six times per week with Pepsodent as sponsor. That year Berg wrote a book about the show. Gertrude also continued to write the scripts and act the role of Molly. Her salary eventually rose to about $7500 per week.

Berg was outearning her husband by a long shot. In order to enhance his authority in front of their children, Gertrude would ask him if it was all right for her to buy a new coat, knowing full well it was her own money that would pay for it.

The radio program attracted millions of listeners and was second in popularity only to *Amos 'n' Andy*. Each episode ended so that listeners would want to tune in the next day to find out what happened. As such, *The Goldbergs* was a forerunner of the family situation comedy TV serials.

The Rise of the Goldbergs ran until 1934, when Pepsodent withdrew due to financial problems. Gertrude then took the cast

on a vaudeville tour. She also came up with a new serial called
The House of Glass, based on her childhood at the Catskill
Mountains resort. It was broadcast for a short time in 1935, but
never achieved the success of *The Goldbergs.* During the 1936-37
period, Berg also wrote several screenplays for Hollywood. In
addition, she wrote a radio serial about a visiting nurse titled
Kate Hopkins.

CBS radio picked up *The Goldbergs* again in 1936, and in 1938
NBC also broadcast the program. The show was heard on both
stations until 1945. Gertrude also acted in the 1937 movie *Make a
Wish.* In 1948 she wrote and performed in a play at the Belasco
Theater in New York. Titled *Me and Molly* the play was based on
The Goldbergs radio serial.

Some critics called it "warm and touching," but *Time* found
her play "commonplace and dull." The reviewer complained that:
"It stands where dialect humor and realistic observation meet—
or, more frequently collide; where characters are little more than
exploited but a great deal less than explained."

Brooks Atkinson of *The New York Times* was more positive:
"Mrs. Berg is a real human being who believes in the people she
writes about and is not ashamed of their simplicity. . . . The
result is a leisurely, intimate, cheerful portrait of interesting people and the humor is kind-hearted. It is something for a playwright to preserve that much integrity amid the gag traps of
Broadway."

The Goldbergs returned to radio for the 1949-50 season. Berg
continued to write all the scripts, star as Molly, and produce the
show. She thus had almost total control.

Over the years the program altered with the times. Dialogue in
early scripts was written with a thick Yiddish accent. Here's a
sample of some of the dialogue from those first scripts: "Molly:
Vat's de matter so late, Sammy? Let me look on your hends.
Playing marbles, ha? For vat is your fadder slaving for vat I'm
esking you? A marble shooter you'll gonna be? A beautiful business for a Jewish boy!"

As the children grew up and the Goldbergs became more established in America, the language altered. Rather than deriving
humor from a comical-sounding Jewish accent, Gertrude shifted
her dialogue to malapropisms (known as Mollypropisms), and
general misuse of English. For example, Molly was heard to say:
"Enter whoever. If it's nobody, I'll call back"; or "It's late Jake,
and time to expire"; and "So who's to know?"

The Goldberg's financial position also improved with time.

Jake, a tailor, started to make big money in his business. Gertrude had him lose a fortune in the Depression, however, so that the mass audience would identify with the family.

What remained constant in the program was the realism of the characters. The Goldbergs and their neighbors were like any other people. There were no plot extremes like murders or love affairs. The episodes revolved around typical family problems or experiences, like Jake's blood pressure, Molly's weight, or Sammy and Rosalie's dates. There were few gags in the dialogue. The humor came from the language and the foibles of the characters.

Molly doled out plenty of homespun philosophy like "Better a crust of bread and enjoy it than a cake that gives you indigestion." Many of her lines were ad libbed.

Gertrude created over 200 characters for the program during the time it was broadcast. Although the show focused on a Jewish family, Berg made certain that people of other nationalities were represented. For example, the janitor of the Goldberg's apartment building was Irish. Nor were all the actors Jewish. Sammy and Rosalie were just two of the roles played by non-Jewish performers. Some of the actors who appeared on the program included Joseph Cotten, Van Heflin, Marjorie Main, John Garfield, Anne Bancroft, and Jan Peerce.

The program was very popular with both non-Jews and Jews. Berg recalled that once a Mother Superior of a Philadelphia convent wrote and asked her for a synopsis of six weeks of programs. It seemed that the nuns were regular Goldberg fans but had given up the program for Lent, and wanted to find out what happened.

Jews enjoyed the program because they were proud to identify with the culture and rituals presented on the show. Non-Jews related to the family interactions, their struggle for financial stability, and the ideal of motherhood. The show was considered an important vehicle for interracial understanding, and was thought to be free of excessive stereotyping. In fact, it won several humanitarian awards. Controversial issues like politics, unionism, and Zionism were avoided.

Time magazine described the Goldberg scripts in 1949 as having an "apple-dumpling flavor—sugary smooth as butter, pastry-thin plot and heavily spiced with Bronxisms. What keeps this confection from cloying is author Berg's tart recognition of human frailties and her blunt but understanding sense of humor."

In 1949 *The Goldbergs* was also seen on television on the CBS network. An estimated thirteen million viewers tuned in to the weekly show. In 1950 Gertrude won an Emmy for her role as

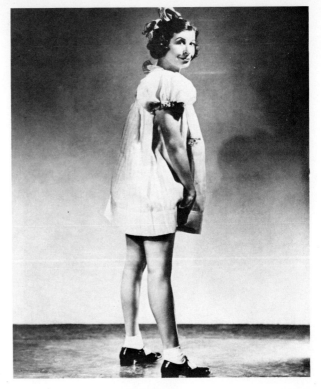

CHARLOTTE GREENWOOD

ZASU PITTS

BEATRICE LILLIE

GRACIE ALLEN

SOPHIE TUCKER

MAE WEST

GERTRUDE BERG

JOAN DAVIS

KAYE BALLARD

GRACIE FIELDS

CAROL CHANNING

IMOGENE COCA

MARIE WILSON

JUDY HOLLIDAY

Molly. The show was to have a short life on CBS, however. In 1951 Philip Loeb, who played Jake Goldberg, was blacklisted during the McCarthy era for left-wing sympathies. Loeb refused to leave the program, even though the sponsor, General Foods, offered to pay off the rest of his salary, a sum of $85,000. Gertrude had no intention of firing him. The sponsor then dropped the program, and it went off the air from the summer of 1951 to early 1952. Loeb was never proven to be a communist but the publicity tarnished his career and morale. In 1955 he committed suicide.

The Goldbergs survived, however, and ran on NBC for part of 1952 and 1953. In 1954 it moved to the now defunct DuMont network. Gertrude had the family living in the suburbs to provide fresh material, but the ratings were slipping.

A reviewer for *Commentary* felt that the scripts for the television show had become dated: "Mrs. Berg's language, cute as it always is, and right as it sometimes is, is contrived to meet outmoded expectations. For one thing, television audiences today do not find the portrait of a domineering, sheltering matriarch exactly comfortable. . . . Mrs. Berg's uncompromising use of Molly's garrulousness, prying, and need for keeping things astir made one often feel involved in an uncomfortable session of gossip."

It was not surprising that in the patriarchal 1950's of *Father Knows Best* there was no longer room for Molly. And would a critic have applied the terms "cute" or "gossip" to a male performer? It would take the Women's Liberation Movement to make a big-hearted, domineering, mother acceptable again on television as *Maude* was in the 1970's.

Gertrude Berg got a lot of mileage out of the Molly Goldberg character, however. In 1951 she co-wrote *Molly* with N. Richard Nash, the Paramount movie version of *The Rise of the Goldbergs*. Gertrude played the title role.

Berg remained involved in acting for the rest of her life. In 1953 she appeared as a Jewish landlady in the MGM film *Main Street to Broadway*. She acted in summer stock comedies in 1956 and 1957. Her 1959 performance in the Broadway play *A Majority of One* earned her a Tony award. Berg played the role of a Jewish widow who on a trip to the Orient became romantically involved with a Japanese widower.

In 1961 she began a new CBS-TV series called *Mrs. G Goes to College*. The program only lasted until April 1962, and had a new title that year, *The Gertrude Berg Show*. Berg played a character named Sarah Green who decided to return to college and complete her education even though middle-aged. Gertrude wryly noted of Sarah Green: "It's the same Molly, just older."

Berg starred in the Broadway musical *Dear Me, the Sky Is Falling* in 1963 and was working on a new production when she died in 1966.

MINERVA PIOUS

Minerva Pious won fame as a dialect comic on radio, most notably on Fred Allen's program, where for close to twenty years she was perhaps the best known and most popular of the various regulars.

Fans remember her more for her character, that of the Jewish housewife from the Bronx, Mrs. Pansy Nussbaum, than for her real name. Due to the wide range of characters she could play, she was once called the "Ruth Draper of Radio."

Pious was born in Odessa, Russia, in 1909, the daughter of a wholesale candy merchant. The family emigrated to the United States when she was two or three years old. She grew up in Bridgeport, Connecticut, where she was involved in high school dramatics, but other than that she had no theatrical training, although she was an accomplished piano player.

She was in New York City in 1933 working as a promotional writer when a friend of hers, Harry Tugend, got an audition with Fred Allen. Tugend was a singer and asked Pious to go along with him as his accompanist. At that audition Tugend happened to tell Allen that Minerva did dialect characterizations and Allen asked for a demonstration. He liked what he heard and signed Minerva up for his radio program *Town Hall Tonight*, which was later called *Allen's Alley*. At the time she was hired Pious referred to herself as "a complete amateur." Nevertheless she remained a regular on the show until she left in 1949.

She did all the female voices on the program and one of her other popular characters was a woman named Blossom Rappaport. It was Mrs. Nussbaum, though, that brought her fame. She played that character for some time before Fred Allen came up with the name Pansy Nussbaum.

Mrs. Nussbaum was an exaggerated caricature of a Jewish immigrant who spoke with an equally exaggerated Bronx and

Yiddish accent. Each week she happily mangled the English language with an onslaught of malapropisms and a variety of other strange and funny speech patterns. She regaled the audience with ridiculous stories about the troubles she had with her radio husband, Pierre, who never appeared on the show, and she also engaged in banter with Allen.

On the show Allen would knock on her door and greet her by saying, "Ah, Mrs. Nussbaum," to which she would reply, "You are expecting maybe Ingrown Bergman?" or "You are expecting the Fink Spots?" She pronounced Mississippi as "Matzos-Zippi" and Massachusetts as "Matzos-chusetts." Her favorite foods were items such as "herring du jour, chopped liver cacciatore (and) pot roast à la king." Allen would ask her a question to solicit her views on some topic or other, to which Nussbaum would reply, "Again I am to be prodded by your poll?" Her lengthy comments were delivered in a loud monotone and always in the present tense.

The stereotypical Jewish character didn't elicit any complaints from listeners and the appearance of Pansy Nussbaum on the show each week invariably brought the largest applause. The similarities between Pious's character and that of Gertrude Berg's Molly Goldberg were obvious. Berg's creation had more charm while Nussbaum had more of the acid wit for which Fred Allen was noted.

Pious was able to do a wide variety of dialects with ease, be they English, French, Scottish, Italian, German, or other. She was equally adept as a Park Avenue matron, a schoolgirl from the Midwest, or a cockney fishwife. Her natural voice was so clear that she once got an award for having diction totally free of affectations or regional influences.

During the time she was a regular with Allen she appeared all over the dial on a host of other radio programs, both day and evening—everything from soaps to drama to comedy variety. She was a frequent guest on *Easy Aces*. On the Sammy Kaye show she was once heard as Gypsy Rose Rabinowitz. She worked with all the big names such as Bob Hope, Bing Crosby, and W.C. Fields. Most of her fans weren't aware of all her radio work, since the performers weren't seen, of course, and billing was often limited to top stars. Appearing under the guise of different voices made it difficult for Pious to establish any kind of fan following from her work on these other programs.

She had no training in dialect and attributed her abilities to powers of observation and to her habit of being an "inveterate eavesdropper in crowded places." Another time she called herself a "parlor comic with an ear." She was once getting ready to play an Irish character and a few seconds before air time the director suddenly announced that her character, for political reasons, would have to be a Scottish woman. Minerva had never done Scottish dialect before but was able, on the spur of the moment, to recall the speech of a Scottish family she had known in the past, and carry off the program successfully.

With the demise of radio came the demise of Pious's career. She had parts in a couple of films in the 1950's, parts in a couple of Broadway productions in the 1960's, the odd TV guest shot and some commercials on both radio and television. She continued with this irregular and infrequent work into the 1970's, and died in March, 1979.

JUDY CANOVA

Judy Canova had hopes of becoming a classical singer but abandoned this aspiration early on when she wasn't able to make any headway. She turned instead to comedy singing of the country and western variety, and cultivated the image of a man-chasing hillbilly. It was a successful endeavor and Canova became popular in vaudeville, movies, and finally in radio, where she achieved her greatest fame. Despite attempts later to change her image, she always remained the "Queen of the Hillbillies."

Born Juliette Canova on November 20, 1916, in the small town of Starke, near Jacksonville, Florida, she was the last of eight children. Her father had once been a cotton broker and later went into the construction business. Before marriage Judy's mother had been a concert singer. The four children who survived infancy all had musical talent and all of them studied piano, singing, and various other instruments. Judy was a natural ham and was singing at various family get togethers and other affairs by the time she was three.

At about the age of twelve she teamed up with a school friend and the pair entered as many amateur night contests as they could, winning many. When the friend dropped out Judy's mother substituted sister Anne and brother Zeke in the act. This young troupe got some air time on a Jacksonville radio station where they sang and did comedy routines. They were billed as the

"Canova Cracker Trio." The family had spent some summers vacationing in the hills of North Carolina and the Canovas had picked up several mountain songs. They did these numbers for their own amusement at that time, and did not use them in their professional appearances.

In high school Judy was an extrovert and constantly entertained and amused her friends. As with so many other women, it was her way of coping with what she considered to be her plain physical appearance. "I got smart and not only accepted my lack of glamor, but made the most of it."

She had been to New York City briefly with her mother, where she studied tap dancing, but returned to Florida when no jobs opened up. At that time Judy wanted to be a concert singer, preferably opera, but her plans for further musical education evaporated when her mother died in 1930. The three Canova siblings journeyed to New York City in 1932, and this time they were determined to carve out show business careers for themselves. It was reported that Judy had to argue with Anne and Zeke to include her in the act because they believed she wasn't "high-tone enough for them."

They made the rounds trying to get bookings for their brand of pop and semi-classical singing but found no takers. In desperation they hauled out their North Carolina hill numbers and began to practice them. Their landlady wouldn't let them practice these numbers in their room, so the Canovas were forced to use Central Park. "Our yodels, grunts, and hog-calls opened windows to see what jungle animals were now invading Broadway." This country singing and hillbilly humor were different enough to land them some paying jobs, one of which was at a Greenwich Village club called the Village Barn, where they did their rustic act for almost two years. Zeke played the guitar and sang while the sisters, billed as the Happiness Girls, played piano and sang.

By this time Judy had adopted her hillbilly costume, which came to be standard over the years. She wore overly big ankle boots, bobby sox, a plain short skirt, and a colored, checked blouse. She had her hair in braids, sported a straw hat on her head, and carried a beat-up old suitcase around.

The group were next signed to a regular spot on Rudy Vallee's radio program and stayed a year. Judy was now the chief attraction of the act. "It was she who performed most of the solo song numbers, with her nasal-twanged singing, yodeling, shouting, and cawing." The act was as successful as it was because it was a new and different experience for an urban audience. (This was in the days before the Grand Ole Opry became a household word.) At the same time they continued to appear on the vaudeville circuit.

The Canovas, joined by brother Pete, made their Broadway debut in 1934 in a musical revue titled *Calling All Stars.* Judy's big number was a tune called "Last of the Hill Billies," done in her usual exaggerated country style. Warner Brothers had financed the revue and subsequently signed the Canovas to a film contract.

In one of their movies, *In Caliente* (1935), Judy had a scene which gave her career a big boost. The movie had a lavish production number of Spanish singing and dancing. At one point the camera swung away from the lead singer to Canova, who had popped out from behind a pillar dressed as a Mexican hillbilly, and she promptly parodied the song being sung. That scene convulsed audiences then, and still does when the movie is shown at revival houses.

From there Judy was signed as a single for Broadway and the *Ziegfeld Follies of 1936.* "Judy Canova endangers the stability of the Winter Garden with her parodies. In one sketch . . . her imitation of a hill billy singer is one of the comedy treats of the evening." After three pictures for Warner Brothers, the Canovas (Pete was no longer performing) were signed by Paramount and did two films. The Canovas did specialty numbers in both films, with Judy doing solo work as well.

During that time, when studios had a lot of stars under contract, the musical or revue film was a common format and was a way for the studio to insert as many of its contract players as it could to sing, dance, etc. Studios felt obliged to do this, since these people were drawing weekly salaries whether they worked or not.

In one of the Paramount movies, *Artists and Models,* which featured Martha Raye as a specialty performer, Judy got to do some straight acting and adopted a style which became her standard "straight" method over the years. She became the sympathetic, empathetic listener with an earnest manner, wide open eyes, clenched chin, and shuffling feet. The Canovas had earned $6,000 a week from Paramount. However, the studio didn't renew its option, which was all right with Judy. "I would have done better getting eighteen bucks a week and a good part." The Canovas left the film world for a while and turned to vaudeville, a booking in London England, and Broadway, where they were more appreciated.

Judy, working mostly solo, was a big hit in the 1939 Broadway musical *Yokel Boy*. "Judy pranced through her parade of performing tricks: yodeling, mugging, shouting, and singing with a voice which 'constantly gets away from her and goes shooting madly off by itself'. . . . A rowdy mixture of Beatrice Lillie and other comediennes along parallel lines in the general direction of Fanny Brice." She was in demand again by film studios and, after weighing offers, she accepted one from Republic Pictures, as a solo. She preferred to be the star of low-budget movies rather than continue to be just a specialty act in more lavish productions.

Starting with *Scatterbrain* in 1940, she starred in a series of "programmers" for Republic. These were movies destined to be the "B" part of double features. *Scatterbrain* marked her first film as the top-billed star and, in addition to appearing in pigtails, calico and doing her stock hillbilly singing, she also lived up to the film's title by appearing somewhat addled. One of the film's high points had her washing a kitchen floor by skating across it with brushes attached to her roller skates. The film did very well at the box office and Republic quickly signed Canova for five years. She was then the studio's fourth hottest property, behind Gene Autry, Roy Rogers, and John Wayne.

In a 1941 release, *Puddin' Head,* she was again the dizzy country rube who, this time, mowed the kitchen floor, because the grass was growing between the cracks. A continuing bit in this film had glass breaking everytime she sang. One reviewer remarked, "Miss Canova, like Martha Raye, doesn't take to the glamourizing process. . . . Corn is okay and so is glamour, but the two just don't mix."

In *Sleepytime Gal* (1942), besides singing, Judy was well into slapstick. She was used as a rug, locked in a fridge, knocked over by a group of waiters, ate several soap-filled creampuffs, and took a dozen pratfalls doing a comic dance. In another release that year, *True to the Army,* Canova, disguised as a man, got to mug her way through standard army humor, with a rifle range and mess hall as backdrops.

Under a loan-out arrangement she made three films for Columbia from 1944 to 1946. Judy had hoped that more money would be spent on those features, but the reality was three shoddy vehicles which didn't endear her to her fans. After those pictures, she stayed away from films for five years. Fortunately, by then her radio show was well established and very popular.

Republic lured Judy back into its fold in 1951 at a time they were in need of a star, Autry and Rogers both having left. The films produced by Republic, cheaply and quickly, were shot in three or four weeks' time. She starred in six films for this studio from 1951 to 1955. None of these films were memorable and Judy mostly played her stock character, the backwoods gal who sang.

She played characters who lived in towns with names like Roaring Gulch and Cactus Junction. Republic stopped producing theatrical films at that time and Canova would only appear in one more film. In 1960 she had a small role in *The Adventures of Huckleberry Finn,* her twenty-third motion picture appearance.

After their stint on the radio with Rudy Vallee, the Canovas appeared as regulars in 1936-37 on a variety program called the *Woodbury Rippling Rhythm Revue,* drawing a $1,700 weekly salary. They were regulars on the Edgar Bergen show for thirteen weeks in 1938, earning $4,300 a week. Having guest starred on most of the major radio shows, Judy finally got her own program *The Judy Canova Show,* without family, in 1943. It began in July of that year on CBS and went off the air the following June due to low ratings.

NBC stepped in and took over the half-hour program, keeping the same name, and debuted it on their network in January 1945. It was the start of a long and successful run. In the CBS format Judy portrayed a country girl who had come to the city for adventure. In the NBC version she hailed from Unadella, Georgia, visited an uncle in Cactus Junction, and her aunt in the big city. The program was a situation comedy format, with Judy usually singing two songs per show. She sang serious songs once in a while, but most were her patented hillbilly variety. She also dressed, for the studio audience's benefit, in her stock bucolic outfit.

There were lots of jokes on the show and they were pure corn, but the audience didn't mind. One running theme on her program was the stock portrayal of a man-hungry, love-starved woman. A second theme was Canova's attempts to crash into society. While she did use some self-deprecating humor, it wasn't very prominent. Playing an essentially dumb character, self-debasing humor wasn't necessary because the female was no real threat to men in any intellectual manner. A woman playing an intelligent character was more likely to be required to use this type of humor, to show her supplication to the male.

The following are samples of some of Canova's radio jokes:

Judy: My Aunt Aggie says nice girls don't kiss.

Suitor: Do you really believe that nice girls shrink from kissing?

Judy: Shucks, no. If that was true, I'd be nothing but skin and bones.

Judy: I'm only human.

Stranger: You're exaggerating?

Aunt Aggie: Being denied the companionship of men is sometimes a healthy thing.

Judy: Take a look at the healthiest girl in California.

Stranger: You will ride in a carriage with four horses.

Judy: With four horses? Won't that be a little crowded?

One of her jokes placed in a May 1946 poll of the most popular comedy lines:

Stranger: One of my ancestors was a Knight of the Royal Order of the Bath—or don't you know the Order of the Bath. Judy: Why, shore—on Saturday night it was Paw first and then all the kids in the order of their ages." Corny or not, audiences ate it up.

In the late 1940's NBC carried the show on 128 stations; it reached an estimated audience of 18 million at its peak, made the top ten in the ratings, and paid Judy Canova a salary of $8,500 per week. In 1946 she received 250,000 fan letters. She also won a magazine contest to name "the corniest actress in the movies." Judy's only comment was that she was flattered to be termed an "actress."

One reviewer of her show wrote that "Miss Canova represents an almost vanishing type of American humor once immortalized by Mack Sennett. She is the girl who is always chasing and never quite catching a man . . . raucous, twangy, and incurably hayseed." The program went off the air in 1953 when Canova left to have a baby. The show had lasted an inordinately long time considering the relentless onslaught of a new medium, television. Even with her movie and radio work she found time to tour cities with her act, to play state fairs, to appear in Las Vegas, and even to do a nightclub tour of Latin American in 1947, for which she was paid $10,000 a week.

Judy's experiences with television were not as fruitful as those with radio. The Canova family did have one distinction, though.

They appeared on May 3, 1939, on NBC television, then in an experimental stage, and became the first hillbilly act to ever appear on commercial TV.

Judy next appeared on television as a guest on *The Colgate Comedy Hour* in 1952. She was part of one lengthy skit in which she and Zsa Zsa Gabor were on a train fighting over a sleeping compartment. Gabor wore a sexy nightgown and reeked of a perfume called "Spring Night in Venice." Canova wore a flannel nightgown and said her perfume was called "Hot Night on a Chicken Farm." From the remarks of one reviewer it was obvious Canova's character hadn't changed. "Miss Canova's talents are specialized. She can yodel; she can grimace; she can twist her mouth into astonishing shapes. She can scream, and she can roughhouse. . . . There are the long pigtails, the straw hat, the checkered jacket and the battered suitcase."

Plans for a televised *Judy Canova Show* were begun in late 1953 but the series never materialized. She continued to make guest appearances on other shows, and talk of a series for her was begun again in 1960, a series which would supposedly have played down the rustic comedy. This, too, failed to materialize. After her 1960 film appearance she received no more "suitable" offers for movies and her TV appearances were mostly confined to game shows. In 1970 plans for a third series were announced and a pilot was actually filmed. However, the abysmal idea, an Ozark version of Romeo and Juliet, didn't sell. After that experience Judy went into semi-retirement. She did the odd television commercial and appeared in a revival of the musical *No, No, Nanette.* Judy Canova died in August of 1983.

By the mid-1960's she had been married and divorced four times, and was one of many women who felt her marriage problems stemmed at least partly from her work. "It is almost impossible to maintain a marriage when you are in the limelight and separated from your husband because of a career." Judy Canova was successful once she adopted the guise of the slightly dizzy hillbilly, anxious to be liked and helpful, and hoping to land a man. Her cornball humor and style allowed listeners to feel, consciously or otherwise, superior to her, which undoubtedly contributed to her success. Her hillbilly style was the model for the enormously popular television series *Beverly Hillbillies,* and its offshoots, which hit the tube in the early 1960's.

When she first adopted the hillbilly style, the rumor had spread that Canova was just playing herself. Judy good humoredly went along with that and said, "We walked up here from Florida in our bare feet, subsisting on betel nuts and the bark of trees along the way." Inside, though, she was hurt by being slighted as a likeable freak. Once her studio had her fill out a questionnaire, and in the space opposite "character" she wrote: "Moody and generally unhappy. I'm a comedienne."

Once Canova adopted this hillbilly character she found her public unwilling to let her modify it or cast it aside. Judy once remarked, "Some folks may have thought my stuff was corny in the beginning, but the public bought it. After I got started doing country stuff with my brother and sister, I couldn't get out of it. . . . A lot of my act was tongue-in-cheek. But I guess I did it so well, that people took me seriously."

MAE WEST

She was an American institution and sex goddess supreme. Mae West was an irreverent iconoclast and mistress of the double entendre. No one could infuse a seemingly innocuous sentence with as much meaning as she could. Most of the other female comedians in this book can be compared in some way with others who preceded them and/or those who followed. But not Mae West. There was nobody like her before her time and there hasn't been anybody since.

She presented women in a totally different light. With her characters women were always the winners. She took on and beat all male comers. She did it through a parody of the age-old femme fatale, a combination of humor and sex which hadn't been done before. At the same time she mocked the male. She was more insatiable than Casanova and more lecherous than the proverbial dirty old man. She ran afoul of the law and the censors a number of times, and even went to jail. But she always turned these seeming setbacks into major victories.

If the Mae West character won on stage or screen, then the real Mae West also triumphed in real life. She got around the vigorous film censorship of the day by writing lines that were innocent enough on the printed page but deadly when delivered in her inimitable style. Her comedy reached the point where Mae West satirized Mae West. She wrote all her own material and that's why she triumphed: she was in control. Her importance to the women's movement, to female comedy, and to the self-image of women can't be overestimated. She was self-assured, flamboyant, and aggressive, an image of women that could only be presented through the softening effect of exaggerated comedy and satire, but she made her point.

Mae West was born in Brooklyn, New York, in August, 1893, the daughter of John Patrick West, who ran a livery stable and was once a heavyweight boxer known as "Battling Jack West." After the automobile supplanted the horse, Mr. West became a private detective. Her mother Matilda (Delker-Doelger) had briefly, before marriage, been a fashion model of such things as corsets. Born Mary Jane, she soon changed her name to the more glamorous Mae, sometimes spelling it May as late as 1913. Mae's schooling was irregular and her formal education came to an end when she was just thirteen. Her mother enjoyed vaudeville and often took Mae to matinees. When she was five, she did, with her father's encouragement, imitations of people such as Eva Tanguay.

At seven she had some dancing lessons and entered an Elks Amateur Night contest at a Brooklyn theater where she appeared in a gaudy outfit of satin and spangles. Her song and dance routine was called "Movin' Day." Billed as "Baby Mae" she won the $10 first prize and went on to enter and win other amateur night contests with routines such as "The Grizzly Bear" and "My Mariooch-a Make-a da Hoochy-ma-cooch," a comic dialect number. At eight she joined a stock company based at Brooklyn's Gotham Theater, which was directed by Hal Clarendon. She stayed with that company for a few years and appeared in all the stock melodramas, such as *Little Nell and the Marchioness* and *Uncle Tom's Cabin,* and played all the famous child parts, such as Little Willie, Little Lord Fauntleroy, and Little Eva. She also sang ballads, did imitations of George M. Cohan and Eddie Foy, and was billed as the "Baby Vamp."

At about fourteen she entered vaudeville, where she had a song-and-dance act with a singer named Frank Wallace. They married when Mae was still a teenager, on the advice of a wiser vaudevillian who told her that marriage would make her more respectable, and presumably enhance her career. She and Frank separated personally and professionally within a few months, although she never bothered getting a divorce for over thirty years. She never married again. Even at that early age, men were always around her in droves, and she was already involved with multiple lovers, a practice she would apparently continue all her life. Two men had a fistfight over her when she was fifteen; it wouldn't be the last time. West once said, "I never set out to make men a career . . . It just happened that way."

In 1911 she appeared on Broadway for the first time, in a musical comedy revue called *A la Broadway*. The one spot she had in the show was to sing a song with two popular comics of the day, Cook and Lorenz. Though she was still a teenager, she was already finding methods to achieve her own ends. While the show was still in rehearsals, she wrote some extra lyrics for the song and then added some "new business" to embellish them. She then approached the comics and told them they had enough hard work to do in the show and that she would be willing to sing alone and let the comics take a well-deserved rest. After they agreed, Mae approached the show's director and explained that Cook and Lorenz didn't want to do the song, but that she could do it solo. He also agreed. The show's opening night proved a triumph for Mae, as she got several encores and the best critical notices of anybody in the cast. She appeared in a couple of other Broadway revues in which she sang ragtime and dialect songs and performed acrobatic dancing.

Around 1913 or 1914 she was back on the vaudeville circuit and toured around, now as a headliner. Her weekly salary went from $350 to $750. She was already accustomed to changing and embellishing material which someone else had written for her. By 1915 she wrote her first song. It was called "The Cave Girl" and she wore a leopard skin costume while she delivered the tune. Her typical stage costume in those days, however, was a forerunner of the style which was to come and which she would always use. She usually wore a long, tight fitting gown of black velvet or white, adorned with rhinestones and silver. It was on the vaudeville stage that she developed elements of her style which would soon become world famous.

A wriggling walk, holding her hand on her hip suggestively, and caressing her hair, were gestures that became Mae's trademarks. One of her first double entendre lines was delivered at the close of her act in vaudeville, "It isn't what you do, it's how you do it." She was heavily influenced in style by Eva Tanguay, the "I Don't Care Girl" with her uninhibited antics. She was billing herself as "The Original Brinkley Girl," a successor to the Gibson Girl.

In 1918 she was appearing in the musical *Sometime* and after a performance one night she went to a New York jazz club and saw black dancers doing a dance they called the "shimmy shawobble." The next night, when it came time for her encore, she introduced the "shimmy" to the white world. Many months later a woman named Gilda Gray would make the dance famous and get credit for introducing it, but it was really Mae.

She continued doing revues into the 1920's, and early in that decade she wrote her own nightclub act and took it on the road. She had discovered that material written for more conventional performers just didn't fit her style. In 1926 the Shuberts were looking for a play suitable for West's talents but not finding anything. Mae's mother urged her to write one herself. West had already written a lot of her own material but considered herself too lazy to sit down and write a full play. This time, though, she realized that the risk of doing an unsuitable vehicle was too great, so she wrote a play and sent it off to the Shuberts. She sent it in under the pen name of Jane Mast, because she felt it would be too egotistical to use her real name. In due course the play was returned, rejected, from the Shuberts. Later West found out the Shuberts hadn't even seen the manuscript and that an office clerk had returned it.

When the play came back Mae's mother suggested they produce the play themselves. So Mae, her mother, and a lawyer friend of the family did just that. During the play's rehearsals the director was enthusiastic about the play's subject and, according to West, "He kept saying the play reeked with sex, sex—he said it so often I began to like the sound of the word." West liked it so much that she changed the name of the play from *The Albatross* to *Sex*. It opened in April 1926 in Manhattan, with Mae playing a waterfront prostitute. The title itself was daring for the times. The word was only used to denote gender, as in the male sex, and New York newspapers refused to carry ads for it, or so Mae said. In truth *The New York Times* did carry ads for the play using the title. Mae was already working on establishing her legend.

The play created a storm of controversy from the beginning. Most nice people professed outrage. The British Embassy was perturbed enough to speak out and say it annoyed them. While half the people wanted her blood, the other half loved the play precisely because of its subject matter. Its open and light approach to the subject of sex was a novelty. Usually sex was taboo, or treated in a ponderous, serious, moralistic manner. Critics overwhelmingly disliked the play. One wrote that it was "A crude, inept play, cheaply produced and poorly acted." The *New Republic* found the play dull and West's performance "crude, ugly and idle," yet admitting she had a certain insolence and magnetism. A New York paper, the *Herald-Tribune,* featured the following headline, *"SEX WINS HIGH PRAISE FOR DEPRAVITY, DULLNESS."*

The production was raided and closed down, but not right away. The critics didn't like it but the public snapped up the tickets. About eighty percent of the audience was male and the play's success spawned a number of so-called "indecent" imitations. *Sex* ran for nearly a year. After 375 performances, which had been seen by a reported 700 policemen and seven assistant district attorneys, the police shut it down, along with a couple of the imitators, under pressure from the Society for the Suppression of Vice. Mae was found guilty of "corrupting the morals of youth," fined $500 and sentenced to ten days at the New York City prison. One of the main pieces of evidence that led to her conviction was the testimony of the arresting officer, who stated that she had "moved her navel up and down and from right to left" in a belly dance. She served eight days of her sentence, getting two off for good behavior.

Papers were full of stories about the hardships of her jail term. Her tender skin, being used to silk underwear, was being irritated by the jail's coarse cotton clothes. Mae West later claimed that she was allowed to wear her own underwear, was housed in an official's office, not a cell, and was taken for drives in the evening by the warden. She even found time to write a couple of articles for magazines, and had an enjoyable time all in all. At least that is how she reported it. While she wasn't likely to have been treated like an ordinary prisoner, West's version is probably something less than the truth. It was her style to convert everything to a victory, if only in her mind. Needless to say, the publicity value of all this was an enormous boost to her career. She may not have been an institution at that point, but she was well on her way.

That same year another of her plays opened. It was titled *The Drag* and was a study of homosexuality. West had always enjoyed high popularity with gay people, due, some think, to her flamboyance and the fact that she herself gave the appearance of a flashy drag queen. About this popularity Mae remarked, "They love to imitate the things I say and the way I act, and they like the way I move my body." *The Drag,* which West didn't appear in, opened for a few days in Bridgeport, Connecticut, and then for a couple weeks in Paterson, New Jersey, preparatory to moving to Broadway. Patrons paid a reported $20 to $50 a ticket to see her latest offering. A theater in Stamford, Connecticut, had been booked first, but the manager cancelled upon learning the nature of the project. Conferences with New York officials and the looming shadow of the Society for the Suppression of Vice convinced her not to take the production to New York after all.

Next was the *The Wicked Age,* which opened in New York in 1927. It was a comic sendup of phony beauty queen contests, and a box-office success. However, Mae closed it after a couple of weeks because she didn't get along with the leading man. In 1928 she wrote, and starred in, *Diamond Lil* on Broadway, her biggest success and perhaps best-known vehicle. It was a comic melodrama, set in New York's Bowery, about a kept dance-hall girl in the Gay Nineties. This play brought together in sharp focus West's recurrent twin themes of sex and shock, and created a character with whom she would always be identified. She portrayed a barroom singer to whom all men would come and pay court. Virtually all of her later roles would be variations of this theme. The play gave her a chance to indulge in all the Westian trademarks. She lounged in a golden bed reading the *Police Gazette,* and she descended a staircase like royalty. She would later rewrite the play and have it published as a novel, and also star in the film version, one of her biggest movie hits. Years later she remarked about herself and the character Diamond Lil, "I'm her and she's me and we're each other."

One of West's motivations for writing *Diamond Lil* was to bring more women into the theater. She wanted to break box-office records, and couldn't do it with her largely male fans. She determined that nobody had written a play about the Gay Nineties and saw a chance to "get three generations of men and women: the young crowd, the mothers and fathers and the grandparents. And the women would love the gorgeous period clothes and hats. That's when I wrote 'Diamond Lil.'" According to West's own observations it worked. "I'm the woman's ego, see. When women'd be leaving the theater at intermission, you'd see them sort of walking like the Mae West character, you know, giving an attitude—and the talk, too." This play was a critical as well as popular success and ran for over nine months on Broadway. Not every critic liked it. *The New Yorker* found it "rough, incoherent. . . . It isn't even dime-novel material." Readers were urged, nevertheless, not to miss it.

Also in 1928 another of her plays opened, *The Pleasure Man,* a vaudeville story that included some female impersonation. The police closed it after two days and West was back in court. In 1929 and 1930 she did national tours, first with *Diamond Lil* and then with a revival of *Sex.* That same year she had time to have a novel published, called *Babe Gordon,* about a woman of pleasure who works her way up from the dives of New York to the high society of that city and of Paris.

The first publishing house she contracted with insisted on certain deletions, to which West agreed. Despite these cuts that house's board quickly refused to publish the work at all. West finally found a more receptive publisher. After the first edition the title was changed to *The Constant Sinner.*

West used this title for a stage adaptation, which played successfully in New York from 1931 to the summer of 1932. One critic called it "simple-minded, lurid and crude." Writing in *The Nation,* this critic felt West's audience were really "little boys" who made rude noises in the theater, giggled at every suggestive line and discovered indecencies even where none existed. He suggested there was no point in jailing Mae again, and if any offense was committed then it was by the audience for "being what they so obviously are." Another critic claimed her plays drew people from the "lower forms of animal life."

By the early 1930's the stage was beginning to suffer economically from the effects of the Depression, so in June of 1932 West accepted a Hollywood film offer. She had already been screen tested by a man named Charles Walsh from Fox who had been unable to sell her either to his own studio or to Warner Brothers. George Raft, though, had requested her for his film *Night After Night* (1932) and Paramount offered her $5,000 a week for ten weeks' work, a staggering sum for what was a minor part. Raft later said of her performance, "Mae West stole everything but the cameras." It was a film she almost didn't make. When she saw the script she wanted out because it wasn't her style. Paramount was determined to keep her, though, and West finally consented to stay when the studio agreed to let her write her own lines.

Many wonderful Westian lines would come out of her films, starting with *Night After Night.* When West flashed on the screen in her usually bejewelled manner, a hat check girl remarked, "Goodness, what lovely diamonds." To which West retorted, "Goodness had nothing to do with it, dearie." She created such a memorable impression in that film that Paramount decided to elevate her to star status. Mae West stayed with the studio, but on her own terms. She wrote the scripts, picked the other cast members, selected the director and picked the music composer if there was one. She also made the decisions on the scenery and costumes.

Her second film and first starring role was the 1933 release, *She Done Him Wrong*. This was the film version of *Diamond Lil,* but because of its notoriety, Paramount and the censors insisted on releasing it under another title, with the lead character having a different name. Faithful to the play, Mae got to strut around in sequins, beads and feathers and to devour every man in sight. She was an enormous box-office hit.

It was in films that the remarkable Westian wit truly came to the fore. She had gotten laughs in vaudeville and in revues, but she regarded her first couple of plays as dramatic vehicles which, while they had funny situations, had no funny lines. Her films tended to be the opposite—situations that weren't by themselves funny, but lines that were. She stated that, "My comedy was a gradual thing. I didn't start putting in all those wisecracks till I started in pictures."

She began that process with *She Done Him Wrong,* and it was in response to pressures from the studio and the censors. No longer would she be allowed such lines as "A hard man is good to find." The pressure in films was much more vigorous than it had been on Broadway, the rationale being that more children attended films. West found she wouldn't be allowed to do certain things, "and so with everybody weakening my drama, I figured I had to put some other element in. I used humor so I could do and say what I wanted and get over the sex. And then they started classifying me as a great comedienne."

Censorship pressures on her were very rigorous, even though she did use an exaggerated humor. Ultimately she wasn't able to do and say everything she wanted to and it hurt her with the fans and made the studios timid in dealing with her. It was a tribute to her ingeniousness that she accomplished as much as she did in the face of so much opposition.

There was some difficulty in casting a leading man for *She Done Him Wrong* until one day Mae spotted an unknown and handsome member of Paramount's chorus line on the studio lot. She declared she would have him for her leading man "if he can talk." He could and his name was Cary Grant. In *She Done Him Wrong* Mae played a woman who judged men by the size of the diamonds they gave her. It was in this film she uttered her most famous line of all, to Cary Grant, "Come up and see me sometime." At least that's what it got loosely translated to. The original version was, "Why don't you come sometime and see me. I'm home every evening. Come up. I'll tell your fortune."

Her next film was *I'm No Angel* (1933) and was a circus picture in which Mae was a female lion tamer. She refused to have a stunt double and entered the lions' cage herself, fulfilling an apparently lifelong childhood dream. In the movie she played "a girl who lost her reputation but never missed it." She also uttered another of her more memorable lines, "Beulah, peel me a grape." Those two films broke box-office and attendance records in the United States and throughout the world, no small feat in the midst of the Depression. The receipts from her movies saved Paramount Studios, who were then in financial difficulties and thinking about selling out to MGM, as well as closing all 1,700 of their theaters and converting them into office buildings. Producer William LeBaron said that *She Done Him Wrong* must be credited with having saved Paramount. . . . Mae West is a lifesaver to the motion picture industry." Her pictures virtually brought to a halt the confession-type movie in which the heroine was punished for her sins.

There was more to the West character than just sex. She was unstintingly honest. Crooked politicians, con artists, hypocritical high society snobs, and other undesirables were often the victims of Westian humor and put downs. In one film a low type claimed he was the "backbone of his family," to which West replied, "Then your family'd better see a chiropractor."

Puritans were still up in arms over her and in 1934 the motion picture industry began to strictly enforce the Hays office censorship code, first set down in 1930 but not enforced until 1934. Mae West wasn't the only target, but her material contributed more to the code's rigid enforcement than that of any other single individual. The code itself changed the face of film making. In that year her fourth film was released, *Belle of the Nineties*. It was originally titled *It Ain't No Sin* but the Hays office demanded a title change. They also objected to some scenes and dialogue, but the final version, with Westian double entendre and suggestive delivery, was still a triumph.

In 1935 *Goin' to Town* was released in which Mae played a cattle rustler's widow who schemed her way into high society and marriage, and always gave better than she got. West had by then become the highest paid entertainer in the country. In 1934 she made $340,000 and the next year $480,000. Of all the salary earners in the country that year she was second only to William Randolph Hearst, who once editorialized in his paper, "Isn't it time Congress did something about Mae West?"

The Mae West phenomenon took hold of the entire country. Women took up her style and her fashions. Professional and amateur imitations of the Diamond Lil-Mae West character "sprang up like a plague." Jokes about Mae could be heard all over the land. She was truly now a legend and a household word. Her fame was such that a wax likeness of West was installed in Madame Tussaud's museum in London. She inked a new deal with Paramount paying her an incredible $300,000 per picture plus another $100,000 for the screenplay, the highest of any Hollywood star. Commenting on the phenomenon, West said, "I became suddenly a star seen in the third person, even to myself. . . . It didn't frighten me. I got fun out of being a legend and an institution."

It was reported that crowds of people stormed theaters in Vienna to protest her pictures. In 1941 British airmen applied her name to their inflatable life jackets, because when inflated the jackets were said to resemble her "awesome chest." With that, the words "Mae West" went so far as to enter the dictionary. It was a Westian age because she was the only person treating sex in a humorous, tongue-in-cheek manner. Everyone else portrayed sex as evil or pornographic.

West gave us a joyous celebration of the delights of sex. She was using high camp humor long before the term was invented. The watchdogs of public morality and other puritans didn't share in the fun, but West was too popular, too influential, and too shrewd to be stopped completely. She was a tonic for the hard times of the 1930's and helped people forget their troubles. Said Mae, "I make fun of vulgarity. . . . I kid sex."

In 1936 *Klondike Annie* was released and ran into more troubles with the censors. The script was watered down by the Hays Production Code office and then when they previewed the film they cut a further eight minutes out of it. All this of course greatly diluted its effect.

In this film Mae impersonated a Salvation Army-type woman, and she was soundly denounced by the Hearst press. The next year *Go West Young Man* came out, and Mae had also started to do radio work. It was a radio appearance that caused Manhattan

College to launch an attack against her in their magazine, claiming that she was "the very personification of sex in its lowest connotation polluting the sacred precincts of homes with shady stories, foul obscenity, smutty suggestions and horrible blasphemy."

The radio program which caused all the fuss was West's first appearance on that medium in December 1937 on the Edgar Bergen program. The show featured an Adam and Eve skit with Bergen cast as the snake, Don Ameche playing Adam, and West as Eve. The script had been cleared by NBC and rehearsals had gone smoothly. The program was aired live. West delivered her lines with her inimitable style and tone, embellishing their meaning. NBC was hit by a flood of protest over the immoral nature of the broadcast.

Two congressmen reprimanded all concerned parties. Newspapers claimed they received a torrent of letters condemning the program as "filthy," "profane," "indecent," etc. Products of the show's sponsor, Chase and Sanborn, were threatened with a boycott and clergymen everywhere raised an uproar. The network responded by placing a ban on Mae. It was an informal ban, but Mae West didn't appear on network radio again for over twelve years, until January of 1950. Not only was she physically banned, but NBC also banned even the mention of her name on their network. She did make a few radio appearances during that time, but only on local, independent stations.

Her next film was *Every Day's a Holiday* (1938). Censorship was much tighter for this film and West wasn't allowed any of her ribald dialogue or double entendre.

It was an attempt to impose discipline on an essentially spontaneous talent. The result was a dull film which was much less successful then her previous endeavors. Based on the receipts of her last two pictures, her popularity had clearly nosedived. This marked the end of West's association with Paramount Studios. Some felt her declining popularity was due to the novelty of her character having worn off, even though the studio had obviously steered her away from the style she was most successful in. Others attributed her decline to the triumph of puritanism. It was certainly true that pressure from the studios, the Hays office, and other groups such as the Legion of Decency greatly reduced the potency of her work, and must have had an effect on her decline.

The Hays office had let the studio use the basic *Diamond Lil* story, subject to many provisions. Ironically they recommended something which contributed to West's career as a comic. "In view of the low tone of backgrounds and characters, comedy should be emphasized." The script for *She Done Him Wrong* was finally approved, but when the Hays office saw the film they demanded some 25 more changes. Even with all those changes the movie was still subject to a variety of deletions by local censor boards in various countries. It was banned outright in Australia and New Zealand. The first script submitted for *Belle of the Nineties* was rejected outright as it was "quite patently a glorification of prostitution and violent crime."

West's character in *Klondike Annie* was that of a nightclub singer who posed as a settlement worker. The Hays office made it clear that West musn't play a character who could in any way be mistaken for a minister. She wasn't allowed to carry a Bible or to utter the word "religion." Despite all of this, Hearst sent a memo to all of his managing editors saying that *Klondike Annie* was a "filthy picture. I think we should have editorials roasting the picture and Mae West."

The pressure was beginning to take its toll, for when the script for *Everyday's a Holiday* was submitted, the producer said he felt "Mae had censored herself to the point of marring the entertainment value" of the film." Still, the Hays office insisted that changes were needed because there was too much drinking and double entendre. When the revised script was received, the Hays office demanded still more changes and deletions. By the time of the last two films of Mae's early film career, producers had pretty well given up trying to insert and retain the more wicked, and inspired, examples of the Westian wit.

She was then off the screen for two years, a victim of the studio's cold feet and censorship, until she teamed up with W.C. Fields in 1939 to make *My Little Chickadee* for Universal. Mae's troubles with the censors had left the studios not knowing how to use her and still meet the restrictions. As a result she was no longer able to impose her will on the studios and was lucky to get a film offer. She signed for $40,000, just one tenth of what she received in her peak years. The film itself was a mock Western with West playing a woman with a bad reputation who enters a never-consummated marriage with Fields to gain respectability. Much had been expected from this monumental pairing of talent, and as usual Mae wrote the script, although Fields wrote his own part. The promise was much greater than the result and the film was disappointing. There was a certain amount of friction between teetotaling Mae and the always-drinking Fields, and both individuals had large egos. Neither one was used to, or enjoyed, being upstaged by anybody. The film marked a major compromise for West who had not co-starred with anybody since her first film. As she put it, "I stepped off m' pedestal."

West negotiated with both Columbia and Universal for future pictures but agreement could never be reached on a script. In 1943 she finally turned out a feature for Columbia, *The Heat's On*. It marked the first time she appeared in a film not dressed in 1890's fashion, and it was a mistake. She was also not allowed to write her own script. It was not a box-office success and her critical notices were worse than usual. The film didn't revive her career, and convinced her to stay away from projects she couldn't control and didn't like. At that point West turned her back on Hollywood and made no more movies for over a quarter of a century.

She had been working on material for a movie of the Russian empress Catherine the Great. But since she couldn't interest any film studio in the project, she turned it into a stage play which opened on Broadway in 1944 and went on tour in 1945. In the play Catherine became just another variation of a familiar character, or as Mae West put it, "a Slavic-Germanic Diamond Lil, just as low in vivid sexuality but on a higher plane of authority." One reviewer found it to be "one of the most tasteless and extravagant displays ever to be presented as a play for adults."

West toured with a couple of other mediocre plays but didn't do particularly well until she revived *Diamond Lil* and toured successfully with it for four years from 1947 to 1951, playing to enthusiastic audiences all over the United States and England. In the revival, "Miss West's walk, or writhe, is certainly one of the most hilarious performances in the theatre." Another critic called the play a "dreary charade." Yet her popularity was still overwhelming. In 1949, according to a public opinion poll, she, along with Eleanor Roosevelt, was the best known woman in the world.

Between 1954 and 1956 Mae toured the United States with a nightclub act spoofing the traditional girlie shows. West was outfitted in her Diamond Lil finery and surrounded by eight young musclemen, all wearing loin clothes, while she sang numbers like "I Like to Do All Day What I Do All Night." Two of these men once came to blows in a Washington, D.C., nightclub over her affections. She was then nearly sixty-five. Having men fight over her was something that didn't bother Mae. It was a state she felt to be "both natural and appropriate."

She claimed she got the idea for her nightclub routine after talking to a group of women whom she met at summer stock. These women told Mae they didn't go to nightclubs because of the nude or semi-nude women there, which didn't make it entertaining for them. From this West got the idea to put semi-nude musclemen into her act to entertain and appeal to women and get them into the audience. Her club act did remarkably well and did break box-office records.

In her act she was carried onstage by nine of the body builders while being borne aloft on a chaise longue. At the end of her act she passed out keys to her hotel room to each of the anxious men, saying, "Don't crowd me, boys. There's enough for everybody." During the routine the men would come out to be reviewed by Mae. They would face her, backs to the audience, and open their capes for inspection, giving the audience the impression they were nude. Mae would look each one up and down and linger on the crotch while delivering lines like, "I feel like a million tonight. But—one at a time," and "I'm glad to meet you face-to-face."

For the next dozen or so years she was out of the limelight. She never cared for television and appeared on the tube only a few times. She taped an interview with Charles Collingwood in October 1959 for the CBS program *Person to Person* but at the last minute network officials cancelled the segment, worried that some of her comments might be "misconstrued." One of the exchanges had Collingwood ask her views on current events, to which Mae replied, "I've always liked foreign affairs." She had refused television series offers, citing as her reason "that some clown in Omaha can turn you on and off. . . . A woman like me must be an event." She had also recorded an album of her best known songs in 1955.

She published her autobiography in 1959, *Goodness Had Nothing to Do with It*. An adviser criticized the manuscript because West didn't include the struggles and disappointments that are a part of every life. Mae said her fans didn't want her to have struggles and disappointments. Revealing more of her own mind set than that of her fans, she said, "Mae West always triumphs."

Towards the end of the 1960's and well into the 1970's, Mae's films underwent a revival, as did those of the other great irreverent and iconoclastic comics from the 1930's, Fields and the Marx Brothers. West released a few rock and roll albums which garnered some good reviews. One album contained songs by the likes of Bob Dylan and Lennon and McCartney. It sold over 100,000 copies. Her *Wild Christmas* album contained her rendition of "Santa Baby" and "Put the Loot in the Boot, Santa." By the end of the 1960's an international fan club was established, started by a fifteen-year-old boy. Most of the members were said to have been teenage boys, and membership reached a peak of 8,000. She got hundreds of fan letters every week. The first fan club to honor Mae West had been set up after her second film.

West returned to the movies, claiming her fans demanded it, and in 1970 appeared in Gore Vidal's sex-change comedy *Myra Breckinridge*. She wrote her own lines and was paid $350,000 for ten day's work. Mae got top billing over the film's lead, Raquel Welch. West also had the exclusive right to wear black or white.

In doing her own dialogue, West completely changed her character, Letitia Van Allen, from a masochistic victim of men into a more normal Westian character who conquers all the men she encounters. Mae and Welch appear together in the film only very briefly. This, too, was part of Mae's philosophy. Raquel was ready to share the screen, but as she said, "Mae didn't write me into her scenes." West's rule was that "I never appear opposite a woman." Generally speaking she didn't. She wanted all the focus on herself.

During filming she was asked her opinion of Raquel. "She's a sweet little thing. She has one or two little scenes in the picture, I believe." It was said that Mae was the only one to have emerged from this film with her reputation unscathed. Two Westian lines from *Breckinridge* were: "Let's forget about the six feet and talk about the seven inches," and "All right, boys, take out your resumes."

Her old films were being shown everywhere, on television and in revival houses, and drawing huge crowds. In 1978 her last film was released, *Sextette,* based on her play *Sex* of some fifty years earlier. She was still playing the same lusty and bawdy character as always, at about age 85. It was something that only a legend would dare to do, something only an institution could pull off. One of the male co-stars of that film was Tony Curtis, and he admitted he signed for the picture without looking at the script or worrying about salary because it was a Mae West film. Critics called the movie so bad that it was good, in the camp tradition. Others said it was so bad that it was just plain awful. West played a movie sex goddess who had just married for the sixth time. Originally, 71-year-old Cesar Romero had been suggested for the part of the husband, but Mae quickly dismissed him as too old. She auditioned 1,000 handsome unknowns before settling on a man more than fifty years younger than herself. When Mae West behaved the way she did it was lewd and crude. When the equally aging George Burns did the same thing it was eccentric and cute.

During the 1970's she continued her career in other ways, appearing in nightclubs and recording suggestive songs, such as "A Guy What Takes His Time." She continued working until her death in November, 1980.

The last years of her career didn't compare with the earlier ones, yet it was astounding that West could still play the same sultry character for so long and still exude such a commanding presence. In a country where youth was worshipped, women many decades younger than West were considered old and non-sexual. But West didn't find it odd at all to find herself on the screen being romanced and courted by men more than half a century younger.

In her private life Mae kept up the Diamond Lil character. She was one of the richest women in America. Her living quarters were furnished right from the 1930's, with gold and ornate trappings everywhere, along with the nude statues and paintings of herself. She often greeted interviewers wearing a nightgown, and conducted the interview while lounging in bed. She had an endless succession of lovers over the years, and toward the end she surrounded herself with young musclemen. In most ways, though, her private life was quiet. She didn't smoke or drink, or go to nightclubs. She rarely went to parties. West was narcissistic enough to have a mirror over her bed. How much was real and how much was false was hard to say. Mae was well aware of what her fans expected of her and she knew they expected her to be "bad."

At least one critic has claimed that West was actually a regressive symbol for modern women. He had missed the point. It was West who almost singlehandedly broke the hammerlock of Victorian morality on the stage and, in fact, paved the way for women to become more emancipated. She can't be blamed if it didn't come about. She did more than her share. In the world that West created, women were free and aggressive. They were intelligent, knew what they wanted, and went after it. No longer timid and passive, they were bold enough to invite a man to come up and see them sometime.

She opened up sexuality through humor and parody. She mocked men and women. Her outlandish clothes, her piles of jewelry, her tons of make-up, her huge and concrete hairdo, once called "a Mount Rushmore of the cosmetician's art," were all her way of caricaturing female characteristics and making them appear ludicrous and perhaps even slightly disgusting. By creating this extreme image she conveyed a double message. She seemed to be saying to women, "Tone it down. Don't dress just to please men or you'll look as absurd as I do." To men she was saying, "You want glamour? You want sex? I'll give it to you."

She did what was impossible for a woman to do up until then — ridicule sex, while at the same time being sexual herself. It was a sexuality that was never obvious or blatant. She was rarely seen or photographed in anything but a full length dress, and while her dialogue could suggest everything, especially with her delivery, there was usually nothing concrete to latch onto for the censor.

Her popularity with fans was enormous but it was much more ambiguous with the critics, who usually gave her vehicles bad reviews but still admitted a fascination with West herself. The critics were largely male and middle-class and in some cases apparently very much offended by West's bawdy approach and view of liberated women. One reviewer called her the worst actress in the world.

Others have mentioned that West was not beautiful, or glamorous, or seductive at all. Which was also not true. Evidence from her own life indicated just the opposite. She did present her sexuality in a humorous way, but the sexuality itself had to be there. Reviewers of her vehicles, while often panning the play or movie, would, at the same time, admit to her magnetism and suggest to people not to miss her.

The Mae West character was a man-chaser, but with a very big difference. She chased, but on her own terms and according to her own rules. And once caught she discarded each man, when it suited her. She wasn't chasing anybody to get married and settle down for life. She just wanted a good time. She was the complete opposite of the more common man-chaser as typified by Eve Arden. Decades later Sandra Bernhard would get on stage and say it, but Mae West lived it. She was after a man, but only for a quick lay.

From a very early age Mae knew what she wanted, knew that she would make her own rules, and that there would be no double standard for her. Nor would men tell her what to do. She always looked out for Number One. As she remarked, "Men have structured society to make a woman feel guilty if she looks after

herself. Well, I beat men at their own game. I don't look down on
men but I certainly don't look up to them either." She did beat
them, and more power to her.

For someone who didn't play by the rules Mae had a few rules
of her own. Paradoxically she believed in censorship, on the
whole. She was in favor of a certain kind of dignity, wouldn't tell
or listen to dirty jokes and wouldn't say certain words. On stage
or screen she would never play the part of a mother, and not usually a wife, preferring to be an illicit girlfriend. She wouldn't play
a mother because she thought of a mother "as a wonderful person
and I don't often play a wonderful person." On the screen she
also wouldn't do something to embarrass women in the audience,
such as taking a man away from a woman on the screen.

West was likely the most quoted woman in history. A small
sampling of the Westian wit, from a variety of her movies might
explain why:

A friend told Mae that ten men were waiting for her at home.
She replied, "I'm tired, send one of them home."

A suitor said to her, "Your lips, your teeth, your eyes, your
hair, your . . ." To which Mae said, "Say, what are you doing,
making love or taking inventory."

"Good women are no fun. The only good woman I can recall in
history was Betsy Ross and all she ever made was a flag."

"A man in the house is worth two in the street."

"I used to be Snow White but I drifted."

"It's not the men in my life, it's the life in my men."

"I always say keep a diary and one day it will keep you."

"Too much of a good thing can be wonderful."

"I generally avoid temptation. Unless I can't resist it."

"It's better to be looked over than overlooked."

"When I'm good, I'm very, very good, but when I'm bad, I'm
better."

"Keep cool and collect."

"Between two evils, I always pick the one I never tried before."

"Give a man a free hand and he'll try to put it all over you."

"The score never interested me, only the game."

"Come up and see me sometime. Come up Wednesday. That's
amateur night."

"Do you have a gun in your pocket, or are you just glad to see
me."

Over a period of 45 years she appeared in only twelve films, but her impact was far in excess of that.

Toward the end of her career she was asked what she wanted to be remembered for, to which she replied, "Everything." In the film *I'm No Angel* a man said to her, "I'll never forget you." Mae answered, "No one ever does." We won't either.

THELMA TODD

Although her career was cut short by sudden death, Thelma Todd, during the early 1930's, became one of Hollywood's top female comedians, with a prodigious output. Including her short films, she appeared in approximately 120 pictures from 1926 until 1935, with close to half of those being feature-length films.

She was born in July 1905 in Lawrence, Massachusetts. Thelma completed her schooling in that state and went on to obtain a teaching certificate. She helped put herself through school by working as a part-time model, something she continued to do when she became a schoolteacher, a career she pursued only briefly.

In 1926 she entered her home state's beauty pageant and won the title of Miss Massachusetts. This brought her to the attention of Paramount Studios who signed her up that year and brought her to New York where they enrolled her in their newly established acting school. After a few months of training she began to appear in bit parts in a few movies. Her breakthrough film as a comic came in 1927 when she appeared opposite Ed Wynn in *Rubber Heels*. She was such a hit that her comedy future was assured.

In 1927 Todd joined the Hal Roach company in Hollywood and worked for that studio until her death, with some freelance work as well. She was described as a "stunningly beautiful blonde" and it marked one of the few times that a woman was given credit for comic skills and beauty at the same time.

The coming of sound enhanced Todd's career and, due to her "timing and her rapport," she quickly became sought after as the leading lady to all the big male comedians of the day.

She co-starred in films with Charley Chase, Jimmy Durante, Harry Langdon, and Wheeler and Woolsey. She played opposite

Joe E. Brown in *Son of a Sailor,* with Buster Keaton in *Speak Easily,* with Laurel and Hardy in *The Bohemian Girl* and opposite the Marx Brothers in both *Monkey Business* and *Horsefeathers.* In general she played the wisecracking woman. She did the odd straight role, such as in *Corsair* (1931), using the name Alison Lloyd for that film. She had hoped it would change her image but it didn't. Obviously she couldn't have been completely satisfied as a comic.

In 1931 she began her own comedy series for Roach, which lasted until 1935 and made her highly popular. Roach had given the world Laurel and Hardy and he set out in 1931 to create a "female Laurel and Hardy." That year Todd was paired with ZaSu Pitts and the team produced 17 comedy shorts until 1933 when Pitts left the studio. Todd was then paired with Patsy Kelly and that twosome made 21 films from 1933 to 1935. In those films a combination of slapstick, sight gags and situation comedy were used, with Todd prepared to do anything for a laugh. In the Todd/Pitts pairing, ZaSu played her stock character, a bewildered and not very bright character, with Thelma usually having to get the two of them out of some predicament caused by Pitts's innocent ignorance. In *Red Noses* the pair went to a Turkish bath to work off a cold. They found themselves stranded out in the country with an escaped lion in *The Old Bull,* and the pair became taxi dancers for a night in *Asleep in the Fleet.*

When the team became Todd and Kelly the same blend of humor was used, but Patsy Kelly came on as wisecracking and headstrong with Todd as more of the comic foil. Pitts had got the pair in trouble by being dumb, Kelly accomplished the same by being headstrong and impulsive. They played two clerks demonstrating washing machines in a department store window who got locked in for the night in *Babes in the Goods.* In *Bum Voyage* they found tickets for a steamship cruise without knowing that a gorilla also occupied the cabin. Todd and Kelly were cornered in a spooky old house complete with strange old man and a robot who hated women in *The Tin Man.*

This series, and Todd's all-too-brief career, came to an end in December 1935 when Todd was found dead of carbon monoxide poisoning in her parked car, at age 30. The circumstances of her death, whether it was suicide, accidental, or foul play, have never been solved, and remain a mystery to this day. The pairing of Todd and Pitts and then Todd and Kelly represented the only time in film history that a female comedy team was ever assembled for any length of time. Dressler and Moran appeared together in about half a dozen films over that many years, from the late 1920's to the early 1930's. But they were not really a team. They only did a few films together and most of the work for which they were known were solo efforts.

The attempt by Roach to create a female duo comparable to Laurel and Hardy was not overly successful. They never caught on the way male teams did, but it certainly wasn't due to being a cheap imitation. Both teams, male and female, worked at the same studio and had access to the same talents, production staffs, and the same type of budgets. There was nothing to suggest that Roach put more effort into the male teams. Some have said the series went wrong because Roach "tried to create situations that were more suited to women than to men, but far too often they miscalculated," and in the roughhouse and physical slapstick portions the results "were often embarrassing." That says more about that particular critic and his image of women than about the films.

Actually the plots of the Todd shorts were very similar to the type done by Laurel and Hardy. The difference, though, seemed to be not in the material, but rather in the perception of the audience as to what was proper and not proper for women to do. By the time of the 1930's the kind of comedy image projected by women which was considered acceptable by the public had changed markedly. A number of female solo comics had scored successes with slapstick during the latter half of the 1910's, but the movement to restrict women to a more confining comic role and image was well underway by Todd's time. By then the audience was only prepared to tolerate either the dumb Dora and/or helpless and dependent female comic. Physically active women were not the norm. And certainly the idea of two women united together, with no regular man in sight, was a threatening one. Women were to be shown as dependent, and dependent on men.

ZASU PITTS

Her career as a comedian in film and television spanned 45 years. She played the befuddled and the bewildered type, the "addle-pated spinster." Her trademarks became her whimpering and quivering voice, delivering the distressful cry of "Dear, oh, dear," and her hands, which constantly weaved about and fluttered in gestures of impotency and ineffectualness. Her specialty in show business was the "flustered, featherbrained, helpless type," which she played to perfection.

Many stars of the silent film era saw their careers go down the drain with the advent of sound pictures, but not ZaSu Pitts. From 1917 until the end of the 1920's she had divided her time between comedy and drama and had a greater reputation for the latter. With the coming of talkies her career as a straight dramatic actress was doomed because her quivering and crackly voice was not suitable. Instead of letting her career evaporate, however, she used her voice and other characteristics to become a top comedian, a distressed "flibbertigibbet," a "fluty-voiced, fluttery-fingered" comic.

She was born in Parsons, Kansas, on an undetermined date, perhaps January, 1898, or March, 1894. Her unusual first name was thought up by her mother and supposedly given to her at birth. Mrs. Pitts couldn't decide which of two paternal aunts to name her daughter after. To avoid picking one name over the other, she compromised and gave her new child a name containing the last syllable of Eliza and the first syllable of Susan. The name was distinctive enough to become one of her trademarks and she was called, early in her career, "The Girl with the Ginger Snap Name." Jazzman Cab Calloway once used a version of it in his nightclub routine.

She was the daughter of Rulandus and Nellie (Shea) Pitts. The family moved to Santa Cruz, California, when ZaSu was quite young. Her father died in 1908, after which her mother made a living running a boardinghouse. Attending high school in Santa Cruz, Pitts wanted to get into the school dramatic club, but was rejected because her looks were unusual. She resorted to performing solo pieces, doing monologues she had picked out of a book, one of which was "Mrs. Smart Learns How to Skate." Her recitals had the students in stitches. Perceiving this gift of mimicry in her daughter Mrs. Pitts decided that ZaSu should go to Hollywood and try to get into show business. ZaSu herself wasn't particularly interested in doing that, but her mother kept coaxing her, arguing that if she failed, "There's always time enough to come back here and work in the five-and-ten."

Influenced by her mother, ZaSu went to Hollywood in the mid 1910's after graduating from high school. She took a room and began making the rounds of the studios. She had no luck initially, since casting offices were filled with beautiful would-be actresses and Pitts "felt like a peg-legged lady who had wandered into a harem." It was reported that one casting director gave her a screen test "just to see how homely a subject could be without affecting the camera."

Eventually, though, screenwriter Frances Marion saw Pitts and her forlorn quality appealed to her. Marion wrote a part for her, and Pitts made her debut in the 1917 release *The Little Princess*, which starred Mary Pickford. In her very early roles ZaSu did mainly comedy and "developed her distinctive woebegone manner." She claimed to have modelled it after one of her school-teachers whom she used to impersonate to the delight of the other students. The image of Pitts as unattractive was firmly entrenched by 1923 when it was reported, with tongue in cheek, that she was "getting so pretty that she's been forced to abandon the wistful ugly duckling parts that brought her before the public eye."

During her first eight years in Hollywood she worked for almost everybody and made a large number of films, some comedy and some straight drama. She had two experiences with Charlie Chaplin whom she admired and wanted to work with. The first time she worked at his studio for six months at $50 a week, but never got near a camera. The next time she spent four paid months there and was in one rehearsed scene, but not in the film itself.

The height of her early career was reached in a dramatic role in the 1924 film *Greed* by famed director Eric von Stroheim. The German filmmaker had seen Pitts working in a comedy part on a set next to his and sent for her to take a screen test. Studio heads didn't want Pitts for the role, claiming she wasn't sexy enough for the part. One executive suggested that "This story of yours is horrible enough without throwing ZaSu in there to frighten the audience." Von Stroheim fought everybody and succeeded in getting Pitts for the part. She was delighted, since she had always wanted dramatic work in preference to comedy.

The finished version of *Greed* ran eight hours but MGM cut it down to two, whereupon von Stroheim loudly disowned the shortened version, which he considered to be hopelessly mutilated. Nevertheless, ZaSu's performance was outstanding, and if there had been doubts about whether she was a comedian or a dramatic actress, this film firmly established her as a first-rate straight actress. Almost a decade later a film historian said of her acting in *Greed* that it "has never been equalled by any other American actress in any time." The film became a classic in time, but when first released it was a commercial bomb. So, it was back to comedy roles for Pitts. By 1926 the style of comedy she specialized in was termed "pathetically humorous or humorously pathetic," and her hands were already famous.

It was said that her hands were so expressive that a slight movement was a syllable, a wrist turn stood for a mood, and she had more expression in a finger than some actresses had in their entire bodies. Her hands had a sense of humor. "Droll, sly humor. Hands that could hang limp at her sides—their very attitude calling for paroxysms of laughter. And a thumb that could go to her lip in a questioning curious manner that broke forth merry howls." Her comedy was that of helplessness, of distress, of pathos, as opposed to the broader slapstick prevalent during that time.

Von Stroheim was still encouraging her dramatic side, however, and called her the "screen's greatest tragedienne." He cast her in *The Wedding March* (1928), in which she turned in another stellar dramatic performance. She appeared in yet another drama that year and seemed to be back on track for a straight dramatic career. But it was her last silent film as that era came to a close. ZaSu feared her career might be over, since the studios had decided her voice was unsuitable for dramatic roles.

She did make one more attempt at drama though, in the 1930 release, *All Quiet on the Western Front,* for which she was hired on von Stroheim's recommendation. She played the mother. But when the film was shown to a preview audience they laughed at her tragic death scene and the studio decided to reshoot all of her scenes with another actress. It was a bitter disappointment for Pitts and it marked the end of her career in straight drama. What the studios had forecast for her with the coming of the talkies had proven true: "It was expected that Pitts' high-pitched cracking voice would rule her out for serious dramatic roles, and indeed thereafter she was almost invariably typecast as a fluttery comedienne."

She had a supporting role in the 1929 release *The Dummy*, a talkie, wherein she re-established herself as a comic and quickly became more popular than ever. In the middle thirties Pitts was still hoping to get a serious part, but it never happened and she reconciled to her typecasting. "I'm always the hired help. . . . Good waiting-on-table parts." She was enormously busy and from 1930 to 1934 appeared in 60 films, leaving her mark as a scatterbrain in most of them. Besides these she found time to team up with Thelma Todd in a series of 17 short comedies from 1931 to 1933. As mentioned before, the Todd/Pitts pairing was produced by Hal Roach and was an attempt by him to create a female equivalent of Laurel and Hardy. Those films were slapstick farces, but the pair never achieved the success of the male team on which they were modeled.

From her long list of screen credits some of ZaSu's most memorable were *Ruggles of Red Gap* (1935), in which she played a whimpering Western maid; *Mrs. Wiggs of the Cabbage Patch* (1934), where, as Mrs. Hazy, she was romanced by W.C. Fields; *Make Me a Star* (1932); *Meet the Baron* (1933); *Dames* (1934); and *Life With Father* (1947). Her last screen appearance was as the confused switchboard operator in the 1963 film *It's a Mad, Mad, Mad, Mad World*, which was released after her death, in June of that year. She once described her movie characterizations as "pathetic comedy."

In the 1940's her film work began to lessen as she turned more to other media. She did a good deal of radio work as well as appearing in a few stage plays. One was the 1944 production, *Ramshackle Inn,* in which she played a librarian who had invested her savings foolishly in a hotel only to find herself surrounded by gangsters. Her role was true to type: "The part is not too great a deviation from her usual role of servant girl and half-witted spinster." The play was not well received critically, but Pitts got her usual good notices.

In the 1950's she made many appearances on television and spent four seasons as a costar on "The Gale Storm Show." She played Esmerelda "Nugey" Nugent, the bewildered and befuddled spinster operator of a beauty shop on a cruise ship. As a comic foil to the ship's social director, played by Storm, the pair were in continual hot water with the ship's blustery captain. Pitts was largely retired by the end of the 1950's.

The idea of a woman as a natural homemaker surfaced in Pitts's case as it had years earlier with May Irwin. In June 1944, *American Home* presented a story outlining how much ZaSu loved to cook. The article gave credit to the public for accepting Pitts as an entertainer "even though she hadn't the first vestige of the full-blown peach-glow beauty requirement." This article also credited Pitts with having said: "Being an actress was second-best in my choice of careers. All I wanted to do was to stay home and

fix good things to eat." In view of her 45-year career, such a pro-
nouncement, as with Irwin, was nonsense. It merely represented
an attempt to portray the "proper" role for women.

In real life ZaSu considered herself a serious person and not
funny at all. Interviewers would often remark on the fact that her
hands moved no more than they do with the average person, that
she didn't look bewildered, and her voice wasn't as whimpering as
on film. As happened with so many other female comics,
interviewers feigned surprise when they found that in real life the
dumb woman didn't turn out to be so dumb after all. This kind of
confusion of a stage persona with an entertainer's actual personality happened much less frequently in interviews with male comics.
For example, no one asked Chaplin if he was really a poor tramp.
No one asked Buster Keaton if he was sad and never smiled in real
life. No one asked Ed Wynn if he was the "Perfect Fool."

While Pitts had resigned herself to her type and was very
easygoing, she did get annoyed with reporters who wrote about
her voice and fluttering hands. She often refused to wave her arms
aimlessly or wring her hands in despair when photographers made
such requests.

During her career she appeared in almost 180 films, as support
more often than star, but was one of America's longest-lasting and
most popular female comics. Yet an article about her in the June
6, 1936, issue of *Collier's* was titled "Mr. Woodall's Wife."
Perhaps to emphasize Zasu's scatterbrained image, the article
claimed she mistakenly called her husband Mr. Woodhall for the
first six months of their marriage. In any event the title of the
article gave some idea of the relationship between the sexes. Her
husband was unknown, a Pasadena real estate broker.

PATSY KELLY

Patsy Kelly achieved fame in the 1930's and early 1940's as a film
comedian. She usually played the star's best friend and was always
ready with some rather loud-mouthed advice, or a dry and witty
retort. She excelled at that style, and became known as "Queen of
the wise-crackers." She was greatly aided in this by her ad libbing
skills, which she had picked up in trial by fire under a master of
standup comedy, Frank Fay. She never really attained the heights

of stardom in her own right but, perhaps from her early pairing with Thelma Todd, came to be considered the "greatest second female lead around." For the most part her films were not of major importance, and Kelly's performance was often the only highlight. Decades later, when her movies still occasionally turned up on the Late Show, newspapers would mark them with such comments as, "worth watching for the Patsy Kelly scenes."

She was born Bridget Veronica Kelly in Brooklyn in January 1910, daughter of a man who washed cars in a garage and later became its foreman. Raised in Manhattan, as a young girl she hung around a neighborhood fire station, where she became an unofficial mascot. She had an ambition to be a firefighter but also had the misfortune to be involved in several accidents on her way to and from the fire hall. She was never seriously hurt but the fire chief asked Mrs. Kelly to keep her daughter away from the station, fearing someday she might be killed. Mrs. Kelly, not happy with her daughter's ambition, complied.

The only thing she could think of doing with Patsy was to send her off to dancing school. At the age of ten Patsy became a pupil at Jack Blue's dancing school, where she stayed for several years. At thirteen she was paid a small amount to teach tap dancing at the school, an art in which she was then quite proficient. One of her classmates at the dancing school was Ruby Keeler, who got a job as a buck dancer when Texas Guinan first opened a nightclub in New York. Kelly also tried it, but only for a week before realizing it wasn't her kind of work.

In 1926, when only sixteen, she happened to cross paths with Frank Fay, which led her into her lifelong career as a comedian. Fay was an enormously talented stand up comic of the day with a caustic and acerbic wit, and truly gifted in ad libbing. Patsy's brother was trying to get into show business and got an audition with Fay. He took his sister along to help him with his dance routine. Fay was impressed, but by Patsy, and he quickly made her a part of his act. She spent a little time dancing in his act, but was soon promoted to the rank of Fay's stooge, a receiver of his insults. Fay had as many as three stooges at a time and Kelly quickly became the best he'd ever had.

She was able to trade quips with him and come up with funny answers to funny questions. The routine had a couple of bits that were always included, but the bulk of the act was totally unstructured and unrehearsed. Fay's routine consisted of whatever was in Fay's head at the time, and Kelly never had any idea what they would do or talk about on the stage. She had to think fast and feed Frank a good line, because if her reply fell short of the mark he would turn to the audience and say, "Isn't that awful? Here I am paying her a big salary and you can see for yourselves how stupid she is." Once in a while she would be forced to respond to a Fay question, "Well, that stumps me; from this point you're on you own, Fay." Generally, though, she gave about as good as she got and the training proved invaluable in making her a quick-thinking, sharp-tongued comic.

Fay, an egomaniac and erratic employer, fired her after a few years and Kelly moved on to Broadway. Forever after, though, she considered Fay to have been her discoverer and acknowledged that she owed him "a debt of gratitude I can never repay."

After leaving Fay, Kelly was put in touch with a Broadway producer by her old friend Ruby Keeler, and she appeared in five revues from the late 1920's until 1933. These included Earl Carroll's *Sketch Book, Vanities,* and *The Wonder Bar.* When she turned to films in 1933, some wondered if she could make the transition due to her stage presence on Broadway, which had been described as follows: "She came out and captured the stage, roamed around like a panther with the hives and raised her shrill voice to the galleries with all the assurance of a district attorney who has just accompanied the judge in from a backroom poker game."

Hal Roach brought her to Hollywood in 1933, after seeing her on Broadway. He teamed her up, as a replacement for ZaSu Pitts, with Thelma Todd. This team made a series of 21 two-reel comedies between 1933 and 1935. These shorts were shot in about a week and involved the whole cast in working out the gags from the initial written idea and synopsis. As noted previously, the Todd/Pitts and the the Todd/Kelly pairings represented two of the very few female comedy teams in film history. The Todd and Kelly pairing ended only as a result of Todd's sudden and untimely death in 1935. The comedies produced by this team "are considered by authorities on screen comedy as among the finest the sound era produced." Kelly made a few more shorts with other partners, but the magic couldn't be recaptured and she turned full time to feature films, her first being *Going Hollywood* (1933).

Some of her best-remembered feature films were *Every Night at Eight* (1935), *Thanks a Million* (1935), and *The Cowboy and the Lady* (1938). The pictures themselves were varied, from comedy to musicals to straight drama, but Kelly's part remained consistent.

She was never the star of the film, except for a few "B" pictures in the early 1940's, and always essayed a comedy role in her films. Her delivery was deadpan style, and she played the wisecracking friend to stars such as Jean Harlow and Loretta Young. She remained a constant ad libber and more than once played a street-smart Irish maid who delivered caustic quips to deflate a few snobbish households. She was a perennial fall guy in her films, "an ideal foil as the plain-Jane confidante of a generation of Hollywood actresses." In 1937 *The New York Times* described her as "dealing out, Parthian shots and deadly, devastating squelchers." They also called her the "best gag-plugger in the movies—a girl who can take a poor author, and does nine cases out of ten, and make him sound like Noel Coward."

By the early 1940's she was appearing in some "B" pictures. The 1943 release, *Danger! Women At Work* was her 31st feature film and proved to be her last screen appearance for almost twenty years. The mid 1940's saw her spending a very brief time on stage, on radio, and with a nightclub act. She also toured for a short time in the stage farce *Dear Charles* in 1955. With these minor exceptions, Kelly disappeared from public view for almost two decades.

The vague term "personal problems" was cited as a reason for her decline, but no satisfactory explanation was ever offered. When asked about her prolonged absence, Patsy herself said, "I don't honestly know, but I believe in cycles. There are just times when it seems you can't do anything wrong. Then there are other times when whatever you do is wrong. . . . I think I could have had more drive. I was never very ambitious." In the 1960's she appeared in films again with bit parts in half a dozen pictures. Her last screen role was the witch in *Rosemary's Baby* (1968) but there was none of the old Kelly visible.

In 1971 she made a triumphant return to Broadway with a small part in *No, No, Nanette,* which featured her old friend Ruby Keeler. Her performance was praised by critics: "Patsy Kelly takes full and rich advantage of the part of the outspoken maid in a glorious display of pure ham"; and she won a Tony. In 1973 she had a part in the musical *Irene* on Broadway, and then toured nationally with the production. She had made the odd TV appearance over the years, and ventured into that medium as a costar of a 1975 situation comedy series "The Cop and the Kid," about an Irish cop who found himself with custody of a black street tough. Kelly played the cop's mother, and the attempts of those two to reform the tough provided the so-called humor. The show was poor and lasted only 13 weeks before being mercifully cancelled.

Patsy Kelly, "the pert, rumpled farceur of knockabout movie comedies," died in September 1981 at the age of 71. In one of her films, *The Girl from Missouri* (1934), she and Jean Harlow were hired, along with other chorus girls, to entertain at a men's smoker. As soon as they got there an old man made a lunge for Kelly, to which she replied in her normal deadpan manner, "Look at this—death takes a holiday." Few could deliver that tart rejoinder the way she could, and her presence in any film during the 1930's guaranteed a lot of laughter.

The 1940's and 1950's

INTRODUCTION

The period of the 1940's and 1950's marked the lowest ebb for female comics in terms of the images they projected. The great majority of the stars from this period were typecast as dumb, ugly man-chasers, or some combination thereof.

World War II came and went with much the same effect on women as World War I. Many more women held down jobs than in peacetime, receiving better pay and more variety of work than usual. For some, it was the first time they had an independent income. But the gains women made during the war were short lived.

At war's end most women were dismissed from their jobs as the returning men took them back. Females were reassigned to lower paying and more menial work, to the unemployment lines, or back to the hearthside. The government ran a sophisticated advertising campaign to accomplish this, and it came about quietly. Women were told their place was in the home, and, practically en masse, females resolutely marched off to their ranch houses in the suburbs.

Feminism was nowhere to be found during this period. Suffrage, the big issue at the turn of the century, had a consciousness-raising affect on women before and after World War I. The vestiges of suffrage helped women to have a more positive and forceful image in society which lasted through the flapper era of the 1920's. This image was reflected by the female comedians of that time. No such influences were forthcoming in the 1940's and 1950's, and this period continued the reversal of women's rights, which had been dealt a blow by the Depression of the 1930's. The images projected by women comics coincided with this reactionary era.

During this time television succeeded radio as the main medium providing home entertainment, and brought about a change in style. Where radio relied on women mangling the language, television, in keeping with its visual nature, relied more on physical sight gags to convey "dumbness." This period thus brought to the fore the combination of dumb, blonde, and buxom. On television, though, most of the women could talk normally, albeit illogically.

Cass Daley was the last to achieve fame through radio. She began as a straight singer, but moved over to being "ugly" and doing comic songs when she found it was the only way to advance her career. When she went into radio she added "man-starved" to her "ugliness" and achieved her peak stardom. Minnie Pearl adopted the guise of the hillbilly clown started by Judy Canova and established a character that was unattractive to men. She performed mainly in one night stands at county fairs and in the Grand Ole Opry.

Anna Russell also performed mainly in concerts across the nation for over three decades. Beginning as a serious classical singer, she found herself drawing laughter when she shouldn't have. She was forty years old before resigning herself to comedy, where she excelled as a musical satirist. Her forte was lampooning classical music and classical musicians. Nancy Walker was yet another from this group who was laughed off the stage as a straight singer only to rebound as a comic. She became a Broadway star portraying rough and rowdy types and then moved over to television, where she played second banana on a number of programs.

Awkwardness as a child led Carol Channing into comedy, where, in Broadway musicals and nightclubs she established herself as the archetypal dumb blonde, a persona she continued for decades. What Channing was to Broadway, Judy Holliday was to film. Both were consummate dimwits; one sang, the other didn't. As a generality, the women cast in the dumb roles didn't complain, at least publicly. Holliday, whose career was cut short by an untimely death, was one of those who did express discontent. She desperately wanted roles with more depth, but never got them.

Martha Raye performed in a number of media but was perhaps best known from TV. Her specialty was comic sketches done in a rough, knockabout style. Imogene Coca also specialized in comic sketches on television. She did a lot of physical comedy as well, although in a subtler way than Raye. Attention was inordinately focused on the physical attractiveness, or lack thereof, for both of these women, particularly Raye.

On TV the housewives were represented in the person of Joan Davis and Lucille Ball, both dizzy scatterbrains who dragged their spouses from one wild crisis to another. Davis had started as a broad slapstick comic, moved on to be a man-starved character on radio, and finished her career as a housewife and airhead. Ball switched from a film career as a glamour girl to become one of the all-time greats in the scatterbrain derby.

The images cast by Davis and Ball represented an improvement of sorts over some of the TV housewives found in the sitcoms. The wife on "Life With Riley" and, the best example, wife Margaret on "Father Knows Best" were lifeless and colorless, contributing little to the programs except completing the nuclear family. At least Davis and Ball had zest and personality, ditsy as they were.

Working women were represented by Arden the schoolteacher on the TV program "Our Miss Brooks." Even though she was financially independent, she didn't live on her own, choosing room and board at a house. Arden represented the frustrated spinster relentlessly pursuing a man.

Sex was brought to television in a not so subtle fashion in the persons of Marie Wilson and Dagmar. Both were blond, played unbelievably dumb characters, and had large bosoms, with the last being emphasized. Wilson was cast in the Allen mold and labored under the additional handicap of playing a character who butchered the language, common in radio but unusual on TV. Perhaps this extra trait was added to water down her sexuality and to stress her dumbness.

Dagmar's characteristics were basically the same as Wilson's. She too wreaked havoc with the language. One difference was that Wilson had costars and some semblance of a plot on her show. Dagmar had none of these. Her main form of comedy was limited to mangling a few poems and appearing on stage with her 40-inch bust encased in a very lowcut and tight gown. Not surprisingly her career was short. But it was spectacular while it lasted, and she was enormously popular during her brief stardom.

In the field of stand-up comedy several women emerged during this period. Moms Mabley had started much earlier but didn't hit her stride until the 1940's when she became a favorite on the black club circuit. She combined raunchy jokes and political and social satire with another stock female role, that of the domineering maternal figure. The color of her skin, in addition to the bawdy and aggressive nature of her comedy, kept her from being "discovered" by whites until well into the 1960's. By then she was old and her effect considerably softened. Whites could then embrace her as a lovable and eccentric character.

Jean Carroll became a popular monologist during the 1940's, using largely "feminine" type material. But she failed to make the transition to television. This may have been due to an image too far ahead of its time. Both Kaye Ballard and Pat Carroll combined monologues with songs in the early phases of their careers in club acts and in revue productions. Both of these women made the transition to television, where they achieved their greatest recognition as comic support on a wide variety of programs.

While the prevailing image for this period was that of the dumb and/or unattractive woman, one notable exception was Elaine May. For a period from the late 1950's to the very early 1960's May, and partner Mike Nichols, enjoyed enormous success. May didn't play dumb, nor did she try to look ugly, or do any self-deprecation. She was an equal partner in the team, not just a foil for the male half. Their material was social satire and they viewed the world with a jaundiced eye. They were hard-edged enough that they couldn't make the transition to television due to violating too many of its taboos.

While the period of the 1940's and 1950's marked a low point for the image of female comics, it was due to turn around in the 1960's. Elaine May was an example of what women could accomplish when given an equal opportunity, and provided a sample of what was to follow as more and more female comics cast off the old images and stereotypes and broadened and extended their place in the field of humor.

CASS DALEY

Cass Daley was another of the women comics who got into comedy not through choice but by accident. Like others she started out as straight singing. She came to epitomize the rubber-faced comic by adding as many unattractive grimaces as she could to her repertoire, thus turning what she felt to be a handicap into an asset. While her time at or near the top was limited to a dozen years or so and she has long been forgotten, she was big in her day and was ranked with women such as Judy Canova, Martha Raye, and Joan Davis.

Catherine Daley was born in Philadelphia in July of 1915, the daughter of a streetcar conductor. As a child she became overly self-conscious about her appearance, which was thin and wiry. What bothered her most were protruding and widely spaced teeth. Other kids gave her nicknames like "Bucky" and "Horseteeth" and she was told her teeth were so big that she could eat corn on the cob through a tennis racket. Not surprisingly Cass developed an inferiority complex over this.

As a child she always had a humorous bent and loved to perform, aping singers like Helen Kane, the boop-boop-a-doop girl. She got her first fee as a performer when she was just ten years old. She was standing on a bread box, singing outside a Philadelphia store, when someone gave her a quarter. While growing up she entered as many vaudeville amateur night contests as she could and would occasionally return home with a prize such as a certificate for dresses, or one for shoe repairing, etc.

By the time she was into her early teens she had to drop out of school to help out her family financially. She worked at small jobs such as candy wrapper, and at fourteen was employed as a stocking trimmer in a hosiery mill. Her facility for making people laugh surfaced at this factory when she mimicked the foreman, behavior for which she was fired. She earned $12 a week tops during this period.

One night at a party she was entertaining the guests with her impressions when a nightclub owner heard her and hired her. This marked the start of her professional career. The Old Mill nightclub was located in Camden, New Jersey, and Cass did double duty as both hatcheck girl and singer. She started at age seventeen and stayed a few years; she made about $85 a week.

In the mid 1930's she got hired as a singer during the intermissions of a Camden Walkathon, which was what they called dance marathons. She was singing the blues during one intermission when the audience suddenly started laughing for no apparent cause. Cass discovered the reason when she turned around and found the emcee holding a lighted candle behind her so the audience could see through her dress. The emcee was Red Skelton.

Despite Daley's flair for comedy, she had never done any professionally. She had remained a straight singer of ballads and the blues. The episode with Red Skelton got her seriously thinking about comedy. From Camden she got a job at a Westchester, New York, nightclub, again doing straight singing; there she also met Frank Kinsella, a part-time agent and part time insurance salesman.

While she sang her ballads she was very much aware of her protruding teeth and in an effort to hide them she tried to keep her upper lip pulled well down while she sang. This didn't sit too well with Kinsella, or some of the other audience members, either. He sought her out and advised her to act naturally and return to the uninhibited comedy of her childhood. After several such sessions, Kinsella's advice prevailed and Daley turned to comedy professionally. Kinsella became her manager and later her husband.

Her first venture was her own wild version of the song "The Music Goes Round," complete with a gagged up trumpet. This number was highly successful with the audience and Cass was launched as a comic. She abandoned glamour and worked up her routine of comedy and music which consisted of "wild parodies and slightly salacious songs." She practiced making faces in front of a mirror until she had a whole series of grimaces at her disposal, which one reviewer said were "worthy of a Chamber of Horrors."

She played vaudeville and presentation houses with increasing success and appeared in the *Ziegfeld Follies* as a replacement for Judy Canova. She did a tour of English music halls in 1938 and drew rave notices from the British critics. Her income had now gone up to $750 a week. During her act she pranced around the stage, sang her songs in a hoarse and screeching voice, and "rode her mike like a streamlined witch on a chromium broomstick." She also threw every exaggerated facial grimace she had at the audience, which loved it all.

In their March 17, 1941, issue *Life* magazine displayed no less than a dozen of those facial poses and proclaimed that Daley was well on her way to becoming "the nation's toothiest, loudest, ugliest singing entertainer." While she made her faces, Cass was likely to yell to the audience, "Am I scaring you to death?" This image of Daley as ugly was purely a stage ruse; in reality she was an attractive woman.

In 1941 Cass signed a seven-year contract with Paramount Pictures and made her screen debut the following year in *The Fleet's*

In. All of her film roles were similar. Daley played a featured part in musical comedies, in which she engaged in manic singing and clowning. Her first film was a vehicle for the star, Dorothy Lamour, but Daley reportedly stole the show. In a 1943 film, *Riding High,* she played dude ranch owner Tess Connors and got to sing something called "Willy the Wolf of the West." A film critic wrote, "Miss Daley, the girl with the dentures, screams and tortures amusingly a couple of comedy numbers." In another film of that year, *Crazy House,* her big number was "Lament of a Laundry Girl." All in all she appeared in thirteen films over her career, the bulk of them before 1948.

It was radio, though, where Cass Daley made her biggest impact and achieved her greatest success. She appeared as a guest star on a number of radio programs, including the Jack Benny show and the Edgar Bergen show. She was a regular on the "Frank Morgan Show" in 1944, playing Morgan's exuburant niece Cassandra on the comedy variety show. On that program she made famous the phrase, "I said it and I'm glad."

The next year she became the chief female comic on "The Fitch Bandwagon" and was remembered for years for her rendition of the program's theme, a ditty praising Fitch shampoo. The summer of 1945 she had her own radio program as a summer replacement for the "Bandwagon." Early in 1946 she reached her apex when she became radio's most popular woman comedian. According to the radio ratings she had briefly supplanted Joan Davis in that position. In 1950 she had another comedy program of her own on the air, "The Cass Daley Show," in which she played a small-town resident forever getting into trouble while trying to help people out.

At the height of her radio popularity she was making $2,000 a week. Her antics on the radio were similar to those onstage. After entering and demurely giving a curtsy, "she suddenly chases the announcer, swings on the velvet curtain, howls a snatch of some unrefined ditty, walks on the side of her heels, pops her teeth and straddles the mike." Radio audiences missed most of that but it didn't lessen her appeal. Another major part of her radio character was the stock role for women of that era. She played a daffy lady who was a "raucous man-starved female."

With her broad, visual comic style and abilities Daley seemed to be a natural for television and was thought to be potentially more successful there than in radio. However, in the early 1950's she retired to the Los Angeles suburb of Newport Beach to raise her young son. And from that day on her career was effectively over. Asked once about being forgotten, she explained, "You know what it's like out here—out of sight, out of mind!" She did admit, though, that she hadn't tried too hard to find television work. She later called moving to Newport Beach the biggest mistake she ever made in her life.

By 1970 she was ready to make a comeback. She was low on money and even had to collect unemployment benefits. Her son was grown and she and her husband were divorced. She appeared in cameo roles in a couple of movies and did some minor stage work, but jobs were very scarce and casting directors no longer recognized her name. "And when I tell them who I am they don't seem to care."

She died in March of 1975 at the age of fifty-nine, the victim of a freak accident. She tripped and fell in her apartment and broke a glass, a piece of which pierced her neck and severed her jugular vein.

Daley had become famous for her "toothy grin, raucous comedy songs and Plain-Jane looks" and for never resisting the impulse to use a facial grimace or a body contortion. Or, as one writer put it, "Cass had learned to capitalize on a face and figure that would have ruined the life of another woman." This last quote came from a 1982 publication, indicating that a woman's appearance was still given priority over her accomplishments. Moreover, Daley was in no way the ugly specimen she was portrayed to be. That was strictly an invention.

MINNIE PEARL

Sarah Ophelia Colley was born in Centerville, Tennessee, in 1912, the youngest of four sisters. Her father owned a sawmill and the family was comfortable financially. From an early age Ophelia, as she was called, loved to entertain by singing or doing imitations. Her ambition was to become a great dramatic actress, something her parents were supportive of. What they didn't like was for Ophelia to "cut the fool." Little did they know that their daughter would achieve fame as a hillbilly clown.

After high school in 1930 Ophelia attended Ward-Belmont College, a fashionable finishing school in Nashville, where she studied drama. The Depression took its toll on her father's sawmill and in 1932 Colley had to return to Centerville. She taught drama to

local schoolchildren, but was miserable in the small town. Her
escape came in 1934 when she joined the Wayne P. Sewell Production Co., a touring group which directed amateur theatricals
in southern towns. Colley stayed with Sewell for six years and it
was during this time that the character Minnie Pearl was born.
Colley discovered the persona for Pearl in a backwoods Alabama
cabin. She based the character on a mountain woman she had
boarded with while on tour. The woman had a son named Kyle
who didn't care for his name. He got everyone to call him
"Brother," and brother became part of Minnie Pearl's routine.
Colley began trying out Pearl stories on her fellow entertainers in
the Sewell company.

In 1938 Minnie Pearl made her debut before the Pilots Club of
Aiken, South Carolina, for a fee of $25. Dressed in an old yellow
dress, scruffy white shoes, white cotton stockings and a flowered
straw hat, Minnie Pearl told stories about the town of Grinders
Switch and about Brother. She made gags about her feller and
established her character as unattractive to men. The audience
loved the act.

Colley would retain this basic costume throughout Pearl's
career, making only minor alterations. One thing she added was a
price tag hanging from her hat, and she changed from white
shoes to black "Mary Janes."

In 1937 Colley's father died and by 1940 her mother needed
support at home. Reluctantly, Ophelia once again returned to
Centerville, where she was hired to run a recreation hall for the
WPA. As a sideline she gave singing and dancing lessons once
again to local children. She was twenty-eight years old, unmarried, broke, and with no dramatic career in sight. It was a low
point for Colley.

One day a banker friend of the family asked Ophelia to perform at a banker's convention and do "that old silly thing,"
meaning her Minnie Pearl sketch. The act went over so well that
one of the bankers used his influence to get Colley an interview
with WSM radio, which broadcast the Grand Ole Opry show from
Nashville. The program had started in 1925 when a few farmers
had fiddled and sung for the radio station. It grew into one of the
most popular country music shows in the United States, and was
broadcast from a hall that seated an audience of several hundred.
Today the program is heard from an auditorium that seats 4,000.

Colley felt her audition for the Opry had not gone well, but she
was hired on a trial basis for a late night spot on the show. Her
Minnie Pearl routine was an immediate hit and Pearl became a

fixture on the show. She was the sole female comic and earned a salary of $10 for her Saturday night broadcasts. She and her sister Virginia wrote the material and Pearl always opened the act by whooping, "Howdy, I'm just so proud to be here."

She also toured with some country musicians, notably Roy Acuff and his band. But Acuff eventually fired her, claiming that she had to loosen up and be sillier with her Pearl character. Colley realized that she did need more experience developing comedy routines.

A chance to really work on her sketches came in 1941 when she was hired to perform for servicemen with the Opry Camel Caravan. Her jokes were often self-deprecating, but she always made them relevant for her soldier audiences. Her favorite gag was about the entrance checkpoints at military bases. Minnie would say, "I felt so at home when I got here. In fact, one feller told me I was the homeliest girl he'd ever seen. They were so cordial and pleasant when we got to the gate. Why, they even had fellers out there with my initials on their sleeve—M.P.—Minnie Pearl."

It was during this tour that Pearl was bothered by her first heckler, a hostile drunk. She left the stage crying. Fellow entertainer, Ford Rush gave her advice which sent her back to complete her act. He told her never to forget that she was in control. She had the powerful mike and could drown out the heckler by being louder. He told her that as a funny person she would always be the target "particularly as a woman . . . it's even worse for a woman because it puts her out of her natural habitat." Pearl recollected: "My feminine ego was hurt, and you can't play comedy and worry about that."

In 1947 Colley married Henry Cannon, a private airline pilot. She never performed as Mrs. Cannon, however; she was by now identified only by her stage name—Minnie Pearl. Cannon flew Pearl across the country for twenty years of one-night stands, mainly on the fair circuit. She also performed twice at Carnegie Hall and once at Madison Square Garden. Every Saturday night, though, she came back to Nashville for the Opry.

In 1939 NBC picked up a 30-minute segment of the Opry program and it was broadcast coast-to-coast. In 1941 Minnie Pearl's act was included in the nationwide segment. Colley and her sister were still writing all of Pearl's material, with stories like this: "My feller and me went to a weddin' the other night, and, oh, it was so pretty and so sad. I cried and cried and had the best time. The bride, she come down the aisle in the prettiest white dress. It'us short in front, but it sagged somethin' awful down the back. Two little younguns had to come along behind and tote it fer 'er. Why, if she'd a had to git away from there in a hurry with that long dress a swingin' out behind her, she'd a fell and broke her leg, they'd a had to shoot her. She looked so happy. I don't blame her. I know how long she'd been after him. We started about the same time, but she outrun me. The groom was awaitin' fer her at the h'alter, and that's what it was, too. He didn't know it, but he found out in a couple of days. He was awaitin' there fer her, and everyone said the bride looked stunnin' but the groom, he jus' looked stunned. He looked like another clean shirt would do him. And the lady at the organ was playing Meddlesome's wedding march and it was so pretty, and they had flow'rs, they had nasty-tursuns and peetunyas and beegonyas; well, hit smelt jus lak a funereal. The groom stood there in front a all them folks and told that girl he'd give her all his worldly goods, and his pappy was a setting' there in front a me and he said, 'Uh, oh! There goes Jed's slingshot.'"

When Minnie Pearl became part of the NBC segment of the Opry they hired agents to write her material. Pearl accepted the offer since she had to turn out a weekly routine, but wasn't always happy with the jokes. This agency-produced gag gave an indication why: "I seen two fellers and one of them said to the other one, 'I believe that's the ugliest girl I ever seen,' and the other one said, 'Oh, she might be a pretty good old girl. You know beauty is only skin deep,' and the first one said, 'Well, let's skin her.'"

Pearl also teamed up on some of the NBC segments with comic Rod Brasfield. He would pop up near the end of her act and the two would ad lib. Their sketch might go like this:

Rod: I brought myself a new car and the first thing I done was grease it all over.
Minnie: Grease it all over? Why'd you do that? . . .
Rod: So the finance company can't get a holt of it.

Rod might ask, "Miss Minnie, I sure do wanna walk you home tonight. I always wanted to walk home with an experienced girl." "But Rod, I'm not experienced," Minnie would protest. "Yes, and you ain't home yet, neither."

The two continued to work together until 1957 when NBC dropped its portion of the Grand Ole Opry.

Minnie Pearl was heard on the radio musical variety show "River Boat Revels" in the early 1940's, as well as the Grand Ole Opry. In 1955-56 ABC aired a television version of the Opry, featuring Minnie Pearl as one of the cast. She appeared on other television variety shows, including the 1966 NBC program "Swinging Country" and "Hee Haw," which ran from 1969-1971 on CBS.

By 1975 Minnie Pearl was semi-retired, but still made the occasional appearance at the Opry, and performed at hospitals, churches and senior citizen homes. As an alter ego of Sarah Ophelia Colley Cannon, Minnie Pearl was a persona that could never retire completely. Cannon referred to her in the third person, saying, "I like to talk about her because she is warm and friendly, and she has all the qualities I wish I had. . . . She is pretty near perfect, you know, and I like her."

ANNA RUSSELL

One of the comics who used singing exclusively to present her comedy skills was Anna Russell. While she satirized all forms of music and singers she hurled the majority of her barbs at opera and the classics. She was forty years old before she had resigned herself to the field of comedy, and abandoned the regular singing career she had envisioned for herself.

With enormous energy she had performed for over thirty years, crisscrossing the globe on numerous concert tours. She gave a series of farewell concerts in 1984 at the age of seventy-two but admitted at the time that she might be amenable to being tempted back for concerts in the future.

She was born Anna Claudia Russell-Brown on December 27, 1911, in London, Ontario, Canada. Her father—and in fact every male for three generations back on his side—had been a career officer in the British Army. Her mother had at one time had briefly been a singer. When Anna was just six months old the family moved to London, England.

In England she was subjected to training designed to ensure she became a "lady." From the ages of nine to eighteen she was a pupil at a "proper" boarding school for young girls at Suffolk called St. Felix. From there she was sent to a finishing school, Pensionnat les Tourelles, in Brussels, for two years. At this school she was given the choice of either sports or music and she chose the latter. This involved going to the opera four times a week.

Back in England she enrolled at the Royal College of Music, since she had decided that music would be her career. She had a talent for singing and the piano. Russell had composed a little when she was young and had once written the music for a school revue. She had a great aunt who had been an opera singer and Russell intended to follow in those footsteps. In fact, becoming an opera singer was Anna's childhood ambition. During this period her training as a debutante continued with a formal presentation at court in 1934. Anna spent five years at the Royal college studying piano, theory, harmony, cello, voice and composition.

After graduation she set out to pursue her career as a serious singer. Her first professional jobs were with the British Broadcasting Company giving folk song recitals on radio programs, and touring England with small opera companies. It was during this time period that Russell shortened her name to it's present form. She performed in several languages, including, German, French, and Spanish. From this period she remembered herself as having "no sense of humor at all, and probably no talent either." She claimed that her singing voice was "horrible."

This wasn't true; she was an accomplished singer, pianist, and composer. A fellow student recalled her as being a beautiful singer. Russell also remembered herself as being socially inept, "as a lumpy, silly sort of person. I was spotty, pimply, fat,"

What did happen during her early, and serious, career was a series of untoward accidents. Her dress would fall off her shoulders, the music would fall to the floor, somebody would trip and fall. The result was that the audience would laugh at inappropriate times. She began to go home and laugh at herself and some of the pretensions of the stage. At one concert in 1937, the big Anna, then 180 pounds, stepped forward to sing and she appeared so much larger and fiercer than the nearby trumpet soloist and conductor that the audience broke into laughter.

Another time, while touring in Birmingham, she was singing in *Cavalleria Rusticana* opposite a tenor half her size. During the duet he was supposed to throw her to the ground. While trying to help her partner accomplish this feat Russell turned her ankle and went careening across the stage. She crashed into the prop church and the whole set came tumbling down. The audience broke up and so did the orchestra, so much so that the performance was ended. Russell was fired. She was still sensitive to the laughter and this experience marked the end of her serious career. After five years of hard work Anna felt it meant, "My life's work was shattered."

Shortly before the outbreak of World War II she returned to Canada with her mother, her father having died. In Toronto,

Ontario, she appeared on the Canadian Broadcasting Corporation radio in soap opera roles. Accidents continued to bedevil her. On one show she was required to yell out the name "Virgil." She did so loudly that a tube blew, throwing the entire CBC off the air. She wasn't happy with the radio work, as she had no audience to play to and she was just reading lines.

Her musical career had lain dormant for several years and wasn't revived until about 1943. Several events then transpired to move her into the realm of comedy. She was called in at the last minute as a substitute speaker for a music teachers convention. Having no time to prepare she delivered a humorous monologue on the art of singing, which was well received.

Someone else asked her to do something amusing, in the Ruth Draper style, for a benefit. Gradually she began to appear at benefits, women's clubs, and at armed forces shows, doing take-offs on serious recitals. The Imperial Order of Daughters of the Empire, equivalent to the DAR, asked her to entertain at a small benefit. She worked up her routine and was aghast to find that the group had booked a large auditorium and sold 1500 tickets. She did her act solo, providing her own musical accompaniment, and was a huge success.

That clinched it for Russell. Comedy was to be her career. "I came to the the conclusion that if I was as funny as all that, I'd better make a buck out of it." Russell was then a musical satirist, spoofing the very thing she had worked so long and hard to become. A local promoter heard her and booked her around Canada. She enjoyed success and built up a following and a reputation as a musical funny woman. However, Anna had her eyes on bigger things, and in 1947 she left Canada and moved to New York City to try her luck in the United States.

She went around to producers and agents but she found most doors closed to her. She had to take other employment and once worked as a soda jerk on Sixth Avenue. She did manage to give a couple of concerts, attended mostly by friends. It was enough, though, to enable her to give a concert at Town Hall in February of 1948. The press gave her good reviews, but not many spectators turned out and Russell was quickly forgotten.

Over the next few years she performed at a variety of places, including a hotel where she had to perform every twenty minutes on a revolving bar. She also appeared at the Harvard Club in Boston, gave a concert for a Milwaukee Wisconsin Women's club, entertained at a stag night in Chicago for a Lumbermen's Convention, complete with strippers and baton twirlers, and was on a variety program at a Long Island vaudeville house.

Finally she came to the attention of concert manager Eastman Boomer of a company called the Columbia Lecture Bureau. He arranged for another Russell concert at Town Hall in November of 1951. There wasn't much money in the box office but the hall itself was packed, thanks to "freebies." The critics reaction to this concert, a month before Russell turned forty was phenomenal. The critics were lavish in their praise and she became another overnight sensation. Her career as a musical satirist was assured.

Critics compared her comic impulses to Beatrice Lillie. She was also compared to Gracie Fields, to whom she bore a physical resemblance. Following her Town Hall smash she embarked on a cross-country concert tour and returned to give two sold-out performances at Town Hall with hundreds turned away. She even managed to fill the auditorium one Sunday afternoon during the World Series. She has been busy ever since.

Anna has regularly given 200 concerts a year and has appeared in a host of countries, including Australia, New Zealand, South Africa, Singapore, India, Hong Kong, the British Isles, North America, and throughout Europe. Her appeal was universal. She has also made numerous guest appearances on television, appeared at music festivals, sung in operas, guested with symphony orchestras of several major U.S. cities, and has performed her one woman show on Broadway. She appeared in films and on the stage, continuing to act occasionally in plays into the 1980's in both musical and non-musical roles, because she loved playing the "dotty old gals."

She also had best-selling records. Two of them, released originally in 1953, were so popular that they were still in the catalog in the 1980's. Her first record was called, "Anna Russell Sings!?," with the subtitle, "Song Selections for Loud Singers With No Brains."

In her act she lampooned opera stars, folk singers, psychoneurotic crooners and pianists of all skill levels. A high point of her act was Russell appearing as a president of a ladies' club and introducing a series of performers, all of them played by her. Her swooning and dying scenes also made big hits. She didn't limit herself to classical music, but spoofed popular material as well, from the earliest "coon shouting" to the popular songs of the current day.

During the course of her act she "tweets like a canary" and

"brays like a mule," taking the pretentious down a peg or two with her wit. She did take-offs of Wagnerian sopranos, particularly the meaty Brunnehilde, and a torch-singing Piaf. She gave her music "depreciation" courses, and lessons on "How to Write Your Own Gilbert and Sullivan Opera."

Her most famous routine was her take-off on Wagner's *Ring of the Nibelung's* which she mocked with soap opera terminology. She had performed this piece unchanged for over thirty years. Russell tried to introduce other operas but always found that her audience demanded The Ring. She performed with great vitality and with an expressive, rubbery face. Her idea for the Wagner spoof came from her days at school in Brussels, where she had to see various operas in the cycle six times during the course of her stay.

Russell created all of her own material. She wrote the text, composed the music, and did her own arranging. She played the piano, French horn, cello, clarinet, castanets, and the bagpipes. Her audience ranged in age from five to ninety. In more recent years she had done a lot of college dates and her best audiences were those "that are up on the classics." She never tested new material she had written, preferring to try it out on a paying audience. When onstage she admitted to ad libbing "frantically."

During the early years of her career she used to make quick costume changes backstage but found that she and her audience were losing contact with each other during those breaks. Thereafter she brought the few props she did use, mostly hats and veils, onstage with her and never left the stage during her performance. When she made her first recording she tried doing it in the studio but the sessions fell flat. She needed the audience and their reactions. After several unsuccessful studio sessions, the record company set up shop backstage and recorded her live in concert, long before it was fashionable to do so.

For Anna Russell the path to comedy was a slow and tortuous one. She never dreamed of being a comic during her time at the Royal College. "I had no more idea of becoming a comedienne than the man in the moon. . . . I was a boring lumpy girl with no sense of humor." Just as she underestimated her own musical abilities so she did her sense of humor. After becoming the foremost musical satirist of her time, she admitted to having no answer to the question of how her comedy worked or what made her funny.

In a conservative family, serious music was about the only acceptable avenue for a female child. Thus Anna was thirty-one before she even started doing any comedy routines at all, and forty when she became a star. Over the years she has insisted that her voice and musical talents were not particularly good. Perhaps by believing this she could ease her conscience about being a comedian, convincing herself that she had no choice in the matter. A couple of years after she had attained stardom Russell's mother was still not impressed. "She thinks all this nonsense I do is the call-girl type of thing," said Anna.

NANCY WALKER

As an aspiring torch singer Myrtle Swoyer was a failure. Physically she didn't present the sultry image necessary to be convincing and vocally she didn't have the talent. Laughed off the stage as a serious singer, she re-emerged as Nancy Walker, star of Broadway musical comedy. During her television career in the 1970's she received her greatest public exposure and popularity in supporting roles and a commerical, only to be unsuccessful as a star on her own show.

She was born Anna Myrtle Swoyer on May 10, 1922, in Philadelphia and came from a long line of show business performers. Her grandfather was Roxy Swoyer, who performed as an acrobat until age slowed him down and he became a Ringling Brothers circus clown. Five of Walker's aunts had been circus acrobats, aerialists, and bareback horse riders. Her mother, Myrtle Lawler, was a dancer in vaudeville with her partner Arnold Grazer, under the name Grazer and Lawler.

Walker's father, Stuart, was also an acrobat and performed with a vaudeville team called the Three Bartos. When he joined this group he changed his name to Barto and his first name to Dewey, in honor of George Dewey, the U.S. naval officer who became a hero at Manila Bay during the Spanish-American War.

Within a month of her birth Nancy went on the road with her mother and was put in a basket in the wings while her mother performed her act. Predictably she crawled out of her basket at the age of ten months and made her way onstage, where she brought down the house. For the first year of her life Nancy's parents were seperated, being booked on different vaudeville circuits. The family was finally reunited in California. Nancy's father joined the act of Grazer and Lawler, now billed as "Singing Comedy Dance Sensations."

In due course Grazer quit the act and the family continued touring. Nancy, who was now too big for her basket backstage, was babysat by anyone who was willing and available. Her education was informal until she was seven years old, when she was enrolled at the New York City Professional Children's School, an institution she would attend sporadically over the years, in person and through correspondence. Due to her father's urgings, Nancy, against her will, was enrolled for ballet, piano, and singing lessons.

In 1930 her mother died shortly after giving birth to a second daughter. Barto then teamed up with Mr. Mann to form the tumbling team of Barto and Mann. Barto did routines such as running straight up columns and then doing a back flip to the stage. He initially tried to tour with both daughters and their maternal grandmother but found it too difficult. Eventually grandmother and infant returned to Philadelphia while Barto took Nancy with him on the circuit, including one junket to Europe.

Reaching her teen years, Nancy was shy around people and felt insecure and inferior, despite constant social interaction in the theater. Her father had trouble even coaxing her to go out for a newspaper. Just two weeks short of her scheduled graduation from the Professional Children's School, Walker announced she was quitting school and that she wanted to go onstage. Barto and Mann were then in the Olsen and Johnson revue, *Hellzapoppin* and splitting $2,000 a week. Barto was against Nancy's decision but reluctantly agreed. He did tell her that she would have to get a job, though, since he didn't intend to support her indefinitely.

With her sense of inferiority, she made no headway in the entertainment industry. When she did get up the nerve to ask, nobody was interested. She bought hundreds of records and played them over and over, studying them rigorously. It was her goal to be a straight singer of sad ballads, a torch singer, and she tried to copy the style of a then popular singer, Helen Morgan. Barto was impressed enough by his daughter's perseverance to get his own agent to try and help her find work.

The agent did get some work for Nancy. One job was for a week at the Bridgeport movie theater. She was back home after one day. A job at a Catskill resort lasted a week and then there was an equally short engagement at a club in Greenwich Village. This was followed by another short stay at a bar in Jersey City.

With a voice later described as resembling a "wounded moose," Walker had been fired from all those straight singing jobs.

In 1941 producer George Abbott was casting for his new musical. Reluctantly Nancy's agent sent her around to the auditions. When she was onstage to perform, she was announced as Helen Walker, an established singer of the day. Nancy, then billing herself as Myrtle Swoyer, had gotten that far only through a case of mistaken identity. Since she was onstage she was allowed to do her stuff, a serious song. Abbott's response was to be convulsed with laughter. He told her there was no part for her in his musical but there would be. Abbott, who had discovered a comic talent that Walker herself was unaware of, had a part written in for her.

So, at the age of nineteen and rechristened Nancy Walker, she made her Broadway debut in the campus musical *Best Foot Forward*. She played the part of Blind Date, a dense and determined coed at Winsocki University. She had twelve lines and two songs especially tailored for her comic ability, and a salary of $75 a week. Recalling her debut, Walker said, "They pushed me on the stage—I was lucky to make it to the other side." Nevertheless, reviews of the play were favorable, with Nancy being singled out for special praise. The play closed after more than 300 performances and Walker promptly signed a seven year contract with MGM at $750 per week and was off to Hollywood.

Her first movie was a film version of *Best Foot Forward* in which Walker played the same rowdy character who roughnecked and cut up with the boys. She made a second film for MGM the same year, 1943, and a third in 1944. Essentially she played the same Blind Date character with minor variations.

However, her relationship with the studio was not a happy one. She was accustomed to the rapid pace of Broadway musicals and never got used to the frequent film shooting delays, or sitting around all day waiting to be called by the director. She was also unhappy about the lack of frequency of her work. She felt the studio was not using her enough.

She began to put more and more pressure on the studio to release her from the contract, which they finally did in 1944 when she returned to Broadway. Ten years later, in 1954, she made her fourth movie, *Lucky Me*. She was again cast in a variation of her Blind Date character, just older. A critic remarked on the waste of her and another featured player's talents in that film: "Nancy Walker and Eddie Foy Jr., having almost nothing to do, do it with desperation."

After her return to New York, Walker opened in the musical *On The Town*, in which she played a man-chasing female cabby. She remained with the show until it closed after 462 performances, drawing praise for her comic performance. In 1946 she appeared in another Abbott campus musical, *Barefoot Boy With Cheek*. The show was not well received but Walker's performance was: "She continues to grow in the finest tradition of clowns."

By this time Nancy was a Broadway star and George Abbott gave her the leading role in his next musical, *Look Ma, I'm Dancing*. The play opened in February of 1948 but Walker had been given the role about a year before that. While she waited for the writers to produce what turned out to be a very corny script, Walker enrolled in a ballet school and spent a year learning ballet so she could make mistakes correctly. The play called for parodies of ballet and Nancy had learned to do everything right so she could do it wrong on stage.

The play was written with Nancy in mind and confirmed her status as an established Broadway star. The plot had Walker portraying a beer company heiress who financially supported a ballet troupe because she wanted to be a ballet star herself. She played a rough, tough, and rowdy character. One reviewer described her acting as "a kind of muted frenzy as if she were stealing apples from a pushcart." Another described her stage presence as a cross between "a swaggering tough advancing on a beer, and a punchy heavy shuffling toward the center of the ring. Her speaking voice is that of a truck driver calling his mate."

While the play was weak, critics loved Walker's performance. One termed her a "hammered-down Bea Lillie" (Walker was slightly less than five feet tall). No less a critic than Brooks Atkinson writing in *The New York Times* called her the "best slapstick comedienne of her generation." It was generally conceded that without Walker the play was a turkey.

As with all women comics Walker's appearance was judged crucial for her style: "she could not claim comeliness as her strong point. . . . Although the swans may win the 'Oh's'and 'Ah's,' it is the ugly ducklings who win the laughs." Miss Walker won them beyond counting. Almost immediately Walker found herself unable to duplicate her success in *Look Ma*. The next year, 1949, she appeared in the revue *Along Fifth Avenue*. It closed after 180 performances and was poorly received, although Walker's performance was again praised. This time she was favorably compared to Fanny Brice.

After that Broadway show she had trouble with her voice and had to resort to going to a singing coach to bring it back. She worked a little summer stock and played Broadway for a few weeks as a fill-in for the show *Pal Joey*. Other than that she remained mostly inactive until 1955, lacking a vehicle for her talent. As she once remarked of that period and lack of job offers, "I couldn't get arrested." She tried nightclubs but found herself not effective, admitting to having bombed at Miami's San Souci Hotel in 1954. She said, "The way I figure it . . . they got me typed as some kind of hoodlum, and when I don't knock the walls down, they get upset."

In 1955 she appeared in a revue called *Phoenix '55* which satirized American middle-class suburban lifestyles. She was able to play a variety of characters and it marked a comeback for Walker. She again drew raves and was called the "funniest woman in the hemisphere." She hadn't been in a Broadway show for three years, since her brief stint in *Pal Joey,* and she was glad of the change in type. "And back when I was working it was always the same loud, hard character. I wasn't going anywhere." She was then expressing an interest in doing situation comedy.

She opened in two more Broadway shows over the next two years. One was Noel Coward's *Fallen Angels,* where the critics again agreed that she was the only bright spot in an otherwise listless show. As for the second vehicle, one reviewer stated: "Miss Walker is a superb and chilling comic. The fact that the theater has nothing better to offer her than *Copper and Brass* strikes me as melancholy indeed."

In 1957 Walker announced that she was heading to Hollywood again, this time to try television. She was convinced that Broadway didn't know what to do with comedians. Over the years she would return to Broadway from time to time to perform with about the same record as before—always getting good reviews herself, but often appearing in a weak play.

After arriving in Hollywood she was soon kept busy appearing as a guest on television variety shows and game shows, something she continued for years. The 1970's saw her achieve her greatest television comic success. She appeared on NBC's "McMillan and Wife" series from 1971 to 1976. She was featured as the McMillans' maid Mildred, a wisecracking, acid-tongued, sarcastic woman. In 1974 she began doing double duty by appearing on the CBS series "Rhoda," portraying the featured and continuing character, Ida Morgenstein, mother of Rhoda. She was a meddle-

some, nosey, know-it-all who soon became the country's favorite
mother. What launched her into such prominence that decade
perhaps more than anything was her best known part of Rosie,
the owner of a diner, who touted the merits of Bounty paper
towels in a commerical.

In 1976 she left both her television shows and joined ABC to
star in her own series, debuting in the fall that year. For Walker
the show represented "a pretty nice capper to a nice career."
"The Nancy Walker Show" aired in September of 1976, but was
dead by December of that year. The producer was the highly successful Norman Lear, but as in the past the material was woefully
weak. Lear and coproducer Rod Parker were determined to make
Walker a star and each had an idea for her show.

Lear wanted it to be about a Hollywood agent who gave up
everything for her clients. Parker opted for a couple who had
been married for 20 years, with the husband off most of each year
in the merchant marine. The husband then retired and the couple had to get used to each other again just like honeymooners.
For some reason these two ideas were simply combined to produce
the so-called plot for Nancy's show. Initially ABC executives were
leery about Walker's first choice for a screen husband. They
feared the man, William Daniels, might have been too young and
handsome and that Walker was not young or pretty enough to
have such a handsome husband. Ultimately Walker prevailed in
that matter, but the show, with Lear trying to present some mixture of middle-aged sexuality on television, did not.

In February of 1977 ABC performed a shuffle and Walker
debuted as the star of "Blansky's Beauties," in which she played
house mother to a group of Las Vegas showgirls at an apartment
house. That series died an equally quick death, expiring in May
of that year. Of the series Nancy admitted that it was "a real
bummer." Never before having been a star of her own show,
Walker achieved the dubious distinction of having two failures in
one season. The next season she returned to her role on "Rhoda,"
determined to stay away from a series of her own for awhile.

Along the way she has also directed some plays, television, and
films. In 1980 she directed her first film, *Can't Stop The Music*.
This movie starred the singing group The Village People, and was
based on the disco craze. It was a film the critics virtually unanimously agreed was one of the most atrocious movies ever made. A
couple of years later Walker directed, and co-starred in with Eve
Arden, a female version of the Neil Simon play *The Odd Couple*,
in Florida dinner theater.

For Walker the stage was always her first love, the place where she felt a comedian could best be an artist and have the time to perfect a piece. She always felt herself forced to turn to films and television due to the lack of appropriate theatrical vehicles. The transition to comedy from the straight singing she had started out in was not an easy switch for Walker: "It took me about seven years to adjust to my stage personality. I was uncomfortable being funny. People expected me to be 'on' and I wasn't. I never am. But I kept at it, and learned to do comedy well."

Throughout her career she has been plagued with the lack of appropriate roles, poor material, and deficient productions. Due to her retiring nature, she has never been the type to approach people to say she wanted to do something; she found chasing after work to be demeaning. She preferred to think about what she wanted to do and wait until somebody picked up on her "wavelength." This lack of ego in a business dominated by huge egos has certainly hampered her career. Still, she has achieved a measure of stardom, perhaps because she has kept on adapting and changing. Nancy Walker has certainly kept at it.

CAROL CHANNING

She parlayed her look of innocence, her wide saucer eyes, and her raspy, much-imitated voice into the part of Lorelei Lee in the 1949 stage production of *Gentlemen Prefer Blondes*. The role made Channing a star. The character of Lorelei, created in 1925 by a woman, was well suited to the year of its Broadway triumph, since the dumb blonde image was in vogue. When Anita Loos created the golddigging character of Lee, it functioned as a backlash against independent and intelligent women at a time when women had just begun to make headway by getting the vote.

By 1950 any such progress, real or perceived, had been rolled back and the Lee character was then simply a reinforcement of the image of the ideal, and idealized, female—pretty but dependent and very, very dumb. Carol Channing played the part exceptionally well and the inevitable questions were raised about her own intelligence. Was Carol as dumb as her character?

Channing was born in January, 1921, in Seattle, Washington, but the family moved to San Francisco a few months after her birth. The only daughter of George and Adelaide (Glaser) Channing, her father was an editor for Christian Science publications and did much to shape the talent of his daughter. He taught her songs which the pair of them sang together, and he showed her how to establish contact with an audience.

According to her mother, Carol was already showing talent by mimicking friends of the family almost before she could talk. During her stay in grammar school Carol had been trained to be dainty and petite by her mother. But Carol was larger than the rest of the kids, and her resultant movements were awkward. She felt rejected by her schoolmates. To overcome this she turned more and more to her skills as a clown. In the fourth grade she became secretary of her class with the task of reading weekly minutes. She turned this into hilarity by impersonating each student whose remarks she read from the minutes. She also did imitations of the school's teachers and continued in this vein throughout high school. Understandably she gained a school reputation as a good-natured clown and early on she developed the intention of establishing a career as a comedian.

After high school in 1939 she went east and enrolled in Bennington College in Vermont, where she planned to major in drama and dance. During the summer of 1940 she worked briefly in the Poconos at the Tamiment Summer Playhouse, where she had been hired as "fourth comedienne." She was fired midway through the season "because of her disorganized habits." During another school break in January of 1941 she appeared in a small role in a straight play, *No For an Answer*. Her pay was $22 a week, but the play only lasted three days before closing. Carol got one line of praise in *The New Yorker* for her efforts, but it encouraged her to leave school, move to New York City and seek a full-time show business career.

Later that year she spent nine months as an understudy in the play *Let's Face It,* but got to go on stage only once. Near the end of 1942 she had a small role in the drama *Proof Through the Night*. That vehicle lasted only eight performances. For three years starting in 1943 Carol tried the nightclub circuit. She had developed a comedy routine which consisted of "satires on topical subjects" and included impersonations of show business stars of the day such as Ethel Waters, Sophie Tucker, and Carmen Miranda. She obtained some work at Manhattan clubs and in Catskill resorts, but it was sporadic and she spent far more time not working. To support herself she held a series of odd jobs such as receptionist, stock girl, model, and sales clerk.

Not making any headway with her career, she returned home to San Francisco in 1946, at her father's request, and spent a year at an artist's colony, where she took up painting and sketching. She still had the show business urge, though, and the next year she was in Los Angeles, where she gave herself six months to make it. Most of that time she spent doing her night club act in a series of one-night stands in front of various clubs and fraternal groups.

Finally, in 1948, she was hired by director Gower Champion for his satirical review *Lend An Ear*. The show enjoyed a successful five-month run in Los Angeles before moving to New York in December 1948, where it was a smash and played for over a year. Channing's performance was singled out for special praise: "A brilliant new comedienne. . . . A deadpan blonde who's really a little too pretty to be funny, but who can't, apparently, help it." It was through this vehicle that she came to the attention of the producers who were casting *Gentlemen Prefer Blondes*. Carol was still a relative unknown and she didn't get the part until the producers had tried without success to sign one of the big names of the day.

The show opened on Broadway on December 8, 1949, where Carol essayed Lorelei for close to two years before taking the show on the road for another year. She became a superstar from the time the play opened and within weeks she was promoted to star billing and had her weekly salary raised "to four figures." The play achieved the biggest advance ticket sales ever recorded up to that time. Critics gave her rave reviews. The New York *Daily News* called her "the funniest female to hit the boards since Fannie Brice and Beatrice Lillie." Brooks Atkinson of *The New York Times* said, "Let us call her portrait of the aureate Lee the most fabulous comic creation of this dreary period in history." Several songs from the show became popular classics, and one in particular, "Diamonds Are a Girl's Best Friend" became, and remains, Channing's signature number.

The character of Lorelei was that of a beautiful but dumb golddigger determined to land a rich man, which she did. Lee couldn't spell and her speech was rife with malapropisms: "Possession is twelve-tenths of the law." The moral from the play was clear, it was the dumb woman who got the rich man, hence the ideal role model. In due course the question arose that since Carol was portraying a "birdbrain" was she really acting or doing what came naturally. One writer commented that "most everybody in the audience would swear that not a thought lurked behind that bland baby-face."

Or, put in a slightly different way, "a goodly part of the audience is convinced that only nature could have arranged so flawless a match of actress and role." Carol herself was quoted as saying that early in her life she would assume an air of idiocy whenever she felt threatened. At school she was often called into the principal's office for one reason or another and when he started to bawl Channing out she'd "just fall into this asinine girl role and sort of stare dumbly at him. It almost always worked."

Channing was only one of many female comics who found themselves in the dumb female role. In 1953 Carol played on Broadway for six months in *Wonderful Town,* and in 1955 she starred on Broadway in *The Vamp,* a musical comedy loosely based on the life of silent film star Theda Bara and put together specifically for Channing's talents. While Carol got good notices — "She looks like an overgrown kewpie. She sings like a moon-mad hillbilly. Her dancing is crazily comic" — the vehicle didn't and closed after 60 performances.

In 1957 she went back to the nightclub circuit with an act that featured impersonations of female show business people, both past and present, as well as songs from *Gentlemen Prefer Blondes.* For three years she toured the posher night spots of the country. She was back on the stage in 1961 in a New York revue, *Show Girl,* which was basically her nightclub material and which lasted for 100 performances. She returned again to the nightclub circuit and in 1962 briefly teamed up in a comedy act with George Burns. Burns was then without Gracie Allen and the Burns and Channing team tried to do Burns and Allen material. It didn't really work.

In January of 1964 she opened on Broadway in what proved to be her second smash hit. In *Hello Dolly!* she played Dolly Gallagher Levi, the redheaded, busybody widow determined to remarry for money. Channing had taken the part on condition that Gower Champion be hired to direct.

Champion said he initially didn't think Carol was right for the part. He changed his mind quickly when she auditioned, and she went on to acclaim and a three-year run. She wore a carrot colored wig instead of the blonde wig she usually wore, and still does, for her professional appearances. She accented her already large eyes with the help of "seven-ply, double-thick false lashes."

A decade after *Dolly,* she would return to Broadway in a reprise of her greatest role, Lorelei. Channing has won Tony, Emmy, and Grammy awards during her career. She has appeared in a few films, the most notable being *Thoroughly Modern Millie* (1967), and has appeared on television numerous times as a guest on most of the variety shows, on panel shows, and as the star of her own specials. However, the bulk of her career has taken place on the stage and in nightclubs, where she remained active into the 1980's. In the late 1970's her club routine consisted of songs such as "Diamonds Are a Girl's Best Friend," some Dolly vamping and impersonations of stars like Marlene Dietrich and Brigitte Bardot. Her stage character still retains many of the characteristics of her most famous role, Lorelei Lee, the quintessential female character.

She had always preferred comedy, since she received instant feedback from her audience. Not so with dramatic actresses, "because they can't hear anxiety in the audience the way I can hear laughter." Her voice has been described as a "well-modulated foghorn with the overtones of a caged canary." Partly because of this, and as a tribute to her talent, she was one of the most imitated show business women — and many of the mimics were men.

JUDY HOLLIDAY

Judy Holliday appeared in only a handful of films, and an even smaller number of stage plays. She had not started out with the intention of becoming a comedian or even an actress. But a comic she became, and a fine one at that. Jack Benny, an acknowledged master at the subtle art of timing, went to see her perform in order to study her timing. Like so many women comics of the early post World War II years she was cast in the mold of the dumb blonde. There were a lot of women trapped in that same box and one critic gave Judy Holliday the dubious distinction of being the "dumbest broad of them all."

Holliday was never happy with the kind of roles she was limited to and searched for a way out, either in dramatic roles or as a writer. She had not managed to escape the typecasting she felt so burdened with, and unfulfilled by, when death cut short her life and career. The number of her credits was relatively small, but she was a superstar from the mid 1940's until 1960. She left behind the image "as filmdon's No. 1 dimbrain." It was an image she had wanted to live without.

She was born Judith Tuvim in New York on June 21, 1921, the daughter of Abraham and Helen. For her birth Helen Tuvim went directly to the hospital after watching a performance by Fanny Brice. Her father was a professional fund raiser, mostly for Israel, and her mother was a piano teacher. Judy's only formal training was in voice lessons, which she took for several years as a child.

In school, at the age of ten, she took an IQ test and achieved a score of 172, a near-genius level. She was a prolific and prodigious reader, going through the classics at an age when most young readers were content with the "Bobsey Twins." At school she wrote plays and acted in them. One Christmas play she wrote featured herself as the director as well as the lead player. She graduated from high school at the age of sixteen and set her sights on entering the Yale School of Drama where she hoped to become a playwright. Her plans were frustrated, however, when she found she was a year too young for admission.

Instead she went to work at New York's Mercury Theatre, then under the direction of Orson Welles, to pick up some theatrical experience. However, she ended up operating the backstage telephone switchboard. She left that post after a bout with a throat infection, and her mother decided to take her off to the Catskills to recuperate. While she was there in the summer of 1938 she met a young man named Adolph Green, who was part of a theatrical group called the "Theater of Six" which toured the eastern seaboard summer resort circuit putting on farces and performances of Chekhov one-act plays. Judy persuaded Green to give her a short stint as stage manager. Her duties included producing the sound effects offstage.

She was back in New York City that fall and at loose ends when one day she got caught in a thunderstorm and took shelter at the nearest place. That happened to be a club called the Village Vanguard, which featured, as their entertainment, poets reading their works. She got talking to the club owner and told him she thought the club needed some new and different entertainment, such as the "Theater of Six." The owner was agreeable to the suggestion, but not prepared to pay very much. Judy quickly got in touch with Green, who also liked the idea. The trouble was that none of the other members were interested in performing on the owner's terms. Green was able to find three new people, including Betty Comden, and the five formed a group called the "Revuers." They were paid $5 each to perform once a week on Sundays.

They proved to be such a big hit that within six months they were performing nightly and were paid $250 a week. They wrote all their own material and their act consisted of songs and skits. Their sketches were often satirical and they lampooned everything under the sun, including Franco, Fascism, Hearst, and political witch hunters of the day. They also did takeoffs on theater personalities and various aspects of show business. One was a sendup of a Joan Crawford fan club, another was a spoof of the lavish type of musical produced by the Shuberts. They also did a "documentary" on the life of a man who invented the shoehorn. They were unsure of the kind of reception they would get initially, so "we walked on backward because we thought it would be safer. Then, if the crowd hated us, we could leave in a hurry."

It took Judy about a year to get over her stage fright. She used to throw up before every performance and hated the whole idea of being an actress. "Finally," she said, "I began to get kind of good." They put on as many as three shows a night and wrote their material in the afternoons. Later Holliday would call this phase of her career the most satisfying. The group spent about five years in various New York night spots, where they became favorites of the intelligentsia and achieved wide critical success. According to Judy they gained a lot of prestige but not much money, and when one day a movie producer gave them an oral promise of a movie if they went to Hollywood, they were only to happy and eager to accept.

When they arrived in Hollywood the four "Revuers" (the fifth person had left the act after the first couple of years) found that the movie wasn't going to be made and their oral promise was worthless. The group got work in area clubs, including the Trocadero, where they earned their highest ever salary, $1,000 a week. They were hoping to attract the attention of movie producers, but while producers did take in their act, they left saying things like "You're smart and you're funny—too damn smart. I understand your stuff, but nobody else does."

It was while she was in Hollywood that Judy changed her name from Tuvim to Holliday. In Hebrew, Tuvim means "holiday" and

Judy was tired of people misspelling and mispronouncing her name. She had been called names like Twin, Turmine, and even Termite. The Revuers may not have been drawing movie offers but Judy was, offers that didn't include the rest of the group. She refused to accept any of these, insisting that the whole group be included. The group was equally adamant that Judy should not miss her chance and should go off on her own.

A compromise was worked out with 20th Century-Fox in 1944 which had Judy signing a seven-year contract, starting at $400 a week, and the Revuers all appearing in the first movie. That film was called *Greenwich Village* and featured three bits by the group, all of which, however, ended up on the cutting room floor. In the film's final version Betty Comden appeared briefly by herself; none of the other Revuers, including Judy, appeared at all.

At that point the group disbanded. Green and Comden went back to New York and on to fame as the writing duo of many Broadway hits. Judy remained in Hollywood but did very little work for the studio. She had small parts in two other 1944 films, but mostly she "didn't do a stitch of work for months and months." In one of the films she had only one line to speak. She was bored, homesick for New York, and disenchanted. Fox must have felt the same way and they mutually agreed to drop her contract.

Holliday returned to New York and renewed acquaintances with Green, who put her in touch with a man casting a play called *Kiss Them for Me*. The play was a fast-paced comedy about a prostitute who tried to comfort war weary fliers on their return home from combat. Holliday played what one critic described as "a dumb but sweet little tart," another referred to the character as a "blonde stumblebum." *Variety* commented that "Judy Holliday . . . scores a decisive triumph as this moronic but devastating nitwit; she's going places." Judy herself called it "the most moronic part I ever played." The show ran for 110 performances and Holliday stole the show, garnering rave critical reviews. The role won her the Clarence Derwent award for best supporting actress of 1945. She spent the next six months unemployed until her big break in January of 1946.

The Garson Kanin play *Born Yesterday* had opened in New England with pre-Broadway tryouts in December of 1945. The lead female role was played by Jean Arthur. In January Arthur had to leave the cast due to illness and the show's producer, remembering her work in *Kiss Them for Me*, put in a call for

Judy. That was on a Wednesday and she opened in Philadelphia on Saturday. The producer was willing to take a chance on Holliday, a relative unknown, because he knew that any name star would demand more than three days' time to prepare for the show. Judy opened in Philadelphia that month and within a few weeks was on Broadway.

The play ran almost four years, closing December 31, 1949, after Judy had given 1,643 performances. She had appeared in all the performances save for a short leave she took in 1949 to appear in a film. She played Billie Dawn, an ex-chorus girl who lived in Washington, D.C., as mistress to a rich junk dealer who tried to build an empire, through bribery and profiteering, out of war scrap. Afraid that Billie was too dumb to take her place with polite society, the tycoon hired a liberal young writer to educate her. After a couple of months of this tutoring, the expected happened. Billie became a solid citizen, got wise to the junk dealer, and brought about his downfall.

She was a smash hit and had created one of the stage's funniest and most memorable characterizations. As Billie Dawn she was described as "using a voice like a rusty diaper pin, a walk as languorous as sap at sugaring-off time and a stare of unblinking vacuity." She had a "floozie's walk, an asparagus tip hairdo, the voice of a truculent Brooklyn urchin and the deceptively innocent eyes of a predatory kitten." Holliday did not consider herself to be particularly attractive, but part of her appeal was that of the blonde sex object.

Judy had become the country's "favorite female dimwit of the day," she was the "quintessence of dumb blondeness." Jack Benny attended this play twice, once specifically to study Holliday's timing.

In 1948 Columbia Pictures acquired the movie rights to the play for the then astronomical sum of $1 million. Logic would seem to dictate that the role go to Holliday. Columbia's headman was Harry Cohn and he thought otherwise. He didn't think Holliday was right for the part, not glamorous enough. He announced he wanted a "name" for the part and launched a futile year-long search for one. He then announced he wanted an unknown for the part, which further insulted and irked Judy.

In 1949 she took a leave from the play to appear in the film *Adam's Rib*, written by Garson Kanin and starring Spencer Tracy and Katherine Hepburn. This was part of an effort by Kanin and Hepburn to help Holliday get the part in the film version of *Born*

Yesterday. They hoped her appearance in *Adam's Rib* would help sway Cohn, for they both admired her work. She portrayed another dizzy dame in a supporting role in the comedy and ended up stealing the show from the two major stars. Her performance was termed one of the funniest features of the movie and her acting "a simply hilarious representation of a dumb but stubborn dame."

After a casting search of some 28 months which was said to have rivalled that done for *Gone With the Wind* Cohn finally announced he had signed Holliday for the film and to a seven-year, one-picture-a-year contract. Cohn then went around saying that "he had her in mind all along." Cohn had hoped she would agree to a three-picture-a-year deal but Judy held out for only one picture per year. She had never been happy in Hollywood and much preferred New York City. She lived simply and quietly and shunned the world of parties and fashion. The one-picture deal allowed her to minimize the amount of time she would have to spend in Hollywood. The film was released in 1950 and was as successful as the play. Her performance earned Judy the Oscar for best actress of 1950.

Holliday had been working on writing a play at that time. She hoped to eventually direct it herself, as a way of escaping from the "dumb" image she had been saddled with. But nothing ever came of the project. She was horrified by the idea of being typed as a dumb blonde and longed for something serious. She was sick of fans coming up to her and demanding she talk like Billie Dawn. After *Born Yesterday* her aim was to never play a dumb blonde again, something she didn't succeed in doing. About her roles she remarked, "I started off as a moron in *Kiss Them for Me,* worked my way up to imbecile in *Adam's Rib,* and have carved my current niche as a noble nitwit. Now I want a part where I can use my own hair, my own voice, and maybe even be literate." She never got that far, as the type-casters confined her to roles she described as the kind where "you see them walk on the stage and you laugh." She cynically wondered where she could go from being an imbecile. "Maybe If I'm lucky, I can be an idiot or cretin." She would make only a half dozen more movies and largely remained the dim-brained airhead. Critics referred to the type as "shrewd featherhead" and "sensible screwball" and as a "female Mortimer Snerd."

In the early 1950's she began to be a frequent guest star on TV variety shows. This aspect of her career came to a quick halt when in March of 1952 she found herself called before the Senate Internal Security Subcommittee to testify. This was at the height of the Joe McCarthy era, in which the Senate was investigating people for supposed Communist connections and sympathies. Holliday was an unlikely candidate to be investigated and she confounded the committee by adopting her Billie Dawn character to the hilt and giving vague, confusing, and nonsensical answers to queries. It was one of the few times that the stereotype came in handy.

The committee drew no conclusions about Judy and made no recommendations. She had done nothing worse than sign an occasional petition about something or other and had once had her photo taken with a group of strikers, for publicity purposes. Nevertheless, she remained on the television blacklist for years. A weekly show she had signed for was abruptly cancelled. She was allowed to keep making movies primarily because Cohn went to bat for her.

In 1956 she was back on Broadway appearing in the musical comedy *Bells Are Ringing* by her old friends Green and Comden in a role especially tailored to her talents. It was her first musical and she sang and danced acceptably. She also got to display her considerable abilities as a mimic and parodied the secretary to the Duchess of Windsor, a French restaurant owner, and a Marlon Brando style female. She played the part of a telephone answering service operator in the play who got mixed up in her client's lives as both friend and advisor. It goes without saying the character wasn't too bright. The play ran more than two years. She appeared in the film version in 1960, her last film.

By 1960 Judy looked back and was unsatisfied with her movie career. She considered it to be respectable but insignificant. She was still searching for roles which would get her away from the Billie Dawn syndrome. That year she got the chance to appear in a play called *Laurette,* a straight dramatic biography based on the life of the actress Laurette Taylor. Holliday quickly grabbed the opportunity, and the play opened in New Haven.

Unfortunately the play that meant so much to her had to be cancelled when she developed throat problems. She was booed one night by the audience when she was able to do no more than mumble her lines. A medical check diagnosed breast cancer and she underwent a mastectomy. The press was told she had a benign throat tumor and when the cancer killed her in 1965 it was reported as throat cancer. It was only years later that it was publicly revealed to have been breast cancer. In those days women didn't publicize breast cancer or mastectomies.

Around 1960 she had begun to write songs, with Gerry Mulligan a jazz saxophonist as a collaborator. One was used by Dinah Shore on a Christmas TV show. It was the closest Holliday got to her childhood dream to be a writer and was very satisfying to her. She went onstage for the last time in a 1963 musical about the Peace Corps called *Hot Spot*. The vehicle was a turkey and Holliday didn't care for it from the start. She did it for the money, as she faced mounting expenses from her illness and the Internal Revenue Service was after back taxes in the amount of $99,000. The show was a short lived disaster but Judy got good notices for her performance. She died June 7, 1965, two years short of her forty-fourth birthday.

Inevitably the question was raised in print as to whether or not she was really dumb. "Is Judy Holliday just a dimwitted dame?" With a near genius I.Q. the answer was obvious. Judy may have hated Billie Dawn type roles but she played them wonderfully well, too well. She had a great rapport with the audience and they always wanted to see another Billie Dawn. Judy Holliday, whom director George Cukor once likened to Chaplin in the way each could touch the depths of emotion, had her own way of handling the dumb blonde image. "All I have to do is remember to be dumb when I'm out, and smart when I'm home."

MARTHA RAYE

Martha Raye was best known as the lady with the big mouth, and has been called "elastic mouth," "rubber mouth," and "tunnel mouth." Like other women comics who have had epithets of a physical nature hurled at them, the ones thrown Martha Raye's way have been exaggerated. She fit the classic personality profile of a comedian in that she was insecure and sought attention and approval. Her personal life had been troubled enough to keep gossip columnists happy. Martha Raye was rarely "off." Put her in contact with strangers and as likely as not she would commence a show.

She was born Margaret Theresa Yvonne Reed on August 27, 1916, in Butte, Montana. Her parents had a song, dance, and

comedy act, specializing in physical comedy, and were on tour on
the vaudeville circuit when Martha's mother gave birth. Her
parents, Pete Reed and Mabelle Hooper, were Irish immigrants
and performed under the name Reed and Hooper. A second
billing they sometimes used was "The Girl and the Traveler." Two
days after giving birth Mabelle was back performing on stage. At
the age of three Martha joined her parents' act by singing, mugging, and making clown faces. Being a performer seemed to be
her destiny. Years later she remarked, "I can't imagine being anything but an entertainer."

Her formal schooling was very erratic, as she was only able to
attend when her family's act settled for a while in one spot. In
addition to the few public schools she attended she also went to
the Professional Children's School in New York City. Most of her
learning came on the road, with her mother teaching her to read
and write. Martha remembers those years as ones in which the
family often didn't have enough to eat, but they were basically
happy. Martha's younger brother Bud was now part of the act
and as the children became more experienced performers they
began to become the central features of the act.

The result was that the name of the act was changed to Bud
and Margie. They sometimes made as much as $400 a week.
Then suddenly the act was less in demand. They slid down to
working only one week out of every three, and then down to one
in six, and then down to club dates and one-night stands such as
a $15 booking for an Elks Club meeting. The family was reduced
to using their car for both eating and sleeping. According to Martha the act was as good as ever but nobody was booking them,
and "We never knew why." Martha was then fifteen and at this
low point in the family career she went to see Paul Ash, a former
vaudevillian who had toured the same circuit as Martha and was
then a rising bandleader. Martha auditioned for Ash and was
hired as the band's singer.

She performed mainly as a band singer for the next few years.
During this period she decided she needed a new stage name, and
from the Manhattan phone book she randomly selected the name
Martha Raye. It was also during this period that she developed
her high-powered, high-volume singing style. She truly belted out
a song with all the emotion and volume she could muster doing
her versions of pop songs of the period. It was a style very much
related to the earlier coon shouters. The reported, and exaggerated, size of Raye's mouth—not tiny to be sure, but nowhere

nearly as large as was suggested—may stem in part from her singing style, which emphasized opening her mouth as wide as possible.

Martha then got a featured part in a Broadway musical revue, *Calling All Stars,* in 1934. As a newcomer many of her songs were cut from the production as it was put into final form, but she did get to play several comic sequences when the woman for whom they were originally intended proved unequal to the task.

One reviewer wasn't overly impressed: "Martha Raye is a shouter of hot songs, and fairly trying in the assignment." It was a pattern that would continue throughout her career. She received more bad reviews than good, unlike many of the other female comics who were often singled out for praise in spite of a bad vehicle. However, the most important critics, those who voted with their wallets, loved Martha Raye and her slapstick antics. Her most memorable routine from *Calling All Stars* was a drunk bit which she would use again and again in the future.

Raye continued to sing at clubs across the country such as the Chez Paree and Riviera in New York, and the Century Club in Hollywood, where she earned $100 a week. However, she often had to play clubs for much lower salaries and at times she had no bookings at all. To earn extra money she worked at the Cedars of Lebanon Hospital in Los Angeles as a nurse's aide, and later actually became a registered nurse. In order to get her career back on track she adopted the practice of singing for free at various Los Angeles clubs. It was at one of those clubs, the Trocadero, where she was doing her loud singing ("When I opened my mouth, they thought it was a cave-in") that she was spotted by film director Norman Taurog, who promptly signed her to a $1,300 a week contract for a part in his Paramount movie *Rhythm on the Range* (1936), which had already begun shooting.

Studios were then heavily into musical revue films to highlight various specialty performers, and the time was right for Martha. As an indication of how threadbare the plots were in these films, and how easily changeable they were, Taurog had no part in his already begun film for Martha, so he simply had one quickly written and inserted.

In the film she played the fourth billed character and performed a great many broad slapstick bits. She did her drunk routine, double takes, tripped over anything and everything, and mugged. She sang a word song titled "Mr. Paganini" which became wildly popular and which she also used repeatedly over the years. Taurog had essentially let Raye run wild in the film with all the bits she had, and applied only loose direction. Despite her rather uncontrolled performance, critics were generally pleased. "Martha Raye is a stridently funny comedienne with a mammoth cave, or early Joe E. Brown, mouth. . . . Hollywood has found a truly remarkable pantomimist." Her career got a quick boost and Paramount signed her to a five-year deal. She got more nightclub bookings and endorsed various makeup products. She also appeared regularly on the Al Jolson radio program in 1938.

About her performance in *College Holiday* (1936), a critic stated, "Martha Raye remains for me a young girl with a big mouth and very little aptitude for clowning." The next year in *Waikiki Wedding* she was the woman with "the elastic mouth, the rubbery legs and the amazing holler." She got to fall off awnings, leap off porches and take lots of pratfalls. One critic remarked, "Martha came up fast and she'll go down the same way if she doesn't richen her mixture." Another film reviewer wrote, "The big-mouthed comedienne works too hard and is continually forcing her comedy."

While critics tended to attack Raye's habit of repetition and overly broad, non-subtle and raucous slapstick, the audience continued to turn out for her in large numbers. Her last film in 1937, *Artists and Models,* involved her in a bizarre story. One of the musical numbers had a Harlem setting with Louis Armstrong on trumpet and Martha Raye made up with burnt cork. At the time it was felt that "the intermingling of the races isn't wise . . . it may hurt her personally." For some years thereafter many people thought Raye was part black, and when she tried to rent an apartment in Greenwich Village in the late 1930's she was turned down for what later turned out to be racial reasons.

Raye continued in the same kinds of roles for Paramount, sometimes man-hungry, sometimes not, but she never played anything near a glamorous or romantic role, despite the fact she had a better figure than some women. In a 1938 release, *Give Me a Sailor,* the studio decided to try an image change. Martha displayed her usual comic behavior by wrestling with a facial mudpack, and turning household duties into slapstick routines. Through a plot twist she inadvertently won a beautiful legs contest and became glamorous for the last half of this film. She even won the film's male lead and love interest away from co-star Betty

Grable. But the fans were displeased with Martha's image. Paramount quickly reverted to slapstick for Martha and ugly duckling characters.

Her film career began to slide as Paramount put her in shoddier and shoddier vehicles. From 1936 to 1938 she appeared in 12 Paramount films, and then only three more over the next two years. On the final day of shooting *The Farmer's Daughter* (1940) Paramount slipped a note under her dressing room door dismissing her. In that film she fell down stairs, tripped over ladders, and caught her foot in cans. "Her stock in trade—mugging, tumbling and strutting—is funny at first, but rapidly becomes tiresome because of continuous repetition," wrote another disenchanted critic. Raye then went freelance and made four films in 1940-41, three for Universal, and two for 20th Century-Fox in 1944, all similar to her previous work. In the 1941 release, *Keep 'Em Flying,* she played second string to the team of Abbott and Costello. Raye played twin sisters and one memorable routine took place at a lunch counter where the hungry Costello tried to eat a piece of cake which was alternately placed before him by the good-hearted twin and taken away by the bad-tempered one.

While her career may have been waning in film, Martha was doing well in other media. She returned to what was left of the vaudeville circuit, attracting large, enthusiastic audiences. One of her strong points was her penchant for ad-libbing, something that went over well in live presentations but not in film. She was a popular and regular guest on many radio variety programs, and she returned to Broadway in the 1940 musical revue *Hold on to Your Hats.* Reviewers were enthusiastic: "She is about three hundred times better on the stage than she was on the screen."

In the mid-1940's Martha went on an extended USO tour of North Africa along with three other female Hollywood personalities. One of her 1944 films, *Four Jills in a Jeep,* was based on that trip, for which she earned critical praise. Her "comedy has never been more raucous, rough and pleasing," said one critic. Yet her professional work had come to a halt by 1946 when Charlie Chaplin suddenly signed her for his 1947 film *Monsieur Verdoux.*

For one of the few times in her career she won near unanimous critical praise for her playing opposite Chaplin in a light comedy. But audiences had apparently been expecting slapstick and the film was a bomb at the box office. Contributing to the lack of success may have been Chaplin's unpopularity in America at the time, with tax troubles and his alleged Communist tendencies. In any event, this box-office disaster put a near end to Raye's film career. She wouldn't make another movie for 15 years.

Chaplin reminded Raye that her strong suit was slapstick and he offered her some advice for future appearances, in whatever medium. It was advice that a good many female comedians would follow in the future, not just Raye. He advised her to dress well and impeccably and to be sure her makeup and hair were perfect. That way she would be even funnier just tripping instead of doing a pratfall in plain clothes.

She continued doing club work and even had a one-month booking at London's Palladium. She was surprised to get good reviews, not being certain if her broad style would appeal to the staid British. She also appeared extensively in one night spot in Miami Beach, the Five O'Clock Club, primarily because she had become the owner of the place. Other than club work though, her career was in a slump after the Chaplin movie. Commenting on those years Raye said, "I couldn't even get arrested in Hollywood. Nobody seemed to give a damn whether I made another picture or not, and the only work I could get was club dates."

She might never have gotten into TV at all if it hadn't been for Milton Berle going to bat for her. He "literally dragged" her into this new medium as a frequent guest on his show. He then badgered the NBC chiefs into giving Raye her own program. He even once proposed tying her into his own contract to ensure she would get a fair deal. She made guest appearances on other shows as well, including the comedy variety *All-Star Revue* during the 1951-52 season. The next year she was one of the many rotating hosts of the show, starring in four one-hour episodes. Her rough and rugged brand of physical comedy caught on with audiences, many of whom had never seen her before.

Finally NBC gave her her own series, "The Martha Raye Show," which debuted in December 1953. For the 1953-54 and 1954-55 seasons the hour show was seen once a month. For the 1955-56 season her show was aired 13 times. Rocky Graziano was featured as her chief comic foil. During the 1954-55 season her show reached ninth spot in the ratings, trailing Lucy, Hope, and Benny, but ahead of George Gobel and Berle. The program was largely unstructured comedy variety during its first two years, but in its final year told a complete story, in a musical comedy format, every episode.

During the peak of her TV career she was earning $150,000 a year and negotiated a 15-year deal with NBC. Her TV character remained consistent with that of the past. On the tube she pranced violently, grimaced, mugged, and shouted her songs. Raye was cast as an addlehead who got into impossible situations and somehow extricated herself, usually through physical, as opposed to mental, means.

She put enormous energy into her work. For her TV shows she rehearsed almost 60 hours and was never content to walk through a rehearsal, always going full tilt. As an example of her never being "off," after she had finished a day at the TV studio she would take the commuter train home to Connecticut from New York. Her custom was to go straight to the bar car, help the crew serve drinks, and generally liven up the trip. At a party she would perform and clown for hours. During the late 1930's, during her sojourn as a radio performer, when she had finished her work she would often make the rounds of nightclubs, as a patron, but still wind up onstage giving a free exhibition of her talents.

In the midst of her TV series at least one critic hailed Raye as "the country's No. I comedienne . . . the unqualified queen of buffoon." But the magic of her show had started to slip by the time of her third and final season. One of the reasons was that chief writer Nat Hiken had left to do the Phil Silvers "Sergeant Bilko" show. The critics were now much less kind. "Martha Raye proved that slapstick can be tasteless." Another said, "Martha Raye is an exasperating girl. When she is given the right material . . . she can be a true mistress of slapstick. But when not afforded every protection, she can exhaust a viewer's patience."

Raye's personal life had its share of troubles, all of which were noted in detail by the press. In the summer of 1956 a new crisis evolved which almost brought her TV career to an end. That summer she commenced divorce proceedings against her fifth husband, all her previous marriages having ended similarly. Late in the previous year she had received a series of threatening phone calls at her Connecticut home. Moving to Florida she hired a number of bodyguards while she established residency in that state to begin divorce proceedings.

In April of 1956, Barbara Ann O'Shea, wife of Bob O'Shea, who was one of the bodyguards, charged Raye with being a homewrecker and stealing her husband. Mrs. O'Shea was then preparing to give birth to her first child. She sued Raye for $50,000 in damages. Added to this were problems she was having in establishing Florida residency. All of this culminated in a suicide attempt by Raye in August. Eventually Martha settled with

Mrs. O'Shea out of court for $20,000 and married Bob. Within a few years this union ended in divorce, with O'Shea claiming Raye had promised him $60,000 if he would marry her.

Television work came to a halt for her at that time, but she still had plenty of nightclub bookings, an area where she could put her talents for ad-libbing and off-the-cuff remarks to their best advantage. She also had a propensity for using blue material, something only acceptable in the clubs. Legend has it that when she guested on the Red Skelton TV show, she and Red would engage, during rehearsal, in a battle to see who could outgross the other. Raye was more than able to hold her own, and Red was notorious for his very "blue" rehearsals. In 1958 she and NBC reached a settlement in which what remained of their 15-year deal was torn up. The network was then doing nothing for her.

That same year Steve Allen was doing a comedy series for NBC and he suggested booking Raye as a guest. He was told she had a reputation for being undependable and "She's dead in the business. Forget her." Allen refused to listen and insisted that she be allowed on his show. Ultimately she appeared a dozen times on the Allen program with good results. It should be noted that Allen also insisted on full control over Martha on his show, telling her she was to "put herself in our hands and trust us to make all the right decisions."

Steve Allen also recognized Martha as one of the very few in the comedy field who could be truly funny without a script, resorting to physical routines to get laughs, rather than verbal wit. Red Skelton was another from the same group.

Her television career was revived and she made the rounds of the comedy shows as a guest star during the 1960's. Early on in that decade she began to do summer stock, appearing in such vehicles as *The Solid Gold Cadillac, Calamity Jane,* and *Wildcat.* She became a tent circuit favorite and often resorted to the ruse of booting her lines so she could then ad lib. Audiences enjoyed the practice but it was hard on the other actors in the show. "One of the difficulties of acting with Martha Raye seems to be that you never know what she's going to say next."

In 1962 she appeared in the MGM musical circus movie *Jumbo.* She played the fortune teller Lulu and displayed her talents as a human cannonball, clown, tattooed lady, and imitation lioness. She appeared as the long-standing fiancée of Jimmy Durante finally dragging him to the altar after some 14 years. Touted as

Raye's comeback film, the movie received a poor critical reception but did fairly well at the box office. Martha's performance was singled out, however, for critical acclaim. She had brief roles in two undistinguished 1970 films. Her own summation of her film career is one of bitterness. She has described herself as being "used." Of her films she has said that "most of them were mindless."

Martha worked entertaining the troops during the Vietnam War, something she had done during World War II and the Korean War. Beginning in 1965 and continuing for the next seven or eight years she spent four months of each year in Vietnam entertaining the troops for nothing. She spent more time there than any other entertainer and received several citations for her work. For Raye the work was important because "I'm military and I'm proud."

She was back on Broadway in 1967 in *Hello Dolly*. In the early 1970's she appeared for a few seasons on a Saturday morning kids' show, "The Bugaloos," in which she portrayed a witch named Benita Bizarre. In the 1976-77 season she appeared on the "McMillan and Wife" series, renamed "McMillan" that year. She played the part of Agatha the maid, replacing Nancy Walker who had played the servant role for the previous five seasons. Walker had left to do her own show. In the 1980's Martha returned to TV as a semi-regular on the CBS situation comedy, "Alice."

In real life Martha Raye has been described as thoughtful, serious, soft spoken, and often lonely, seeking attention and affection. But because of her strength of character she has never been described as "vulnerable." She has devoted her life to her craft: "My career is my whole life. I'll always work," she said. Raye had been at her best when engaging in that lowest form of comedy, broad slapstick, portrayed through a good-natured buffoon character. Both Nancy Walker and Carol Burnett have been influenced by her. She was a superior mimic and pantomimist, but her image of the schnook was the one that has prevailed. She was best remembered as the "homely knockabout," the "brash, slapstick, not-too-bright lady clown." This image has never seemed to bother her: "She has the wisdom to allow people to think of her as the professional dunce."

Steve Allen admitted that the size of Raye's mouth was exaggerated for the purpose of publicity and easy laughs. He has acted as a male apologist of sorts by pointing out the same thing has happened to male comics of that era such as Hope, and Durante with jokes about their noses, Eddie Cantor's eyes, and Joe E. Brown's mouth, and that it was typical of the times. Up to a point that's true.

But when jokes about the men were made, such as the ones about Durante's nose, there was no ridicule or viciousness involved. The size of the object in the case of the men made it a source of pride, something to be admired and to be proud of. *The New York Times* reported that once, long ago, Raye sued a magazine to restrain them from publishing a photo comparing her to a chimpanzee. Another writer commented on Raye's mouth by saying "it stretched to a gargantuan shape, the mouth of an ape or cow." No doubt crude insults like these made Raye conclude, "I'm a clown . . . not a comedienne. . . . It is hard . . . for a woman to get laughs in a fast-fire situation and remain feminine."

IMOGENE COCA

Imogene Coca became known as the woman with the rubber face. Like so many other women comics she was pursuing a career as a straight performer when she accidentally got into comedy. She then parlayed her amazing facial grimaces and other comic attributes to become one of the top comedians around in the early 1950's. Teamed with Sid Caesar in the television series "Your Show of Shows," she and the program became a classic.

She was born in Philadelphia in 1911, or thereabouts, the daughter of Joseph Coca, the orchestra conductor for Philadelphia's Chestnut Street Opera House. His father had been a music teacher. Her mother, Sadie Brady, had run away from home at an early age to join the traveling company of a magician, Howard Thurston. She later became a dancer and actress in vaudeville. Imogene's father was of Spanish descent and the family name had at one time been Fernandez y Coca.

Imogene got an early induction into show business and was enrolled for piano, singing, and dancing lessons between the ages of five and seven. Thanks to her father's theatrical connections she made her stage debut early. She recalled with shudders the amateur nature of those child parts. "I began [on the stage] as one of those horrible little children who sing with no voice." At nine she made a vaudeville appearance as a tap dancer and at eleven had an engagement at Philadelphia's Dixie Theater singing "personality" songs.

When she finished grade school her parents asked her if she wanted to continue on at school or begin her career full time. The choice was easy for Coca, and at fourteen she became a full-time trouper. At the age of fifteen she left home and made her way to New York City. Her first stage appearance was during the 1925-26 season, when she appeared as a dancer in the chorus of the musical *When You Smile*. Over the following decade she appeared in the chorus of several other shows and performed in supper clubs and night clubs such as Jimmy Durante's Silver Slipper Club and the Fifth Avenue Club. She also appeared in vaudeville, as a dancing partner with Leonard Sillman, and later in an act with Solly Ward, whom she later married.

Her early years in New York were difficult financially and on occasion she went hungry in seedy hotels, or slept in Grand Central Station. Up until 1934 her roles had all been minor and straight. In that year her ex-vaudeville partner Leonard Sillman was producing a revue called *New Faces* and hired Imogene at a salary of $40 per week.

During a pause in rehearsals at the cold theater, Coca borrowed a topcoat from a man to help keep her warm. The coat was far too large for her and, being struck by her own ludicrous appearance, Coca began to clown around the stage doing an imitation fan dance with the loose hanging ends of the coat. Sillman saw it and liked the ad-lib routine enough to insert it into the show, along with a few other routines he then thought up for her. The reviews were good and she was marked by the critics as a "rising young comedienne."

During the next ten years she appeared in featured roles as a comic in a number of Broadway shows, including seven produced by Sillman. She also performed in nightclubs and at Catskill resorts. In the Catskills she got room and board and $700 a season. In her club act she satirized everything from torch singers to fur fashion shows and was described as having the "light lunatic touch." She played a water sprite and did a takeoff of Carmen Miranda.

During the early 1940's her husband joined the armed forces and Coca was still having a difficult time financially. She had not achieved any sort of wide fame and was not assured of a steady income. She went back to Philadelphia to live with her mother

and seriously considered dropping out of show business. She
remarked that, "I'm spending three-fourths of my life out of
work."

Things picked up for her and the mid 1940's saw her receive
more and more nightclub engagements. Among others she
appeared at New York City's Le Ruban Bleu, Cafe Society
Uptown, Blue Angel, as well as the Park Plaza in St. Louis and
the Palmer House in Chicago. The "elfin satirist" poked fun at
all-girl bands and lampooned the changing style in Hollywood
femme fatales over the previous twenty years. She received critical
praise and began to build a bigger following.

By the end of the 1940's she had a loyal, but not large, following. This would soon be altered by her breakthrough into television. In 1949 she appeared as a featured player on NBC's
"Admiral Broadway Revue," after being signed by Max Liebman,
a producer she had worked for previously in summer stock. The
show's advertising agency had reservations and objected to Coca's
signing. Over the years she had achieved a highbrow reputation,
since she had appeared in "Broadway shows of the ultrasophisti-
cated type, [and] played in nightclubs catering to the smart set."
When Coca had complained that she only worked about one-
fourth of the time, she had also said that she spent that time
"among people so chic you can hardly stand them."

The qualms about her appeal to the masses were groundless, of
course. Coca was an immediate hit on the show, along with Sid
Caesar. This was actually not her first stint as a regular on a
television series, but the first was so swift it was hardly noticeable.
Coca appeared in an ABC comedy variety show called "Buzzy
Wuzzy" in November 1948. She and comedian Jerry Bergen were
the regulars on this once-a-week fifteen-minute show which lasted
only four weeks.

The "Admiral Broadway Revue" ran from January to June of
1949 and resembled a Broadway show, with well-known guest
stars, lavish production numbers and, of course, lots of comedy
skits. It was many weeks before Coca and Caesar actually worked
together on the show. Initially the writers weren't writing for Coca
and she was on her own in terms of providing material. They
were then primarily writing for Caesar, who had come to the
show with the biggest string of successes behind him.

Imogene went along from show to show using the material she
had developed for her night club routines and summer resort
work. Finally she was out of fresh material and she asked pro-

ducer Liebman for ideas. He suggested she do a pantomime piece she had done on Broadway some twelve years previous. It was a two-person piece which she had done with her husband. Coca hoped the producer would hire her husband for the part, but instead Liebman suggested she do it with Caesar. She barely knew Sid then, since the performers worked in separate cubicles. Nevertheless, the routine went well and was successful.

The next week Coca and Caesar did another routine which was a smash. From then on they worked together on the show, doing about four routines as a team and maybe one each on their own. The writers began to write for both of them.

The next year NBC brought out a successor to the "Broadway Revue" which debuted in February 1950 and went off the air in June 1954. It starred Coca and Caesar and was called "Your Show of Shows." It was one of the most ambitious programs undertaken in television history. It was a live, 90-minute, original comedy show broadcast weekly on Saturday nights. It had singers and dancers, but mostly sketches. Each week featured a different big-name star who functioned as the nominal host.

Some 25 years after the program began, "Saturday Night Live" copied the same format and become a big hit on television. Years after "Your Show of Shows" had left the air, a movie was released called *Ten From Your Show of Shows* which consisted of a series of skits from the program.

This Caesar-Coca series came to dominate its time spot and would become something of a cult classic. What set it apart from other shows quite simply was that it was good. One of the reasons was an excellent supporting cast, including Carl Reiner and Howard Morris. The show also had outstanding writers who would go on to even greater successes. These included Neil Simon, Mel Brooks, and Woody Allen. However, it was the comic interplay between Coca and Caesar for which the show was remembered.

They appeared in regular bits on the show, such as "History As She Ain't" and in full-blown satires of other television shows and current movies. they also did a sketch as a battling husband and wife in "The Hickenloopers." Among her solo routines Coca did songs, impersonations, dances, pantomimes, and monologues. She also did a satire on ballet, spoofed torch singers, impersonated a spinster giving a lecture, and did her regular pantomime as a happy hobo, one of her best-known and popular routines. She received acclaim from critics for her "astonishing versatility" and was called a "master of pantomime."

A poll taken by the Hearst newspaper chain rated her the top comedienne in television, and in 1951 she was named the "Tops in TV". in a poll conducted by the *Saturday Review of Literature*. The "pixyish" Imogene Coca, in real life described as a shy and gentle person, had attained the lofty heights of being called by at least one critic, "The finest comedienne in the country today."

She was being compared to the likes of Beatrice Lillie and Charlie Chaplin. The weekly audience for "Your Show of Shows" peaked at about fifteen million viewers. One of her most memorable skits, performed in pantomime with Caesar, reinforced her image of a rubber face. Caesar was a photographer who was trying to rearrange the features of his model, Coca, to make them more photogenic. He pushed, pulled, and kneaded her features and they stayed wherever he put them. He pulled her mouth down and there it stayed. He twisted her nose which "sags like an overwarm candle" and it remained out of kilter. As Liebman once noted, "her left nostril never knows what the right one is doing." For Imogene the whole rubber face thing was accidental, something that just occurred. "It just sort of happens, unplanned. I mean, I never even set out to be a comedienne."

She also earned praise from the critics for her subtle, low-keyed approach to satire as opposed to the sledgehammer, overkill method. She remembers the show as being partly improvisational, with the cast sitting around at weekly meetings generating ideas. From the beginning Coca and Caesar worked well together, and they complemented each other in timing. A certain chemistry existed between them so that each could sense when a routine wasn't going well. Little or no verbal communication was necessary to perfect routines. It was a matter of instinct.

Nowhere was that chemistry more apparent than when they played a married couple on the show. From the time they first did such a routine on the air, many in the audience failed to distinguish between fantasy and reality. Fans sent in floods of mail containing knickknacks for their home and toys and trinkets for their kids. The number of children the mythical Hickenloopers had varied from none to over a dozen, depending on the needs of the skit. Letters would come to one or the other with advice on how to handle their mate. When some fans heard the pair weren't really married to each other, they refused to believe it. If Coca or Caesar were out in public with their real spouses they would often get knowing looks and sly winks from passersby.

When the show left the air in June 1954 the parting was a friendly one, with Coca and Caesar each going on to pursue individual careers. One of the reasons for the show's demise was given as a slow but steady slippage in the ratings. More importantly was the question of cost. Each show was then budgeted at $220,000. As a spokesman for NBC said at the time, "It's just not economical to put Caesar and Coca together." As it turned out "Your Show of Shows" marked the high point in the careers of both Coca and Caesar. Neither one would ever do as well again, either in mass popularity or in critical acclaim.

By the end of the program Coca was as much the star of the show as Caesar. It detracts from Caesar not at all to say that Coca was as versatile and as good a comedian as he. But they were treated quite differently, marking the difference between a male and female comic. They both starred on NBC in the fall of 1954 in their own shows, but Caesar was given a full hour program. Coca got only 30 minutes from the network.

At the close of "Your Show of Shows" Caesar had been making $25,000 a week. Some half-hour shows of that time had weekly total production budgets which were no higher. In comparison Coca's salary was just $10,000 a week. Caesar was said to have approached his new show by taking charge of every aspect, such as writing, producing and directing. On the other hand Coca, who was a retiring and self-effacing type, approached her series with much less enthusiasm and zeal, and no assertiveness. She said before it debuted, almost hopefully, "Maybe I'll get sick, or have an accident."

Caesar's show lasted three seasons before being cancelled. Howard Morris and Carl Reiner remained on the show, thus providing Caesar with three of the four-person, almost repertory group from "Your Show of Shows." Given that fact, NBC's idea of saving money seemed to have been to get Coca off the show. Perhaps other reasons, still not public, were responsible for the restructuring. Caesar's show had a high turnover of women paired with the three men, none making anywhere near the impact of Coca.

Imogene's show, "The Imogene Coca Show," lasted only one season and the critics were unimpressed from the beginning, mostly because of the weak material. The show began in October 1954 and never really knew where it was going. It started as a situation comedy with Coca playing an actress with comic adventures in the "real world." After only two weeks this format was dropped and replaced by a variety format with guests, production numbers, and skits. In a few months, February 1955, the format was again changed. This time Coca played one half of a couple of newlyweds, the Cranes, in a situation comedy. With all these format changes it wasn't surprising the show was cancelled that spring after just one season.

About this time Coca asked NBC to release her from their ten-year contract, which guaranteed her $100,000 annually. The contract had nine years to go, having been signed after the demise of "Your Show of Shows." She wanted to enjoy more artistic freedom and NBC complied. She had hoped that being free of commitments would revitalize her.

Over the next few years she limited herself mainly to nightclub engagements as well as one 90-minute TV special. That show was not well received and was rated a disappointment by critics. The consensus was that Coca was burdened with defective material and was trying too hard, to the detriment of her timing and her overall performance.

In January 1958 Coca and Caesar were reunited on a half hour ABC comedy series, "Sid Caesar Invites You." The reunion was looked forward to with much anticipation but the magic which had existed in previous years could not be recaptured. Despite strong regulars such as Carl Reiner and writers Neil Simon and Mel Brooks, the show was cancelled in May, just four months after it began.

Coca returned as a series star on NBC in the fall of 1963 in a situation comedy called "Grindl." She played a domestic worker for an employment agency who was sent out on a different job assignment each week. This forgettable series lasted one season. Her next, and last, series was for CBS in the fall of 1966. She was a featured performer rather than the star of this terrible sitcom called "It's About Time." The plot had two astronauts getting lost in time and ending up in the middle of the Stone Age. Coca was one of the prehistoric people for the astronauts to adjust to. After five months the format was changed. The astronauts found their way back to the twentieth century and a few of the prehistoric people, including Coca, stowed away on the ship. The comedy now derived from the prehistoric people adjusting to modern times. Mercifully, this series expired after one season.

After that Coca limited her work mainly to the relative obscurity of the dinner theater circuit and in the 1970's she celebrated her 50th anniversary in show business. By the end of the 1970's she had returned to Broadway as part of the hit musical *On the Twentieth Century*. Someone asked her if that show marked her comeback. With characteristic modesty she replied, "I don't think my part in this is large enough to be called 'comeback' material."

The following quote, from 1951, while dealing specifically with Coca, offered some insight into the perception of female comics in general in that decade and the kind of disdain they were subjected to:

"The good comedienne, of course, is a rarity, especially in America. Most American women, particularly the determined kind who are likely to go into the theater, like to be glamorous. Few actresses go in for comedy unless they have some physical peculiarity which forces them against their will to abandon romantic roles. Martha Raye, for example, has a Mammoth-Cave mouth which no make-up can disguise. Cass Daley has buck teeth. Since they drift into the business by necessity, comediennes as a rule seem to view their jobs with distaste or even with humiliation, and they go about their work with a vicious energy that suggests they are hell-bent on destroying their music, scripts, stages, microphones, audiences and possibly even themselves. The theater world regards them as a kind of necessary evil, as likely to set the customer's teeth on edge as to amuse him. Miss Coca, a good comedienne and a non-destructive one, has no serious physical defects. Her figure is adequate and her face, while not beautiful, would hardly stop a clock. She had no trouble finding a husband." In 1939 *Collier's* magazine described Coca as a woman "with the face of a junior gargoyle, the shape of a suspender strap."

Again there is the excessive concern with physical appearance. Granted Coca was not cast in the Marilyn Monroe mold. But Caesar was not cast in the Cary Grant mold either. No one had bothered to analyze Caesar's physical attractiveness, or lack thereof, and how it did or didn't force him to be a comedian. Nor of course should they. It was an irrelevant standard, but one that was applied consistently to women.

Coca was a modest, unassuming, non-assertive woman, traits instilled in females to a greater degree than males, and traits that work against women in a business that was aggressive, to say the least. Coca had remarked, "I've just never really been what they called 'career-smart.' I don't speak up. . . . It just doesn't occur to me to object. I'm accustomed to doing what directors say to do."

The main reason for the cancellation of "Your Show of Shows" apparently was financial, although the reason put forth was that Caesar and Coca were to pursue separate careers. The net result was that Caesar's show was very much "Your Show of Shows" reduced from 90 to 60 minutes. Coca was the only major figure to be severed. Was there perhaps too much ego on the show to work with Coca? A fear that Coca might become the show's top banana?

Imogene Coca's career peaked in the first half of the 1950's and, despite her comic talents, she was never again able to reach those heights. Hollywood had again wasted a talent, something they do with women far more so than men, through bad material or no material at all.

JOAN DAVIS

She was noisy, awkward, and she was man hungry. It was a stock role for female comics of the 1930's and 1940's who didn't have stage husbands. Other examples were Judy Canova and Eve Arden. This stereotype was as common as the "dumb female" image so often evoked by women with stage husbands. Nor was it uncommon for both of these traits to be found at the same time in the same comedienne.

One of the most popular of these types was Joan Davis, who for a time in the mid-1940's, when she was at the peak of her career, was called the top woman comic in the business. She was unusual in that she had decided early on in her life that comedy was to be her career. Most women have looked elsewhere for their future, and stumbled into comedy through chance or circumstance. Few women have ever viewed comedy as a first career choice.

Davis achieved her first real fame in the movies and then rode that fame to the peak of her popularity in radio. When the public seemed to tire of her, she switched to television and was modestly successful for a few years but continued her drift toward obscurity until her early death. It is more than a little ironic that one of the most physical of all women comics—famed for her mugging, her rubber face, and her pratfalls—should achieve her greatest success and popularity in radio, a non-visual medium.

She was born Madonna Josephine Davis on June 29, 1907, in St. Paul Minnesota, the only child of Nina Davis and LeRoy Davis, who worked as a train dispatcher. Some accounts have listed 1912 as her year of birth. Her parents had no connection

with the world of show business, nor did they have any theatrical
background. Despite this Davis seemed to have been born an
entertainer. By the time she was three she was already performing
before local gatherings and church groups by reciting, dancing,
and singing. One of her routines had her playing cupid and
clutching a gilded coat hanger for a bow.

At six she was appearing at a local theater in an amateur night
contest. Joan was doing a serious recital and had her first taste of
audience disapproval. The crowd first laughed at her and then,
showing no mercy even to a child of her age, they booed her off
the stage. They even went so far in their critical assessment to
deliver that timeless judgment of her performance, a barrage of
rotting vegetables hurled at the stage. After that fiasco her father
offered her some advice. "Joan, you lay beautiful eggs. Better be
funny, not serious. . . . Keep moving! It spoils their aim."

Showing more nerve and presence of mind than most adults,
Joan was back at the same theater the next week. This time she
did a comedy routine and a song. The audience found her new
act more acceptable and she won applause. Talent scouts were
duly impressed with the precocious youngster and successfully persuaded her family to allow her to tour on the prestigious Pantages
Theatre vaudeville circuit. She had a 14-minute act and was
billed as "Cyclonic Josephine Davis" and "The Toy Comedienne."
On the road Joan was accompanied by her mother and a tutor.
During the times she was laid off the group would return home to
St. Paul in order for her to get a month or two of regular schooling.

Sometime by her early teens her popularity was beginning to
drop. She was no longer a small child and the novelty was wearing thin with the audience. Her parents wanted her to attend regular school, so Davis retired, temporarily, from show business.
She returned home and graduated as class valedictorian from St.
Paul's Mechanic Arts High School. She then took a brief stab at
regular employment. She got an $8 a week job clerking at a local
five-and-dime. Her sense of the absurd quickly surfaced, however.
She worked at the goldfish counter and used to do a series of tripping and sliding gags along the floor. She also asked customers if
they wanted their goldfish wrapped. She quickly returned to her
first love, the vaudeville circuit.

She was "certain that her metier was comedy" and she devoted
herself to improving her style and learning new routines. She stu-

died the techniques of various comedians and concentrated on the style of one of her favorites, Charlie Chaplin. At that time vaudeville had begun a period of decline owing to the competition from films, and Davis found herself unable to get any bookings on the circuit. What Davis did do was to play summer camps, Elks' lodges, one night engagements, and amusement parks.

Her act was made up of slapstick routines, mugging with rubbery facial expressions, and running her gravelly voice through its entire range. One of her better known bits was that of juggling an immense stack of dishes which arranged themselves at gravitationally impossible angles. She had by then included in her act her version of Chaplin's routines. She also dressed in outrageous clothes onstage: "She wore green ruffled drawers down to her ankles and a hat even a queen wouldn't be seen in."

Davis had been considering adding a straight man to her act in order to strengthen and stabilize it. In 1931 her manager introduced her to Serenus (Si) Wills, already an established veteran of vaudeville. By this time Davis was billing herself as Joan, rather than the earlier Josephine, or Jo. The two decided to team up and went on the road as Wills and Davis. Later in 1931 they married. Wills later did some of the writing for Joan's radio and television shows, although the couple divorced in 1948.

The team barnstormed the country for several years and they developed into a "smart outfit." By 1935 they had worked their way to the west coast and Joan was determined to break into movies. She felt this was the best medium for her brand of zaniness, since the decline of vaudeville had continued unabated.

She first attempted to get an assignment with a company called Educational Films, which was then grinding out 20-minute shorts as fillers for playbills. Mack Sennett was directing there. When Davis got no further than the reception area she arranged to get invited to a party at which Sennett was also a guest. Davis performed some of her routines at the party and this led to her appearance in a Sennett hillbilly short called *Way Up Thar*. She sang a couple of songs and did her balancing dishes routine.

As a result of her performance RKO Pictures signed her to a stock contract. She appeared in a featured comedy role in one picture, but RKO seemed disinterested in giving her further work and so the parties, by mutual agreement, terminated the contract. With no further film work forthcoming, Wills and Davis returned east and got an engagement at New York City's Palace

Theater, then a goal for all variety players. In what was their big time stage debut they bombed and were reduced to returning to play the lesser vaudeville circuits.

In 1936 Joan managed to sign a contract with 20th Century-Fox studio. This studio was then embarking on an extended program of musical and comedy films and were looking for more specialty acts to fill out these forthcoming productions. She remained with this studio from 1937 until 1941. During that time she appeared in 24 of their films, a staggering 11 of them in her first year, 1937. In her very first film, *The Holy Terror,* she had established the style she would use throughout her career, her bizarre brand of slapstick. She was described in that film as a "strange female curtain-climber, with a trick of punching herself in the jaw and a curious resemblance to Olive Oyl in the cartoons."

Of another of her films that year, *Time Out for Romance,* a reviewer said: "Thanks to the presence of that spidery-legged comedienne Joan Davis, who is in the habit of knocking herself out in a form of protest against her human limitations . . . the film may be classified as endurable second rate." Throughout her career with 20th Century-Fox Davis played short-featured roles in grade "B" pictures. Often Davis's part was the only aspect of a film that reviewers found worthwhile. She sang in some and performed frantic dance numbers in others.

She played a nurse in one, *The Great Hospital Mystery,* and had ample opportunity to destroy medical equipment and slip and slide through the hospital corridors on her "collapsible legs." A critic remarked, "Sole relief from the picture's dullness is provided by Joan Davis, who does her round-heeled slide juggling a bed pan and never spilling a drop." She was at that time being compared to Martha Raye, the reigning slapstick queen of films.

Subtle nuances were important to Davis in her routines despite their broad effects, and she remarked that even with her natural-looking brand of "hokum comedy" she needed to constantly study and work at it, since a slip of the finger or a slightly different facial expression could make the difference between indifference and a laugh from the audience.

Some observers of her work did give her credit for more than what superficially met the eye. Regarding her style, one commented, "Superficially it is slapstick, but on second consideration it appears rather to be a super-sophisticated distillation of the most elegant type of humor. The comedienne goes directly to the heart of her material in an almost savage manner without once sacrificing method to mugging."

Often she was on screen for only a few minutes to do some outrageous bit and then to quickly disappear again. But audiences remembered her. She knew how to make the most of her brief moments. "I've always had to sneak in and make good." One of her 1938 films *Hold That Co-Ed* had her disguised as a male playing on the football team. She was able to make flying tackles, fly around with limbs akimbo, and come to earth with an enormous crash that "shakes the inherent faith of man in the frailty of women."

By the end of 1938 she was making over $50,000 yearly from her film work. She had reached the top of the featured players. Darryl Zanuck, head of the studio, carefully monitored her screen time to keep the audience wanting to see more of her and yet preventing her from becoming stale. To this end she was essentially tossed into any picture, regardless of quality or type, for comic relief and to expose her to a wide spectrum of filmgoers.

She continued to play a man-hungry woman with no success in dragging a man to the altar, to do frenetic dance numbers, to play characters such as a maid who bungled her cleaning tasks, and to sock herself in the chin, in this latter case to punish herself for stuttering. She had received offers to take her act to England on tour but was unable to accept. While she was allowed to do this within her contract, the studio had the right to call her back on notice, thus effectively allowing Davis to book her stage act no more than two weeks ahead.

Joan made the following comments when asked about her success in the film industry. "Most of the good comedians on the screen today started out in vaudeville. And I think that's the only way in which one may learn the important business of timing one's act to get the best laugh return. After you'd been on the vaudeville circuit grind for a couple of years, facing all sorts of audiences, you developed a 'feel' for the comedy situations that carried you through. . . . Laughs are based on other people's misfortunes — it's awful, isn't it? A good fall always gets a laugh."

Dressing in unbecoming clothes in her film roles didn't bother Davis. She felt that due to this lack of glamor she would "last longer." By early 1940 she was the only major woman comic then under contract to a Hollywood studio. Others such as Martha Raye, Marie Wilson, and Patsy Kelly had had their contracts terminated. One factor contributing to her success was that she had remained a featured player and didn't run the risk of boring her audience through the overexposure of being a star in film after film. That happened easily in those days when actresses and actors made many more pictures in a given time than they do today.

In 1941 she refused to renegotiate her contract with 20th Century-Fox, feeling the studio wasn't going to come up with any good parts for her. Part of her must have wanted to try different types of comedy, or even straight drama, for she remarked at the time of her contract termination: "In my heart, I feel I am so much more than a screwball."

She moved on to freelance in films. Her first movie under this system was *Hold That Ghost,* starring Abbott and Costello. Davis and Costello did a memorable and madcap slapstick waltz. At this time Joan was commanding $50,000 per picture. By the mid-1940's her fee was $75,000 per film, as much as major stars at top studios received. She continued her mugging and slapstick in these films, which had now been long established as her stock in trade. She also continued to be pushed around and kicked in the pants. A highlight from a film called *Kansas City Kitty* had her serving dinner to two male callers at the same time in different rooms. She would later use this routine on her TV series.

Of the films she did after 20th Century-Fox, she was again often referred to as their only saving grace. In some of these pictures she was the star, and sometimes the critics found her too energetic and raucous, or too heavy-handed, or not able to rise above the poor vehicle she was appearing in. Generally, her talents were considered to be superior to the films she appeared in. In 1952 she starred in *Harem Girl.* It was a second-rate, lacklustre film, Davis' 44th feature film appearance and her last. She was then concentrating her talents in other mediums, first radio and then television.

Early in 1941 she made her first appearance on radio. People in the industry were apprehensive and had many doubts about her ability to transfer her visual grimaces, pratfalls, pantomimes, and body language to the medium of the radio. Davis was herself somewhat leery and adopted a slightly different style. She did a parody of a popular song by singing the first few lines of the song as they were written and then changing the rest into a monologue. It worked and in August of 1941 she was a guest on the "Rudy Vallee Show."

She was so well received that in 1942 she was made one of the show's regulars. Her major function was to play "a man-crazy, scatterbrained dame whose chief aim in life was to snare Vallee." Rudy left the show in July 1943, and it became the "Sealtest Village Store."

Joan Davis remained as the star. Critics doubted the ability of the show to survive with Vallee gone. Others felt that Davis was well enough established to carry the lead alone. The producers of the show were uncomfortable with only a female lead and they immediately signed Jack Haley as co-star and as an "essential" male lead.

The show became a situation comedy program with Davis as operator of the Village Store. Davis would leave this show in a couple of years and the store's manager would become Eve Arden. The fears about Davis's ability to carry the show were unfounded and at the end of 1943 polls conducted by the Scripps-Howard newspapers and Cleveland's *Plain Dealer* voted her radio's top comedienne for 1943. In 1944, radio ratings placed her show among the top five comedy shows. She made guest appearances on many other radio variety programs, at one point doing eight different ones in a week.

In 1945 she reached her radio peak, trailing only Bob Hope and Fibber McGee and Molly in the race for the top comedy show on radio. Part of her success was said to be due to the outstanding versatility of her deep voice, "which could transcend from a low screech to a high-pitched, cracking quiver in no time flat. The timbre of her voice gave substance to her jokes and aided tremendously in her song renditions."

In September 1945 she moved from NBC to CBS network and began a new program, "Joanie's Tea Room." She was paid $1 million a year by the sponsor, United Drugs Company, and easily became the top paid female comic in the business. As befitting the show's status, it had six writers on staff, a large number for radio shows of the day. While Davis was then in charge of a tea room on the air instead of a general store, reviewers couldn't detect any other differences. It was the same Joan Davis unleashing her routines of mayhem, the same man-chaser, or as it was then put, "uneasy about having so much virtue so long."

The following interchange perhaps is typical of her man hungry ways:

> JOAN: Did you just get into town cowboy?
> COWBOY: Yep!
> JOAN: Do you know any girls in town?
> COWBOY: Nope!
> JOAN: Would you like to go out with a girl?
> COWBOY: Yep!
> JOAN: Would you like to go out with me?

COWBOY: Nope!

JOAN: Why, pardner, how can you stand there and say no to me? Me, Gower Gulch Gertie!

COWBOY: But ma'am, you don't look like you've ever been on a horse.

JOAN: Never been on a horse? Look again, pardner—I didn't get these here bow-legs from ridin' a pickel barrel!

By the fall of 1947 United Drugs had dropped her two-year-old show, claiming she was too expensive a package. That year CBS used the cooperative sponsor system for her show, selling it to individual stations for a fee based on the station's power rating and potential audience. In turn the station tried to sell the cued blank spots to local sponsors. In New York, 50,000-watt WCBS paid $810 for Davis's half-hour program and charged the sponsor $1,000. In Jacksonville Florida 250-watt WMBR paid $78 for each program and sold the commercials for the same amount.

Joan Davis's salary had dropped, but she still received a substantial $10,000-a-week guarantee. From this amount she had to pay her writers and cast members. The American Federation of Musicians wouldn't allow its members to appear on a show with multiple sponsors, which ruled out the cooperative system. Joan Davis needed a musical break on her shows, so she got around this regulation by hiring an a capella group.

After two years, in July 1949, her last radio program debuted, "Leave It to Joan." This was sponsored on CBS by American Tobacco Company and Davis received a salary of $8,250 a week. The series was set in a department store, with Joan portraying a man-chasing salesgirl. As one reviewer remarked, "Miss Davis is changeless as the tides. She's still a sex-starved, addled and very, very noisy girl. It's been the standard comedy role for women since the days of Mack Sennett and Miss Davis is not a girl to rough up tradition. . . . The jokes concerning Miss Davis's difficulties in catching a man have been honed to such a fine thin point it's almost a mathematical exercise thinking up new ones. This has produced what might be described as the inevitable joke."

Radio was then in a decline thanks to television and this show went off the air in 1950. There was no reason for a comic, especially a highly visual one like Davis, not to move over to the new medium. This she did and in October 1952 her television series,

"I Married Joan," debuted on NBC. Davis owned the show and paid herself $7,500 a week in salary. Jim Backus played her husband, Judge Bradley Stevens, who presided over a domestic court in California.

As each episode began Judge Stevens was on the bench trying to sort out some couple's domestic difficulties. He would tell them of a similar problem he had dealt with with his own wife and the courtroom scene would start to fade as he began the story, and the tale would then be enacted.

The man-chasing character was gone, of course, but Joan Davis was now the typical well-meaning but addled scatterbrain. She spent half her time launching herself and her husband into various ridiculous escapades. The rest of her time and energy went into finding ways to keep her foolish mistakes and harebrained schemes from being discovered by her husband, who, while occasionally exasperated, was eternally patient. She continued to mug and cut up but was found to be a slightly subdued version of her movie self. In explaining her television style, Davis said, "It's the first time I've ever done a domestic comedy. But since I made a reputation as a physical comedienne, I had to continue."

The series remained on the air until the April 6, 1955, episode, at which time 98 episodes had been done. Some of the plots included: Joan substituting for her husband's secretary and then losing a check for a large amount, Joan filling in for an opera star at a woman's club performance, Joan borrowing a rare stamp from her husband's collection and then mistakenly using it to mail a letter. Her slapstick routines involved her climbing into upstairs windows on a very shaky ladder, moving household furniture, and winding up inside a dryer at the laundromat. She also tossed out self-deprecating one-line wisecracks about her own frailties.

The writers did leave a good deal of slapstick for Davis to perform, and wrote the show to a formula that contained two domestic crises, no more or less, in each half-hour episode. When the series left the air it was not doing well in the ratings. It was third in its time slot with a rating of 21.5. In comparison, that year the top show, "I Love Lucy," had a rating of 49.3.

Davis signed a television contract with ABC in 1956 and a new series was announced for that fall, but nothing came of it. In 1957 a format was announced for her new series pilot. It was to be about the first female astronaut getting ready for a moon flight. Davis was enthusiastic about what she called the first comedy science-fiction series on television. Nothing came of that.

At this point her career was effectively over, despite her acknowledged talents.

In the 1940's Fanny Brice had been asked her choice for an actress to portray her. (Barbra Streisand eventually did in *Funny Girl*.) Brice had replied, "There's one dame that could play me, that's Joan Davis." On May 24, 1961, at the age of 53, Joan Davis had a heart attack and died.

Davis, with a specialty of "sitting down hard," had worked her way to superstardom through broad slapstick, subtle nuances, and a canny sense of timing. Her character was a gawky, man-hungry woman, and later, a birdbrained housewife. Self-deprecation for Davis was usually delivered physically. Only occasionally would she say critical words about herself out loud. Her more usual response when she became disenchanted with her own clumsiness on stage was to slap herself in reproach.

She turned to television at a time when Lucille Ball had already entrenched herself as the chief scatterbrain. Many shows, openly copies, were trying unsuccessfully to usurp her. Davis perhaps had a chance, since she was a much bigger star going into the 1950's than Ball was. However, the public seemed to be growing accustomed to, and possibly tired of, Davis's brand of humor. A more subtle form of comedy was also beginning to vie with the slapstick style, as in Even Arden's "Our Miss Brooks."

Davis's supporting cast did not have the variety and talents to match the outstanding group that Ball worked with. Jim Backus did yeoman service as the husband, but the idea that a judge had married a character such as the one Joan portrayed was just not believable. The character of the judge was also too bland, uninteresting, and insipid to go up against the formidable and quirky trio of Ricky, Fred, and Ethel who were backing up Ball.

A couple of years after her series had been terminated and nothing new had emerged, Davis was in a somewhat bitter mood and remarked, "I've been afraid all along that I just wouldn't be funny or pretty enough for the long-time big time. I've kept going on a mixture of gall, guts, and gumption." She was perhaps right.

LUCILLE BALL

"I Love Lucy" was more than just the name of a television program. It was a sentiment felt by the millions of viewers who had tuned into the program over the thirty years it has been aired as both an original and as a rerun series. Lucille Ball's comic talent enraptured audiences the world over, and brought her unqualified praise from critics and overwhelming respect from fellow performers. But it had been a long struggle to the top. Ball was forty years old when "I Love Lucy" premiered.

Lucy had been born in 1911 in Jamestown, New York. She was of mixed Scottish, Irish, English, and French ancestry. Her father, Henry Ball, was a telephone lineman. Her mother Desiree, a pianist, never realized her ambition of appearing on the concert stage. In 1915 Ball's father died of typhoid fever. When Desiree remarried, she and her new salesman husband moved to Detroit. Lucy and her younger brother were left with her stepfather's parents, who were extremely strict. This unsettling time after her father died made Lucy very insecure. Later in life she felt this period had an effect on her as a performer: "Most comedy successes stem from long-standing inferiority complexes, and I had mine. . . . My father died when I was four. . . . My step-grandparents had stern, old-country ideas. . . . It gave me a feeling of frustration and of reaching-out-and-trying-to-please. I found the quickest and easiest way to do that was to make people laugh."

Desiree's second marriage lasted only a short while and she returned to Jamestown where her children once again lived with her. Life improved for Lucy and she became involved in amateur theatricals. In high school she played the lead in *Charley's Aunt* and told an interviewer for *Time* in 1952: "I played the lead, directed it, cast it, sold tickets, printed the posters, and hauled furniture to the school for scenery and props." She also had a role in a community theatre production of *Within the Law*. Lucy remembered being taken to see some vaudeville shows which made a tremendous impression on her.

Like many other female comedians, Ball did not aim for comedy. She just knew that school did not interest her, and that show business did. Any kind of performing would do, as long as she was on stage.

In 1926 at the age of fifteen, Lucy convinced her mother to let her enroll in drama school in New York City. She became a pupil at the John Murray Anderson-Robert Milton academy. Recalling this experience Ball said: "I was a tongue-tied teenager spellbound by the school's star pupil—Bette Davis." Her teacher felt Lucy showed no aptitude for acting and wrote to her mother: "Lucy's wasting her time and mine. She's too shy and reticent to put her best foot forward."

Despite her failure at drama school, Lucy hung around New York, taking odd jobs to support herself, such as salesgirl or soda jerk. In her spare time she auditioned for chorus girl roles. She was picked for the road company of the Broadway show *Rio Rita,* but after several weeks of rehearsal the stage manager fired her, saying: "You're not meant for show business. Go home!" After being fired from a second show, Lucy decided to try modeling under the glamorous name of "Diane Belmont." With her striking five foot six inch beauty and newly dyed blonde hair, Lucy did well as a model.

It was during this time that Lucy suffered a physical breakdown. The reasons for her illness have not been confirmed, but have been cited variously as a car accident, malnutrition, or arthritis. Whatever the cause, Lucy's legs were paralyzed for two years, and she was confined to a wheelchair. Her mother nursed her back to health.

Undaunted, Lucy resumed her modeling career in New York. She also had her first walk-on bit part in the 1933 film *Broadway Thru a Keyhole.* In addition, she achieved some fame as the poster girl for Chesterfield cigarettes. This brought her to the attention of a Hollywood agent, and she was cast as one of twelve Goldwyn Girls in the Eddie Cantor film *Roman Scandal,* directed by Busby Berkeley, in 1933. When Berkeley asked which of the showgirls was willing to take a mud pie in the face, only one girl volunteered—Lucille Ball. Said Berkeley: "Get that girl's name. That's the one who will make it." Even at that early stage of her career Ball was willing to do anything for a laugh.

Within a year she had appeared in eight bit parts in United Artists and Fox features. At the end of 1933 she accepted a $75 dollar a week offer from Columbia to be cast as a dumb blonde type in burlesque style comedies. As the Depression deepened, however, she was laid off from Columbia when they reduced staff.

RKO hired her in 1934, but only as a bit player again, and at a lower salary of $50 a week. By 1935 Lucy was working her way up

to supporting roles, but was limited to "B" pictures. Yet she began
to receive some attention from critics, and her first set of notices
came for a 1936 film, *That Girl from Paris,* in which Ball was
fifth-billed as a rejected girlfriend. The New York *Daily Mirror*
praised her as "an able actress and an agile dancer," saying she
"contributes an exquisite scene as a dancer with soaped
shoes. . . . Miss Ball plays it quite straight, intensifying the
comedy of each disaster. She rates, thereby, more conspicuous
roles and more intense promotion. She is a comedienne, which
always means a 'find.' "

Lucy was still stuck in supporting roles in "B" pictures despite
good notices. Thus in 1936 she decided to try out for the
Broadway-bound play *Hey Diddle Diddle*. She landed a role, but
the play died before it ever reached Broadway. Lucy, however,
received an excellent review in *Variety:* She "fattens a fat part and
almost walks off with play. She outlines a consistent character and
continuously gives it logical substance. Has a sense of timing and,
with a few exceptions, keeps her comedy under control." Already
her comic talent was appreciated.

By 1938 Lucy had made seven films for RKO, all frustratingly
"B" level pictures with small roles. Most were of the "screwball"
comedy genre with plenty of slapstick. Lucy was often picked out
by critics and *The New York Times* in 1938 felt she was "rapidly
becoming one of our brightest comediennes."

Lucy might have been less resentful of her comic roles in "B"
pictures if she had been able to foresee the tremendous success she
would have in the frequently slapstick "I Love Lucy" television
series. Moreover, even though many of the films were Grade "B,"
she often worked with "A"-level talent. She appeared with the
Three Stooges, the Marx Brothers, Buster Keaton and Laurel and
Hardy. But Lucy didn't feel that she gained much from these
experiences: "I didn't learn a thing from them except when to
duck. Buster Keaton taught me about props."

In 1939 Lucy had set her sights on being a dramatic star in "A"
pictures and she was nowhere nearer her goal. She was, on the
other hand, beginning to get top-billing in RKO "B" pictures. In
1949 she had the lead in the film *Too Many Girls*. Also in this
film was a young Cuban-born actor named Desi Arnaz. Arnaz was
born in Santiago in 1917. His father was the mayor of the city,
and his family was impressively wealthy. They lost everything in
the 1933 revolution, and Desi's father was imprisoned for a time.
The family fled to Miami, and Desi eventually made a living by

forming a Cuban rumba band. He played the guitar and sang. Later he became a vocalist with Xavier Cugat's orchestra.

Striking out on his own again, Desi became proficient on the drums when he introduced the conga line to United States audiences. His band became known and respected in clubs in major cities. In 1939 he was offered a part in the stage production of the musical *Too Many Girls*. He played a Cuban football hero. When the play was filmed in Hollywood in 1940, Arnaz was kept on in the role.

Lucy and Desi began dating during the filming. In November of that year they eloped to Greenwich, Connecticut, where they married. Hollywood gossips predicted the marriage would fall apart in six weeks. Arnaz, six years younger than Lucy, was known as a temperamental playboy. The marriage did indeed get off to a bad start and remained rocky.

Lucy and Desi purchased a ranch in the San Fernando Valley, but they seldom spent time there together. Desi was drafted into the U.S. army in 1943. Released in 1945 he made a few "B" movies which did not advance his career in any way. He then continued touring the country with his band. Desi was doing well in nightclubs, earning over $100,000 per year.

Lucy meanwhile was still at RKO churning out "B" films. Although her contract was renewed in 1941, her salary of $1,500 per week was less than Desi earned as a musician. And there was no future for Lucy at RKO. The studio decided that for the types of roles and movies that Lucy appeared in, they could hire cheaper actresses. They let her option expire in 1942.

MGM promptly hired Lucy for the musical film *Du Barry Was a Lady,* starring Red Skelton. This 1943 movie gave Ball a trademark which would become one of her best known features—her red hair. The shade started out more towards a pinky-orange color and later evolved into bright red. She dyed it that color because it looked good in technicolor.

Lucy appeared in three other supporting roles for MGM, but her career was still not taking off and she did not have star status. Adding to her worries was her marriage to Arnaz. The relationship was shaky and Desi was rarely around. They were apart so frequently during the first eleven years of their marriage that they spent $29,000 on long distance telephone calls and telegrams. Lucy filed for divorce in 1944 but the couple reconciled before the decree was final.

Lucy made several other lackluster films in 1944 and 1945. In 1946 she had a substantial role in the movie *Easy to Wed,* co-

starring Van Johnson, Esther Williams, and Keenan Wynn. The
New York *Herald-Tribune* lauded Ball: "She snaps her lines over
the heads of the other characters . . . and in pantomime manages
to be as scatterbrained and indignant as a wet hen." Another critic enthused: "Keenan Wynn and Lucille Ball . . . make it clear
that they are the funniest comic team on the screen just now—
and by a wide margin."

Praise such as this frustrated Lucy more than ever because she
was still not offered movie roles worthy of her talent. As a result,
a thirty-six-year-old, disenchanted Lucy decided to branch out
into radio. She had appeared in 60 movies by that time and still
wasn't a star.

In 1947 Ball joined the cast of the radio program *My Favorite
Husband*. She played Liz Cooper, the scatterbrained wife of a
midwestern banker, George Cooper, played first by Lee Bowman
and then by Richard Denning. It was a typical domestic comedy.
Supporting cast included George's boss Rudolph Atterbury,
played by Gale Gordon, and his wife, Iris, played by Bea
Benaderet. One of the best remembered lines from the show was
Iris's greeting "Ah, Liz-girl, George-Boy." It was on this program
that Lucy perfected her famous crying fits.

Lucy's decision to join the radio program was more momentous
than she could have imagined. It would form the basis of the "I
Love Lucy" television show using the same writers—Jess
Oppenheimer, Bob Carroll, and Madelyn Pugh. Gale Gordon
would become a featured player (again in the role of a banker) in
later Lucy television series. *My Favorite Husband* remained on the
air until 1951.

In the meantime Lucy had not abandoned her movie career
entirely. In 1949 she appeared in a small role in *Sorrowful Jones,*
with Bob Hope, and again with Hope in the 1950 movie *Fancy
Pants*. Between 1949-1951 she made a total of seven more films—
none of them really showing off Lucy's potential. This waste was
noted by the *Los Angeles Times* critic Edwin Schallert who had
seen Lucy in the 1948 stage production of *Dream Girls*. Schallert
wrote: "She is, in a sense, wasting her talents in pictures. . . .
Miss Ball is a striking presence in the footlight world. She has
efficiency as a comedienne. She can tinge a scene delicately with
pathos. She has special facility in dealing with sharp-edged repartee."

Ball's marriage to Arnaz had been deteriorating with each passing year. Desi continued to tour with his band and the couple saw
each other infrequently.

Lucy was now forty years old. Stardom had eluded her, and her marriage was unstable. She needed a radical change in her life and she set about accomplishing it. Lucy and Desi decided to put more effort into their marriage. They planned to do a series similar to *My Favorite Husband* on television. This would not only allow them to live together on a regular basis, but to work together as well.

Although Arnaz was condescendingly referred to as a "clean-cut Latin," his image was still exotic enough to make CBS executives hesitant about casting him as Lucy's husband. "Nobody will believe you two as a married couple," said one studio executive. But Lucy refused to appear without Desi.

To prove that the public would accept them as man and wife, Lucy and Desi put together a musical-comedy act and took it on the road. Their routine included gags in which Lucy played the cello, imitated a seal, and sang a "Cuban Pete — Sally Sweet" medley with Desi. Some of the advice for the gags came from an old Spanish clown, Pepito, who had played the vaudeville circuit for years.

Audiences loved the show, but CBS still considered a television series with Desi a risky proposition. So Ball and Arnaz set up their own company, Desilu Inc. Arnaz was president, Lucy vice-president. They convinced Philip Morris Cigarettes to sponsor "I Love Lucy."

Desilu retained ownership of all the films and tapes of their show. After the success of the series they sold the reruns to CBS for about five million dollars. The reruns were translated into almost every language for international distribution.

Arnaz and Ball introduced several television firsts for their half-hour show. Karl Freund, the famous cameraman who filmed several Garbo films including *Camille,* came out of retirement to do the "I Love Lucy" show because of the technical challenge. In the early 1950's kinescope was used by the television industry. This recorded images from the face of a television picture tube. By having Freund film the shows, reproduction quality was higher.

Freund innovated the three-camera technique for television while filming "I Love Lucy." It is still in use today. Prior to that TV shows had been filmed in separate shots. Freund's "multicam" approach filmed the action continuously. This meant that each episode of the program could be performed live at the "Desilu Playhouse," like a three-act play. The live audience precluded the need for a sound track and gave the show more vitality and spontaneity. Later an editor spliced the best shots together.

The action took place on four sets. Two of them represented the Ricardo's Manhattan apartment, one was the nightclub where Ricky's band played, and the fourth was used for miscellaneous scenes. The company rehearsed from six to ten hours, three days a week. An average cast and crew of 93 people were involved in the production. Costs ranged between $23-25,000 per week for Desilu during the 1951-52 season.

The method of filming "I Love Lucy" in Hollywood had an impact on the TV industry. Much of television production shifted from New York to California, because that was where the film facilities were.

"I Love Lucy" was in many ways a typical family situation comedy. Lucy played Lucy Ricardo (an American of Scottish ancestry with the maiden name of MacGillicuddy). Her husband Ricky, a Cuban bandleader, was of course played by Desi Arnaz.

Ricky was employed by the Tropicana Club and many of the plots involved Lucy trying to get on stage while Ricky tried to keep her off. Her schemes to appear at the Tropicana would evoke an outburst of Spanish from the exasperated Ricky.

Other themes for the program involved Lucy trying to get Ricky to prove how much he loved her, Lucy trying to outclass her affluent acquaintances, or Lucy trying to get out of some horrible scrape she had gotten into.

The Ricardos lived in a middle-class apartment building in Manhattan. Their neighbors and best friends were the landlords Fred and Ethel Mertz. Vivian Vance, who played Ethel, was Lucy's cohort and partner in her zany schemes. Fred, played by William Frawley, was Ricky's counterpart as another long-suffering husband.

The show debuted on October 15, 1951. The first episode revolved around a fight between Lucy and Ethel and their husbands. The men wanted to go to a boxing match while the women wanted to go to a nightclub. The men intended to get blind dates if their wives refused to go, so Lucy and Ethel dressed up as hillbillies and showed up as the blind dates.

From this first episode onward, the show was an overwhelming success. The actors were praised for their performances and Desi was called "refreshingly unpretentious." He was described as having "a sprightly sense of fun, a young and handsome facade, acting ability . . . and a marvellous parallel aptitude for nonsense that bounces slickly and affectionately alongside his wife's."

But although the company played beautifully together, it was Lucy who carried the show. Arnaz credited her with 90 percent of the program's popularity. A reporter for *Time* described Lucy as "a redheaded, uninhibited comedienne who takes pratfalls and pie-throwing in her stride, manages to add on an extra wriggle or a rubber-faced doubletake to each funny line."

Lucy was praised for her physical comedy and excellent sense of timing, which was compared to that of Jack Benny. The props and outrageous gags on the show were reminiscent of old-time vaudeville. Lucy's exaggerated facial expressions gave a visual focus to her comedy and made her less dependent on jokes. She appeared in an enormous variety of guises, including everything from a Martian to a matador. Lucy's wild stunts on roller skates or stilts provided much of the comedy.

Only Vivian Vance voiced any resentment about Lucy being the star attraction. As Ethel Mertz her character was supposed to be matronly, even though Vance was actually one year younger than Ball. Vivian's contract, much to her dismay, stipulated that she always remain twenty pounds overweight.

Yet relations on the set were generally cooperative despite the pressure of staying number one in the ratings, and despite the problems in the Ball-Arnaz marriage, which were recurring. In essence they were professionals who put work first. It was said that Desi could memorize his part in a 40-50 page script after one reading.

Critics were enthusiastic about the series. Jack Gould of *The New York Times* wrote in 1953: "An extraordinary discipline and intuitive understanding of farce give 'I Love Lucy' an engaging lilt. . . . Only after a firm foundation of credibility has been established is the element of absurdity introduced. It is in the smooth transition from sense to nonsense that 'I Love Lucy' imparts both a warmth and a reality to the slapstick romp which comes at the climax."

In 1952 *Time* featured Lucy on its cover and had this to say about "I Love Lucy:" "This is the sort of cheerful rowdiness that has been rare since the days of the silent movies' Keystone comedies. Lucille submits enthusiastically to being hit with pies; falls over furniture; gets locked in home freezers; is chased by knife-wielding fanatics. Tricked out as a ballerina or a Hindu maharani or a toothless hillbilly, she takes her assorted lumps and pratfalls with unflagging zest and good humor."

Her manager, Don Sharpe, described Lucy's style as "close to the Chaplin school of comedy—she's got warmth and sympathy, and people believe in her, even while they're laughing at her."

If the critics like Lucy, audiences adored her. At the start of its second season, "I Love Lucy" was the biggest hit in television history. It was estimated that 11,055,000 American families were tuned in weekly, making the program the first TV show to be seen in over ten million homes, an even more impressive figure when one took into account the fact that only fifteen million sets in total were in operation.

There were Lucy dolls, songs, aprons and furniture. In 1952 when Adlai Stevenson interrupted the show with a five-minute campaign message, his office was inundated with hate mail.

During the original run of the series it never ranked lower than third in the ratings and was often first. Lucy won an Emmy in 1952 and 1955 (as well as in 1966 and 1967 for her later TV series.) In 1952 the Academy of Television Arts and Sciences honored Ball as Comedienne of the Year.

Lucy's show was important in terms of female comedy. While it's true that she played the scatterbrained housewife, her program's themes, like her red hair, were a transition between the sexy dumb blonde and the witty independent brunette. Lucy was a housewife to be sure. But what kind of a housewife was she?

Lucy Ricardo was not content to stay at home. She wanted to be in show business. Ricky preferred her to be a housewife. Lucy Ricardo did not take orders from her husband. She wanted her own way. As a result the couple were almost constantly quarreling. As in all comedies, programs were happily resolved at the end of each show, but conflict between husbands and wives was often the focal point of the plot. Lucy Ricardo was a far cry from the meek wives appearing in shows like "Father Knows Best" or "Leave It to Beaver."

Her homemaking skills left much to be desired, and she was frequently getting into messes because of her inept cooking and cleaning abilities. Once she put too much yeast in bread she was baking, and the giant loaf pinned her against the sink. Another time she set fire to Ricky's newspaper at the breakfast table. Lucy Ricardo displayed a subtle hostility towards her role as housewife which verged on the rebellious.

The cast of "I Love Lucy" used real props as much as possible. Actual bread was used for the loaf gag. When one plot called for two sixty-pound tunas, real fish were brought in, and the grimaces on the actors' faces were authentic when they handled the gamy tunas. In one segment the plot called for Lucy to hide raw eggs in her clothes which would later break and trickle down her body. She used fake eggs in rehearsals so that when she used the real eggs during filming, her reaction would be genuine.

Female viewers identified with Lucy's rebellious spirit and wished they had the nerve to assert themselves the way she did. At the time she gave them a sense of competency, because they knew that however insufficient they were at running a perfect house-hold, they were never as extreme as Lucy Ricardo.

Male viewers were also comfortable with the Lucy character. Her ineptness made them feel superior, and her sex appeal held their interest. Lucille Ball's good looks were not the norm for a comedian. Many were amazed that a beautiful woman would allow a camera to record her getting a pie in the face, wearing curlers, face cream, or ridiculous costumes. It was understandable why Imogene Coca or Fanny Brice might turn to comedy, but more of an anomaly when a former model like Ball did. As *Time* magazine noted: "Lucille belongs to a rare comic aristocracy: the clown with glamour."

Ricky was very much the boss of the household, but Lucy was constantly testing his authority. When Ricky wanted to grow a mustache that Lucy disliked, she glued on Santa Claus whiskers in protest.

As Karyn Kay, a co-editor of *Women and the Cinema,* com-mented: "Lucy, you were a voice of rebellion for a pre-liberation . . . group of women. You shared a big secret with us: that women do not necessarily want neat, orderly homes and spic 'n' span lives, quietly serving their husbands. You rejected the expected, Lucy, and refused to behave correctly. You spoke a lunatic language of female discontent—you were an inspired feminist clown in the dog days before feminist consciousness."

Yet the Lucy character never quite made it as an independent strong female. Even in her later Lucy series, when she played a widow, she was always conniving against her male boss. Lucy has stated, "I need a strong father or husband figure as a catalyst. I have to be an inadequate somebody because I don't want the authority for Lucy."

Although Lucy tended to downplay feminist politics she did tell an interviewer in 1980 that women "can use my name for equal rights, but I don't get out there and raise hell because I've been so liberated I have nothing to squawk about."

"I Love Lucy" added another feminist first for television to its credit when Lucy became pregnant on the show. In real life Lucy had a daughter, and was pregnant with her second child, a boy. Writers for the program decided to incorporate the pregnancy into the series. So radical was this idea at the time, that a priest, minister, and rabbi were invited to all the rehearsals to ensure nothing offensive was included. CBS management found the word "pregnant" objectionable and "expectant" was substituted.

When Lucy gave birth to her TV child in 1953, 40 million Americans or 71.7 percent of people with television sets were tuned into the show. (Compare this with the 33 million who watched Queen Elizabeth's coronation, or the 29 million who watched President Eisenhower's inauguration).

The popularity of the "I Love Lucy" show was undisputed and Lucy and Desi were the highest paid stars on TV at eight million per year. But in 1953 the acid test of audience loyalty came when Lucy was accused of being a communist. In the hysterical days of McCarthy's reign of terror at the helm of the House Committee on Un-American Activities, it was discovered that Lucy had registered to vote on the Communist ticket in 1936. Lucy who now described herself as apolitical and whose ideas tended toward the conservative, had been prompted to register as a Communist by her socialist grandfather. She did so to please him, and not because of any conviction of her own. Nevertheless, the Los Angeles *Herald Express* ran a banner headline: "Lucille Ball Named Red." Other newspapers, magazines, and radio stations picked up the story.

Lucy was officially cleared by the Committee of being a Communist after she testified at their hearings. Anxious that their show would be cancelled and Desilu ruined, Ball and Arnaz were relieved when the sponsors stood behind them, giving total support. But there was still the public to face. When they filmed their first show after the news broke, Desi made a short speech to the studio audience saying that the only thing red about Lucille was her hair and even that was phony. Her fans broke into applause to show their unqualified support and approval.

After this crisis it was smooth sailing again for the "I Love Lucy" show. The Ricardos moved to Hollywood when Ricky got a movie offer and the change of locale and plot provided for the introduction of big-name guest stars like Harpo Marx and William Holden.

Additional writers, Bob Schiller and Bob Weiskopf, were hired, and new story lines took the Ricardos to Europe where they visited Britain, France, Switzerland, Italy, and Monaco. During the trip, Lucy got stuck in a ship's porthole, dangled from a helicopter and fought with a professional stomper in a vat of grapes. On the plane home she disguised a large overweight cheese as a baby.

During the 1956-57 season Little Ricky first appeared on the show, played by child actor Keith Thibodeaux, an expert young drummer. Previous to this, Lucy's infant had been seen only on occasional episodes played by hired babies. The Arnazes had decided not to use their own son, Desi Jr., in the show because it might make their daughter Lucie jealous.

Other changes to the program's plot came when Ricky returned to New York and bought an interest in the Tropicana Club, renaming it the Babalu. This provided a stage for more guest stars like Bob Hope. The series went through a final change when the Ricardos and Mertzes moved to a Connecticut suburb. Two new neighbors, Ralph and Betty Ramsey, were cast, and Lucy was up to her usual tricks. In one episode Lucy and Ethel dismantled a barbecue trying to find Lucy's lost wedding ring.

May 1957 brought the series to an end. It was difficult to keep the show fresh after so many years, and the demands on Ball and Arnaz were enormous. They needed a break. After they sold the rerun rights to CBS, Desilu acquired RKO Studios for 6.15 million dollars.

The "I Love Lucy" cast continued to do 13 one-hour-long "Lucille Ball-Desi Arnaz Show" specials over the next three years. The format and content of the programs were similar to the weekly shows, only less frequent.

As well as the hour-long specials, Arnaz and Ball had made two comic movies, *The Long, Long Trailer* in 1954 and *Forever, Darling* in 1956. Neither were critically acclaimed, although they were box-office hits.

Despite the enormous television success of the Ricardo marriage, the real life Arnaz-Ball relationship had gone downhill. Desi was a drinker, gambler, and womanizer. Lucy needed someone to feed her ego. They divorced in 1960.

Lucy was awarded half of Desilu Productions. Both remarried, Lucy to comedian Gary Morton in 1961, and Desi to a wealthy divorcee, Edith Hirsch in 1963. Ball's marriage to Morton has lasted for over twenty years, no doubt because of Morton's strong sense of self-identity. He has never felt like "Mr. Ball." When

Morton later became an executive at Desilu, he had to put in five years before Lucy gave him a title.

Career-wise Lucille Ball was on her own again. She had made it big in "I Love Lucy" and now she had to prove she could draw an audience on her own: "I know better than most people," she said, "how much the 'I Love Lucy' legend was built around the marriage of Desi and me. Now that I have to go it alone, I am not frightened. I know it will not be as satisfying to me, because I loved the legend while it lasted."

Ball accepted a starring role in the Broadway musical *Wildcat,* which opened in 1960. Audiences turned out for 171 performances but reviewers were critical of the production. Lucy became ill and the show closed in 1961.

But Lucy was always ready for another challenge. At the age of fifty-one she started a new series on television "The Lucy Show." Although the new show never matched the artistic quality of "I Love Lucy," TV audiences tuned in faithfully. Lucy felt her continued popularity was due to the fact that "people seem grateful that Lucy is there, the same character and unchanging view. There's so much chaos in the world, that's important."

"The Lucy Show" ran for five and one-half years. Ball played a widow sharing a house with her two children and with a friend played by Vivian Vance. She worked for a banker, Mr. Mooney, played by Gale Gordon.

In 1968 the series was changed to "Here's Lucy" and this time she played a widow with her own two children appearing on the show in the roles of her television offspring. Gale Gordon stayed on this time in the role of "Uncle Harry." The series was shown on CBS from 1968 to 1974.

Not content with television alone, Lucy, with her tremendous energy, also appeared in five more films during the 1960 to 1974 period, including *The Facts of Life* with Bob Hope in 1960; *Critic's Choice* in 1963, again with Hope; *A Guide for the Married Man* 1967; *Yours Mine and Ours* 1968; and *Mame* 1974. Lucy had appeared in an incredible 74 movies during her career as a performer. Moreover, after her television series ended in 1974, she made several television specials and guest appearances on other shows. In the fall of 1986 she returned to TV with another series.

Nor did Lucy need the work. She was making a fortune from Desilu Productions. In 1962 she had bought out Desi's half of the business for close to three million dollars, making her the first woman to head a major Hollywood film company.

When Desi was president of the company, Lucy credited him with all the business decisions. But seven years later under Lucy's management Desilu grossed $30 million. She obviously had a knack for business. Some of the television shows that Desilu produced were "The Ann Sothern Show," "The Danny Thomas Show," "The Untouchables," "Mannix," "Mission Impossible," and "Star Trek."

Just as Ball has been low-key about feminism, she also tended to downplay her business expertise. She claimed she cried a lot at first and found it difficult to boss men: "I'm all wrong as an executive, I feel out of place. . . . I'm too easily hurt and intimidated." Yet she acknowledged that "I can make quick surgical decisions." And Lucy was not timid either when it came to confrontations with her stockholders. In 1965 at the Desilu annual meeting some of the shareholders complained that she was making too large a salary. Lucy fought it out with them, and proved that as president she deserved every penny she got.

Modest as she may have been about her business acumen, friends were more outspoken. Bob Hope said: "It's startling to find out that a comedienne as capable as Lucy is also a very smart business person." Noted her husband Gary Morton, "Don't be fooled. Lucy has an innate business sense." And Vivian Vance added: "Believe you me. I wish she were my business agent."

In 1967 Ball sold Desilu to Gulf and Western for $17 million. She then formed the smaller Lucille Ball Productions Inc., which continued to be involved with producing movies and TV shows. Lucy was considered the wealthiest woman in Hollywood with a fortune estimated at between 50 and 75 million dollars.

It may be easy to measure Lucy's wealth in dollars but her real legacy was the "I Love Lucy" program, where her wonderful talent as a comedian was showcased. Lucy did not believe in entertainment as propaganda. She had no "message." Her main purpose she said was to provide "hope, faith and fun." With "I Love Lucy" still being rerun on television thirty years after its premiere, her purpose has certainly been fulfilled.

EVE ARDEN

Eve Arden was a busy and active entertainer for about twenty years before she attained her greatest fame as the high school teacher Miss Brooks, on both radio and television. Until that point she had appeared in all of the entertainment media, from stock companies, to Broadway revues, to summer theatre, to motion pictures. She made dozens of films, most of them "B" features in which she offered comic relief. She never got the man in the film, or went out on dates, and was usually a best friend to the star, or a shoulder to cry on for somebody. Her main character type was a woman with an acid tongue and a caustic, acerbic wit, or in more popular parlance she was "catty" or "bitchy." She was also very funny.

Her parts were small but she embellished them whenever possible with her own unique touches and drew enough notice to be more steadily employed than most. As Miss Brooks she combined most of the traits which Hollywood had already typed her with, albeit in a softer and more humane way. Few entertainers have ever been so strongly identified with a single character as Eve Arden was. Over a quarter-century after that high school teacher left the air, one can't see or hear Eve Arden without thinking of Miss Brooks.

Arden was born Eunice Quedens in April 1912 just outside of San Francisco. The child of divorced parents, she was raised by her mother (who had some experience in acting) and by a couple of aunts. The aunts in particular encouraged Eve's theatrical ambitions. As a youngster she was involved in staged child dramas and in dialect recitals. In a W.C.T.U. contest at the age of seven, she did a reading of "No Kicka My Dog," and won a gold medal. Her only other theatrical experience of note took place in high school when she had the lead in her senior year in a play called *Dulcy*.

At the age of sixteen her aunts drove her into San Francisco, dropped her off in front of a theater which housed one of the city's better known repertory companies, the Henry Duffy Players, and told her to get an acting job. Somewhat surprisingly she did just that, and spent the next eighteen months doing mostly bit parts with that group before leaving to join a four-person vagabond group calling themselves the "Bandbox Repertory Theatre."

This group traveled throughout the state of California and performed skits and plays wherever they could; in the streets, in desert resorts, private homes, hotel lobbies, and even in barns. This West Coast equivalent of the Borscht Belt was known as the Citrus Circuit, and it was here that Arden got experience in comic delivery and the art of timing.

From that job she moved to a Leonard Sillman revue, *Lo and Behold,* in Pasadena, and while in that production she was noticed by Lee Shubert who signed her up for the *Ziegfeld Follies,* which opened in New York City in 1934. It was at that time Eunice took her stage name of Eve Arden. Up until then she had been performing under her real name. She came up with the new name one evening when she scanned her cosmetic bottles and combined "Evening in Paris" with "Elizabeth Arden." The following year she appeared in the Broadway production *Parade,* and critic Brooks Atkinson said it was "Eve Arden's lorgnette humor which turns a song entitled 'Send for the Militia' into highly amusing satire." She next appeared in the *Ziegfeld Follies* (1936), at which time she was a featured member of the cast and earning $100 a week. She understudied for the star, Fanny Brice.

In 1937 she returned to California when her mother died, and while there landed her first film role. She played a gun moll in a "B" comedy melodrama, *Oh, Doctor.* Regarding that experience, she said, "Things like that shouldn't happen to anybody." It marked the beginning of a long and ambivalent relationship between her and the film industry. Her mother had always been one of Arden's toughest critics and had told her she'd "be happier with a home and a dozen children than [she] would be on the stage." After her mother's death, there was enough guilt involved for Arden to be in psychoanalysis for a number of years.

Her second film was *Stage Door* (1937), in which she was cast as a wisecracking stage hopeful. The film also had a cat named Henry in it and Arden convinced the director to let her wear the live cat around her neck instead of a fur piece. It was her way of enhancing her role. In *The Doughgirls* she beefed up her part of a Russian guerrilla by adding some comedy routines with her rifle. It was this film that caused audiences to finally take note of her name. In *My Dream Is Yours* Eve had a scene where she washed a dog. To enliven this she appeared in a pair of conspicuous leopard skin pants which she herself designed. At one point a producer heard that she was rewriting and improving some of her dialogue on the set. The producer sent down word that she should cease and desist.

The films she appeared in ran the gamut from comedy to musicals to serious drama, but her parts remained essentially the same—comic relief. She rarely played a straight role, and by 1950 she had appeared in 49 features. By 1980 this total was 57. She also found time to appear in a number of Broadway productions as well as in summer stock.

From the beginning she was typed as the character who delivered brittle and caustic humor. "Without exception, her roles had always required her to appear as a well-tailored, barb-tongued female who casually skewered her victims with a caustic line." In *The Unfaithful* (1947) she played Ann Sheridan's "bitchy" sister-in-law. The next year in *Voice of the Turtle* she was a busybody actress friend described this time as just "catty." In *Mildred Pierce* (1945) she delivered one of her best remembered lines when she commented about Joan Crawford's screen daughter, "Alligators have the right idea, they eat their young." She had a wide range of facial expressions and was able to express an array of emotions from distaste to surprise to disapproval almost at the same time. This, combined with her dialogue, caused one observer to classify her stock in trade as "elegant bitchery."

Audiences loved her cruel retorts, but the character type didn't sit easy with Arden. She didn't care much for Hollywood because "the star got everything and the comedians what's left." She had started doing radio work in 1945 and was a regular on "The Danny Kaye Show" and "The Sealtest Village Store," where she replaced Joan Davis. During her first three years on radio she played the same wisecracking, sharp-tongued woman she was doing in films. She had almost always been uneasy playing that type of character.

As time went by the roles became more and more repugnant to her, but by then she was well and truly typed and trapped. Audiences enjoyed her and producers kept her working, for they knew her comic skills would keep their films from wallowing in too much sentiment. Arden's dislike for her film alter ego was strong enough that she never saw any of the films she appeared in until *Mildred Pierce*, which was her thirty-third feature. It was one of her stronger films and earned her an Oscar nomination, but the character Eve saw wasn't the warm, sentimental, or sympathetic person she wanted to play. Eve saw "a sarcastic, unmannerly, two-dimensional character type she cordially despised." As Arden said of her character, "I just don't like that dame. She is hard-boiled, unsentimental — and not me."

From the time she saw that film she vowed to herself that she would take the first "human being" part that came her way. She got her chance in 1948 when she auditioned for the role of high school teacher Connie Brooks in a new radio series, "Our Miss Brooks." Some thought the move was a mistake on Eve's part. One film director said to her, "What are you trying to do? . . . Louse up your career?" But Arden was determined to break type, and Miss Brooks was the kind of likeable and sentimental character she was after. A short while after the show had started, a studio called and offered her a $50,000 part in a film, the typical character she had played so long. The reply was no, because "Eve Arden isn't playing Eve Arden parts any more."

The show premiered in July of 1948 on CBS radio and was one of the most popular comedy shows almost from the start. Jack Gould of *The New York Times* wrote, "Eve Arden, who can deliver a line with a decidedly sophisticated and acerbic wallop, finally has won a program of her own." Another critic said "Miss Arden wisecracks indefatigably and courageously . . . there just isn't anyone in the business who can handle feline dialogue as well as Miss Arden." Connie Brooks taught English at Madison High School, located somewhere in Middle America.

The show revolved around Connie's efforts to snag the school's shy biology teacher, Philip Boynton, and the problem of trying to live on the low salary paid to teachers in those days. The show had an outstanding supporting cast as well. Gale Gordon, an expert in the role of blustery windbag, did perhaps his best windbag as the school principal, Osgood Conklin. Richard Crenna played student Walter Denton, who regularly drove Miss Brooks to school in his jalopy. Connie rented a room in a house owned by Mrs. Davis, played by Jane Morgan. As the landlady Mrs. Davis was partly naive and partly senile, cast in the same mold of logical lunacy that Marie Wilson and Gracie Allen were found in. Boynton was played by Jeff Chandler in his only stab at comedy, unusual for the usually macho actor. Nevertheless he did the role well on radio.

Teachers across the country took the program to heart. They were pleased that the low salary conditions of the profession were brought to light. Arden got hundreds of letters every week from grateful teachers. She received numerous honors and citations from teacher groups and spoke at many functions and meetings of teachers. In another example of confusing reality and illusion, six high school principals reportedly offered Eve jobs teaching in their English departments. In any event, Arden wouldn't have been able to afford such a job. In the early 1950's she was making about $200,000 a year, mostly from "Our Miss Brooks." Not all teachers were favorably disposed toward the series. Quite a few complained, and one said the show "sets the teaching profession back 100 years." Complaints centered around undermining the profession by presenting undignified caricatures of teachers and a bullying principal.

The Connie Brooks character was not as far removed from Arden's other roles as might be thought. The Brooks character had a "sarcastic wit that became its strongest trademark." On her show Eve remarked, "Teaching school can be a very rich life for a young woman—that is, if she happens to be a very rich young woman." Another time she and Mrs. Davis were discussing Mr. Boynton. Connie was somewhat disconsolate over not being able to land him. Mrs. Davis remarked that there were lots more fish in the sea, to which Connie replied, "Yes, but on my salary I can't make the bait as attractive as it should be.'

The series debuted on CBS television in October 1952. The half-hour program was on both radio and television in the mid 1950's. The program transferred to television with the cast virtually intact, except for Mr. Boynton. The show's staff knew he was too macho to come across visually, and Jeff Chandler was then starting to make an impact as an actor in films. The producers persuaded him that that was where his future lay, and so Robert Rockwell took over the part of the shy and indifferent Mr. Boynton. The TV format remained the same and involved Arden's interaction with the other regulars and her major activity, the unending and ultimately futile pursuit of Boynton, a man who liked and understood his frogs better than women. The series usually had short fast scenes and sight gags.

The program peaked in popularity in the 1953-54 season, when it made the top fifteen shows. Arden won an Emmy in 1954 as the best comedienne. Ratings were slipping at the start of the 1955-56 season and the program underwent a massive overhaul. Madison High was bulldozed for a highway and Connie found herself teaching at a private school. Miraculously, Conklin turned up there as principal. A new love interest was found, a physical education teacher who, in a turnaround, chased Eve. As might be expected, these changes did nothing to enhance the show and ratings sank lower. In the early part of 1956 Mr. Boynton was rushed back into the program as a last-minute emergency transfusion, but it was too late; the series died that spring. It was, however, one of those series that was rerun for years, everywhere, and it was there that it achieved its greatest popularity.

Arden saw the Brooks role as a loving person who cared about her students and kept them out of trouble while getting into trouble herself, and chasing Boynton. The Brooks role was certainly softer and more human than her other roles, but not that far removed. Nor was she that different from the stereotype of the teacher in those days. She was a spinster and getting a bit "vinegary" because of it. "Her cynical comments on life were always devastatingly illusion-shattering, but delivered with a saving grace of humor; bitter Miss Brooks may have been, but she never lost her sense of proportion." Following the tradition in those days set by such as Lucy and "My Friend Irma," the series was turned into a movie, *Our Miss Brooks* (1956). The basic cast were all there but the film was neither successful nor particularly funny.

Arden returned to TV in the fall of 1957 with her own comedy show, "The Eve Arden Show." She played a widowed novelist who made extra money on the lecture circuit. The show was undistinguished and expired after one year, in the spring of 1958. A decade later she was back in a series called "The Mothers-In-Law" which debuted in September 1967. Eve co-starred with Kaye Ballard as mothers of children who had just married each other, and dealt with their tribulations. She played a wisecracking role similar to Miss Brooks. This series was not as well written but managed to last two years, terminating in the spring of 1968. Over the past couple of decades Arden has kept busy doing some Broadway work, TV guest spots, lots of summer theater, a few movies and has toured with road versions of musicals like *Mame* and *Hello Dolly*.

Eve Arden did manage to escape the "dumb woman" stereotype during her career, but she was caught in others. As Miss Brooks she didn't have her own apartment, she just rented a room in somebody's house. This was done not so much to point out that teachers had low salaries but to deal with the image of the lone female. It was most common for those not married on stage to live with a roommate, such as Irma, or to live as a roomer, such as Miss Brooks. Thus the image of the independent lone woman was counteracted by the image of the timid and passive creature, not alone by choice, who didn't even have the nerve, gumption, or independence to set up her own household. The idea of the lone woman as a threatening and possibly free sexual object was also neutralized with those conditions. It was difficult to have an affair if your roommate was always around or if your landlady was forever dropping in. Her good looks and witty humor made her a sexually attractive woman, but the writers suppressed this in Connie Brooks by making her a perpetual pal, and never a lover.

Stories about the "real" Eve emphasized her devotion to home. She was called a slave to nothing "except possibly her own diligent domesticity." Home was "obviously her primary interest." Arden it was said was a "frustrated homebody almost all her life." Obviously she was nothing of the sort; her own life and career were evidence to the contrary. But in the 1950's the media was determined to emphasize the idea of a woman's place.

The other stereotype that Miss Brooks fell into was the man chaser. Not perhaps the raucous type like Judy Canova but a chaser just the same. Many of her programs, year after year, dealt with no other topic than how to catch this one man. It was even the focus of her conversations with her landlady. The message here was very clear, a lone woman had really only one worthwhile goal to pursue, that of capturing a man. A lone woman was not a complete being on her own. It would be decades before shows like "Mary Tyler Moore" came along which could show a female living independently in her own apartment and not devoting the better part of her free time, and even some of her work time, to catching a man. Brooks was a misfit in a society that dictated that a woman should marry and stay home and raise kids. She used laughter to cover her pain, but she did suffer pain.

The role of Connie Brooks was a step up for women, though, in some ways. She was an intelligent woman and held a full-time outside job, albeit woman's work, and she presented a more subtle, intelligent, and verbal style of humor. She got out of the broad physical slapstick style that so many women of the period favored. She played the character wonderfully well, and ever since, Eve Arden and Connie Brooks have been one in the public's mind. A reflection of, and a tribute to, her comic skills and abilities.

MARIE WILSON

One of the most favorite dumb, blond, female comedians was Marie Wilson. She was a success with her character in three different mediums—movies, radio, and television. As a nitwit and dunderhead in radio, where she became nationally famous, she followed such classic comics as Jane Ace and Gracie Allen in the "dummy" role. Her style of illogic most closely followed that of Allen, on whom her character of Irma Peterson was modelled. Some enthusiasts even felt she was able to outdo Allen in the peabrain sweepstakes.

She differed from those radio comics in that her ample bosom was played up. In her stage and television appearances she often appeared in tight and low cut dresses. She became a prototype for the dumb and sexy blond funnywoman, a popular creature of the 1950's. The humor of those women lay not in their saying something witty or funny. It lay in their incredible stupidity, the preposterous situations they found themselves in, their butchering of the language, and their totally illogical thought processes.

Wilson parlayed the character of Irma into seven years on radio, two on television, and two movies. Her trademarks came to be her sexy innocence, her baby voice raised in eternal puzzlement, a wide-eyed stare and her generally dazed and bewildered manner.

She was born Katherine Elizabeth Wilson in 1916 in Anaheim, California. She later decided her name was too long for a theatre marquee and adopted the name of a sister, Marie. Her father was a realtor who owned an orange grove as well. Her parents were divorced. When her father died he left his estate of $11,000 to Marie. Instead of putting the money into a trust fund until she was 21, he stipulated that she could use the money immediately even though she was just a teenager. So in 1932 Marie took the money and moved the family to Hollywood where she hoped to become an actress. The family consisted of mother, stepfather, half and stepsiblings, and a few other relatives. She rented a house, paying a year's rent in advance, bought a mink coat, a convertible, and stocked the house with months' and months' worth of canned goods. The money was gone in a month.

Marie kept herself and her family alive by doing movie extra work and other odd jobs. She once worked in the toy department of a store but was fired for talking a customer out of spending $25 for a teddy bear, and for giving toys from the store away to poor children. Her break came in 1934, thanks largely to her own initiative. She knew where a producer lived and that he cut his grass at a certain time of the day. Marie conveniently arranged for her car to run out of gas in front of this man's home. One thing led to another and she was given a screen test by MGM. That studio didn't act on the test, but Jack Warner, who had also seen it, did, signing Marie to a Warner Brothers contract on the strength of the test.

Until her contract expired in 1941 she appeared in a number of Warner movies. Marie had wanted to do straight roles, but the studio had different ideas. In her first year with Warner she had already been tapped for the dumb blonde role, the forerunner of her Irma character. The movies she appeared in were all eminently forgettable. Mostly she played daffy blondes in programmers, the "B" film on a double bill. Her films were demolished by critics but were successful enough at the box office to give Wilson steady employment for quite a while. By the time her contract expired she found herself not yet a star and with bleak future prospects.

Vaudeville and radio comic Ken Murray rescued her fading career the next year. He was producing a vaudeville style revue called *Blackouts of 1942* and was looking for a leading lady. Murray was familiar with Wilson from radio work the two had done, and he offered her the spot. He was aware of her ample bust and was the first to truly exploit it, feeling she could be funny and sexy. He had her appear on stage in black lace underwear and billed her as the "Mattress of Ceremonies." One bit of patter from the show had Murray ask where she was born. Wilson would reply she was born in an Anaheim grapefruit grove. Murray would then leer at her bust and say that that explained a couple of things.

Blackouts played in Hollywood for seven years, with Marie doing ten shows a week. During her tenure on the show she missed only 28 performances out of 3,567. Wilson started out at $250 a week and was earning $1,000 a week from the show by 1949, the year she left. During the first two years of her Irma radio program she continued her gruelling schedule in *Blackouts*. How important she was to the success of that show can perhaps be seen from its fate after Wilson's departure. Murray took the show to Broadway in 1949 but it closed after just 51 performances.

In 1947 radio producer Cy Howard was casting for the role of Irma in the show he had created, "My Friend Irma." He had seen

Wilson in *Blackouts* and offered her the role. Wilson hesitated, saying she was nervous about doing a full-length script before a microphone and that she would ruin the program for Howard. However, he persisted and helped her to overcome her "sense of inferiority." Thus one of America's most lovable and durable nitwits began a lengthy run.

The character of Irma remained largely unchanged whether it was on radio or television. Irma worked as a stenographer in a law firm and was enthusiastic, friendly, a good samaritan, and just plain dumb. She lived with a roommate who was level-headed, and the stories revolved around the trials and tribulations of her roommate as she affectionately tried to cope with Irma and her harebrained schemes and scatterbrained antics.

All of the "dumb" women of this era lived with someone. Some, such as the characters of Joan Davis and Lucille Ball, had husbands; Irma had a roommate. In all cases the other half was more or less normal and level-headed. The function of this person was to bail out the dumb woman. These women were portrayed as being so inept that they obviously would never be capable of functioning if they lived alone. They had to have someone to care for them, normally a man, although that was not always neces- sary, especially if the female in question was projecting any kind of sexual image as well as her stupidity. This helplessness was of course the intended message.

The epitome of dumb blondes was reached with the creation of Irma. When asked about compulsory military service, Irma replied that "a girl shouldn't have to go out with a sailor unless she wants to." The show quickly reached the point where a laugh could be generated merely by having Irma state that she had pur- chased a set of the Encyclopedia Britannica. In one half-hour program, among her many absurdities, Irma knitted a pair of gloves and forgot to leave an opening for the hands, told a friend that Shakespeare's Hamlet was a new breakfast food, and doubled the amount on her employer's income tax return so nobody would think that he wasn't doing well. The show rapidly became popu- lar and was rated among the top handful of programs in radio. It was also the first successful comedy show to break into radio in the previous ten years.

The distinction between a stage character and the performer who plays that character is often a blurred and fuzzy line. For Marie Wilson and Irma an attempt was made to erase that dis- tinction entirely. Part of this came from Cy Howard. He claimed half of what occurred on the show he got from observing Marie's behavior. The other half of Marie's behavior was so outlandish that Howard claimed he had to rewrite it to make it believable. According to legend, Cy once waved a cue at Marie while the show was in progress and Marie waved back in a daze. Another time Howard told Marie that Senator Taft was coming on in place of them. Wilson pouted that Howard had promised her there would be no guest stars. During a media interview it was reported that Marie couldn't remember her husband's last name when asked.

Wilson herself played up the idea that she was dumb. She once said, "People like me because I'm dumb. . . . It gives them a good feeling to be smarter than I am." She had been a bright student at high school but later decided to say she was never able to finish high school, because she thought it fit better with her character. It was said that the world wanted to think of Marie as a dumb blonde. But it might be more accurate to say the world insisted. The media certainly did. One article titled "My Friend Irma Is Not So Dumb" turned around and drew the reverse conclusion that "Marie Wilson at Base Is the Dumb Blonde."

Another article was even more extreme. "Never in the history of mankind has there been a more perfect mating of role and actor. Marie is not only Irma on the air but in real life. She is the flutter-headed Samaritan who has the brains of a chipmunk."

The radio show received about 500 letters a week. Most of them offered suggestions to improve Irma's deplorable state. Some felt she should move out of her boarding house because they thought her roommate didn't always treat her properly. Others thought Irma needed a good psychiatrist and a few even offered to pay for the costs.

Hal Wallis produced the first of the two Irma pictures in 1949. The first bore the same title as both the radio and the television shows, *My Friend Irma*. When Wallis announced the movie it was rumored that the part would go to Betty Hutton. Wilson promptly hired a press agent to advance her case and worked with him in lining up fan clubs and other pressure groups to threaten a boycott unless Wilson got the part. She was successful and the movie became one of the biggest grossers of 1949. It was a notable film in that it introduced an unknown male comedy team in their screen debut, Martin and Lewis.

For Marie Wilson being a dumb blonde was "profitable and nice. I'll work at it until I'm an old lady." She did admit though that thinking up all those dumb remarks she made was a chore. The show ran on television for a couple of years, going off the air in June of 1954, although it continued in reruns for many years. It didn't achieve the same dominant position in the ratings that the radio show had captured.

The show's humor, on both radio and television, was broad and not subtle, and was given out in weekly doses. While these were often the ingredients of monotony, the show enjoyed a long run. Like the even briefer run of Dagmar, Wilson found the public eventually tired of her character and were turning to other female comedians such as Lucille Ball and Joan Davis.

Wilson's career waned after the show left the air. She did a number of TV pilots but none were sold. She played Las Vegas a number of times as well as doing a resurrection of *Blackouts* in 1960 for a few months. During the sixties she toured in stage productions of *Gentlemen Prefer Blondes* and *Born Yesterday*.

Marie Wilson died in 1972. Shortly before her death, she remarked on some of the problems of being typecast and stereotyped with a "dumb" image. "It has been very good to me and I'm not complaining, but some day I just wish someone would offer me a different kind of role. My closest friends admit that whenever they tell someone they know me they have to convince them that I'm really not dumb. To tell you the truth, I think people are disappointed that I'm not."

JACKIE "MOMS" MABLEY

Jackie Mabley was born Loretta Mary Aiken in 1897 in North Carolina. She was one of twelve children, and her father Jim owned the town grocery store. Mabley was of mixed black, Cherokee, and Irish heritage. Her great-grandmother, Harriet Smith, had been a slave.

Stories of Mabley's early life vary. One version she gave was that she ran away from home when a marriage was arranged between her and a man so old that "somebody threw one grain of rice and it knocked him out."

Another story she told a *Washington Post* reporter was that she was an unwed mother: "We didn't get married up in the mountains. I did get engaged two or three times, but they always wanted a free sample. That's how I got stuck."

For whatever reason, Mabley did leave North Carolina and lived for a time in Washington, D.C., and Cleveland. She became an entertainer in her early teens to support herself because, as she said in a 1974 interview, she "was very pretty and didn't want to become a prostitute."

Mabley's religious feelings guided her: "I prayed and it came to me more in a vision than a dream: Go on stage." She started out in black vaudeville on the old T.O.B.A. (Theatre Owners Booking Association) circuit. It was a rough grind and racism on the road was rampant. Mabley joked that star performers had to have stand-ins in case they got lynched.

On the road, Moms met a handsome young entertainer named Jackie Mabley. "He took a lot off me," she said of Mabley. "The least I could do was take his name." It has been suggested that Mabley referred to him in her act as the man who said he'd roll over in his grave if she went out with anyone else after he died. Mabley joked, "I went back to see him a year after he was buried, but I couldn't see him 'cause he had rolled all the way down the hill." Moms had several love affairs going in her vaudeville days. Cab Calloway was one of her big heart throbs.

Mabley later got the nickname "Moms" because of her maternal attitude towards fellow performers and audiences. She incorporated her "Moms" character into her stage act when she was in her early twenties. She began wearing loose house dresses, and addressing her audience as "children."

She remembered "letting granny grow. . . . I had in my mind a woman about sixty or sixty-five, even, when I first came up. . . . She's a good woman, with an eye for shady dealings. . . . She was like my granny, the most beautiful woman I ever knew. She was the one who convinced me to go make something of myself. . . . She was so gentle, but she kept her children in line, best believe that."

Moms was making about $14 a week before she got her first big break. She was appearing in Dallas in 1921 when the dance team of Butterbeans and Susie saw her act. They introduced her to an agent who booked her in Baltimore for $90 a week.

By 1923 she was playing Connie's Inn and the Cotton Club in New York City, and touring on the "Chitlin Circuit," travelling from one northern ghetto to another. She appeared at famous black clubs like The Howard in Washington, D.C., Club Harlem in Atlantic City, and The Monogram in Chicago. Also headlining these clubs were musicians like Louis Armstrong, Duke Ellington, and Count Basie.

Moms teamed up with entertainers like Pigmeat Markham, Tim "Kingfish" Moore, and Bill "Bojangles" Robinson. She often did jailhouse routines.

Her vaudeville act brought her some bit parts in movies. In 1929 she appeared in *Boarding House Blues,* and in *Emperor Jones* in 1933.

In 1939 Mabley was the first woman comic to appear at the Apollo Theater in New York City. She became a regular performer at the Apollo, playing fifteen-week stints and changing her act every week. Her routine included singing and dancing as well as comedy. Many comedians including whites caught her act and she claimed they all stole her material except Jack Benny, but she didn't mind: "It makes no difference. God always gives me some more." Her younger brother Eddie Parton also helped out by writing some of her material.

In the forties and fifties Mabley did stand-up comedy in black clubs. Her humor was raunchy and her jokes often centered around the merits of young versus old men. She used to crack: "The only thing an old man can do for me is bring a message from a young one," or "I can't do nothing with an old man, 'cause he can't do nothing with himself." When Moms herself became old she wasn't any more sympathetic to old men: "A woman is a woman until the day she dies, but a man's a man only as long as he can."

She liked to joke about the ugly old man whose job it was to stand outside a doctor's office and make people sick. Her formula for attracting a young man? "All you have to do is knock on their door and ask them: 'Say, doll, do you have change for a hundred dollar bill.'"

Mabley became known outside the black entertainment world in 1960 when Chess Records produced her first album *Moms Mabley—The Funniest Woman in the World.* It sold over 1,000,000 copies and went gold. In 1966 Mercury Records issued the album *Now Hear This,* with humor so blue it was popular at stag parties.

Acceptance in the white world had been a long time coming, and Moms had said: "I don't care if you could stand on your head, if you was colored you couldn't get no work at all." In 1975 she told a *New York Times* reporter: "There was some horrible things done to me. I've played every state in the union—except Mississippi. I won't go there. They ain't ready."

LUCILLE BALL

PHYLLIS DILLER

TOTIE FIELDS

NANCY WALKER

EVE ARDEN

JUDY CANOVA

MINNIE PEARL

MARTHA RAYE

ELAINE MAY

ANNA RUSSELL

LILY TOMLIN

CAROL BURNETT

JOAN RIVERS

GOLDIE HAWN

GILDA RADNER

SANDRA BERNHARD

WHOOPI GOLDBERG

© 1984 MARTHA SWOPE

One of the stories she told her audiences was about two bank robbers, one black, one white. They killed three tellers, two policemen and wounded a bystander. Sentenced to hang for their crime, the white man was overcome by terror. "I don't want to be hung. I don't want to be hung," he pleaded. The black man admonished him: "Oh man, we done killed up all them people and you talk about you don't want to be hung. . . . They gonna hang you, so why don't you face it like a man?" "That's easy for you to say," replied the white man, "You're used to it."

Yet Moms was philosophical about racism: "I try not to be bitter. I would have liked to have gotten my chance earlier, but that's the way things were in those days. . . . Better times are coming." In fact, Mabley could be called a political moderate. When riots broke out in black ghettos after Martin Luther King's assassination, she commented, "That ain't civil rights people, they're looting people using the least excuse for their own selfish use. They're the craziest people in the world. God created all men equal. Ain't that enough?"

But Moms didn't leave politics out of her act altogether. One routine involved giving advice in fictional telephone conversations to various world leaders, including President Lyndon Johnson, whom she called "Boy." Two of her record albums, *Moms Mabley at the Geneva Conference,* and *Moms Mabley at the UN* spoofed international affairs. She warned Cuban leader Fidel Castro about attending a performance at the Apollo Theater: "You gonna sit in a box at the Apollo Theater with all that hair on your chin? That's how Lincoln got it, remember."

She could also become sentimental on stage about her political heroes and often ended her act with the song, "Abraham, Martin and John."

In 1967 Harry Belafonte produced the first all-black comedy special on NBC television called *A Time for Laughter.* This was Mabley's TV debut, and she played the maid of a black suburban couple who thought of themselves as white. She followed this by appearances on such shows as Merv Griffin, Smothers Brothers, Bill Cosby, Flip Wilson, and Mike Douglas. Mabley earned about $8,500 per television show. When Ed Sullivan offered her a four-minute spot on his show, she declined, saying, "Honey, it takes Moms four minutes just to get on the stage."

Of her television success Mabley commented: "Instead of looking at the audience as my children, I looked at the world as my children. TV's been good to people like me and Redd Foxx. We came up when it was tough. We've been everything but hung. And now we've made it. It's too bad it took so long, though. Now that we've got some money, we have to use it all for doctor bills."

Mabley had used her femininity on stage, but of course the dumb blonde image wasn't available to her. Instead, she adopted another archetypal female persona, "mother." As Moms she was able to come across as earthy and bossy. Dressed in a garish housedress, knit cap, Argyle socks and large, floppy shoes, she lampooned the housewife's uniform. And audiences were delighted to hear racy jokes coming from such a maternal character.

With this persona Mabley was able to work into her old age without worrying about being young and attractive. In fact Mabley made the most out of being a feisty old lady with bulging eyes and rubbery face. One of her favorite lines about old age was: "You wake up one morning, and you got it." She even capitalized on her toothlessness. Moms claimed she could never work with her false teeth in, and kept them "parked" in a box she called "the garage." When she appeared on TV's 1973 Grammy Awards she took her teeth out in front of the audience. One of her frequent gags was to hold up an apple and say," "I may not be able to bite 'em, but I bet I could gum 'em to death."

Mabley, a devout Baptist, believed her talent was a gift from God: "When I get up there, what comes up comes out. I don't have a set routine . . . I really just talk about life . . . I've always asked the Lord to lead me, and He has."

Her religion didn't inhibit her ribald humor: "I do the double entendre," she said. "And I never did anything you haven't heard on the streets. . . . Well, now, when you say 'religion,' I guess that means I try to do what's right. I don't believe in cheatin' or doin' anybody out of nothin'." Her religion also made her take a stand against abortion. Mabley herself had four children and two husbands. She had separated from her second husband in the 1950's.

In 1974 the United Artists movie *Amazing Grace* was released. Mabley starred in the role of a woman who makes certain a corrupt black politician is reformed so that the black community can get behind him in the election. When producer and writer Matt Robinson began casting for the part he thought Moms might be too old. But he told a reporter, "She just came in and took over.

Her timing is so great, that face is so . . . different, she's just overwhelming."

Unfortunately the film was a poor vehicle for Mabley. Critics complained that it was silly and full of stereotypes. (A sample line: "We're all just the dark meat of God's great chicken.")

The movie premiered in white neighborhoods in New York. The Apollo Theater where Moms had performed for 35 years couldn't get the film on a first-run basis. It did well at the box office, though, and earned plenty of money for Mabley, who wanted to do the movie "to make my children and great-grandchildren proud of me, like all mothers do."

Unfortunately Mabley had suffered a heart attack during filming, and her health deteriorated after that. She died in 1975.

JEAN CARROLL

Jean Carroll started out in vaudeville in the 1920's in the traditional way for a woman, as a singer and a dancer. Her natural comedy bent led her quickly to that field, first as a member of a team and finally as a single. She was one of the very few true stand-up female comics working solo in the 1940's.

Born circa 1915 she entered amateur shows as a youngster and had attracted the attention of the theatrical agency, MCA, by the time she reached her teens. The agency convinced Carroll's mother to let her sign with their company and go on tour on the vaudeville circuit. At the age of fourteen she was part of a four-person act doing unison dancing. She was also the act's manager and one night gave one of the two male members a dressing down for flirting with a woman while the act was in progress, making precision dancing very difficult. Jean and the second female member moved on to the next town on the circuit the next morning, and the two men were to follow later that day with the wardrobes and the music. Apparently angered, they never showed up again and the two women had to struggle through as a two-person act, without their usual equipment.

She had brief stints with other acts before turning to comedy in the early 1930's. In the backstage "Green Room" where performers could relax while waiting their turn to go onstage, Jean sometimes did comedy bits. One involved stuffing a pillow over her stomach and doing an impression of a Kentucky colonel. Vaudeville comic Marty May, then a star of the bill, saw the bit and was impressed by Carroll. He convinced her to become his partner. While she was working with May, nothing was ever written down or even prepared ahead of time. The pair walked onstage and May just started talking to Carroll and she would answer whatever came into her head. This was her initiation into comedy.

One day she worked on a bill which also contained Buddy Howe, a dancer. The couple began to date and fell in love. They wanted to be together, so Jean wrote an act for them and the team of Carroll and Howe was born, around 1934-35. The pair married shortly thereafter. The act was a comedy dance act, with Howe doing the dancing and acting as straight man to Carroll's comedy. Jean did all the writing and taught Buddy how to deliver his straight lines. Howe had never had any lines at all on stage before, being strictly a dancer.

The act was initially broken in at state fairs where they did the talking routine if the audience wasn't too big, and a dancing act if the audience was large. The team was very successful and played all the major theaters from coast to coast, including New York's Palace. By 1935 Jean Carroll was doing comedy monologues on stage alone. She dressed elegantly and her routines were ten-minute or so bits which she often based on real events.

Carroll had gone shopping one day and admired a blouse in a store. She asked the clerk what size it was and the clerk said it wouldn't fit. Carroll said again that she wanted to know the size, was it a twelve? The clerk told Carroll she would never get into a twelve. From this incident Carroll built a ten-minute routine which she used countless times. It was one of her funniest and most popular.

In 1936 Carroll and Howe went to England for a three-week booking. They stayed for three years. They became superstars in England and were said to rank second only to Burns and Allen. Back in the U.S., they spent the next two years with the USO before Howe was called into the service. When he was discharged in 1945, Jean was doing a single act so successfully it didn't make sense for Howe to go back to a double. Howe had never been really comfortable as the act's straight man. He delivered the lines exactly as written and if Jean ad-libbed, as she often did, he was at a loss. Howe admitted that Carroll "was too good" to need him in the act. `

Starting about 1943, Jean was doing a solo comedy routine with no singing or dancing or other extraneous material, just verbal patter. She tended to favor monologues over one- or two-line jokes, and continued to write all her own material. Another routine of hers that became a favorite was one about buying a mink coat wholesale. The content of her material tended toward her own domestic life, and current customs. Her material was described as "droll commentaries upon everyday situations." Her delivery was called "sardonic." She believed her material should be tailored to her audience and that what was funny in small towns was different from what she would use in a place like New York City. To this end she made it a practice to listen in on conversations in public places such as stores and restaurants to gather material.

She often used her family as the butt of her jokes, including her daughter, mother, and especially her husband. Some of her fans complained, feeling it wasn't right for her to be doing that. Due to such complaints Carroll once said, "I can't say I'm fat, I can't talk about my mother, my husband, my child. You know, there is really very little left to say."

As a team Carroll and Howe had done a good deal of radio work, and as a solo Carroll reached the peak of her career in the late 1940's from both nightclubs and theater work, building a national following. She made guest appearances on TV shows and got her own series in 1953. This half hour ABC sitcom was titled "Take It From Me" and was also known as "The Jean Carroll Show." Jean played a New York City housewife complete with an inept husband and daughter. She opened each show with a monologue and delivered comic asides to the audience during the program. Many of the plots involved Carroll trying to trick her husband into doing what she wanted.

One critic termed the show "weak and inadequate." Audiences agreed. The show debuted in November 1953 and was cancelled in January 1954, lasting just twelve weeks. Carroll's career had by then passed its peak and little was heard from her again. Not long after she retired from show business.

Her material was largely domestic and she didn't tackle any social or political issues. But she made an important contribution to women comedians in being one of the very few stand-up female comics in the 1930's and 1940's. She also wrote all of her own material. The failure of her TV show could have been due to reasons other than its quality or lack thereof. Successful women comics on the tube then, such as Lucille Ball, Joan Davis, and Marie Wilson, projected a different image. They were all of the "dumb" variety, getting involved in outrageous situations. If they weren't dumb they were man-chasers like Eve Arden. The other type of female on sitcoms were like the wives in "Father Knows Best" and "Life Of Riley," essentially reduced to the role of decorative nonentities.

Carroll's image was that of a stronger woman, one in control, a dominant female able to manipulate without whining, pleading, or hysterics. She also did monologues, not then being done on TV by women to any extent. This put Jean Carroll ahead of her time, and her image of a woman with equal power to men was too threatening to the male ego and the females who swallowed such ideology. It was an image which was not acceptable to TV viewers in the early 1950's. It didn't conform to the norm of what a woman was, or how she was supposed to behave. Perhaps this had more to do with the quick demise of her show than anything else.

KAYE BALLARD

From the time she was five years old, Kaye Ballard wanted to be an actress. But her high school drama teacher wouldn't even allow her in his classes because she wasn't pretty enough. Ballard, like other "plain" aspiring actresses, turned to comedy as an alternative. "I did it out of self-consciousness," she said in 1966. "I just wasn't pretty enough for what I wanted to be. My present style of comedy is based on this self-consciousness."

Ballard was born in Cleveland, Ohio, in 1926. Her real name was Catherine Balotta, and her Italian father was a construction worker. Kaye was musical and played the flute, a talent she would later use in her nightclub act. Although she received no encouragement from her family, she joined a burlesque show as a straight woman after leaving high school in 1944. Ballard eventually created her own act of songs, jokes and impersonations.

Spike Jones was in the audience one night when Kaye was playing the Bowery, a Detroit nightclub in 1945. He was impressed by her talent and told her to look him up if she was ever in Hollywood. A month later she was in Los Angeles and was hired as a singer and comedienne by Jones, and toured with his band on the RKO vaudeville circuit.

In 1946 Ballard moved to New York City and had a small part in her first Broadway revue *Three to Make Ready.* She was to appear in numerous musical comedies both on and off Broadway throughout her career. One of her funniest roles was as Helen in the 1956 production of *The Golden Apple* by John Latouche and Jerome Moross. Ballard played a bored, sensual, small-town housewife only too happy to be abducted. One New York critic noted that she delivered "her songs with a daffy attitude all her own."

Kaye replaced Beatrice Little in the 1957 *Ziegfeld Follies* and was seen in several other plays during the early 1960's. In 1965 she appeared in the Square East Theater Off Broadway in *The Decline and Fall of the Entire World As Seen Through the Eyes of Cole Porter, Revisited.* Ballard impersonated Mable Mercer and Sophie Tucker. In a take-off on Bea Lillie, Kaye wore a red boa and sang "When I Was a Little Cuckoo."

A 1973 musical *Mollie,* based on Gertrude Berg's radio and television series "The Goldbergs," ran only for four months in New York, but Ballard wasn't finished with theater. In 1981 she worked in a play written for her by George Tibbales—*That's All the Love I Got—Go to Hell.* It was the story of two Italian sisters who lived together in a brownstone but only spoke to each other on holidays and shopping days.

And in 1984 Ballard opened on Broadway in a one-woman autobiographical musical called *Hey, Ma . . . Kaye Ballard.* Her famous impersonations of Fanny Brice, Sophie Tucker, and Bea Lillie were featured. She also did material on mother-daughter relationships.

Although Ballard appeared on stage frequently, her real popularity grew on the nightclub circuit. She performed annually at the hungry i in San Francisco, Mr. Kelly's in Chicago, The Flamingo in Las Vegas, and the Bon Soir in New York. Her act once ran for 62 weeks at the Blue Angel in New York. In 1954 she did a routine called, "A Tribute to Fanny Brice," reviving Brice's old songs like, "Oh, I'm an Indian." Other acts included comic songs such as, "I Just Kissed My Nose Goodnight," and "The Skin Diver's Passionate Ode." Arthur Siegel was Ballard's piano accompanist and he worked with her for over twenty years. In 1957 a reviewer for *The New Yorker* saw Ballard's act at the Bon Soir. He praised her as "a comedienne who is capable of addressing her audience in both booming and deceptively gentle tones, as she dashes recklessly about the small stage in the cause of her wild exhibition."

Two years later, Robert Dana, critic for the New York *World-Telegram and Sun* also saw her perform again at the Bon Soir. He wrote with admiration that "Miss Ballard's sense of the hilarious accompanies a strong singing voice not unlike Judy Garland's in quality. The performance is presented in vignettes full of her sense of the ridiculous. A fine pantomimist, she has a stage presence that immediately relaxes an audience."

Although Kaye was tiring of nightclub work and complained that two one-hour shows per night were hard work, she was still playing clubs in recent years. In 1981, for example, she appeared at Les Mouches in New York City.

Television was also an important medium for Ballard. She made guest appearances on "The Perry Como Show," "The Colgate Comedy Hour," and "The Johnny Carson Show" as well as many other variety, talk, and game shows. The height of her television career came during the years 1967 to 1969 when she co-starred with Eve Arden in NBC's situation comedy "The Mothers-in-Law." The two women played stereotypical roles of interfering in-laws who badger their newlywed children. Arden played a sophisticated Ango-Saxon matron, while Ballard was the emotional earthy Italian. The rivalry and bickering between the two women were used as comic ploys.

Critics rated the show as funny, although some complained of its slapstick quality. The fact that it held its own in the same time slot as "The Ed Sullivan Show" on CBS was an accomplishment in itself.

Ballard's foray into movies was less successful, and she was only in a couple of films. Nor were her record albums big sellers, due mainly to poor promotion. Her recordings included musicals she had performed in, a rendition of Lucy from the "Peanuts" comic strip, and highlights from her nightclub act.

Ballard had struggled with a weight problem, and had undergone analysis to deal with anxiety. But she has worked steadily as an entertainer for more than forty years. Not being "pretty enough" didn't turn out to be such a terrible handicap.

PAT CARROLL

For over thirty years Pat Carroll has been entertaining audiences in nightclubs, theaters, and television. Born to a middle-class family in 1927 in Shreveport, Louisiana, Carroll showed an enthusiasm for acting in her high school drama class. By then her parents had moved to Los Angeles, and Carroll worked part-time as an usher at the Biltmore Theater and at CBS radio in the sound effects department, while attending Immaculate Heart College.

Deciding to pursue a full-time acting career, Pat left college in 1947 to work in summer stock in Massachusetts. Her first job was a role in a comedy starring Gloria Swanson. In 1948 Carroll worked as an acting instructor for the U.S. Army in Florida, and then decided to resume her education by enrolling at Catholic University in Washington, D.C. Her schooling was once again cut short by acting. Carroll was getting too many job offers to stay with the university. Between 1947 and 1950 she appeared in hundreds of stock productions, which included musical comedies. Carroll was to continue on the stage throughout her career in comedies like *Oh, Men! Oh, Women!* by Edward Chodrov, and *Who Was That Lady I Saw You With,* by Norman Krasna.

An appearance in the Off-Broadway revue *Talent '50* led to Carroll's club act. She made her debut in 1951 at Manhattan's Le Ruban Blue and later performed at the Village Vanguard, the Blue Angel, Tamiment in the Poconos, and One Fifth Avenue. Her act consisted of pastiches of songs and monologues such as "My Girlfriend's Best Boyfriend's My Best Boyfriend Now," and "Look Vogue, Look Glamour, Look Harper's Bazaar." She also spoofed fairy tales and used literary material, impersonating Dame Edith Sitwell, for example. Carroll's act was not easily labelled, and as she told a *New York Herald Tribune* reporter in 1960: "I'm not offbeat enough for little intimate clubs, and I'm too highbrow for the big clubs."

Yet Carroll continued with stage work. In 1955 she appeared in the revue *Catch a Star!* which played the Plymouth Theater on Broadway. Carroll satirized the plays of Tennessee Williams among others. William Hawkins of the New York *World-Telegram and Sun* called her "a madcap clown whose greatest trick springs from lightning changes of mood. She is an excellent actress, at least in flashes, so her comic sketches are always solid."

Television became the major showcase for Carroll's talents. She was a regular on the Red Buttons comedy-variety show on CBS in 1952-1953, and in 1954 was seen on NBC's "Saturday Night Revue." In 1956-57 she was cast as Alice Brewster on Sid Caesar's comedy-variety show "Caesar's Hour." She won an Emmy for her role as the wife of suburban commuter, Fred Brewster, played by Howard Morris. Morris would later direct her in her one and only movie role in the 1968 film *With Six You Get Eggroll.*

Carroll's early television work led to parts in three situation comedies. During 1961 to 1964 she was Bunny Halper, the wife of the Copa Club owner on "The Danny Thomas Show." Between 1971 and 1972, Pat was cast as landlady Rita Simon on "Getting Together," and in 1977 she played a Jewish mother, Pearl Markowitz, in "Busting Loose." She made guest appearances on numerous other television series.

Because of her wit and sense of humor Carroll became a fixture on several television quiz shows, including "Who Said That" (1955), "Masquerade Party" (1958), "Keep Talking" (1958-1960), and "You're In the Picture" (1961).

Carroll also made an effort to appear before live audiences as much as possible. She worked the dinner-theater circuit in the 1970's, and made no apologies for the lightweight material presented. As long as people were relaxed and amused she felt her work worthwhile. She even wrote an autobiographical piece called "An Evening With Who?" for the Coachlight Dinner Theater in Connecticut.

Pat wanted to be remembered for something other than game shows and light comedies, however. After her marriage of 20 years to theatrical agent Lee Karsian (which yielded three kids) ended in divorce in 1975, Carroll was at a low point. She began looking around for an appropriate vehicle.

Because of being overweight, she thought of doing a one-woman show about Sarah Caldwell, Bella Abzug, or Dixie Lee Ray. She finally decided on Gertrude Stein, partly because of her humor and hearty laugh. Solo theater pieces had fascinated Carroll since the age of thirteen when she had first seen Ruth Draper perform. Pat recalled that she actually "saw" the people that Draper evoked in her monologues and felt she used dialect brilliantly.

Gertude Stein Gertrude Stein Gertrude Stein opened at New York's Circle Repertory Theater in June 1979. In October it moved to the Provincetown Playhouse in Greenwich Village where it played until August 1980. Carroll then took the play on tour. Her performance was such a success that the play won the 1980 Drama Desk Award and Outer Critics Circle Award.

ELAINE MAY

Elaine May was one half of the comedy team Nichols and May that took the country by storm in the late 1950's and early 1960's. Their style was a mixture of skits, and improvisational bits done essentially without props. A satirical view of human behavior and the absurdities of ordinary events formed their material. The team set a standard of excellence and their reputation has continued to grow over the decades since they disbanded. Today's teams are still judged by their standard.

Elaine May was born in 1932 in Philadelphia. Her father was Jack Berlin who was the writer, director, and main actor in his own traveling Jewish theatrical troupe. He took his troupe all over the United States putting on Yiddish plays. Elaine made her stage debut literally in her father's arms. By the time she was three she was doing toddler roles. Throughout her childhood she continued to act in her father's company, playing, as she recalls it, little boys who were all called Benny, a practice she had to give up at eleven when she began to develop breasts.

Her father died about this time and the family settled shortly thereafter in Los Angeles. Because of the constant moving about the country, her schooling had been very sporadic. She hadn't started until she was eight and within a few years had attended over 50 schools, some for only a few weeks. She disliked school and at about age fourteen she quit going permanently in Los Angeles. At sixteen she was married. The marriage produced one child and ended in divorce while she was still a teenager. It was from this union that Elaine took the last name, May.

During this Los Angeles period she held a number of unusual odd jobs: roofing salesman, pitchman for a sidewalk photographer, and private detective. Later, at the height of her popularity, Elaine would say that she hadn't felt an urge at that time, or as a teenager, to be an actress, or "be anything," nevertheless she drifted into Method acting classes in California. A standard exercise involved having the actor pretend to be a seed planted in the ground which then sprouts, becomes a tree, buds, and develops leaves. Independently Mike Nichols also studied Method acting.

Some of the people May associated with in Los Angeles theater moved on to Chicago and Elaine decided to follow along. She never formally enrolled at the University of Chicago, but drifted in and out of classes there for a couple of years. Mike Nichols was another semi-student at that institution who was involved in student drama productions, as was May.

The couple knew each other only by sight when one evening they accidentally met in the waiting room of a train station in the spring of 1954. According to Nichols, people had often told him he should meet May since the two of them "had the cruelest tongues on the campus." May also had a reputation for toughness. That evening in the train station they performed what became their first improvisational piece. They spontaneously engaged in a half spy, half pick-up routine complete with dialect. Eventually this routine would become a part of their act.

They discovered they had an instant rapport. Before the end of that year, however, Nichols returned to New York to study acting. Elaine stayed on in Chicago. She joined the Playwright's Theatre, a group Nichols had been associated with, and acted in a variety of plays. Within a few months her salary was raised to $25 a week from $12. In the spring of 1955 this group disbanded when its theatre was closed by the Fire Department. One of the producers organized a new company, Compass Theatre. This troupe operated out of a nightclub and consisted of six players, four male and two female.

These performers presented brief skits based on their own ideas, or ideas generated by the audience. Elaine was a charter member of the group, and was paid $55 a week. Late in 1955 a vacancy came up at Compass and Nichols, then in Philadelphia, was asked to fill it. A contemporary of Nichols and May at the $55 a week Compass was Shelley Berman. The pair stayed with Compass until the fall of 1957 when the group disbanded due to a series of business problems. While they were in New York during abortive negotiations to bring Compass to that city, the pair contacted a manager looking for new talent. This led to a club appearance at the Blue Angel. They were so well received that the owner immediately offered them a booking in ten days when he was changing shows. Nichols and May were forlorn at the prospect of waiting for ten days, since they were down to $40 between them. The owner decided to immediately put them into another one of his clubs, the Village Vanguard. There they served as the opening act for Mort Sahl. These successes led to appearances on television in late 1957, once on the Jack Paar show and once on the Steve Allen show. The latter appearance attracted the interest of a producer and led to a January 1958 shot on the "Omnibus" television show. It was this appearance which catapulted the pair to stardom.

Within a few days of that program they received several offers from producers to do their own TV specials, and requests for guest shots. their manager upped their fee for a guest appearance to $5,000 per shot. Just three months earlier Nichols and May had been making $136 a week in the New York clubs.

That fifteen-minute spot on "Omnibus" established some of their routines as comic classics. The awkward teenagers making out in the back seat of a car and trying to manage cigarettes at the same time; a mother phoning her scientist son and reducing him to sniveling tears; and a man at a pay phone dealing with a series of operators while desperately trying to retrieve his last, and now lost, dime.

Over the next three and a half years the team appeared on numerous television shows, such as the Dinah Shore show and the Perry Como show as well as various specials. In addition they performed in nightclubs throughout the country. In May 1959 Nichols and May appeared at New York City's Town Hall, a first for comedians since the venue was normally reserved for concert attractions. They brought their show to Broadway in October of 1960, where they played to almost full houses until July 1961, when the pair broke up their act.

While a few critics had some reservations, wherever they played reviews were almost unanimously enthusiastic. The public loved them. They released a couple of records, one of which was the first spoken comedy record to become a best seller. By 1961 the team commanded $30,000 for a television guest appearance.

Their act consisted of a series of sketches and improvisational pieces. The sketches were never written down and consequently lines could and did change from performance to performance. They wrote all their own material, with Nichols creating his part and May creating her part. Most of their major set pieces had their beginnings at Compass, where Nichols and May would refine and hone a particular piece which they found to be enthusiastically received by the audience. Neither one of them made any great effort to find an idea for a new skit. It would usually begin with a remark such as, "You be a dentist, I'll be a patient."

The other part of their act was the improvised bits in which the audience would randomly call out two lines and Nichols and May would improvise a five- to ten-minute sketch beginning with the first line and ending with the last. The audience also called out what style they wanted the bit done in. From Euripides to *Reader's Digest,* from Samuel Beckett to Li'l Abner, the pair would oblige.

In their material they dealt sardonically with all aspects of contemporary society. They viewed with cynicism such targets as mother love, radio journalism, female civic mindedness, industrial bureaucracy, space travel, summer camps, psychiatry, Christmas, comic books, and cocktail parties. They cast the same jaundiced and disenchanted eye at their favorite targets, the family, mother and father, mother and son, brother and sister, and lover and mistress.

Some of their fans elevated them to social critics, not merely entertainers. Early in their careers it was believed the pair might not find an audience that was equipped intellectually to handle them. One early review even referred to them as "eggheads." Those fears proved to be groundless in the face of their huge popularity. As one writer put it, "They have both snob and mob appeal."

Elaine May could play a wide range of characters convincingly: a clubwoman with a shrill cackle, a mother with sagging shoulders and a whine, an Englishwoman with clipped diction, and a husky-voiced movie starlet. Nichols and May were in the forefront of a new style of humor, a comedy that traversed a cultural, sociological, and psychological range. Their style was one of indignation at man's inhumanity to man and they treated their characters in a rigorously unsentimental way. Within their act the characters imparted the same message—that anybody and everybody treated each other in the same fashion, hideously.

Critics were divided as to whether some of their humor could be classified as "sick" or not. Sensitive items such as false teeth, protruding ears, baldness and obesity often occurred in their work. Both had their personal eccentricities on stage. Nichols blinked nervously, a tic that was more pronounced onstage than off. May obsessively wore black dresses onstage and off.

Their experiences with television were not all successful. The satirical skits often caused disagreements with officials and sponsors. They had been scheduled to appear on the 1960 telecast of the Emmy awards. However, since one of their sketches took a dim view of home permanents and suggested TV was under the control of sponsors, they were prevented from making that appearance, since a manufacturer of home permanents happened to be a sponsor of the Emmy show. They had been engaged in 1959 by NBC to be regular panel members of a show called "Laugh Line." Just three weeks after being hired they quit, unable to mold their talents to the demands of a television panel show. Also working against them in television was their improvisational routines, which would be hampered by the various taboos imposed by the medium.

Since Nichols and May never worked from a script, this produced problems for the stage manager of their Broadway show. He had difficulties in knowing when to cue the backstage people and so, with the aid of a tape recorder and a typist, he produced a script. Elaine May happened to come across it and read one of the sketches, something she had never done before. She was horrified to find that "there isn't a joke in it" and was so self-conscious of this fact that her performance was affected for a couple of weeks until she convinced herself to put it out of her mind completely.

By early in 1961 May and Nichols were beginning to have doubts about their future. They had done an enormous amount of improvisational work but they had developed very few new set pieces. Most of this type of material dated back to their days at Compass. They were turning down chances to do many TV specials of their own each year but the truth was that they didn't have enough set material to do more than one or two such shows, and they couldn't improvise because of the problems of censorship. Television was a medium that could quickly drain a performer due to the massive exposure, particularly performers who wrote their own material. They could use the same material touring in clubs almost indefinitely, but only once on television. While the pair could have generated new material, they weren't sure it was what they wanted, fearing they might be stuck doing something long after they had ceased being satisfied with it.

Finally, in July of 1961, they closed their Broadway show, still successfully running to large houses, and dissolved the act. The split was described as amicable and at the request of Elaine May. Nichols reported that May told him she was tired of what they had been doing for so many years and that she wanted to write. In some ways May had been the major force behind the act. She was acknowledged as "the term's virtuoso actor." Nichols structured the material for the skits, but May "came up with most of the ideas."

It also seemed to have been May who provided the team with its hard, satirical edge. She once remarked that, "I feel in opposition to almost everything." Nichols commented that he had no message to deliver or sense of mission in their comedy work. "I have nothing I want to tell people." May certainly did. She likened her mission in their work to Swift and his satirical solution to the problem of Irish babies, "That's the way you have to go."

Nichols was the better at public relations of the two. May tended to give outrageous answers to questions and to be less than cooperative in interviews. The reasons that May gave for splitting up the team are vague and unsatisfying. "'I told Mike there was no way we could top ourselves," says Elaine. Besides, she thought privately, Kennedy's election had changed the country's mood and the bland and foolish targets at which they had been slashing with such precision no longer really existed. In any event, one of the brightest and most innovative comedy teams was finished at the peak of their popularity.

On the surface one might have expected Elaine to do as well or better than Nichols as a single, but such was not the case. The career change didn't faze Mike Nichols at all. Within a few years he was one of the country's most-in-demand directors after an unbroken string of hits, including both Broadway plays and Hollywood movies.

For Elaine May, 1962 was a dismal year. Two plays she wrote were produced and bombed. A third writing attempt, a film script, was abandoned by mutual consent of the parties after a series of clashes between May and the film's director and producer. She had a brief second marriage which ended in divorce that year as well. In 1963 she married again and withdrew from show business completely for the role of homemaker.

After a few years she emerged again to succeed in the role of actress. By the beginning of the 1970's she had achieved further success, having directed her first Off Broadway play and her first two movies, *A New Leaf* and *The Heartbreak Kid*. She still had a reputation of being demanding and of not being the easiest person in the world to work with. It had taken her a lot longer and been a lot more difficult for her to make the same transition that Mike Nichols had made with such ease. Elaine May admitted she faced a lot of "agitation" over being a female director, but dismissed it as "a bit of a bore."

Elaine May had used comedy as an outlet for her own cynicism and irreverency and came to full power after she teamed up with a complementary personality in the form of Mike Nichols. Perhaps their success mellowed Elaine May and she disbanded the act because her anger had subsided.

The 1960's to the 1980's

------◆◆------

INTRODUCTION

The 1960's were transitional years for women comics. The first half of that decade was one of the leanest periods in the history of female comedy. The movie industry had long been established, and it was almost impossible for a young comedienne to break into films. Radio comedy was dead, and television, no longer in its infancy, was harder to get into. Perhaps one well-known comedian in one hundred was female.

There were a handful of superstars during that decade, though, and they marked the turning point from the dizzy airhead to the feminist consciousness of many current comediennes. Some like Totie Fields, with her fat jokes, remained entrenched in the self-deprecatory style. Others like Ann Meara broke away from the dumb blonde stereotype. She gave as good as she got from her partner Jerry Stiller.

Carol Burnett represented a performer who straddled the line between independence and submissiveness. She became the star of her own television comedy show in 1967, but she let others tell her what to do. Burnett did not write her own material, and for the first seven years of the show she never attended production meetings. Her financial success and mass exposure were nevertheless impressive, as was her unique comedy style. Burnett was also a comic who had grown in depth over the years. She eventually came to regret her emphasis on self-deprecation in her show.

Phyllis Diller and Joan Rivers both maintained the tradition of self-deprecation in the 1960's and had trouble letting it go later. But their razor sharp wits carried them far beyond the dizzy dunderhead and even the man-chaser. Their aggressive humor had to be made palatable to the mass audience, and one way of doing it was self-deprecation.

Yet both women broke new ground. For one thing, they were almost the only females performing stand-up. Many of Diller's jokes were extremely hostile towards husbands, children, families, the rigid role of housewives and female suppression in general. When Diller started out, there was no Women's Movement to back her up. By distracting people with her outrageous looks and self-disparaging remarks, she could nail her target before the audience realized what hit them.

Barry Sand, producer of the television comedy show "Late Night with David Letterman," spoke of what it was like for women working in the sixties: "Female comics in the old days didn't want to be too pretty or too threatening to women. I mean they were playing in clubs, and they didn't want to threaten the women the guys were with." The result, noted Sand, was, "Phyllis Diller wearing bizarre outfits and talking about how ugly she was."

Joan Rivers, like Diller, used self-deprecation for the same ends, but she also had different techniques. Rivers was super aggressive and hostile, describing herself as a "victim who strikes back." This description crystallized the ambivalence in Rivers's material. On the one hand, she came across as a powerful abrasive performer, daring to offend anyone by her act. But she had to divert attention away from her forceful attacks, not trusting the audience to accept a woman who wasn't the stereotypical "victim" or masochist. She did this through self-deprecation, and by adopting a catty or bitchy or back-stabbing manner so often associated with the stereotypical female personality.

It was in 1968 that television provided a major chance for female comics. That was the year "Laugh-In" hit the airwaves. Goldie Hawn, Ruth Buzzi, JoAnne Worley and Lily Tomlin all got their big breaks on this program. It was the first time that so many comedians had so much exposure since vaudeville days. The show brought all of these women to national prominence.

Lily Tomlin has since used her intelligence and feminist consciousness to create new comic characters, and has presented first-
rate stage concerts. Her foray into film has been less impressive
artistically, and she has appeared in some pretty poor vehicles.
Goldie Hawn had branched out primarily into movies. Her comic
roles, unfortunately, have remained safely within the realm of
dizzy blonde airhead showing off the body beautiful in a bikini.

Ruth Buzzi was in a mediocre TV sitcom in the mid 1970's,
which had a short run. She was also in one film, a Disney movie.
Buzzi would have loved to be in more films working with top comics like Mel Brooks, but the offers were not forthcoming. JoAnne
Worley had practically dropped from sight by the 1980's, which
was a shame, considering her wonderfully brash persona.

The late 1960's and early 1970's marked the beginnings of the
Women's Movement in America. It's attack on sexism and the
double standard radically altered the feminine sensibility. It was
bound to have an effect on women in comedy, and it did. Female
comics were becoming less of a rarity.

Bette Midler, a 1970's Sophie Tucker, with her vulgar vamping
and campy singing, made it big on the concert circuit and on
television. Madeleine Kahn established her reputation in Mel
Brooks's comedy films, also by singing and vamping. In fact, the
tradition of singing in connection with female comics goes back to
vaudeville. Stand-ups like Sandra Bernhard and Marilyn Sokol
continued doing it. Male comics almost never sing. Can one imagine Woody Allen bursting into song? Phyllis Diller dropped singing from her act almost immediately, recognizing it as excess baggage. Perhaps some comediennes retain the singing format
because they are still reluctant to devote themselves to comedy.

One comedienne who used singing to her advantage was Mari-
lyn Michaels, an impressionist. She did imitations of Julie
Andrews, Dolly Parton, Lily Tomlin, and Bette Midler. She was
the only female among the country's top impressionists like Rich
Little and George Kirby to get on the ABC Comedy Hour Series
"KopyKats."

Like "Laugh-In," the television programs "Saturday Night
Live" and "SCTV" were important for comediennes Gilda Radner
and Andrea Martin, among others. Both became household
names in the mid- to late 1970's. Writing their own material and
attending production meetings, Radner and Martin made certain
that they were not overshadowed by the show's male writer/
performers. As alumnae of the Toronto offshoot of Chicago's

Second City improvisational group, Radner and Martin brought quick wits and spontaneity to their humor. The original Second City had started in Chicago in 1959 and spawned talents like Elaine May and Anne Meara.

The most phenomenal rise, however, in terms of sheer numbers, were the women doing stand-up routines in the burgeoning comedy clubs. Marilyn Sokol, Zora Rasmussen, Elayne Boosler, Robin Tyler and Sandra Bernhard all achieved a measure of fame. Their material varied. Some like Zora Rasmussen were still self-deprecatory. With the exception of Robin Tyler, most were not militant feminists. Many dealt with so-called women's topics like fashion, menstruation, weight, hygiene, being single, sex and relationships. Sometimes these subjects were used in an almost self-deprecatory style, but mainly because these were areas in which women have been victimized or were vulnerable. Since humor was a way of dealing with pain, it was inevitable that these topics would crop up repeatedly. The politics were essentially personal.

Only one male/female comedy team came to the fore in the 1970's—Monteith and Rand. They were so concerned with equality in their work that neither wanted to dominate the act. As a result, their style was a bit bland and their careers have stagnated. Their attempt at integrated comedy was a brave one in an era when couples were hypersensitive and confused about sex roles. It was not surprising they couldn't solve the dilemma.

Apart from Jews, minority women had almost never gotten into comedy. Moms Mabley was the rare exception, and she had plenty of problems gaining acceptance in the white entertainment world. With the advent of civil rights and more racial tolerance, two black women, Whoopi Goldberg and Marsha Warfield, have made some headway as comediennes. Liz Torres, a Puerto Rican, was the sole well-known Latino, and Robin Tyler was one of the first openly lesbian comics. Thus not only have women been more accepted into the comedy field, but so have more minority women.

The Women's Movement can take much of the credit. A general resurgence of stand-up comedy in the mid-1970's was also an important development for comediennes. There had always been clubs in the major U.S. cities, but the 1970's saw a remarkable proliferation of not just clubs, but clubs devoted entirely to comedy.

In the 1970's and 1980's some of the clubs and cabarets in New

York City showcasing comics were the Bitter End, Max's Kansas City, the Playboy Club, Jimmy's, Catch a Rising Star, the Duplex, s.n.a.f.u., The Comic Strip, Big Apple Comedy Room, Mickey's, The Fives, Good Times, Mostly Magic, Palsson's, Carline's, Dangerfield's, and the Other End. In 1984 there were an estimated 200 comedy rooms in the U.S. Comedy was a growing business.

Despite the expansion of the industry, and the increasing number of women auditioning, it still was not easy for females to break into comedy. Samuel Janus, a New York psychologist, explained: "Comediennes are simply reflecting cultural expectations: women are supposed to whine and nag, but they've never been taken seriously, or comically as social critics." Irene Pinn, who managed Lily Tomlin for twelve years, commented in 1983: "It's still difficult to book a comedienne in the Midwest, and most club managers refuse to have a female comic open for a female singer." Some of the stars who refused to have female comics as openers were Diana Ross and Melissa Manchester.

In most clubs no two women comics could go on in a row. They were interspersed between the men. The implication was that they couldn't sustain audience interest, and were more of a novelty. Richie Tienken, owner of New York's Comic Strip, which opened in 1973, noted that in 1983 there were only ten or eleven well-known female comics as opposed to fifty or sixty well-known male comedians. "This is a very tough business for women," he said.

Rick Newman, co-owner of New York's Catch a Rising Star, which also opened in 1973, remarked on the rampant sexism he encountered at his club: "Back in the mid-1970's, when we first started seeing young female comics, a lot of agents and managers who came into the club, and even network [television] people, couldn't accept them. In fact, sometimes I'd put on a female singer between comedians just to balance the show. And she would do humorous patter between her songs—it's infectious, I guess, when you work in a comedy club. Well, some of those old-school managers and producers—the typical cigar-smoking characters—would holler from the audience rudely: 'Just sing!' Like that. And that was the kind of attitude there was —no acceptance of a female doing comedy."

Things weren't improving that much in the 1980's. Comediennes with anything to say were being labeled "hostile" or "too masculine." Phil Berger, a writer for *The New York Times Maga-*

zine, concluded that if Sandra Bernhard "didn't have her movie celebrity to trade on, one suspects the act would be hard to sell on the comedy circuit because of its acerbic quality."

Said Newman of Catch A Rising Star, "I think that definitely some people in the business are still a bit close-minded to female stand-up comics." Budd Friedman of Los Angeles' Improvisation club reinforced this perception by noting, "It has to be some ingrained discrimination on somebody's part, because we just don't see the acts on television that we should be seeing."

Talk shows have traditionally given important exposure to comics, and of course, an appearance on Carson's "Tonight Show" was the ultimate plum. And the program had given airtime to comediennes. In 1983, for example, five comediennes were on the show—Sandra Bernhard, Gilda Radner, Andrea Martin, Victoria Jackson and Maureen Murphy. Joseph Bleeden, NBC publicist for the program, said, "Female comics get on the show in proportion to their numbers."

Carson has done an enormous amount for Joan Rivers. She had often filled in for Carson as host, when he was absent, and in 1983 she hosted the show for the entire nine weeks of Carson's vacation, the first time any guest had done so.

But Carson rarely had women comics performing on a repeat basis. In a 1979 quote from a *Rolling Stone* interview, Carson explained why: "It's because of the old role models that are assigned. A woman is feminine, a woman is not abrasive, a woman is not a hustler. . . . I think it's much tougher for women. You don't see many of them around. And the ones that try, sometimes are a little aggressive for my taste. I'll take it from a guy, but from women, sometimes, it just doesn't fit too well."

A young staff writer for *Square Pegs,* Marjorie Gross, thought that Carson hyped Rivers because "she doesn't change the status quo much. What she says—'Get the ring, the husband, the coat'—for Carson that works."

Carson had had only one other comedienne on his show on a regular basis—Maureen Murphy. She didn't uphold the status quo with jokes like, "Maybe we should have a woman president. She'd save the country money because she'd only make half what a man makes." But Murphy was described in a 1984 *Newsweek* article as "a pixieish, sweet blonde." Perhaps that's why Carson had a soft spot for her.

If talk shows weren't going all out for female comics, TV sitcoms were not offering much either. Many had the classic dizzy blonde airhead as star, and seemed to prefer high fashion model types to any woman with experience as a comic.

One comedienne who was interviewed in 1981, and wished to remain anonymous, spoke of her working conflicts: "The men comics were always trying to hit on me. Double whammy: I was a threat not only because I was doing well, but because I was female. Oh, Christ, so many of them really do hate women."

Jan Hoffmann, a reporter for *The Village Voice,* felt that comedy was "the quintessential old-boy network. Its form and substance have been defined by men. Its manner is violent, brazen, loudly aggressive. . . . To be a comic is to wrestle with a classic feminist dilemma: Is her goal to succeed in the traditional male-dominated circuit world, or to break from it altogether, and find a comic language and venue to accommodate her own divergent humor?"

Abby Stein, a New York stand-up, delivered lines like, "A Jewish guy's idea of oral sex is talking about himself." Stein commented on the sexism she encountered as a woman: "You know the kind of stuff we hear? I'll tell you. 'Show me a funny woman and I'll show you a man'. That's what it's all about. . . . A very, very big fear is that the audience is going to be looking at your body instead of listening to what you say." Stein admitted to being imitative of male comics "because that's the only role model you have." Not all comics felt that way, however. Carol Leifer, a stand-up at the Comic Strip, said, "I can't storm a stage like the men. It doesn't feel right. I try to come across much softer, friendlier."

One of the older and best known clubs in New York was the Improvisation, which had opened in 1964. Bette Midler, Lily Tomlin, and Elayne Boosler among others have played the Improv. Performers received good exposure, but no pay. Silver Saunders Friedman, owner of New York's Improvisation, said that one in five comics who auditioned in 1984 were female. This was about five times the number auditioning in 1964. Friedman told *Ms.* interviewer Julia Klein in 1984: "Fifteen years ago most women couldn't get through their pain. It was not very entertaining. Now they don't feel they're the only victims. Out of knowing that they get a little lighter on it. They find things to really laugh at. Now they have a perspective. They have a little distance on it. They see they're only one of a thousand."

In the mid-1970's Bud Friedman, who previously ran N.Y.'s Improvisation, opened an L.A. branch of the club. He cited one in three auditioning comics as female in 1984.

Carol Siskind, stand-up comic and emcee in 1984 at the New York Improvisation used a lot of material about relationships in her act. Joked Carol, "I want to meet someone special, someone I can take for granted. Someone I can look at in the morning and say, 'You're not what I had in mind,'" or "If you come home and he's using your diaphragm for an ashtray, you know it's over."

Siskind's humor focused on female vulnerability, and gender differences: "You guys put on thirty pounds, we call it cuddly. We put on one ounce, you call us taxis"; or "I respect men. I think they're the braver sex. It's bad enough to wake up in the morning and face your face, but to do it with a razor blade?" Siskind's material could sometimes be borderline self-deprecation: "We had one of those love-hate things. We both loved him and hated me." But she made fun of female conditioning. When a secretary friend of Carol's cut her leg shaving, she covered it with white out.

Siskind recognized that "Comedy is a very assertive, aggressive thing to do. You're expressing discontent and irony." Yet as a woman, Carol was reluctant to give full expression to her aggressiveness: "In a way we have to be more careful," she said, talking of females. "Men can be gross and get away with it. We have to be very careful not to step on the male ego. There are things you learn early on to phrase very carefully." Siskind dropped this line from her act because it offended men: "I think some of the guys we date, if they were women, we wouldn't want to have lunch with them."

Outdoing the Improvisation in prestige as the ultimate comedy club was the Comedy Store in Los Angeles. The club was originally opened in 1972 by comedian Sammy Shore. It was a casual place for comics to hang out and ad-lib if they felt so inclined. When his wife Mitzi Shore took over in 1973, as stipulated in the divorce settlement, she turned it into a thriving business, making several hundred thousand dollars profit per year. She opened a branch of the Comedy Store in L.A.'s Westwood district. The Comedy Store could showcase 45 comedians per night. Needless to say, Shore became a very powerful force in the comedy business. About one in ten comics performing at the Comedy Store was female.

The Comedy Store had a special room just for women standups. Shore opened The Belly Room because she felt women were floundering in the highly competitive 450-seat Mainroom.

"Women came late to stand-up comedy," Shore explained, "like they did to everything else. . . . They use to be working downstairs in the Mainroom, but it was difficult for them. They get psychologically blocked when they're working on the same level as a man."

Comics in The Belly Room did their half-hour routines on a stage that wasn't raised, with the idea that the performer would be more intimate with the audience. The room held 75 people.

Many of the comics who played The Belly Room were happy about the segregation. Lotus Weinstock was one of them. She started out in comedy in the early sixties at the Bitter End in New York City, but didn't go over with audiences. "Somehow," she said, "the audience had a hard time accepting hip humor from a woman in pumps and a beehive."

Weinstock moved to California where she met and became engaged to Lenny Bruce just before he died in 1966. He inspired her to put substance in her comedy. Like many of today's stand-up comediennes, Weinstock joked about relationships: "It seems that in order to be the kind of woman who's strong enough to live with a man, you tend to be the kind of woman no man wants to live with. . . . My husband is very open. He says, 'Honey, you can have an open relationship with anyone you want. As long as it's not mental. Or spiritual. Or physical. Or emotional.' If the person's in a coma, I can be totally open, just hang out." Weinstock's humor was urban and trendy: "I find it very difficult to be a dope-smoking mother," she said. "The last time I had a hit of good Colombian on laundry day, it took me six hours to sort two pairs of white identical socks."

Weinstock explained why she preferred The Belly Room. In the Mainroom she felt a need to "put out, put out, get to the punch quicker. . . . If you come on after four men, forget it. The audience has to get out of that yang aggressive thing. The only time gender doesn't get in the way is when confidence speaks louder than gender, and the only way to do that is to work at it."

Dottie Archibald was another comic who worked The Belly Room, with jokes like: "*The Los Angeles Times* is boring; sometimes as my dog is carrying it up the driveway, he falls asleep. Now the *National Enquirer* is what I call exciting; it's like getting an obscene phone call at the grocery store."

Archibald was aware of the discrimination in comedy: "There is still a saying in this business, that when a woman bombs it takes two weeks to get the stink out of the room. Women are more vulnerable, so people are more sensitive to you. If a man bombs, you don't feel bad; but if a woman does, you talk about the poor girl and how she's suffering."

Weinstock and Archibald were standing on dangerous ground by promoting segregation. In effect, they were saying that women couldn't hold their own with men and had to be coddled.

Many of the comics who worked The Belly Room had been humiliated by males in integrated rooms. Emily Levine remembered some terrible introductions: "Once a guy I didn't even know was the emcee, and he said, 'Here's a woman who fucked her way to the top.' So I said, 'Oh, he just hates it when I'm on top.' Another time a guy yelled, 'Take it off.' So I said, 'Mine doesn't come off.' Castration anxiety set the mood for the evening. Boy, did I alienate that audience."

Carol Montgomery, another stand-up comic, was introduced by a male emcee as "a lovely lady with big tits."

Emily Levine mainly used gags about sexism, making fun of the "Total Woman" by jokingly advising women to cut off their arms to be more like the Venus de Milo. Levine, like many contemporary comediennes, made light of sex: "Sometimes men yell, 'I'm coming, I'm coming.' What are they yelling? I'm not going anywhere. I think maybe they think I don't know what's going on. Then I think I'm not in bed with them as a partner, I'm there as a witness. Next week I'll get a subpoena to appear in his mother's kitchen to testify he's a man."

Levine also did political jokes: "The Reagans were so disgusted with the Carter's life-style, that they threw out the china, the furniture—and the Constitution."

Not everyone was happy with The Belly Room, however. In the spring of 1979, the comics in L.A. formed a group called Comedians for Compensation (CFC). One of their demands was to be paid for performing (they had up until then been working the Comedy Store and Improv for nothing). Their other demand was that The Belly Room be integrated, so that men could also work the room. Both demands were met. Those working the small rooms were paid $25 per night; $150 a night was the wage in the Mainroom. In 1984 New York clubs like Catch a Rising Star and the Comic Strip were paying comics $10 per night. Those who went on the road touring in posher clubs earned between $150 to $650 per date. Obviously, it was hard to make a living as a stand-up comedienne, and few do. The Improv also began to pay their performers. There has been some argument about how well

Mitzi Shore has kept her part of the bargain.

Stand-up comic Elayne Boosler saw the assimilation of women as very progressive: "The Belly Room," she said, "created a problem to begin with by making those women dependent and insecure." Moreover, one would think hecklers might be attracted to a room where they knew the performers to be all female.

Boosler, along with Sandra Bernhard, was against segregation in any form. Both refused to do articles about women in comedy, fearing the permanent label of "female comic."

Yet Robin Tyler, a militant feminist, spoke out against integrating The Belly Room, maintaining that "The CFC is trying to be very fair, but they don't understand. You've got to have an affirmative action program, and The Belly Room is it. What they didn't recognize is the tremendous discrimination against women."

Segregation, of course, was one of the most blatant forms of discrimination. But perhaps for Tyler, a militant lesbian, any interaction with men was to be avoided.

Several clubs like Comedy U. in New York City continued to have showcase nights for women comics only. Once Upon a Stove, another New York club, had Friday and Saturday night all-female amateur comedy revues. Even with the emphasis on the female sensibility, comics like Audrey Buslik performing at the Stove in 1977 were still doing self-deprecation with jokes such as, "My thighs—five more pounds and they'll be eligible for statehood." The man-chasing gag was still alive and well in 1981, although with a slightly jaded perspective: "I know there are no well-adjusted men in New York. But I'd be happy to find one that's treatable."

Yet there were women whose material placed the blame for sexism clearly where it belonged, "Yeah, I used to be married," cracked Adrienne Tolsch, "but after a while 'wife' sounded too much like 'woof.'" . . . My marriage was childless, except for my husband."

Tolsch, who also made fun of cosmetics and fashion, dropped lines like, "I've been trying the new line of turtle oil cosmetics and they're great except that I'm late for everything." Tolsch, a regular master of ceremonies at Catch a Rising Star, and voted Best Female Comic in 1981 by the Association of Comedy Artists, said that only four or five out of a dozen female stand-ups made a living at it. "You have to fight harder to be accepted," she said.

Asked why she stayed in a business that was so tough for

women, Tolsch replied: "I got a standing ovation in Cleveland, Ohio. With moments like that, I don't have to date for months."

Other comics were dealing with the differences between their own and their mother's generation. Joked New York stand-up Rita Rudner, "My mother had her own version of natural childbirth. She took off her make-up. . . . You know what really amazes me about having babies these days? Doctors can tell so much about them while they're still inside you. My girlfriend's pregnant, and she had these tests run. It seems the baby is normal and it's a boy . . . and it's a lawyer." Rudner also made cracks about the break-up of relationships: "He wanted to get married, and I didn't want him to."

Beverly Mickins, a black comic, and one of the emcees at Catch a Rising Star in 1983, joked about sexual come-ons, "I love the lines men use to get us into bed: 'Please — I'll only put it in for a minute.' What am I, a microwave?"

Like all artists, comics owed a debt to those who came before them. Jane Anderson was a comic working the Duplex in 1981. Her inspiration came from Fanny Brice's Baby Snooks, and Lily Tomlin's Edith Ann. Anderson used a child character, Baby Leslie, in her routines. Dressed in a pink leotard and enormous diapers, Anderson's material revolved around prepubescent sexuality, pop culture, and childrearing. She also did political satire and opened her monologue with this statement: "Comedy is not nice. It never was and never will be. And I hope to keep it that way."

Women were still laughing about motherhood and there was still plenty of pain underlying that role. Susan Schneider, a stand-up working small clubs in 1984, did a character called Pauline who belonged to a self-help group called Count Your Blessings. They helped her decide it was classy to have a gay son.

If some comediennes were still talking about their mothers, or what it was like to be a mother themselves, others were taking on a much more taboo subject — their fathers. The all-powerful male authority figure was becoming the butt of jokes. Margaret Smith, a 1980's comic who has appeared on the Letterman show, told this story about her father: "He's a real loser. He's an alcoholic and a gambler. But he's vain. He gave up his vices for a hair transplant. Next day, he got drunk on a $20 bet, and shaved his head." The Letterman show, which went on the air in 1982, has also been a boost for comediennes.

Kate Clinton, a lesbian comic who "de-dyked" her apartment

or "straightened up" before relatives visited, was told by her brother not to tell her father she was a lesbian, or it would "kill him." Kate had visions of "the neutron lesbian": "Hey, Mr. Reagan! I'm a lesbian. Kaboom!" Clinton noted that there was a phrase like "the family man," but you never heard of a "family woman" because it was redundant.

Stand-ups like Clinton and Smith were not worried about offending men. Explained Smith: "I'm not a goo-goo girl. I couldn't be bubbly and sparkly and happy for the audience. And that's what typically is accepted from a woman. I mean, in one place when I was first starting out, they told me: Be more like a woman, talk about normal stuff the audience can relate to. I knew what they were saying. Like, how come you're not talking about how hard it is to get a guy and how important it is to look pretty."

Attempts to make Smith toe the line have not discouraged her—just the opposite, in fact. "What it did for me," she said, "was give me anger . . . It gave me enough anger to say to myself: 'I'm going to show you. I'll be back.'"

Smith's attitude wasn't the exception. Noted Barry Sand, producer of the Letterman show: "Nowadays, if comediennes are threatening, their attitude is too bad." Some stand-ups can be downright devastating especially when harassed. Said one comedienne to a heckler: "See my nose? It's bigger than your dick. I like blowing my nose better." Female comics are no longer just tickling the funny bone. They know how to hit below the belt.

TOTIE FIELDS

Sophie Feldman, the daughter of a shopping center owner, was born in 1931 in Hartford, Connecticut. As a child she pronounced her own name "Totie" and it stuck for a lifetime. Feldman was later changed to the more Anglo "Fields" for professional reasons.

Totie began her career at four years of age singing on local radio. By fourteen she was performing in the Borscht belt and later worked as a comic in Boston strip joints like the Frolics Club. During this period she married her husband George, a fellow comic who eventually became her music director. They had two daughters.

Totie was four feet ten inches and weighed up to 190 pounds. Like Sophie Tucker, Fields used her weight as material for her act. "I come right out and say, 'I'm fat!'", she explained. "This deprives the wise alecks from mouthing loud asides all night." Her favorite meal she joked was "breakfast, lunch, dinner and in between. Obese, hefty, overweight, rotund. I never knew there were so many ways to say fatty." Despite her girth, Fields maintained her femininity, and like Sophie Tucker, she had a certain sensuality. "I'm a comedienne," she remarked, "but I'm a woman first, last and always."

Totie left Boston for New York but worked for three years without much success. Her routine consisted of songs interspersed with comic patter. Finally in 1963 she appeared at the Copacabana in what critics described as a "slambang" performance. This act won her more than two dozen spots on CBS-TV's "Ed Sullivan Show." She worked clubs across the country, but Las Vegas and talk shows became her forte. She gradually dropped the singing part of her act and went all out for comedy. In the 1960's she was earning $200,000 per year, giving her an income in a league with Phyllis Diller and Joan Rivers. In 1970 Earl Wilson named her "the hottest comedienne in the country," and in 1975 *Playgirl* magazine called her "the number one stand-up comedienne on the saloon circuit."

Draped in furs, ruffles, and feathers, Fields made no apologies for her style: "You look fat in fox anyway, so if you start fat, you only look a little fatter." One critic described her as "a snowman in drag." Totie used herself as the butt of her jokes. Once when she was co-hosting "The Mike Douglas Show" Arlene Dahl was a guest. After Dahl delivered some beauty tips to the audience Fields called out, "Why do you listen to her? Chances are you'll never look like her. Better you should listen to me because the chances are you will look like me."

Fields joked that happiness was "getting a brown gravy stain on a brown dress," and then berated herself, asking "Why am I such a slob? Maybe it's 'cause the target's so big." Her humor was also very commercial. Noted John J. O'Connor, television critic for *The New York Times:* "Onstage, Miss Fields' act was tailored snugly to the demands of Las Vegas."

Fields's success as a comedian was marred by ill-health. She suffered from diabetes, a mastectomy, and a heart attack. In 1976 she lost a leg to phlebitis. Determined to continue as a comic, Totie made gags about her artificial leg just as she had joked about her weight. She made a point of calling her amputation a "stump." After her operation she lost 70 pounds. Worried about her balance onstage, Fields stoically remarked, "If I fall on my ass, so what? I'll get up and do my act."

Totie continued to perform during the last two years of her life mainly at the Sahara Hotel in Las Vegas. In 1978 she was named "Entertainer of the Year" at an awards ceremony at the Sahara. "I don't want anyone feeling sorry for me," she said, as she received the honor. Later that year she had another heart attack which brought about her death. She was only forty-eight. As the jolly fat woman and later the dying comic, Fields evoked the pathos of the tragic clown.

ANNE MEARA

Anne Meara was born in 1933, the only child of a well-to-do Irish Catholic lawyer in Long Island, New York. She began her career in New York in the early 1950's, starting out as a serious stage actress. She performed on and off Broadway, experienced periods of unemployment, and spent years pounding on doors in search of work. In 1953, at an agent's call for summer stock actors, she met Jerry Stiller, a head shorter than Anne and the son of a Jewish bus driver from Brooklyn.

The pair married in 1954 and continued the search for acting jobs. Anne landed occasional work, did bits on soap operas and worked at various odd jobs, as well as undergoing bouts of unemployment. Sometimes one would get work, sometimes the other, but never together. At one casting call for a married couple Stiller and Meara thought their luck might be turning. But the producer refused to consider them because he thought nobody would believe they were married to each other. Towards the end of the 50's, after four years of marriage, they both got jobs with Joseph Papp's New York Shakespeare Festival. They were also being paid $5 a week less than unemployment benefits. The couple wanted to become known so they wouldn't have to wait for calls, and, for economic reasons, they decided to give up serious acting and turn to comedy. Thus the team of Stiller and Meara was born.

They apparently had no particular background in comedy. Stiller thought that Meara was funny and their personalities offered an effective contrast. Meara was outgoing and brash compared to the more subdued Stiller. They wrote all of their own material and tested their act with Chicago's Compass Players. They got their big break when they landed a spot to appear on television on "The Ed Sullivan Show."

Their comic material came largely from the improbability of people of their diverse backgrounds being married to each other. They were nervous about how such material would be received by audiences, since ethnic humor wasn't particularly popular then (around 1960). Their fears proved to be groundless and the act became widely and wildly successful. They played clubs as stand-up comics, made albums, numerous television variety show appearances and, over the years, appeared 34 times on "Ed Sullivan." They quickly became the country's favorite ethnic comedy team. While Nichols and May dwelt on the absurdities of life, Stiller and Meara presented small sketches taken from life. Having distinctly different styles, Stiller and Meara were never compared with Nichols and May, as later teams would be. While they shared the writing, Stiller has said that Anne was brilliant and quick and could sometimes write a skit in as quickly as 20 minutes.

They achieved perhaps their greatest public exposure through the unlikely medium of commercials, particularly on radio. One night in 1961 they were doing their routine at a Greenwich Village nightclub when one of the audience members was impressed enough to remember the couple eight years later. By 1969 this man, Jerry Della Femina, had formed his own advertising agency and just landed the account of a little known German wine called Blue Nun. When Stiller and Meara were hired for the commercials the wine was selling 43,000 cases a year in the United States. In 1979 when the campaign ended, sales stood at over one million cases a year. The Blue Nun commercials revolved around the naive consumer mistaking the wine for someone who has taken religious vows. Their success led them to make comic commercials for other major companies such as United Van Lines and Amalgamated Bank of New York. The bank found itself receiving complimentary letters about the ads. Stiller and Meara's radio commercial antics were likened to those of Burns and Allen, and Bob and Ray.

They created images of a pseudo-sophisticated couple who in reality "mistake chocolate mousse for an endangered species and Beef Wellington for a wrestler." Their world of commercials was once described as "plastic Americana run amok." The team were winners in 1983 of the Big Apple Radio Award for the best commercial from a new national advertiser and were introduced at the award ceremony as a couple who had done more for radio than any other announcers.

Despite their success for Blue Nun they were dropped from the ad campaign because executives felt they could sell a bottle of wine costing $1.79 but not one costing $5. Sales of the product have remained static in the first few years since Stiller and Meara and the company parted in 1979. All of the radio ads were performed and written by Stiller and Meara themselves, and they remained radio's best paid salespeople into the 1980's. A fee of $35,000 to $70,000 was considered a great fee for a radio-only spot, an amount that the couple was said to exceed on every deal. Their irreverent and brash commercial sketches were considered to be works of art, even by other comedy writers.

After more than a decade as stand-up comics, the team began to diversify. They branched out by returning to acting in summer stock, first together and then alone. They also did film and television work. Meara had her own very short-lived show on CBS in a series called "Kate McShane." It was a straight dramatic program. For the couple, becoming a name act as comedians allowed them to branch out, which was precisely what they did. As Meara said, "We earned the luxury of acting together again in stock after we became known for comedy."

Stiller once candidly admitted he felt jealous of Meara at one time. People would tell him, "I like you but I LOVE her." Stiller, though, was never really threatened by this, as some other men have been in their relations with famous women comedians. It was the strong and enduring bond between the couple that has led to their success.

The stand-up comedy team of Stiller and Meara will probably not make many future appearances together. Anne Meara no longer wants to be typecast as a comedian. Even after all those years of comedy it turns out to still have been her second choice. "I'm an actress first, then a comedian. I get upset when comedy and drama are separated. I started out as an actress, and that is what I have always been. If the truth be known, though, I have always used my humor to get along, to make people like me. It's almost an obsequious streak in me."

CAROL BURNETT

In July of 1957 at a New York City club called the Blue Angel patrons were convulsed by a singer who delivered a comic song. The song was a satire on the adoration teenagers bestowed on rock singers. The tune was called "I Made a Fool of Myself Over John Foster Dulles." The then Secretary of State was picked as the target since he was a most unlikely sex object. The song had been specially written for the singer, who was the second of four twenty-minute acts on the bill. She wanted an opening number that would grab the customers' attention.

The satire was a success and Carol Burnett's career was launched. She was born in 1933 in San Antonio, Texas, the daughter of a movie theater manager. Her parents were constantly fighting, separating, and reuniting, and in 1935 they moved to California, leaving Carol in Texas to be looked after by her grandmother. In 1940 Carol joined her parents in Los Angeles. Her family was poor and her father had spent much of the 1930's on WPA relief. The new start in California didn't pan out and Mr. Burnett rose no higher than coupon salesman for a photography studio. Her parents drank excessively and finally divorced in 1946. They both died in the 1950's.

During much of her time in Los Angeles, Carol continued to be raised by her grandmother. They lived in a single-room apartment in a building just off Hollywood Boulevard. Her mother lived in the same building across the hall.

Carol grew up gangly and bucktoothed, an image she would never live down. Her favorite activity as a child was drawing, and at that young age she hoped to be an artist when she grew up.

In those early years she was also a closet radio performer. When she came home from school she would pretend to be various characters on radio programs that she had listened to. Her grandmother took her to the movies as many as seven or eight times a week. It was a pastime Carol loved and years later she would spoof many of those same films on her show.

She was never a cutup as a child, never a school funny girl. While she was growing up her mother had whacked her a few times for crossing her eyes and making funny faces. Her grandmother was a comic, however. She used to take out her false teeth and pull her lip up over her nose, or belch with glee, to amuse Carol.

Carol attending Hollywood High School, where she had lots of friends, was a good athlete, and editor of the school newspaper. Being tall and awkward she didn't have a very active social life as an adolescent.

Carol felt one of the reasons she turned to drawing was because it was something her mother couldn't do, while Carol couldn't match her beautiful mother in the date department. Her mother drummed into Carol that it would be useless for her to try to be beautiful, something which no doubt sparked the beginnings of her sense of inferiority and later self-deprecation.

Burnett did well in high school and when she graduated in 1952 she enrolled at UCLA, hoping to major in journalism. Her mother had wanted her to be a writer, reasoning that "No matter what you look like, you can always write." Carol had never considered acting because to her acting was movies and movies were beautiful people. At UCLA there was no journalism major, so Carol signed up for Theater Arts/English. She explained to her mother that this major offered a playwriting course.

The playwriting course had a requirement that all students do acting as well. Although up to that point Carol had never considered a show business career, she changed her mind after appearing on stage and getting some laughs. She admits to becoming hooked. Her goal then became musical comedy. She wanted to be another Ethel Merman.

This abrupt switch in career plans got no encouragement from her mother, who stated flatly, "You'll never make it." Carol, nevertheless, performed with several campus theater groups, usually getting the funny and rowdy parts, and won an award for her acting.

In 1954 near the end of her junior year members of her class were asked to perform at a private party in San Diego. Burnett and fellow student Don Saroyan did a scene from *Annie Get Your Gun*. A wealthy building contractor was impressed enough to ask them their plans for the future, and both said they would like to go to New York City to try and make it, but lack of money prevented them. The contractor asked how much money they would need and Burnett replied that $1,000 seemed about right. The contractor said fine, "It's yours."

Since the man was slightly drunk at the time, the two students thought it was just the liquor talking. But when they phoned him the next week he kept his word and gave them each a $1,000 interest-free loan. The conditions were that the money was to be used to launch their careers, it must be repaid within five years, they were to help other young people break into the business if and when they became financially successful, and the benefactor's name was never to be revealed. The conditions were all honored.

In August of 1954 Burnett came to New York and took up residence at the Rehearsal Club, a famous hotel for aspiring actresses. Don came shortly after and the couple married the following year. In 1959 the money was repaid, Carol Burnett hit the big time and the couple separated. They had suffered a problem which has plagued many successful women. As Carol said, "It's hard on a marriage when the woman makes more money than the man does." It didn't bother her but it bothered him.

Out of her original stake money she had spent $130 for air fare, $60 for a winter coat, and another $300 to get her teeth fixed. After settling in at the Rehearsal Club she got a three-day-a-week job as a hat check girl at a restaurant near Rockefeller Center. She made $30 a week in tips and her room and board cost $18. She made the rounds of the agents and met with nothing but discouragement. They told her, "You've got a good loud voice, but not much personality, and you're not that attractive. . . . Go home and get married."

The other problem was a familiar Catch-22 situation. Agents told her again and again they couldn't give her a job until they had seen her work. When Burnett pointed out that she couldn't gain that experience until someone gave her a job, one agent told her to put on her own show.

By now Burnett was president of the Rehearsal Club and she decided to do just that. She convinced a couple dozen residents of the hotel to chip in money to rent a hall. Then she badgered unemployed writers and lyricists to help prepare material, and finally they did put on their own show before a crowd of agents, producers, and any other theatrical people of influence they could persuade to come. Carol was the only comedian in the show and its star.

Her major routine was a spoof of one of Eartha Kitt's sexy tunes called "Monotonous." Kitt had done the number wearing a negligee. As a portent of characters to come, Burnett performed that song with her hair in curlers and wearing an old bathrobe. "I knew I wasn't going to win any glamour prizes. . . . I was going to have to establish myself as a slob."

The result was that she did acquire an agent and began to get work. She did some summer stock and had a one-week engagement at an industrial show in Chicago where she sang about the benefits of aluminum foil. Her first television appearance was on ventriloquist Paul Winchell's children's show. For thirteen weeks she played the girlfriend of Winchell's dummies. She did straight singing only, no comedy. Next was a stint on the short-lived television series "Stanley," in which she played Buddy Hackett's girl friend.

In 1956 she met Garry Moore and auditioned for him with a seven-minute routine, the only one she had. It was impressive enough and in November 1956 she appeared on Moore's morning show. Over the next three years she appeared a number of times on that program, as well as making guest appearances on many other variety shows. Still, by early 1957 things weren't looking too bright as her major source of income was $36 a week from unemployment benefits.

The long-needed boost to her career was from the Dulles song. In August she did the song on Jack Paar's "Tonight" show and later on the Ed Sullivan show. The song created a minor furor, with many complaints about satirizing the Secretary of State. Dulles himself was reportedly amused. In May of 1959 she opened in the lead role of the Off Broadway musical *Once Upon a Mattress*. Burnett was successful enough playing the rowdy princess that the play moved to Broadway and didn't close until July of 1960.

Her biggest public exposure came in November 1959 when she became a regular on the CBS evening "Garry Moore Show." She had appeared earlier that year as a last-minute guest, replacing an ailing Martha Raye. That led to her eventually becoming a regular.

She did both the play and television series until the former closed, working herself almost to the point of collapse. She did the TV show during the day and the play every night plus a couple of matinees. Her stint on the Moore show firmly established her as a great new comic star. Modestly she attributed her success to luck, feeling there were plenty of funny women out there, but she was just at the right place at the right time.

Her style of humor was very physical and at various times she had injured a hip, damaged foot cartilage, and sprained her back doing her numerous pratfalls. During a typical Moore show she might play half a dozen widely different characters. She had an endless series of jumps, trips, leaps, and limps. She could fall around the stage like a doll, sing soaking wet, and make noises like a dog. She was equally convincing whether she played the slob or the seductress.

She was one of the few performers who could perform with her back to the audience and be tremendously funny, just by using the motions of her hands over her back and body language. On the show the troupe satirized Grimm's Fairy Tales and the National Safety Council. Burnett did Scarlett O'Hara and once played a barking seal.

One of her best skits on the Moore show was a satire of the fairy tale Cinderella in which Burnett played the maiden with a hangover on the morning after the ball. She mugged outrageously with a mobile face, expressive eyes, and a body she could contort almost at will. A trademark phrase in skits became, "Watch it," which she virtuously delivered in a loud voice, after some cad had gotten fresh with her. Playing characters was very necessary for her in those early years. She claimed she had to be introduced as some character before she could face an audience. "I have to be somebody else to do anything at all before a camera."

Given her style, it was to be expected that she would be considered not feminine. It was said that she was prepared to sacrifice beauty for comic effect and that she was engaged in "self-uglification." She was described as having an "anteater nose" and that she "looks in profile like a monkey wrench."

Such remarks about her appearance became so commonplace that she engaged in self-deprecation herself. She once said that between Marilyn Monroe and Tony Curtis she more closely resembled the latter. Part of her style was of the girl who grew up believing she wasn't pretty, and being funny about it. It took years for her to accept compliments about her appearance without protest.

In what was then the era of the beat or sick comic, she likened herself to neither, calling herself commercial and hip square. More hip than her grandmother, but square enough to be commercial. At that early point in her career her popularity was already said to rival that of Lucille Ball and she was being compared with the likes of Beatrice Lillie and Martha Raye. All three comedians were among her favorites.

She drew a distinction between comic and comedienne. Burnett saw herself as a comedian, that is an actress who took on funny roles or someone who said things funny as opposed to somebody who said funny things. In that era of cerebral comedians like Elaine May, Burnett was a throwback to old style comedy. She went for the belly laugh.

In 1962 she had the following comments about why there were so few female comics around. "If you're a woman it's difficult to break through the barrier of having others accept you as funny. There's all that training you've had since you were three. Be a lady! Don't yell or try to be funny. Just be a nice little girl. Sit quietly with your knees close together and speak only when you're spoken to. Women are afraid to make themselves unattractive. I'm not afraid of that, goodness knows! But all but one in a million women are afraid to mess up their hair, not wear lipstick, slouch, look flat-chested. . . . Most women are obsessed with an outmoded sense of modesty. They labor under the necessity of being ladylike. They are afraid that being funny is unfeminine. Most men seem to have the same idea about comediennes. They laugh at us, but they're wary of us as women."

Her work on the Moore show earned her an Emmy in 1962. This was a tribute to Burnett's ability to bring added dimensions to the material. Many of the characters she portrayed on the show, beneath the surface, were very similar, "a belligerent and grimly bubble-headed young man-trap who will do nearly anything . . . to get a ring on her finger." Her comic skills prevented such characters from becoming boring or grotesque over the years.

That same year she announced she was leaving the show as a regular after three seasons. She wanted to move on and try different things, Broadway shows in particular. The stage remained her major love and she said, "I'd love to do musical comedies for the rest of my life." In August of 1962 she signed a ten-year contract with CBS which guaranteed her $100,000 a year for making two guest shots and starring in one special each year. Her importance to the Moore show could be seen from the slump in ratings after she left. She had received movie offers by this time, but she had declined them all. She had no interest in playing serious drama because "I would miss the laughs. And probably if I did something serious, I'd get them."

At that time she wasn't interested in doing her own television series in the immediate future. Even if someone came up with a great idea for "The Carol Burnett Show," "I wouldn't do it. The last thing I want is to shove myself down people's throats every week." After leaving Moore's show she did some night club work and TV guest appearances, many on the Moore show.

Burnett's career entered a low period after she left that show. By 1963 she was engaged in a romance with the producer of the Moore show, Joe Hamilton. He was married with eight children and, being Catholic, his wife refused at first to give him a divorce. She later relented, and Burnett and Hamilton were free to marry, but only after a year of very negative and unpleasant publicity in which Burnett was cast as a husband stealer and a home wrecker by some of the movie magazines. Fans began to write nasty letters. Her stock fell as executives in the industry wondered if she hadn't perhaps been overrated.

In 1964 she opened in a Broadway show *Fade Out—Fade In* which was a flop. An old injury acted up and caused her to miss a number of performances, and she was threatened with a lawsuit over her recurring absences. That same year she co-starred as one of the three hosts, with Bob Newhart and Caterina Valente, in a big-budget CBS series called "The Entertainers." This was also a short-lived flop. Burnett's love of the stage and musical comedy was shaken and drastically altered after this Broadway experience, "I don't think I would ever again do another Broadway show." And through to the mid-1980's she hasn't yet returned to Broadway.

This low ebb in Carol's career was broken in September 1967 when her own comedy variety series debuted on CBS, "The Carol Burnett Show." The show became popular and lasted until the spring of 1978 when, after eleven full seasons, Carol decided to end the series. The success of the show came despite the fact that during this period variety shows in general were in a decline. Eleven years was a long time in television. Only about thirty programs had longer runs in television history, and Burnett's show picked up numerous Emmys.

When the series debuted, few predicted any success for it and, given the attitudes on both sides, it was ironic that it even got on the air. Burnett was then still thought to be more "out" than "in" and "television and advertising experts considered the show one of the least likely to succeed." When the program was proposed to Burnett she was hesitant. She felt her real place was on the stage and was certain that a weekly series would bomb: "It'll never last the season."

Both sides were completely wrong of course, and Carol quickly reestablished herself as the "Queen of Zanies." She went on to greater fame than on the old Moore show. She was soon earning about $1 million a year, attracting close to 50 million weekly viewers, and had been called a "female Chaplin." By 1977 the Gallup Poll rated her one of the most admired women in America.

Her style of comedy remained largely the same as it had been on the Moore show. The cast did lampoons on everything from opera to the nuclear family. They did sketches spoofing other TV shows, old movies, and various forms of entertainment. And of course Burnett did lots of characters, and she did them wonderfully. Her style remained highly physical, a reckless slapstick. She did Nixon sketches, Johnson sketches, and Doris Day sketches. She spoofed Esther Williams, and did a Cher takeoff, played a Sophia Loren Italian-style Cinderella. She was a housewife, siren, mother, tramp, tomboy, nurse, secretary, frump, queen and one of her regular characters, the charwoman who mimed on many of the shows.

She belted out songs in an Ethel Merman manner, did soap opera send ups, "As the Stomach Turns," and loved to use outlandish props such as huge false eyelashes and glasses, and eccentric clothes. In her old Hollywood movie takeoffs she did Joan Crawford in "Mildred Fierce," Barbara Stanwyck in "Double Calamity," Rita Hayworth in "Golda," Gloria Swanson, and Jeannette MacDonald.

Two recurring sketches that lasted for years had Carol and series regular Harvey Korman playing an old couple rocking on their porch and contemplating life. In the other sketch the same two played a constantly fighting and arguing, uptight married couple. Burnett's character was Eunice, a screaming Southern banshee married to a lard-headed husband, Ed. The character of Eunice was the only one with which Burnett had any kind of emotional attachment. She likened the character, created by the show's writers, to her mother in that they both suffered a "pitiful frustration." After her series ended Burnett would go on to do a television movie, *Eunice,* based on this character.

The audience that watched Burnett has been described as people in or from small towns, more women than men, more children than adults, more poor than rich, and the less educated. In short, they comprised those who were not in the mainstream of money and power. There is some truth to this. Burnett has said she tried to tailor her routines to "Fred and Maude, a mythical all-American couple who identify with the movies that once infused her own adolescent fantasies." The humor on the show was certainly not biting or cutting. But since the show played the ten to eleven time slot for all of its run, except for one year, it was unlikely that her audience was mostly children.

While Burnett has been categorized as very private and hard to know, as thin-skinned, hypersensitive, naive and easily hurt, the terms most often used have been friendly and nice. She had become known in Hollywood as "Ms. Nice Guy." In many ways she has been the personification of many Middle American virtues: helpful, decent, down to earth, punctual. About her humor on the show, she has said, "There's no soapbox to my humor—I like purely physical humor. . . . A lot of what I do is just silly. . . . I go after laughs."

In real life she described herself as having an average life and being "really dull." "My life is centered around my family." She adored her family and job. She had a home with a front and back yard, two cars, and called herself content.

Some critics have claimed that Burnett's characters were degrading American women. Carol had done a character named Wanda Wiggins, a secretary with a big rear, big breasts, and not too smart. "I'm not saying all secretaries are like that, but maybe one is." She always approached her characters from an individual, rather than group, point of view. And she has played a variety of secretarial types, although "Mrs. Wiggins just happened to be the most popular one."

Her self-deprecation was most evident in a regular segment of the show. This was the question-and-answer session which took place between Carol and her studio audience, and sometimes her guest star, usually at the beginning of the show. This bantering with the audience was genuine, not rehearsed, and Carol fielded questions from the audience. It took the place of a monologue, which she claimed to have been terrified of doing by herself. The dialogue likely contributed to her popularity by increasing audience participation. It also broke down some of the formality between performer and fans so they could identify with her and relax.

During these sessions she appeared as herself and was pleasant, normal, and open. She did put-downs of her figure, her face and her flat chest. Her theory was to strike first before anyone else did. "I used to belittle my looks constantly on the show." By the end of the show's run she still felt she shouldn't sing a song straight. Apparently very early in the show's run she had done a straight solo song and a top male singer sent her a telegram telling her to stick to comedy. It was something that Burnett has not forgotten.

By the 1980's, influenced by various events including the feminist movement, she had changed her mind on the self-deprecation routines, even though they were big laugh getters, and said she wouldn't do them again. "I don't think it does any of us any good to put ourselves down. If other people are going to have negative thoughts, that's their problem. I shouldn't add to it by substantiating what they might be thinking. It's anti-feminine."

Her own early sense of inferiority was evident in connection with the preparation of the show, and her relationship with her husband. In 1972 she told an interviewer that she would like to do some sketches for the entire hour of her show. The interviewer asked why she didn't insist on them, and she replied, "I do what they tell me to do." She didn't want to make any waves or have any enemies. She wanted everybody to love her. Of those early years, series regular Vicki Lawrence said, "People could walk all over Carol and get away with it." By her own description Burnett was "Wishy-washy, a real Charlie Brown."

In her role as wife Burnett clearly deferred to her husband and producer of her show, Joe Hamilton: "We've never had any problem about who's boss. Joe's smarter than I am." A staffer on the show claimed that "She actually goes out of her way to let people know who is boss." Hamilton himself reportedly said, "I don't even think she knows what she makes. . . . She'd rather leave that to me. She's happy just taking care of our children." Part of this may have been a carryover from her first marriage in which her income proved to be such a negative factor.

During the first seven years of her show she never attended the production meetings where the show was planned and written. She just did whatever the staff and her producer-husband had prepared. She could usually be talked into doing things on the show she didn't want to do.

Burnett didn't want to be categorized as "masculine" or as the type of female who wanted to run the show. An assertive male was considered a great guy, but Carol felt an aggressive female was not accepted: "They think she's emasculating everyone, and they have names for women like that." She readily admitted that one of her weaknesses was in going along with other people's suggestions, even when she felt they were wrong for her, because she wanted to be admired and liked.

During the 1970's she underwent a change and gradually became more assertive, due largely to the influence of the women's movement. She began to attend production meetings of the show and to stop being afraid to voice her opinion just because she was female. She got to the point where she was able to cut a whole skit from the show that she felt was openly anti-female. She was then less afraid of being classed as a woman who made decisions. By the early 1980's Burnett had given a few speeches in favor of the ERA and donated money to the cause. It was the first political issue that she had supported in public.

She declined to continue with her series after the spring of 1978 because she had been doing the same thing for eleven years and wanted a change. Burnett wanted the challenge of more serious and riskier roles. Some of her new-found assertiveness carried over into her personal life. She launched a libel suit against the *National Enquirer* after that publication implied, in 1976, that during a raucous conversation with Henry Kissinger Burnett had been drunk. She won that suit in 1981.

When a drug problem involving her daughter surfaced in 1979, she went public to warn other parents. In 1981 she had oral dental surgery done to correct her bite and give her a more prominent chin. She had hated her buck teeth and receding chin for all 48 years of her life and finally got them corrected. In 1982 she separated from husband Joe Hamilton.

The media had always alternated between pointing out Burnett's being ugly on stage and constantly rediscovering in interviews that she was actually attractive in real life. This preoccupation with beauty and looks didn't extend to male comics.

Burnett's motto for comedy was, "Comedy is tragedy plus time." When she first began as a comedian, the Burnett style was raucous slapstick that not many females were willing or able to do. It was an age of kooky comedy with little or no bite. Burnett felt her comedy came out of the fun and nonsense era that also gave us Lucille Ball.

For Carol the big difference between her and Ball was that "Lucy always played one character—brilliantly. It's as if I were to do Eunice every night." Some critics found Burnett to be a little darker and more violent than Ball. Burnett also admired Lily Tomlin and considered her one of the "hippest comedy minds around."

Over the years Carol had maintained that she was not a clown but an actress who dealt mainly in comedy. She didn't consider herself a true satirist, "because I do not write it." The physical comedy was the more enjoyable part for her. "I love being socked and slapped and thrown out of windows."

As Burnett explained her start in comedy: "When I started out . . . it was the era of mugging. And I had a great face for mugging. So I became known as 'The Mugger.' I thought that's what they wanted. It wasn't until about six or seven years into the show that I started to realize I didn't have to do it, that I was a mature woman who could still be funny without crossing my eyes all the time. It was a sense of insecurity that made me do that, and a growing security that made me stop. That's when I stopped putting down my looks."

Since leaving her television series Burnett's career has followed a busy, if somewhat ragged, course. She has appeared on TV specials and been in a number of made-for-TV movies as well as big-screen films. While she has garnered some critical praise for her performances and been in some box office successes, the majority of her vehicles have been critical and financial failures. Much of her work in these areas has not been comedy, but straight drama.

She's appeared in *Who's Been Sleeping in My Bed* with Dean Martin, *Pete 'n' Tillie* with Walter Matthau, *The Front Page* with Matthau and Jack Lemmon, and Robert Altman's *A Wedding*. All of those roles, except the last, were very forgettable. Of *The Front Page* Burnett admitted, "I knew from day one that I stunk. . . . I was out of my element." When she mentioned her film work during that period, she found herself apologizing for it.

When Burnett first ventured into film she claimed that she wasn't hesitant, that she just plunged in, although many years earlier she had said she couldn't imagine herself doing drama. Part of her sense of inferiority carried over into her movie work. She was conscious of the idea that television stars were "smaller than life" and lacked the stature to make it in films. "I'm television. And let's face it, the industry considers us second-class citizens."

She credited Robert Altman with her breakthrough in films. After *A Wedding* she went on to appear in some bombs like *Chu Chu and the Philly Flash,* but she also scored her first box office smash in Alan Alda's *The Four Seasons* as well as landing her biggest film role in *Annie.* She also continued to make TV movies. By the mid 1980's Burnett was trying to put together scripts and production ideas of her own for future film and television development.

Carol Burnett started with the goal of being a musical comedy performer and then came to "adore doing violent slapstick comedy." She believed that people still stereotyped funny women as unattractive. Her gawky, pratfalling, mugging and screechy characters made her famous, but Carol Burnett is looking for a new image.

PHYLLIS DILLER

Phyllis Diller was born in Lima, Ohio, in 1917. The only child of an insurance sales manager father, Perry Driver, and housewife mother, Frances, she described her childhood as secure. Although Diller realized she could make people laugh in grade school, she didn't act up in class. In fact, joking around was not the focus of her energies.

Phyllis was much more interested in music, and she sang at school and in church. After high school in 1935 she enrolled in the Sherwood Music Conservatory in Chicago, intending to become a professional musician. But Phyllis soon felt that she would never be good enough for the concert stage. Her other professional goal, to sing in nightclubs, was thwarted when she was told she was too plain.

Discouraged, Phyllis transferred to Bluffton College in Ohio, where she worked toward a degree in music education. A significant extra-curricular activity for Diller was her position as humor editor of the college paper.

At Bluffton Phyllis met Sherwood Diller, whom she married in 1939. She never finished her degree. Their first child was born in 1940, and the couple moved to California where Sherwood found employment at the Alameda Naval Air Station. In the next ten years Phyllis had four more children, and her husband held a succession of jobs, none for very long. For a while the family income was supplemented by money Phyllis inherited from her parents. This money evaporated when the Dillers made an unfortunate real estate investment. With Sherwood working erratically, the couple lived through a rough time under extreme financial pressure, which created tension in their marriage.

To lift her spirits, Phyllis told jokes to neighborhood housewives at the corner laundromat. But she also realized she had to look for a job. Diller was hired to write a shopping column for the San Leandro *News-Observer*. She moved on to writing advertising copy for an Oakland department store, and then moved into radio, first at station KROW in Oakland, and then at KFSO in San Francisco, where she did work in advertising and merchandising. When Diller auditioned for a talent spot, the station rejected her. Reflecting on this, she commented: "I was an office girl to them. They couldn't see me at all."

Phyllis kept up her clowning anyway. She joked with her family, her co-workers, and polished her material at the laundromat, making up gags like: "I'm nine years behind in my ironing. I bury a lot in the backyard."

Her success with family and friends encouraged Diller to volunteer and act for church groups, PTA meetings, the Kiwanis club, and the Red Cross. She played the piano and joked between pieces. Her son played the banjo.

Diller's husband nagged her about becoming a professional comedienne. He was convinced of her talent, and she credits him with pushing her into action. A self-help book, *The Magic of Believing*, gave her the added boost. She then hired a drama coach to help her with delivery and style. Diller wrote some comedy routines and worked for an entire year on her act.

Her first audition was at the Purple Onion in San Francisco. Fortunately, for Diller, the club's comedian had just left for a temporary engagement in New York, so there was a two-week opening, and she was hired to fill in at $60.00 per week. She quit her radio job.

In 1955 at the age of 37, Phyllis Diller appeared on the professional stage for the first time. Her Purple Onion act consisted of spoofing singers like Eartha Kitt, and telling jokes between songs. The audience received her politely. She used the two weeks to try out new material, satirizing ridiculous ads from *Vogue* and *Bazaar*, making funny faces, and using various props, from comic glasses to tatty furs. Diller's act became so good that she rose to top billing at the Purple Onion and her two-week stint was extended to 89 weeks.

She next took her act on the road, playing clubs all over the U.S. Her husband Sherwood traveled with her, acting as business manager, and her children stayed with relatives. Diller tightened up her routines and dropped the songs and impersonations because, as she told Alex Haley in a 1962 interview: "They sagged the pace." She wrote all of her own material and focused on what she knew best—family relations and housework.

Her act was a success. In 1958 when she played Boston, a reviewer described her as "a mugger . . . Miss Diller's grimaces are priceless, and frequently take the place of words. Secondly, she has a hollerer's laughter, one who throws back her head and really lets go. Who can resist it? And third, her material is slick, sanguine, and frequently macabre."

The greatest thrill of her early career came in 1959 when Bob Hope caught her act in Washington, D.C. After the show he got up from his table, and told her she was great. Diller said this often helped her over rough times: "I'd think: If Bob Hope likes my work, I must have something." And there were rough times. She was, for example, fired after one night at the Fontainebleau Hotel in Miami.

But Diller set her sights high. Her ambition was to headline the hungry i in San Francisco, a club which showcased comedians like Mort Sahl, Bob Newhart and Jonathan Winters. By 1961 she had achieved her goal. Phyllis Diller the comedian was established. In 1961 she also played the Bon Soir in New York's Greenwich Village, a club so sophisticated Diller cracked that "a nine-year-old boy came in here the other night, and when he left he was 38."

By this time Diller was famous enough to be profiled in *Time* magazine, which commended her high-flying imagination: "She sketches one woman who wears bronzed baby shoes for earrings. The kid is still in them, and he has hiccups." Another routine she did was about her fastidious neighbor Mrs. Clean and her two boys Spic and Span.

What really catapulted Diller to fame was her appearances on TV's "Jack Paar Show." Paar kidded that Phyllis looked like "someone you avoid in supermarkets." By mid-1961, she had been on Paar's show 30 times.

In 1965 when Diller celebrated her tenth anniversary in show business 55,000 fans showed up at Soldier Field in Chicago. By 1966, Phyllis was earning $35,000 a week in nightclubs and $55,000 a week in Las Vegas.

Television became a vehicle for Diller and she appeared on most major variety and comedy shows like Ed Sullivan's, Red Skelton's, Andy Williams's, Dean Martin's, Steve Lawrence's, and Jack Benny's.

In September 1966 Diller got her own television series on ABC-TV's "The Pruitts of Southhamptom." She played the role of Mrs. Phyllis Poindexter Pruitt, "an improverished socialite trying to keep up appearances." In January 1967 the show was renamed "The Phyllis Diller Show" to highlight its star, but the series was unsuccessful and was cancelled in the fall of 1967. Critics complained of her "inept slapstick."

Further TV efforts were no greater success. On October 25, 1967, Phyllis starred in an NBC special "The Phyllis Diller Happening" with Bob Hope, Sonny & Cher, and other guest stars. A *New York Times* review censured that while Diller was "an engaging hostess, she doesn't seem strong enough as a comedienne or as a personality to carry a program without a Bob Hope to bring it alive."

Another series, "The Beautiful Phyllis Diller Show" was a variety show hosted by Diller. It lasted for only four months on NBC in 1968. *The New York Times* complained that Phyllis engaged in too much "horseplay" and wasn't enough of a "gracious human being."

Diller also tried her hand on the stage, appearing in several road plays between 1961 and 1963. She also broke into the movies in 1961 with a bit part in *Splendor in the Grass.* Her first co-starring comedy role came in the 1965 film *The Fat Spy* with Jack E. Leonard. Several films followed in which she co-starred with Bob Hope, including the 1966 movie *Boy Did I Get a Wrong Number.* Her 1967 film, *Eight on the Lam,* was not well received by critics, but Phyllis was. A reviewer in *The New York Times* of April 27, 1967, praised her zany energy: "The woman of the day is Miss Diller, as a raucous babysitter, streaking through the picture like a berserk comet, every hair standing on end." On the whole, though, the six comedy films that Phyllis appeared in were too weak and crudely plotted to display her talent.

In addition to appearing in films, Diller has also cut several comedy albums and written a number of humor books spoofing housekeeping and marriage manuals.

Her own twenty-six year marriage to Sherwood ended in divorce in 1965. That year she married the singer Warde Donovan, but later she also separated from Donovan.

Phyllis did not neglect her musical ability. She used her talent publicly between 1971 and 1981, when she performed in close to 100 fund-raising symphony concerts. She did gags between her piano solos, but the playing was serious.

Diller considered herself a feminist and refused to wear hosiery, claiming they were a waste of money. In 1961 Diller cracked: "The older I get the funnier I get. . . . Think what I'll save in not having my face lifted." Yet eleven years later she did get a facelift because she felt she looked "horrible" on TV. Phyllis admitted she used to "poke fun" at women who got facelifts — "women like me."

It's ironic that Diller worried about her appearance when her stage persona involved looking ridiculous. She deliberately masked her good figure and pleasant face by wearing gaudy clothing, fright wigs, shaved eyebrows, false eyelashes, and high-heeled ankle boots. She had a collection of blue, green, pink, yellow and turquoise contact lenses for the stage. She delivered her gags standing with her legs wide apart and her shoulders slightly hunched.

Dressed in this outlandish manner, Diller reeled off one-liners, putting herself down with cracks like: "They just elected me Miss Phonograph Record of 1966. They discovered my measurements were 33 1/3, 45, 78!"

Phyllis explained the reasons behind her wacky get-up and self-deprecation: "To make it on stage, I had to make fun of myself first. I had to dress funny, I had to cover my figure—or I couldn't make any body jokes. Of course, I was accused of being self-deprecatory. I've got to be. . . . Comedy is tragedy revisited or hostility. It is mock hostility, of course, or it would be ugly. . . . But I would come out on stage and put everybody down—myself, the children, the lady next door, the cops. Everybody has got to be bad. See, if everything is good, you've got Grace Kelly and that's not funny."

Diller delivered 12 punch lines per minute in her routine contributing to her fast-talking wild style, and earning her the appellation "Killer Diller." (Bob Hope by comparison delivers six punch lines per minute.)

Diller also had a few other trademarks. One was the unlit cigarette she waved around in a foot-long holder. She used the holder as an excuse to have her arm up in the air, and said it was a way of calling attention to herself. She also flicked off an imaginary ash from time to time when she wanted a pause.

Another trademark was her famous gusty "Aah-ha-ha-haa" laugh which she started in order to counter a lack of response from an audience, or "priming the pump" as she called it. Some have criticized the laugh for its grating cackling quality, but Diller recognized that people identified her with the laugh, and she retained it.

One of her best-known targets was Fang, a single-toothed fictitious husband. She created Fang at the Purple Onion, ad libbing a one-liner. The audience loved it, so she added more Fang jokes. Here's a typical one: "I realized on our first wedding anniversary that our marriage was in trouble. Fang gave me luggage. It was packed. My mother damn near suffocated in there." Diller enjoyed the Fang jokes because she said it was a chance to get back at male comics who have put down wives for years. Diller was never sentimental or romantic about family life. She talked about a Mother's Day present she once received from her children—an oven that flushes.

And instead of the wife's mother, Phyllis attacked the husband's. One of her stock characters was a mother-in-law, Moby Dick. There was also a sister-in-law, Captain Bligh. Diller said she stuck close to the truth for her material using the day-to-day problems that housewives had with husbands, children, relatives, food, and housework.

It seemed that with Moby Dick and Captain Bligh, Phyllis got a little too close to the truth for comfort. After her divorce from Sherwood, his mother and sister demanded that Phyllis omit those two characters from her act. Diller sued them on the grounds that these characters were "an integral and component part of a unique style of humor developed over a number of years at a great cost." The case was settled out of court.

Phyllis started with a one-liner and topped it. She kept adding toppers building to the punch lines—often working it out right on stage. Once she became successful, Diller was able to buy jokes from free-lance writers. One of her main sources was a housewife from Wisconsin.

Phyllis only used what she called gags or one-liners in her act, explaining the format as a set-up, pause, and pay-off with the funny word always coming towards the end. She cited Bob Hope as her idol and inspiration, and claimed she wasn't that influenced by other female comics, although she did mention Joan Davis.

It was not easy breaking into the traditionally male world of stand-up comedy. Diller felt that at first people were not accepting of a female comic, especially one that wasn't dumb or cute, and wondered what she was trying to do. They were ready to conclude that she was butch or nasty: "Being a woman, right away you walk out to almost total rejection. Almost nobody wants you to be a female comic and they give you a lot of static just because of your sex. . . . Keep women in their place. . . . Men have this silly, witchy . . . attitude that a woman who is a comic has lost her femininity."

Perhaps the difficulty that men have had with accepting female comics can be seen in this 1970 review of Diller by Charles Marowitz that appeared in *The Village Voice:* "Diller is a mugger and a mouthpiece. I believe she shares some of Hope's writers; I guessed as much because behind her endless stream of abuse against ugly women, fat women, horrid in-laws, there is something mechanistically routine. Like some oddly chosen go-between, she conveys what the committee intellect has conceived. She has all the traditional equipment: timing, a sense of comic delivery, the ability to milk and to mug, and yet one feels, after 40 minutes in her company, she is a stranger. A stranger, albeit, with some marvelously wrought comedy material to dispense. . . . There is more to stand-up comedy than a manic committment to anatomical derision. I suppose she would say that's her 'thing.' She is an odd-looking lady making capital out of being unlovely. But she pushes unloveliness so far it almost conjures up a need for its opposite. We want her to say something funny about being pretty or wanted or sympathetic. . . .

"She is a true pro, and her professionalism is clearly seen. But I felt all through the evening her material was preventing me from touching her, from knowing her, and I grew to dislike it the way one does a host who elongates introductions when you're anxious to shake somebody by the hand."

This piece was interesting because it seemed that subconsciously the reviewer was lamenting Diller's inability or lack of desire to seduce him as a woman should. He couldn't "touch her." Marowitz got a "stream of abuse" when he wanted sweet talk, and an "odd-looking lady" rather than a pretty, lovely creature.

Diller's very intentions were to mock the whole fantasy of the beautiful sought-after blonde. She did a wonderful lampoon of the *Playboy* centerfold when she posed for a pin-up photo in *Field & Stream* magazine. Dressed in black waterproof waders, Diller was "Miss Fun Fishing of 1973."

Diller remembered that at first she did experience anger and resentment from males in the audience, although homosexual men were her initial supporters. Housewives became her next group of fans because she joked about things "that they wanted to say but couldn't." Moreover, she was living proof that a plain housewife could make good. Through the women she got the husbands listening, and through TV got kids enthusiastic.

Diller has had trouble with elderly audiences, though. In 1976 when she performed at a Pacific National Exhibition Show in Vancouver, Canada, for "golden agers," many found her references to "breasts, knees, sex, and Kleenex" too "dirty." Six hundred requested the return of their $1 admission fee and about one third of the 6,000 spectators walked out. Diller took exception to the labeling of her humor as offensive: "Adult, sophisticated—yes;

dirty—no." Nor did she bring up race, religion, or politics in her jokes.

Diller felt that there weren't that many female stand-up comedians because "It takes so much to make it. Once you've made it, you're the queen and life is beautiful and everybody wants your body and they want to give you gifts. But, man, before you make it, you're nothin'! You're negative nothin'. You're below zero and you know it."

Perhaps even more significant to the relatively few number of female stand-up comics was the fact that until recently women did not pursue a career of any kind, let alone comedy. Because her husband wasn't supporting the family, Phyllis was forced to work. As she noted: "My big motivation was making money for my kids."

And despite sometimes harsh critical reception, Diller did make money, big money. A million a year. In the ranks of stand-up comics she did more than hold her own. She became one of the top comedians in the country. As Eugene Boe of *Cue* magazine noted: "She is brave to venture into an area so dangerous for women, and she is clever to be even intermittently successful in this elusive craft."

JOAN RIVERS

Joan Rivers has been called everything from the "most intuitively funny woman alive," to a self-loathing misogynist. She has described herself as the "meanest bitch in America." Through the early and mid 1980's she was the most popular and highly paid comic in the country. She tended to draw extreme reactions from her audiences. They either loved her or hated her. Some critics have vilified her in a way that few other comedians, regardless of sex, have been vilified. Much of the scorn heaped on her stems from the threat she posed.

She was not demure or sedate but used a hostile mouth in the manner of Babe Ruth wielding a baseball bat. She was a victim who struck back. Men preferred women who remained mute victims. Mixed in with her brand of assault humor was a large dose of self-deprecation, for which she has been condemned by feminists. It was this very aspect of her act which has allowed her to attain the heights of popularity that she has reached. It was the sugar coating on the pill. It was an obtuse form of an apology as well as a manifestation of her own insecurity. It helped make her act palatable to a large audience in a way that Lenny Bruce wasn't.

Few comics have worked as hard at their craft as Joan Rivers. She was born Joan Molinsky in Brooklyn, New York, in about 1935. She was raised there and later in Larchmont, New York, where her father, Dr. Molinsky, practiced as an internist. Her father was successful financially, but her mother, who had been born to wealth, liked to spend money. The result was that the family spent beyond its means and Joan grew up in constant fear of poverty and financial distress.

She wanted to be an actress all of her life and she was involved in dramatics in high school at Adelphi Academy. After graduation in 1951 she had a bit part in a United Artists picture, *Mr. Universe*. From there she attended Barnard College at Columbia University, where she studied English and social anthropology, graduating with a B.A. degree in the latter subject. At Columbia she wrote for the school literary magazine and school newspaper and acted in school plays.

In 1954, after graduation, Joan took a job with the Bond clothing stores, working as a fashion coordinator. While she was successful in her job, she wasn't happy and quit after several years to pursue her first love, a career in show business. During her time at Bonds she was married briefly, to James Sanger, the Bond clothing store heir, a union that ended in divorce after six months. Leaving her job was not that easy, as she faced parental disapproval. She was living at home when she quit Bonds in 1958. Her family was appalled that she wanted to go into show business. Her mother was so ashamed that she asked Joan to refer to herself as a writer. "Don't call yourself a comedian." When she left home to begin her new career, she and her parents didn't speak to one another for a year.

That began a seven-year period of trials, tribulations and humiliations as she ventured into comedy, before she got her first break on the Johnny Carson show in 1965. For the first two years of her career she played a series of "discovery" clubs in Greenwich Village, for which she received no pay. Her parents refused to give her any money, so she did secretarial work as an office temporary to support herself. During the worst of this period she slept in her car and washed up at the YWCA.

In 1960 she set off on a tour along the East coast of cheap clubs, strip joints, and run-down resorts in the Catskill mountains. She appeared in one club in Boston billed as "Pepper January, comedy and spice." She was fired her first night. In fact, during that first year, 1960, she was fired from every booking she had. In one club, an owner yelled over the loudspeaker, "Get her off." At another place she was paid just $5 for her performance and her manager demanded the standard ten percent, in this case 50 cents. As Rivers recalled that period, "If a trash can had a bulb, I played it."

In November of 1963 she toured with a comedy team which called themselves Jim, Jake, and Joan. This group enjoyed a degree of success, but Joan wasn't happy with the act. They specialized in satirical songs on current events, and dialogues. She was frustrated with the material she felt was contrived, and left the team. In November of 1964 Joan began a long-term booking at the Duplex in Greenwich Village, a more sophisticated venue than she had appeared in in the past.

By then she was using the name Joan Rivers. According to Joan she happened to take that name when an agent she had told her to adopt a different stage name. She said fine, and that she would use the agent's name, which was Rivers. This agent was so rattled that Rivers said he never booked her anyplace again.

While working at the Duplex she came to the attention of an agent named Roy Silver, who was astute enough to see her potential. She had sent dozens of postcards to agents asking them to come and see her performance. He persuaded her to make national television her goal. To make her material more appropriate for a mass medium, commercial audience, Silver went over tapes of her performances and helped Rivers to refine her material. With his help she ejected from her act any blue material, literary references, ethnic material, homosexual references, and esoteric show business jokes. She picked up assignments writing material for comics such as Phyllis Diller, Bob Newhart, and Phil Foster. She also worked creating ideas for the television show "Candid Camera."

Rivers had already auditioned for the Johnny Carson show on seven different occasions and had been turned down seven times. She made her television debut on the Carson show on February 17, 1965. Just three weeks before that appearance, her agent had advised her to quit show business, since everybody had seen her and she was too old. She got on the show as a favor to another of her manager's clients—Bill Cosby—as a last-minute replacement when the show was desperate. Rivers has referred to her appearance as a "mercy booking."

On that appearance she was billed not as a comedian but as a comedy writer come to talk about her work and her life. Her material that night consisted of the self-deprecatory humor for which she would become famous. She told the story about driving along the highway and having her wig come off and land on the road, whereupon it was run over by another driver. This motorist apologized to Rivers for having killed her dog. She related stories about her fat childhood and her desperate attempts to find a husband. Her fat jokes consisted of observations such as, "I was my own buddy at camp." To cheer her up her parents would take her for drives and "they'd take me with them in the U-Haul-It." Rivers claimed her mother legally changed her name to "Poor Joan" and put a sign in the front yard, "Last Girl Before Freeway." She was an instant hit after that appearance. She had once been on the "Tonight" show sometime before Jack Paar left in 1962, but she made no impression and Paar "hated" her. Her success with Carson was perhaps a tribute to Silver's reworking of her material.

While her self-deprecation has annoyed feminists, it's easy to see why she stuck with it after it helped her to become an instant hit. As Rivers once said: "For five and a half years I had been telling jokes about my Kafkaesque past. I didn't make a dime, so now I'm looking for universals." One of those universals was self-deprecation. Without it she probably never would have achieved the popularity that she did. She was one of only a couple of successful female stand-up comics at the time, and the public was not then ready to accept an overly aggressive female who, in some fashion, didn't pay her dues.

While she and Diller did use, and still do, this type of humor, they both provided a more positive role model for women and they were certainly light years in advance of the type of female characters created by the likes of Gracie Allen and Lucille Ball. Rivers and Diller, by creating a bridge, made it easier for a future group of female comics to rely less and less on that brand of humor and to choose from a wider variety of styles and material, as men have always done.

Since her first television appearance Rivers has played most of the other variety and talk shows on the air. She hosted her own program, "That Show," a daily morning talk program in 1968-69.

She has appeared in nightclubs numerous times in centers such as Las Vegas and Miami, as well as given concert tours throughout the United States. By the end of the 1970's, in Las Vegas, she had become the highest-priced opening act in show business history, at $55,000 per week. By 1983 she was commanding about $200,000 a week in Las Vegas. She remained a regular guest on the Carson show, having appeared on it, including hosting it when Carson was away, over one hundred times. At times her ratings on the program have been higher than those for Carson himself. In the summer of 1983 she signed to host the "Tonight" show for all nine weeks of Carson's vacation, the first guest host to achieve that distinction. The next year the contract was renewed for the 1984-85 season. She and Carson never mention her sometimes higher ratings. "Johnny and I choose to ignore it. I owe my entire career to him." Despite this success, she used to take her stage makeup home with her every night until 1971, always worried that she would be fired imminently.

Her rapport and tenure on the Carson show ended in the summer of 1986 when Rivers announced she would host her own late night talk show later that year on a newly forming TV network. Carson had not been forewarned about the news and was miffed enough about his substitute preparing to become his competition that he cancelled all the remaining scheduled appearances by Joan.

She was one of three co-authors of a play called *Fun City* which opened in New York in 1971, and which starred Rivers. It received bad reviews on all counts. In 1978 she co-authored and directed a movie called *Rabbit Test,* produced by her husband Edgar Rosenberg. The movie was budgeted for $1 million and Rivers and her husband spent a year trying to find backers for the project. When their efforts fell short, they raised the money by putting a second mortgage of $425,000 on their home. Edgar refused at first, but Joan insisted and threatened to raise the money by getting a divorce and using her half of the settlement. Edgar relented. The movie itself received mixed reviews, ranging from fair to mediocre. Regardless of the reviews, Rivers was adamant that it was a funny script and that her effort was comparable to the early films of Woody Allen and Mel Brooks. She has also been successful as an author, with a book, *Having a Baby Can Be a Scream,* being a regular best-seller for years.

The style of her comedy act remained the same as it did when she first made it big, a mixture of self-deprecation and other

material: "I was such an ugly baby a furrier tried to club me."
And on the subject of her body, "They show my picture to men
on death row to get their minds off women." Jokes about her
obese childhood were still popular. She also joked about her
inadequate sexuality and sexual response: "The only reason I had
a kid," she said, "is because my husband tossed and turned in his
sleep." None if it was true. She was an attractive woman and
appeared that way on stage, making no attempt to make herself
grotesque as Diller was wont to do. According to statements
made by her mother, Rivers was never fat as a child, the obesity
coming solely from her imagination.

The rest of her act, outrageous and bitchy, consisted of a rough
and raunchy ride through middle America in an irreverent,
blasphemous, cathartic rampage. An America where California
morticians say, "Have a nice day," where a Jewish pornographic
film had one minute of sex followed by six minutes of guilt.
Where a Hollywood conservationist threw a brick into his swim-
ming pool as his contribution to saving water.

Celebrity bashing was one of River's favorite sports: Nancy
Reagan's appearance, Willie Nelson's smell, and Bo Derek's stupidity, so dumb she studied for her Pap test. On Queen Elizabeth's
clothes: "Gowns by Helen Keller." Perhaps her favorite celebrity
target was Elizabeth Taylor's weight: "She pierced her ears and
gravy came out." "Mosquitos see her and scream 'Buffet.'" "I
took her to Jack in the Box and she ate Jack." Like Diller's mate
Fang, "Edgah" provided lots of material. When asked once if anybody was safe from her barbs she replied, "Deformed children
and religion."

On stage she thought and talked fast, and moved even quicker.
Her style was frenetic and frantic, manic movements, jerks and
shrugs bordering on the neurotic and hyperactive. Her delivery
was rapid-fire and machine-gun deadly. Having emptied her
weapon she paused not at all before reloading and resuming. She
appeared to be neurotic about almost everything. Her stage
manner has been likened to "a pug in the last throes of brain
damage." "She walks like a child with bed springs tied to tennis
shoes." And "rocket[s] around the stage like a billiard ball possessed."

She punctuated her dialogue with her now famous line, "Can
we talk?" which she has had registered as a trademark. The
suggestion has been made that the relationship between her and
the audience is that of two slightly drunk well-to-do housewives

exchanging gossip over the back fence. Ringsiders are often singled out and pelted with assaults on fashion, marriage, and
babies. In this form of public confessional, someone was picked
out and Rivers asked, "The truth Barbara! Is marriage what you
thought it would be?" She asked another, "Would you have slept
with Onassis for $26 million dollars?" She stated only the brutal
truths of life—in a funny way.

Her personal hero was comedian Lenny Bruce, whose offspring
she feels she was. Her style was more that of a Woody Allen or a
Mort Sahl on stage as she darted rapidly from one train of
thought to another. Despite her brash manner in public she was,
in real life, "excruciatingly shy." She has characterized her own
comic stance as that of "the victim who strikes back." Laughing
at something was a way to get through life, and humor afforded
relief from a sad and tough life, said Rivers. And that's what her
act was about—as well as being therapy for her.

Those early years of struggle have left their mark on Rivers.
"My whole career has been one rejection after another . . . and
then going back and back and pushing against everything and
everybody. Getting ahead by small, ugly steps."

The down-side of Hollywood has been a revelation to her. She
wasn't prepared for the lies. An executive who once told her a
picture deal was all set called her shortly thereafter, on Christmas
Eve, to tell her it was cancelled. She classed herself as being
upset, angry and sensitive about everything. "When you've had a
lot of unkindness done to you, you become a walking wound."
This love/hate relationship with Hollywood was undoubtedly one
of the reasons that show business stars were the major victims of
her assault humor.

Insecurity still dogged her in spite of her enormous success and
popularity. She remained terrified of ending up penniless in a
nursing home. "I wake up at night and say, 'What if I'm not
funny in the morning?'" Success was something she regarded as
fickle, something that could disappear at any time. To forestall
any such possibilities she worked incredibly hard on her material.
For Joan Rivers, work was vacation and vacation was work. She
didn't like to leave Beverly Hills, her home, because "they may
not want you back."

There was very little time in her day when she was not polish-
ing her material. She taped her performances and studied them
to see what was effective and what wasn't. She read voraciously to
keep up with events and admitted to using the *National Enquirer*

for inspiration, since she felt that's what her audience wanted to know about when she performed—that Princess Caroline was a tramp, that Caroline Kennedy was a bore, etc. She wouldn't do the Carson show without five minutes or so of new material, and she wouldn't go on stage without seven or eight new jokes to try out.

It was said that every three months she turned over 60 percent of her material. In the early 1970's she once turned down a three-week Las Vegas engagement that would have paid her $80,000. Instead she performed for very little money in a small New York club to try out new material. In the early years of her career she continued to haunt nightclubs, scouting out the comedy competition. She continued to write 85 percent of her material herself. She kept her jokes written down and catalogued and cross-indexed in file drawers. Of the various subject headings she used, the one with the most entries was, "No Sex Appeal."

Her determination and high energy level carried over into every aspect of her career. One time in New York she was walking along the street with a reporter during the time her movie was running. On every mailbox and lamppost she passed, Rivers stuck on a sticker that read, "Critics Say Rabbit Test Funniest Movie Ever."

On stage her material seemed unstructured and conversational, but she was also taking the audience's pulse during her act and adding and dropping material as she went, when necessary. A twelve-minute bit on Jackie Kennedy Onassis was cut to two when the audience grew bored with it. In the early 1970's she had prepared a six-minute bit on women's liberation only to discard it when she concluded the subject was not funny to America's women. Her audiences found little humor in the youth culture or pollution jokes. She did get good mileage, though, from putting down domestic responsibilities, housekeeping, tampons, and feminine hygiene spray. In the early 1970's Rivers remarked that the fastest way to throw a pall of gloom on her audience was to tell a joke on one of three subjects: narcotics, death, or Vietnam.

Among the female comics, her favorites were Lucille Ball, Carol Burnett and Lily Tomlin. She felt that a lot of women doing comedy today shouldn't be, but she refused to name them. She had her own ideas about women telling dirty jokes and being accepted as funny women. "I don't like funny women. I come out of that generation where the woman should be beautiful and sexy and a wonderful flower attached to a man, even though my whole life has been the antithesis of this. To this day you don't

expect a woman to be funny. . . . Nobody likes funny women.
We're a threat. I don't like funny women. I don't think I'm
funny. I think I'm witty. . . . Onstage I complain for every
woman in America. . . . I don't like to see a woman telling dirty
jokes. People say I'm dirty and I always stare at them. My areas
are just very 'women's' kinds of areas. I have a routine now, which
my husband hates, that for Christmas he gave me a box of Rely
tampons. That's not dirty. I think that's very funny. It's such a
woman's joke."

Rivers thought that there were relatively few female stand-up
comics due to the lonely life on the road. A woman just couldn't
go out alone at night after her act, the way a man could go, for
example, into a bar.

Rivers claimed at one time that she herself had no trouble with
acceptance when she entered comedy. She found no doors closed
in her face and attributed this to being in the right place at the
right time. The times were ripe, she felt, for a female comedian
with her style and material. Her long years of struggle, however,
would seem to belie this idea. And she did admit in 1984 that, "I
had a very hard time getting to where I am, and a lot of it was
because I was a woman doing it."

She started out as an actress but nobody cared. And then a
writer, but nobody cared. Then she turned to comedy to make a
living. Her experience with the film industry has been dishearten-
ing. "I've had nothing but doors shut in my face in the movies.
I've never come across so many closed doors, so many people
thinking I was incapable, that a woman could not deal with it, a
woman could not handle a crew, a woman could not in any way,
shape or form be able to control a movie set or know what is
funny."

Rivers has called her stage persona "Harriet Hostile," and
pointed out that while she loved that vulgar and common woman
up there on the stage it was a different person altogether from the
real Rivers. "I wouldn't want to be that woman's friend. I
wouldn't want her at my dinner party."

She felt that a comic had to be abrasive to be good. Take away
the abrasiveness and all that remained was pap. She would like
ten percent of the audience to hate her, as a measure of
effectiveness. Rivers countered the charge that her material was
tasteless by pointing out that the times themselves were tasteless
and humor itself was tasteless, with Rivers just riding the trend.
She defended her jokes about celebrities by pointing out that

when you become famous you also become a target. And if you allow yourself to be treated as a national institution, then you should behave like one.

She claimed she once tried to remove Elizabeth Taylor jokes from her routine but the audience demanded them from her, along with flat-chested jokes, and so on. She argued that she could never be a friend of the greats, an insider, for if she were she could no longer be funny. For Rivers the use of celebrity jokes was part of her right to articulate what America was saying and thinking about those celebrities. She made jokes about Taylor being fat because Taylor was fat and the truth was vicious. Part of her role was to be the one to tell the emperor that he wasn't wearing any clothes.

Another part of her philosophy was that humor should be on the edge, always on the brink of disaster. That comedy should always be on the border of going too far. Otherwise the material was banal and boring and no one cared. She has put that philosophy into practice with material such as the joke about Roman Polanski's new girlfriend dying from crib death. Or a joke about singer Karen Carpenter, who died from anorexia, being thin enough to be buried in pleats. She tried the last one out three times and drew only gasps from the audience. Deciding they weren't ready for it, she dropped it, but picked it up again later.

While Rivers herself declared nothing to be sacred, she let the audience decide which topics were to be taboo through their reactions. When she did offer up too-hard-edged material for her audience she sneered at them, "Gone too far eh? Stepped over the line, eh?" To her credit she offered no apologies. Unlike Don Rickles, another master of hostile humor, who ended his act with a weak, wimpy, apologetic, "God bless you, please forgive me," Rivers simply took aim at the next target. She was one of the most aggressive stand-up comics of them all.

Rivers felt there was no women's humor. What's funny was funny. Yet she refused to perform before an all-male audience, saying her material bombed in such cases. Her comedy came from a woman's point of view and Rivers felt she needed females in the audience. The males then related to her through the women they were with. This would appear to suggest that there was in fact, women's humor, or material whose impact on an audience varied depending on the sex of the comic and the sex of the audience.

Despite her popularity there were lots of people who detested her. The gentler critics were content to label her as abrasive, neu-

rotic, and tasteless and let it go at that. Rivers herself admitted
that she was not for everybody. She felt that in her act she
appealed to the "brighties," to people who have read what she's
read, to those who were totally urban. Certainly this prosperous
type of audience, concerned with status and appearance, especially women in her age range, were among her most enthusiastic
fans. Women are her biggest fans partly because they can see
another woman on stage telling them it's okay if their body isn't
perfect and it's all right to say you're not happy sexually.

Some critics who didn't like her seemed almost to despise her.
She once told some jokes about Farrah Fawcett-Major's hair and
scalp to which a critic responded: "Rivers has always been
masochistic to the point of idiocy, and a sickening detail like that
is what makes her a misogynist harpie—she projects her self-
loathing onto other women."

A Vancouver reporter was upset that she could sell out two
shows in that city at the price of $25 a ticket in 1983. He felt she
commanded that price only because of the furor she created on
the 1983 Emmy telecast. During that program she joked about
herpes, AIDS, and let fly with a "goddamn." NBC received
thousands of angry phone calls. Yet earlier that year she had sold
out Carnegie Hall in New York and scalpers were getting up to
$150 a ticket.

Another critic labelled her crude and deafening with a cannonball mouth. He condemned her for her "savage diatribes" aimed
at the stars. In a series of snide remarks, the critic complimented
Rivers on finding the right makeup person, designer, and hair-
dresser, "after all these years." He also admired Rivers's energy
and said, "I wish she'd clean my apartment when she's on hiatus."

Much of the heat that Rivers drew was because she often cut
too close with her material. And much of the hostility centered on
the simple fact that she was a woman. Comics such as Buddy
Hackett and Richard Pryor, in their club acts, often delivered just
so much unfiltered filth, and yet they drew nowhere near the
amount of heat that Rivers attracted. Many men were not
prepared to accept an aggressive woman comic who could dish
out hostility the way Rivers could, and who remained unrepentant
after delivery. She flew in the face of an acceptable role model
that was sweet, docile, obsequious.

Rivers countered feminist complaints about her image by saying
she was the first woman to go on television and laugh about being
single. That she did her own movie, the casting, the fund-raising,

the editing, the writing, and the directing. Yet she once told Carson that she hated being called Ms. because she had worked so hard finding a husband and deserved to be addressed as Mrs.

One of the reasons her brand of humor was so popular was because she attacked herself with as much, if not more, vigor than she leveled at the celebrities. This removed any trace of superiority which might be implied in the absence of self-deprecation, particularly in view of her non-apologetic stance. Since she pointed out all of her own warts, she had earned the right to kid about the warts of others.

The self-deprecation was also necessary because she was a woman, and such behavior was part of the price of admission to the ranks. Her timing was also important and Rivers knew exactly how long to stay on a particular course and exactly when to change direction. Also effective was the shock value of her act. People didn't expect a woman who looked like her to use the type of language she sometimes did. The jokes about her own lack of sex appeal were obviously not true, and thus her jokes about other people need not be taken seriously either. It helped to arrest any suspicion of malice in her act.

By the early 1980's she had long since ceased being an act, and was a bonafide star. She continued at a hectic pace. Besides the Carson show she toured 40 weeks a year, 10 at Las Vegas, to standing room only crowds. She had a best-selling comedy album, an autobiography, *Enter Talking,* published in 1986, and was working on film projects. Those who thought, or hoped, she and the likes of Diller might fade away because of their so-called reactionary female consciousness were wrong. In 1984 she came out with another book, *The Life and Hard Times of Heidi Abromowitz,* about one of her characters which was very popular at the time. Heidi was the town tramp from her school days who did things like sleep with the U.S. Navy.

Rivers has continued to serve up her own brand of controversy and irreverance. When she wanted to do a joke about lepers network officials vetoed it because, "You can't do that. We've had letters from lepers." In 1984 she was asked what the biggest risk in her act was, and she replied that it was jokes about women and their periods — something she did in concert but still wasn't allowed to do on television.

Rivers verbalized the secret thoughts of the audience, although some denied the existence of such thoughts in themselves or refused to hear them uttered by a woman. Rivers once said, in the late 1970's, that she hoped to get out of performing someday. Yet with her drive and determination, and the effort she puts into her material, it's likely she'll be up there performing just as long as there's a willing audience.

GOLDIE HAWN

"Rowan and Martin's Laugh-In" was a phenomenally successful television comedy show for five years, starting in the late 1960's. It consisted of skits, sight gags, slapstick, blackouts, and had a large cast of regulars who appeared as various characters. It was a unique show in that it propelled a number of then unknown women to various degrees of stardom as comics. This single program did more for women comedians than anything before or since. The most notable women from "Laugh-In" were JoAnne Worley, Ruth Buzzi, Lily Tomlin, and Goldie Hawn.

The Hawn character was the most stereotypical, most sexist, and least original on the show. She also became the most popular performer on the program. She was the basic dumb blonde who giggled, jiggled, and wiggled, appearing from time to time in a bikini and gyrating before the camera. The Hawn character had been variously, and accurately, described as: airhead, bubblehead, dizzy blonde, birdbrain, dimwit, daffy damsel, ding-a-ling, and dingbat. Goldie Hawn parlayed her image and popularity to become the nation's leading female comic actress in the movies.

She was born in Washington, D.C., in November of 1945 and raised in Takoma Park, Maryland, a suburb of the nation's capital. Her first name is real; she was named in honor of a great-aunt. Her father was a professional musician who played saxophone, violin, and clarinet and often performed with bands at the White House and embassy affairs.

Her mother managed jewelry stores and a dance studio. Goldie began taking ballet and tap dancing lessons at the age of three. The lessons were instituted by her mother with "considerable firmness" on the theory that it might someday open doors for her, or she might want to teach dancing herself one day. Goldie added jazz and modern dance lessons from the age of eleven and continued daily dance lessons through high school. Her father gave her voice lessons.

During her teens Goldie participated in school and community
drama shows and appeared in summer stock. After high school
she stayed in Washington and studied drama at American University for about a year and a half. During this time she did briefly
teach dancing at her own school, Goldie's Dancing School. At the
age of nineteen she left home and headed for New York to see if
she could make it in show business. Her parents were reportedly
encouraging and supportive of her plans.

Her first job was as a can-can dancer at the Texas Pavilion of
the World's Fair in New York, 1964-65. She also danced in
choruses in summer stock and did some go-go dancing, once
appearing at the Peppermint Box in New Jersey for $25 a night.
She danced on a table top in a flimsy outfit she had made herself.
She also performed at a Manhattan disco called Dudes 'n' Dolls.
The pace was often frantic, sometimes with four shows a night,
each lasting one and a half hours. Goldie pointed out that she
never appeared topless, but admitted to playing some dives.

At one particularly sleazy club Goldie was confronted by a customer who exposed himself. Another time she was "discovered" by
an agent for a famous cartoonist. Upon meeting the man and
finding out just what was expected of her in the way of being
"nice," she stormed out. Adding to her troubles was her
cockroach-infested apartment in the city's old Hell's Kitchen area.

A phone call from a friend led her to California where she
worked as a dancer at the Meadowland Theatre in Anaheim.
When that job ended she got a job at the Desert Inn in Las Vegas
in a lounge show as a go-go dancer. She worked from ten at night
until five in the morning and hated it. When she couldn't stand it
any more, she quit and moved to Los Angeles where she gave herself nine months to see if her career would break. The whole go-
go period was the "saddest part" of her life as she found herself
"temperamentally and morally unsuited" to nightclubs and Las
Vegas.

Back in California Hawn got a job dancing in the chorus line
on an Andy Griffith television special, where she was spotted by
an agent who asked her to give him a call. She did and within a
week she had landed a spot on a short-lived CBS comedy series
called "Good Morning World," which debuted in the fall of 1967.
Goldie played a wacky neighbor with lines like, "I have to go
home and get my toast out of the clothes dryer."

When that series was cancelled she came to the attention of
George Schlatter, the producer who was then looking for

"Laugh-In" talent. Confronted with the resultant success, she had a breakdown during this period and would spend seven years in classic analysis. For Goldie, "It was the toughest period of my life. . . . I wasn't doing what I was trained to do."

Schlatter recalled that Hawn was hired because she looked cute and could dance. Beyond that, though, the producers didn't know what to do with her. It was decided to try her with brief introductions. She had had no experience with cue cards and got mixed up and read the wrong words. (She is dyslexic.) When she had blown her simple line three times during one rehearsal, she broke into a mortified giggle. Schlatter was watching the proceedings and told her not to stop, that it was "adorable."

They figured confusion was her thing, and Hawn's "Laugh-In" character was born at that moment. It would remain unchanged for the duration of her two-year run on the show. The audience response to the character was phenomenal. She had been hired initially for a three-show trial and in her first show she was on camera for only about 48 seconds out of the hour. She did little more than stare at the camera and giggle. Before long, however, she was getting more mail than anybody else on the show.

To keep the giggling spontaneous, the crew worked harder and harder devising new ways to distract her. They began to switch cue cards deliberately on her. They held up pictures and dirty words. So, with a combination of sex appeal and innocence, Goldie delivered her famous up and down the scale giggle, her naive expressions, memorized one-liners such as, "What do I care? I'm Polish," flubbed her lines, and dealt out malapropisms and non sequiturs, such as the following answer to Dan Rowan's comment that the Russians were having trouble with their Chinese border: "Why don't they tell him to pay his rent or get out?"

The lovable waif quickly became television's "dumbest and most delectable bonbon." Inevitably the question was raised as to whether or not Goldie was dumb. Just as obviously the answer was no, but Schlatter once said, "She's not dumb. . . . Her head wanders a little, that's all." She was once called "Laugh-In's" answer to Gracie Allen. Hawn considered the character to be childlike rather than stupid; to be naive and gullible with an innocent spontaneity. "I'm like her only in small ways," she said.

Goldie remembered her childhood as being pleasant with no pushing, competition or conflict. She described herself as being "always uninhibited," with an idea that she could act, but she was never a cut-up or a clown for her friends. She claimed she wasn't an entertainer because she needed attention, which was something she got plenty of as a child. She remarked once that she never wanted to be a star, "but my agent shoved me." During her "Laugh-In" stint her mother received a phone call from her confused daughter, who said, "I don't want to be a star! I just want to get married."

The celebrity status made things difficult for Hawn. She found she wasn't able to go grocery shopping without a crowd gathering. And the crowd expected her to clown it up. "I either have to be somebody I'm not or hide." By her own admission, Goldie was very much an old-fashioned person with middle-class values. She wanted children and a nice house. Very domestic, she regarded herself as a compulsive housewife and was into knitting, cooking, and dressmaking. As she once said, "What I really want is to be pregnant and unemployed." She considered raising children to be the most creative thing of all.

As time went by Goldie found her character to be harder and harder to play. The character was unchanging and there was no room for growth. After a couple of years on "Laugh-In" she decided to leave. She was under a lot of pressure to stay and was offered a great deal of money, but she felt it was time for her to try and shed the dumb blonde image. For Hawn it was time to prove that she could play something besides the television kook she portrayed on "Laugh-In."

Before leaving the show, she made her film debut in 1969 in *Cactus Flower,* for which she subsequently won an Academy Award for best supporting actress. In 1970 she starred in the film *There's a Girl in My Soup,* with Peter Sellers. From that point on Goldie confined her career to movies with the occasional appearance on television as a guest or in her own special. She worked with Warren Beatty in *Shampoo,* with George Segal in *The Duchess and the Dirtwater Fox,* and Burt Reynolds in *Best Friends.* She starred in Steven Spielberg's first film as director, *The Sugarland Express,* and in *Butterflies Are Free.*

In many of her films, the characters she played were all "kookie blondes," but not as extreme or one-dimensional as the "Laugh-In" girl. Hawn received $50,000 for her part in *Cactus Flower.* Only a dozen or so years later she commanded $2.5 million per picture. She did have a six-year absence from television which ended in 1978. "I was afraid to go back to TV and do that giggly person who doesn't have much sense."

By 1976 she had appeared in her eighth movie in eight years. Then she took a two and a half year hiatus to be a full time wife and mother. She was lured back to films in 1978 for *Foul Play,* with Chevy Chase, which boosted her again to national prominence. Her following two movies *Private Benjamin* (1980) and *Seems Like Old Times* (1981) reinforced her superstar status. These pictures were box-office hits. *Private Benjamin,* a hilarious comedy about a Jewish princess who joined the army, grossed $175,000,000 by January 1985.

At that stage Hawn was able to command the high salary. With a touch of bitterness not usually her style, Goldie said she was aware that with the inequities of being a female in Hollywood it had taken her a decade of solid box-office success to achieve a salary level that a male star would have attained after only two or three big hits.

The *Private Benjamin* film was a turning point for Hawn, because not only did she star in the movie but she was also the executive producer. When the project was set, Goldie went around to the studios to find the $10 million the project required. It was then that she ran into the problem of her dumb blonde image. "In the beginning, they patted me on the head. I was cute little Goldie. But the minute you stand up, you qualify as a bitch."

Despite her star status, several studios turned the project down. They didn't think she could function as an executive producer. They also weren't happy with the film's feminist tone, which was actually very mild. They expected it from some people perhaps, "but not from sweet Goldie." The studios wanted to stay with what worked, to keep her a "lovable victim." One studio head told Goldie she was "making one of the biggest mistakes of your career."

Finally Warner Brothers, who were at first wary, accepted the project. The movie was a stunning success, one of the top three movies of that year. As the executive producer she was involved in script revisions, casting, and daily discussions between Warner executives and the set. The picture not only reaffirmed her as a star, but also established her as a person with clout. Lucille Ball was another woman comic who had become a powerful producer. Inevitably Hawn was starting to be compared to Ball.

Hawn felt she had to fight hard for the kinds of roles she wanted. "I kept having to prove over and over that I'm not that cute little go-go dancer in a bikini." While Hawn fought to keep all of her favorite scenes intact in *Private Benjamin,* the final product had about an hour cut out of it, down from the original running time of three hours plus, because Hollywood wisdom decreed that a comedy couldn't be any longer.

Despite her apparent change in image since her "Laugh-In" days, the media still claimed the public saw the old Goldie. When *Newsweek* annointed her a superstar with clout in their January 12, 1981, issue they also claimed "what people invariably expect is the giggly dimwit." *TV Guide* in their May 8, 1982, number said, "Her public image is that of a dimwit dame." So entrenched was her airhead persona that an interviewer for *Playboy* in 1985 expected to be talking with a "giggle-voiced daffy blonde." He was surprised to find that Goldie's voice was "pitched lower than expected," and that she was "thoughtful, even serious."

Part of her dumb-blonde image stemmed from the movie roles she had undertaken. Most of her characters were kooky or wacky, less extreme than "Laugh-In" perhaps, but a fairly close relative. She had changed only from airhead to a more mature cuteness. Her movie characters have been wholesome, pretty, honest, decent, warm, etc. The films themselves have been superficial in their dealings with problems. Hawn's intonation in films has often remained childish.

While her movies have been successful and entertaining, critics have agreed that they lack any substance. Hawn's characters have been upright, mainstream, and solid. "She presents no threat to Middle America."

Hawn, herself, has contributed to reinforcing her ditsy image. Regarding her "Laugh-In" role, Goldie has said that she never resented her work although she admitted the character was essentially an object. Commented Goldie: "I never looked at myself as a nitwit. I never looked at anything I did as vacant or dumb or bubble-headed. There was always a sensibility about what I did. Because someone is hopeful, because someone likes to have fun, because someone is trusting and open, does not necessarily mean that someone is stupid."

She felt the character worked for her and established her career. Yet at other times she had made different comments on the old "Laugh-In" image. In 1980 she remarked, "I certainly couldn't work with that image at this point." Obviously she was ambivalent about a dumb persona that had made her a millionaire.

This ambivalence about her identity has shown up in her personal life. Goldie was first married in 1969 to Gus Trikonis, a then-aspiring director. They separated in 1973. She then married Bill Hudson, a member of the singing/comedy group the Hudson

Brothers, in 1976. They had two children, but that union ended in 1980. In both marriages Goldie's career was by far the more successful of the two.

In the first marriage Goldie felt Gus was the stronger, and that was fine with her since "a woman is the passive sex, right? A woman cannot and should not compete with a man." It was said that Trikonis was "breaking Goldie's heart from time to time." Hawn didn't complain, though, and ultimately she blamed the marriage breakup on her own success. Wanting children badly, she risked a second marriage. She was even prepared, she said, to give up her career if Bill asked her to. She was reported as "desperate" to make the marriage work. It was at this juncture that Goldie retired for two and a half years as she pursued the fairy tale.

In both of her marriages she tried to downplay her career, to maintain the unions. "I was very cognizant of not relishing my achievements too much. I never wanted to come back home and say, hey, I won! You hold back. Because it was more important that I keep my man. Because that basically was what kept me happy. Working on 'Laugh-In' didn't keep me happy . . . money has screwed me up in my relationships with men. I'm a woman who was raised to believe that you are not complete unless you have a man. Well, in some ways it's true."

When asked if she resented bottling up her achievements, Hawn responded that the result was she had lost her men anyway. Her marriages ended because her husbands couldn't deal with her fame or wealth. Many other women comics had the same conflict with their mates. Some such as Joan Rivers have enjoyed long unions with a man able to cope with their success. Others such as Sophie Tucker never found a strong partner.

The amount of media publicity given to Goldie's pronouncements about needing a man worked against her developing a strong, independent persona. Much was made of the fact that for Goldie Hawn stardom and stability, marriage and career, were mutually exclusive. The image of Goldie as a passive and dependent creature was reinforced. It was in keeping with her stage character of the lovable, childlike, and vulnerable waif. This unthreatening persona was undoubtedly one of the factors involved in her rise to superstardom. The subtle message was that a female might rise to the top, but there was a price that had to be paid.

Curiously feminists have rarely targeted Hawn as they have Rivers or Diller. Yet Hawn has presented a less liberated image than the other two. Again, perhaps it's because of her image of vulnerability and innocence and her basic kindness. No one wants to hurt Goldie. Rivers and Diller dished it out. Therefore, they must, presumably, stand ready to take it.

In 1984 Hawn was involved in filming on her fourteenth feature, *Protocol*. It was her second film as an executive producer. It was a comedy and Goldie was playing "a ditsy blonde cocktail waitress," Sunny Davis. Regarding her own stereotypical barmaid/bimbo character Hawn reported she had " no problem." Critics saw plenty of problems with the character and the movie, however. Jay Scott, writing for the Toronto *Globe & Mail,* talked of Goldie's "sad descent into the heights of superstardom." He felt the movie had "a reactionary premise—dumb blonde peaches patriotism—set in Reagan's Washington, D.C." Scott noted that Hawn's character was "less dizzy than retarded." Goldie was too mature for the "daffy" role.

Hawn had realized that it was time for her to develop further. She commented, "I do have this quality that is very childlike. But how long can it last? How long can you be cute?"

Nevertheless, in the mid-1980's Hawn stood out as the most successful and entertaining film comedian and one of Hollywood's superstars. To this day she doesn't think of herself as being funny, not in a joke-telling sense. She attributed her comic success to her timing, body language, expression, and openness. Goldie Hawn had often mentioned wanting to escape from the dingbat stereotype. She has had plenty of chances to develop as a comic actress. But she never strayed far from the dumb blonde persona. Perhaps she doesn't really want to.

RUTH BUZZI

Gladys Ormphby sat nervously on a park bench. Her dog face was set in a frown. Her hair was parted severely in the middle and plastered to her skull. The hairnet which covered this was put on backwards so it looked as though she had been hit smack in the middle of her forehead with a bullet, or as one fan described it, it was as if "the mad doctor had flubbed the brain operation." In her baggy dress, lisle stockings, and sensible shoes, Gladys was ugliness personified.

But even the homeliest of women have their admirers, and Gladys was no exception. A seedy man muttering to himself shuffled up to Gladys's bench and sat leeringly beside her. Indignantly Gladys moved to the far end of the bench. Undaunted the dirty old man proposed, "How would you like to call me your consort."

Unspeakably repelled by this obscene invitation, Gladys beaned the old fellow with her huge handbag and, still in a sitting position, he toppled off the bench.

Gladys Ormphby, better known as Ruth Buzzi, played out this scene with Arte Johnson on the weekly television program "Rowan and Martin's Laugh-In." Her Gladys character would make Buzzi one of the best-known comediennes in television history.

The creation of Gladys took place long before "Laugh-In" went on the air. It evolved after years of work by Ruth Buzzi as she experimented with developing the role.

Buzzi had not been born into a show business family. Her father sold graveyard monuments in Ruth's hometown of Wequetequock, Connecticut. Buzzi remembered clowning around in school and getting a taste for performing as a comic dancer.

In 1954, at the age of seventeen, she enrolled as a student at the Pasadena Playhouse. By 1956 she had landed a part in the San Francisco production of *Jenny Kissed Me*, starring Rudy Vallee. Between 1957 and 1960 Ruth did summer stock in places like Albuquerque and Connecticut, always playing character parts.

An important turning point in her career came in 1961 when she was hired for an off-Broadway comedy revue called *Misguided Tour*. At the audition the director told her to do something funny and Ruth improvised a hostess on a cut-rate airline.

During this revue Buzzi invented a character called Shakuntula, who was a magician's assistant too shy to speak, and who bungled all the magician's tricks. Buzzi continued to work on and develop this character in future acts. Dom DeLuise remembered working with her at the Madera Club in Provincetown, where she did Shakuntula.

"She was marvellous," he said. "She wore thrift-shop bloomers, cotton socks at half mast underneath her harem pants, and blotches of rouge that didn't quite hit the center of her cheeks. I did all the talking, she did all the listening. She got the big laughs. At playing desperate ladies, she had no peer."

In 1961 Buzzi also appeared as Agnes Gooch in the play *Auntie Mame* for the Mountain Playhouse in Jennerstown, Pa. She was intrigued by the stage direction, which indicated that Agnes "schlumped" on stage. Ruth asked herself "what would a person look like who schlumped—rotten posture, draggy feet, baggy stockings, speech kind of constipated." Ruth never let go of the Agnes persona, which would later evolve into Gladys Ormphby.

Buzzi's success with her Shakuntula character led to other work. Carol Burnett invited her on her television show in 1965 and Steve Allen had her as a regular on his "Comedy Hour" in 1967. She also appeared as Margie "Pete" Peterson on the television comedy series "That Girl" between 1967 and 1968, and did hundreds of television commercials.

Buzzi continued to perform live and appeared in over 18 revues, all the while developing the Gladys Ormphby character. Ruth would sometimes have fun with Ormphby off stage. She would slip into costume in airplane washrooms and then find out how fellow passengers would react.

It was Gladys who eventually landed Buzzi a part on "Laugh-In." She showed producer George Schlatter pictures of herself as Gladys standing in a basket labelled "Keep New York City Clean." Schlatter loved it.

According to Buzzi his enthusiasm for Gladys was obsessive. He wouldn't allow her to do anything but that part for the entire first year of "Laugh-In." Ruth came to resent the role, but Schlatter insisted, "Don't you know that character can put you on the map." Of course, it did.

Buzzi was one of the few performers who stayed with "Laugh-In" during the entire run of the program from January 1968 to May 1973. During this time she also guest starred on other variety shows like Dean Martin's or Flip Wilson's. Ruth did branch out into other characters, notably Doris Sidebottom the bedraggled drunk, and she did have her own lightweight TV comedy series on ABC-TV from September 1975-1976 in which she played an android from outer space who captured earthlings. Her co-star was Jim Nabors.

But it was her role as Gladys Ormphby that has established Ruth's reputation for comedy. One of her favorite bits was when she played Gladys as a worn-out stripper. While belting out "Let Me Entertain You," the audience threw vegetables at her and hooted, "Don't take it off!" Buzzi called Gladys "a born loser. She can't do anything right. Her inability to get a man leaves her frustrated and unhappy . . . and yet . . . there is a wonderful innocence there and the hope that one day, somehow, a man will come her way. Maybe that's what makes half the women in the world able to identify."

Dan Rowan explained to *TV Guide* interviewer Dwight Whitney in 1969 that Gladys was "not a pitiful object. You really feel sorry for her, but underneath you know she is indomitable. There is something reassuring about that. Life has already treated her as badly as it can and there are no big bumps ahead."

Paul Keyes, "Laugh-In's" head writer told Whitney that he felt women were not threatened by Gladys because her ugliness made them feel superior. Men enjoyed the attempted seduction of Gladys by the dirty old man, Keyes believed, because it was a bizarre form of the sex game where males tried to score. And men also felt superior to Johnson's character of the seedy derelict.

Buzzi had used a formula that had worked for numerous comedians over the years. She was the plain, man-chasing spinster. Ruth took the character to such an extreme that she gave it a perverse kind of power. The power to reject a dirty old man. Even a hag had her limits.

As so often happened with comedians who played unattractive characters, the public wondered if Ruth Buzzi was really as ugly as she appeared on television. Reporters often commented on how pleasantly surprised they were to find her appearance normal if not "ravishing," and to discover that she had been contentedly married since 1966 to writer Basil (Bill) Keko.

By 1977 Buzzi was becoming disenchanted with comedy, saying, "I don't want to be 'typed' as a comedienne." She had hoped to establish a film career, but there was a dearth of comedy parts for females. She was reduced to taking a cameo in the 1977 Disney film *Freaky Friday*. Buzzi had dreamed of working with Mel Brooks but he never offered her a role. She is still waiting.

LILY TOMLIN

Lily Tomlin has taken a strong position on feminism. She was one of the few female comics embraced by the Women's Movement. During her years on TV's "Laugh-In" she refused to do breast jokes or any gags with sexist or racist overtones. In 1972 she walked off the "Dick Cavett Show" when his guest, Chad Everett, referred to his wife as a possession. Tomlin has appeared at benefits for the Equal Rights Amendment, and she campaigned for congresswoman Bella Abzug, and Connecticut Governor Ella Grasso.

Commenting on the repressive body language of some of her audience, Tomlin noted: "I see these very stiff, inhibited women . . . and I think it's criminal. This is what the culture has done to a lot of women — made them so uptight, so uncertain, so thwarted. It's a matter of power and powerlessness."

Lily had never officially acknowledged being bisexual, but she has certainly hinted at the possibility. In one of her gags she said: "In the fifties . . . no one was gay then, we were shy." She shares her Hollywood house with TV and film writer Jane Wagner, who also writes some of Tomlin's material.

When asked in a 1981 interview if she thought of having children, Tomlin said yes, but then admitted that she had publicly stated on the 'Tonight Show" that having a child was not a major goal in her life. Besides, she joked, she had a puppy at home to look after "who won't grow up and spit on me."

Lily's politics have generally been up front. She spoke out against the Vietnam War and campaigned for George McGovern in 1972. When she was being interviewed on TV by Barbara Walters, she attacked Walters for her use of hair spray and its danger to the environment because of the aerosol container.

Once when Tomlin appeared on the "Mike Douglas Show" after Ronald Reagan, who had been defending the death penalty, she couldn't avoid shaking his hand: "His hand was out. There was nothing I could do. But I felt real crummy afterward."

Although Tomlin has stated that she believed that she was being politically active when she performed, she also denied being a propangandist. After all, her forte is comedy, and she saw the humorous side of issues. "What" for example, she asked, "would be your position on women's lib if you were a passenger on the *Titanic*."

Yet Tomlin's sensitivity to female freedom has made her a role model for others. Said Gilda Radner: "She's paving the way for other women like me who want to do comedy." When Diane Judge of *Redbook* magazine interviewed Lily in 1981 and asked, "Has the Women's Movement had an impact on your career?" Tomlin responded: "If it hadn't been for the Women's Movement, people would call it my hobby."

Lily had also theorized on why it has been difficult for female comics. In an interview published in *The Village Voice* in 1975,

Tomlin felt it was the way in which a comedian had the power to evoke laughter that was unacceptable: "Funny is probably threatening, 'cause for people to laugh . . . it's submissive. When people laugh they're vulnerable." Since females had traditionally had a submissive role, audiences, and males in particular, resisted being influenced by a woman comic. In the past female comedians had to be grotesque or scatterbrained, therefore making themselves vulnerable.

Lorne Michaels, producer of "Saturday Night Live," and two of Tomlins TV specials, noted that there was a "female esthetic" in Lily's comedy: "Male comedy is punchy, broad, aggressive; it assaults you. Men shy away from the 'moment' and go for the joke."

Tomlin's background prepared her for both her career and her feminist stance. Her father had advised: "Babe, pay your own way. Don't owe anybody anything." Lily had been born Mary Jean Tomlin in Detroit in 1939. She changed her name to Lily in the 1960's when she auditioned for the role of an Englishwoman, thinking Lily sounded more British than Mary Jean. It was also her mother's name, and the name of a performer she admired— Beatrice Lillie.

Tomlin's mother had worked as a nurse's aide. Her father worked as a job-setter in a brass parts factory. He was a drinker and a gambler, and died of alcoholism at the age of 57. Yet Lily remembered him fondly because he was the one who encouraged her to "show out" as a child. He often took her to a local bar where she would sing for his friends. She also did take-offs of TV characters, and imitated the neighbors.

The outlets for a performer were limited in Detroit high schools. Lily joined the cheerleading squad, and recalled that she was "possibly the best white cheerleader Detroit ever had." However, she was eventually dropped for being too vulgar. Her penchant for drama was served by "The Scarlet Angels," a club for high school girls. The red angel emblems which they wore on the back of their jackets came from a religious goods store.

Tomlin entered Wayne State University as a pre-med student. She wanted to become a doctor because of the autonomy. While at Wayne State she got a walk-on part in *The Madwoman of Chaillot,* and improvised so well in the role that she made an impression on the audience. Realizing that she had a flair for comedy, Tomlin began to seriously consider becoming a performer. At a university variety show she created her first character, Mrs. Earbore, the Tasteful Lady. The character was partly based on a neighbor woman who had taken an interest in Lily when she was a girl. She had coached Lily on lady-like behavior, such as never blowing your nose in public, and crossing your legs at the ankle. Mrs. Earbore was also a take-off on upper middle-class values, and a lampoon of elites like Henry Ford's debutante daughters.

Tomlin began to entertain at coffee houses near the university, and she appeared on local radio and television talk shows. After her second year at the university, Lily dropped out of school and went to New York City. There she studied mime with Paul Curtis. Overwhelmed by the drive and dedication of New York performers, Lily retreated to Detroit, where she continued to work in coffee houses.

In 1965 at the age of twenty-six she made the decision to commit herself to comedy, and returned to New York. Her career progressed steadily. Most of her initial performances were at the Improv, a restaurant-bar where she worked out routines.

To support herself she did office work or collected unemployment insurance. For a short time she was a waitress at a Howard Johnson restaurant. One night she got double her usual tips when she announced over the loud-speaker: "Attention diners. Your Howard Johnson's waitress of the week, Miss Lily Tomlin, is about to make her appearance on the floor. Let's all give her a big hand!" She was fired.

Tomlin tried her hand at television commercials but found the work "totally corrupting." Even this had given her some exposure, though. Steve Allen spotted her in a breakfast cereal commercial, and had her on his show in 1969.

But that wasn't her first big break. Tomlin had been appearing at several New York clubs such as Cafe Au Go Go and Downstairs at the Upstairs. In 1966 Gary Moore hired her for his television show. Moore wasn't certain how he was going to use her when he saw her characters, but Tomlin kept pushing, and actually offered to tap dance for him. The taps were taped to the bottom of her bare feet. Her enthusiasm won him over.

Lily lasted only three shows, arguing with writers and calling their material "unintelligent." (The Moore show itself, went off the air soon after.) But Tomlin kept in the public eye. She had a guest appearance on the "Merv Griffin Show" in 1967, and she was signed by the Ashley-Famous talent agency.

In 1969 she accepted a contract for an ABC-TV comedy series

"The Music Scene." Just after that George Schlatter, producer of "Laugh-In," offered her a spot on his show, but as she was already committed, she had to turn it down.

Meanwhile, "The Music Scene" failed almost immediately after going on the air. Released from her contract, Tomlin got in touch with Schlatter and he signed her for "Laugh-In." Her first appearance on this program was in December 1969. The show with its weekly audience of 40,000,000 promoted her to celebrity status.

And Tomlin earned her fame. She had something special to offer in the characters she created. Perhaps her best-known one was Ernestine, the telephone switchboard operator. With her sausage rolled hair, tight clothing, platform shoes, and face which was a cross between a pickle and a horse, Ernestine ruled the telephone wires with a series of snorts and whinnies. Disagreeable and power hungry, Ernestine aligned herself with her employer, A.T. & T.: "We may be the only phone company in town but we screw everybody."

Dialing the telephone, Ernestine uttered her now famous lines: "One ringy-dingy . . . two, ringy-dingy . . . A gracious good afternoon to you. . . . Have I reached the party to whom I am speaking?"

Haughty and self-assured, Ernestine was awed by no one. Placing a call to J. Edgar Hoover, she exclaimed: "I want to tell you, Mr. Hoover, how much I admire your vacuum cleaners." Ernestine had an overt eroticism, massaging her cleavage and rubbing her thighs together as she handled the phone. Tomlin claimed to like this aspect of her character: "Doing Ernestine is really a very sexual experience. I just squeeze myself very tight from the face down. The bottom line with Ernestine is that she's a very sexual person. . . . She's a woman who knows she has a very appealing body and likes to show it off."

In 1970 California's telephone operators gave Tomlin a "Cracked Bell" award and made her an honorary member of their union. Less pleased with the character was A.T.&T. However they soon realized that Ernestine was a potential commodity. They offered Tomlin $500,000 to do a year of phone commercials as Ernestine. Tomlin told *The New York Times Magazine* in 1976 that she was so insulted by this offer that tears came into her eyes: "First, they try to get it bumped. Then, it's going over real good; so they say, 'Let's buy that.' It's the ultimate comment on the culture," said Tomlin.

The other popular character from "Laugh-In" was Edith Ann, portrayed by Tomlin as a snotty but lovable five-year-old. Lily wore child's clothing and sat in a giant chair to convey the image of a small girl. "Laugh-In" producers wanted Edith Ann to be like Shirley Temple, but Tomlin insisted on her being scruffy. Edith Ann combined both an innocent and world-weary spirit in lines like: "I didn't ask to be born. If I did, Mama would have said, No." On examining an empty box of animal crackers, Edith Ann decided, "They have eaten up each other."

Tomlin's knowledge of a child's psychology of guilt and rebellion, which of course continues into adulthood, came through in Edith Ann's confession: "Sometimes I like to sit on the drain in the bathtub when the water's running out. It feel so inneresting."

And finally, Tomlin used Edith Ann's childish imagination to paint vivid emotional images: "You know what happens when you get angry? First your face gets just like a fist, and then your heart gets like a bunch of bees and flies up and stings your brain. . . . And then your two eyes is like dark clouds looking for trouble. And your blood is like a tornado and then you have bad weather inside your body."

In 1972 Tomlin sued the producer of "Laugh-In" for sole rights to her characters. A year later the show went off the air. Lily claimed to be relieved because she felt her characters "were losing their integrity to bad scripts and overexposure." Nor had "Laugh-In" been the only platform for Tomlin's talent. During the five years of the program, she had also been appearing at clubs like the Bitter End in New York and the Ice House in Pasadena. She had gone on concert tours both alone and with other Laugh-In performers and appeared at Carnegie Hall among other places.

Tomlin wrote much of her own material but also received help from gag writers and friends like Cynthia Buchanan. She called her sketches "comedy documentaries" in the style of Nichols and May. (Tomlin, the feminist, prefers to call them May and Nichols.) Lily remembered when their first record came out: "I probably listened to it about two thousand times. I don't think there's been anybody better."

Tomlin's own first comedy album was issued in 1971 by Polydor. Called *This Is a Recording*, it featured her character Ernestine, and earned her a Grammy award for the year's best comedy recording. Three other albums followed, including *And That's the Truth* with Edith Ann, and *On Stage*, a recording of her 1977

Broadway concert.

After "Laugh-In" Tomlin had several of her own television specials. In March 1973 a one-hour comedy variety show was aired on CBS-TV. She and Richard Pryor wrote the material and he was a guest on her show. In a segment called "Juke and Opal," Pryor played a guy strung out on methadone. CBS management was not comfortable with the sketch, but Tomlin was adamant about leaving it in, and was willing to sue over it. It was left in but put at the end of the show so audiences wouldn't be offended right off, and a laugh track was added to "sweeten" it.

Tomlin defended her artistic integrity, commenting in *Ms.* in 1974: "You can make all the money in the world—and I make a lot of money—but if you've got it on somebody else's terms, if you've had to make so many compromises that it's no longer satisfying, then what's the point?"

Yet Tomlin was willing to give a little. A 90-second sketch she did called "War Games," which satirized the military and violent toys, and in which a mother calling her son said, "Come on, leg or no leg, supper's on the table," was axed from her TV specials. Tomlin let it go.

CBS took a chance on another Tomlin special in November 1973, but weren't happy with that one either. One executive called it a "$360,000 jerk-off." Nevertheless, the writers for both shows received Emmys. Tomlin has stated that TV management does not consider her safe. "Commercial television," she noted, "specialized in escapist fantasy. I deal with cultural reality." Her friend and co-writer Jane Wagner has commented, "The network bosses think Lily is a genius but they are also scared to death of her."

After her difficult time with CBS Lily moved over to ABC-TV. Her luck was no better there. One special she did was never aired because it was considered "too long and artistic." In 1975 a special was finally shown by ABC. The American Academy of Humor cited it as the funniest TV comedy special of the year. They also awarded Tomlin with funniest performance in a nightclub or concert (male or female), and funniest woman in America.

Tomlin did not do another television special until 1981, and she was back at CBS. The show was not well received by critics. Steve Allen called it a disaster. Marvin Kitman of *Newsday* said: "There was no laugh track for the jokes but that was no problem. There was nothing funny in the script."

Tomlin would probably be defensive about this criticism, stressing that her prime interest is characterization. She told an interviewer for *New York Times Magazine* in 1976: "Most sketch comedy makes me feel bad. It has no intelligence behind it. I want a glimmer of hope, a little spirit. It's not that I don't want a laugh; I want both—but I'd rather have the spirit."

Yet Tomlin does not exclude jokes entirely. She's been known for gags like: "I read in an interview that Henry Kissinger said power is the ultimate aphrodisiac—imagine what it might take for him to get it up."

Some of her sketches bordered on the bizarre. In one sketch she did of a funeral scene, she used a dummy corpse "Fred" as a prop. She gossiped about the deceased's pregnant secretary to his wife Betty Lou: "You know, Betty, I tell you, it's just a pity you couldn't of had Fred's children; everybody else did." Then she smartened up the corpse with rouge and a blond wig and played ventriloquist with it.

If television did not always show Tomlin at her best, as her stage performances did, movies were an even greater letdown. Ironically, *Nashville*, the 1974 movie she was most praised for, was one in which she played a straight dramatic role. This was followed by *The Late Show* in 1976 with Art Carney.

In 1978 she played the part of a bored housewife involved with a drifter (John Travolta). This movie, *Moment by Moment*, written by Jane Wagner, was acknowledged by all who saw it as a "turkey."

Nine to Five, the 1980 film in which Tomlin co-starred with Jane Fonda and Dolly Parton was supposed to be a feminist statement about secretarial work. In a *Rolling Stone* review the movie was criticized as a "trash-compacted mini-series. . . . Fonda and company get the raising of consciousness confused with the lowering of sensibility."

Tomlin made no apologies for that film, nor was she unhappy with her 1981 movie *The Incredible Shrinking Woman*, again written by Jane Wagner. It was panned by the critics. The film satirized the conspicuous consumption of the suburban family, and Tomlin played a housewife whose exposure to supermarket products caused her to shrink. In February 1981 Richard Corliss of *Time* compared this movie to the original *Incredible Shrinking Man*, a 1957 sci-fi thriller which Corliss felt worked well as a "parable of mankind's impotence and heroism in the atomic age." Tomlin's film, said Corliss, was just "a laff-a-minute movie that will offend nobody—except the comic's most ardent fans who will buy tickets and then yell, 'Sell-out!' " Michael Sragow of *Rolling Stone* felt the movie reduced "nearly everyone to unpleasant cartoons."

In her most recent film, *All Of Me* (1984), Tomlin played Edwina Cutwater, a rich invalid woman who buys a body to have her soul put into when she dies. The body belonged to a man, Roger Cobb, played by Steve Martin, and the screwball comedy dealt with the problem of putting a female's spirit into a male brain. As a vehicle for Martin, the movie was not much of a showcase for Tomlin.

It was the live concert stage that really did justice to Tomlin's genius. In 1977 she made it to Broadway and appeared in concert at the Biltmore Theater. Her show *Appearing Nitely* received rave reviews, and she won a Tony for her work. She took it on a five-city tour, and it grossed two million dollars.

Lily had been working hard in clubs and on campuses creating new characters and gathering new material which culminated in her Broadway success. From Ernestine and Edith Ann she had branched out to include a whole range of personalities in her repertoire. Tomlin had been strongly influenced by Ruth Draper's satiric monologues. She said she responded to Draper "because she did women and because she did them with humanity." Since characters are the essence of Lily's act, it is necessary to introduce them.

Tess ("the loony woman") was a shopping bag lady who just got out of a mental hospital: "Hey! Howya doing'? I just got out! Did ya miss me? Ya wanna buy a potholder? I made these potholders when I was inside to keep from goin' bats! . . . The reason I got in is somebody told 'em I think I'm God. They don't like anyone thinkin' they're God 'cause they think they're God! . . . I didn't say I was God, I said I seen God."

Tess communicated with other non-visible beings, including creatures from outer space. One alien visitor told her: "Take this message to your people—the earth is cracked! I said I know that!"

Tess also believed that secret death rays attacked people through the telephone: "You pick up the telephone, and it just kills you, you just fall down, and you're layin' there, you're dead, people come in, and they see you layin' there, and they see the phone, they just think you died from bad news."

For all her craziness, Tess had moments of common sense, which of course showed up the rest of the world as being in confusion: "How do we relieve the condition of the needy? Simple, give 'em what they need," said Tess. Tomlin has stated that she perceived Tess as "all there . . . she's like energy."

In March 1977, "Laugh-In" producer George Schlatter told *Newsweek*: "Lily doesn't just do her characters, she becomes them. She can describe Edith Ann's room to you. She can tell you about Ernestine's sex life." Others who know Tomlin well said the same about her ability to lose herself. Jane Wagner told a *Time* interviewer in March 1977: "I don't know how she takes on the personalities of these characters. I've never seen her rehearse to get them, or stand in front of a mirror experimenting. She just gets up and does them. It's a comedic possession, but maybe demonic possession is just around the bend."

Richard Pryor considered Tomlin a "soul mate" explaining: "I mean the characters we do literally take possession of us. You're O.K. as long as you keep an eye on what's happening, as long as you don't get scared and tighten up. Because then you lose control over yourself, and the character takes over completely. I've never seen it happen to any other entertainers but Lily and me. You can see the physical change take place when she's working. It is eerie."

A good illustration of this possession was Lily's use of the character Mrs. Judith Beasley during her Broadway concert. Mrs. Beasley was a harassed housewife from Calumet City, Illinois, and many of her monologues were concerned with issues like impulse buying. She once bought a box of Pampers even though she had no baby at home. "When my husband questioned the purchase," said Mrs. Beasley, "I had to think quickly. I told him I was pregnant. Luckily it slipped his mind and never came up again."

Mrs. Beasley's brain has been described as a "pincushion of anxiety." These days," she worried, "it's not enough for a housewife to be loving and neat as a pin. We must be creative. There are some things you can make so cleverly that it is virtually impossible for anyone to tell if you have talent or not."

Tomlin used Mrs. Beasley to make contact with the crowds lined up in the cold for her Broadway performance. Mrs. Beasley, dressed in a Red Cross uniform, handed out coffee and donuts to those waiting. "I wouldn't go out there," Tomlin claimed, "so Mrs. Beasley did."

Other characters that Tomlin introduced were Suzie Sorority, who confessed, "I love the Lennon Sisters. I'm not ashamed to play their records"; Lupe, the world's oldest beauty expert, who

chanted: "Lines, lines go away, go and visit Doris Day"; Bobbie
Jeanine, a cocktail lounge organist; and Wanda Wilford, queen of
country music. Dressed in white boots and a tacky hairdo, Wanda
is a lampoon of singers like Dolly Parton. Yet Tomlin treated
Wanda with some depth, pointing out the childhood poverty, and
the rigors and loneliness of touring on the road.

In fact, Tomlin has tried to ensure that audiences will identify
with the characters and laugh with them, not at them. "There is
bite in her comedy," said producer George Schlatter, "but she
never goes for a joke outside the character. She won't burn herself
out because people are interested in her characters, who are real
people."

Tomlin herself has explained: "I construct a compressed accu-
racy, a character essence that is as true and real as I can get it. I
don't go for laughter. I never play for a joke, per se. If the joke
gets in the way, I take it out."

Sister Boogie, a septuagenarian radio evangelist, shouted:
"Boogie's not a meanin', boogie's a feelin' . . . Boogie takes the
question marks outa yer eyes, puts little exclamation marks in
they place." When Tomlin did this character, her voice mounted
to a fever pitch, her body shook and bounced, her arms waved
and she wheezed, huffed, scowled and squawked.

Sister Boogie urged her audience: "I say think of yourself as a
potato chip and life as a dip. I say think of yourself as a chicken
leg and life as Shake 'n Bake. Let me hear you say I got Boogie!"
When her listeners failed to respond adequately, Sister berated
them, saying: "Oh, that's pitiful. There's a bunch of dried-up
peach pits in this auditorium."

Tomlin has said of her characters: "I don't necessarily admire
them, but I do them all with love. . . . I love them for their
humanity. . . . After all, in private we're all misfits."

One of Tomlin's most controversial characters was Crystal, "the
terrible tumbleweed." A quadraplegic in a CB-equipped wheelchair, Crystal was on her way across the U.S. headed for Big Sur
where she intended to go hang-gliding. At an amusement park a
little kid asks Crystal if she was a ride.

The idea of Crystal came from a fan, the mother of a crippled
child who felt it would be "terrifically inspiring" if Tomlin did a
handicapped character. Lily maintained that she wanted "every
character to be triumphant. Especially Crystal."

Commenting on the character of Crystal in *Psychology Today*
(July 1977), Elizabeth Stone noted: "The greater the characters'

leaning toward the grotesque, the more generously does Tomlin endow them with a rich and resonant spirit. They have more self-knowledge than most of us, no self-pity, and a shrewd insight into the society—precisely because they don't belong. . . . Like Lily Tomlin herself, they are conscious and intentional comedians. Crystal's first words to us, as she sits unmoving from the neck down, are: 'My body is paralyzed . . . and I have a sunburn.' "

Glenna, "the sixties person," has changed her name to "Plumb" and delivers lines like: "What's your sign? I knew it! Pisces just blow me away," and "Wow, TV is so heavy—no, man, don't turn it on." She groaned: "I can't even remember who was assassinated in order anymore."

Glenna was on her way to a fundraising for a "new magazine Gloria Steinem wants to start." However, on her way out, she called out to her maid Rosita, reminding her to do the laundry and grocery shopping: "And remember no grapes and no lettuce."

Tomlin has used almost entirely female characters in her act. But she did add a male to her repertoire when she included Rick, a singles bar habitué. Rick, with his swagger and boorish come-ons to women like: "I promised my buddy there he could have first crack at you," was Tomlin's satirization of macho males. It would have been easy for Tomlin to demolish a character like Rick. But true to her style she treats him with humanity. We find out that his wife has recently left him and he's not sure why, and he spends too much money buying his buddies drinks. Tomlin has explained: "The comic who stands up there and tells mother-in-law jokes is being himself telling those jokes. I'd rather be the mother-in-law. I'd rather be the characters themselves, and try to capture their essence." As with Rick, she did this by presenting their background, unique mannerisms and outlooks.

Reviews of Lily's work have been mixed, though her live concerts have had generally glowing praise. At least one reviewer, however, has called her characters "too cute." Ron Wetzsteon of *The Village Voice* (April 4, 1977) was a critic who interpreted Tomlin's work, not as an affirmation of the human condition, but as a way of "mocking, ridiculing and exposing" others. The characters he felt were 'all outcasts of one sort or another—linked not so much by their common loneliness as by their common hostility. . . . The outcast has to come to terms with what other people regard as his inferiority and does so by defining his affliction as a sign of superiority. . . . It's this feeling of a sensitive, victimized minority embittered by a vulgar, repressive society that accounts for the Tomlin cult. If a following can be characterized as a group with a common purpose, a cult involves a shared estrangement. I wouldn't object to her cult's sense of solidarity if it didn't attach so much value to its victimization—if it didn't, in fact, regard its weakness as virtues, its hostility as vivacity, its scorn as warmth, its snobbery as compassion. . . .

"Tomlin, then, doesn't deeply identify with her characters so much as she deeply resents those who've rejected them—and we're asked to love them not because they're lovable but because the people who victimize them are so hateful."

A completely different interpretation of Lily's work came from Elizabeth Stone, writing in *Psychology Today* (July 1977). Stone felt that Tomlin's humor, rather than attacking anyone, uplifted all: "Most comedians," she noted, "work by demoting those presumed to be 'up a peg.' The ensuing laughter has a tinge of niggardly pleasure; . . . But Tomlin . . . most often works by bringing her characters 'up a peg,' on revealing the humanness of those in whom it had not been so apparent. Everyone gains in stature, and the resulting laughter is inclusive, glad at the enrichment of the human province."

Moreover, Stone believed that Lily's ability to distance herself was her strength as a performer: "In that the characters are herself, or perhaps psychic fragments of herself, she gives to them the compassion, the benefits of the doubt that one normally gives to oneself, but in that the characters are equally not herself, she views them with the dispassion, the distance that in equal measure comprises the comic perspective."

Just as reviewers have had mixed reactions to Lily's work, so did audiences. It was true that Tomlin had a cult following, many of them feminists. Not everyone, however, related to her act, and Tomlin has commented: "Sometimes the audience gives energy, sometimes they take it."

Whether pro or con, audiences and critics were never indifferent to Tomlin. The media coverage she received was phenomenal, and in 1977 alone she was on the cover of *Time*, *Ms.* and *Rolling Stone*. It was not surprising, then, that one of the characters she incorporated in her act was Dierdre Dutton, and obnoxious reporter. Using a character like Dierdre was perfect for Tomlin's technique of using a video screen on stage, a device she began experimenting with in 1975. Tomlin's characters would appear in costume on the screen, and Lily interacted with them. Dierdre Dutton, dressed in a floppy hat and glasses, annoyed Tomlin with prying questions: "Uh, Lily I hope you're not going to hold back. I want this interview very much to reveal the real you. Uh, it's a long way, Lily, from Detroit, the city of cars, to Hooray for Hollywood, the city of stars. Uh, do you find it corrupting?" "Of, course," Tomlin replied, "that's why I moved out there."

In some of her concerts Lily had a video of herself preparing for her act before she actually came on stage in person. We see her shaving her legs, plucking her eyebrows, putting on cold cream, gargling toothpaste with beer, leafing through *Psychology Today*, and finally snorting coke.

Admiring her use of video, a reviewer for *The Village Voice* on November 3, 1975 commented on Lily's act: "Tomlin's imagination is so visual, her characters are so beautifully realized, that when she uses video, it seems perfectly natural and wonderful. She dances with Margo, the hoody teenager; she plays with Dierdre Dutton, the reporter who wields platitudes like billy clubs. And when she is just using it to magnify her facial gestures, as in her portrayal of the world's oldest beauty expert, it brings a whole other crazy dimension to the show.

"Even when the equipment breaks down, Lily handles it ('there's a lot of technology in art'), and the audience buys the stall."

In television and film, Tomlin, of course, worked in costume. For her stage appearances, apart from video, she remarkably works with no props or costumes. She uses her face, body and voice to portray her characters.

Tomlin has frequently been accused of abandoning comedy. A writer for *Ms.* in 1974 called her style "low-key documentary" and felt her performances could "no longer appropriately be called comedy. Increasingly, she is simply lifting pieces from the culture."

Yet Tomlin's reputation has been built on comedy. It has merely been her approach that has been different: "The comedy to Lily is incidental, a side-effect. . . . Most comics hope that if they tell enough jokes some kind of coherent vision will emerge; Lily starts with a vision so powerful and unique that laughter is inevitable."

A *Newsweek* reviewer gave her the ultimate compliment by comparing her to Chaucer and describing her act as a "one-woman *Canterbury Tales*, a rich and savory collage of human types and destinies."

GILDA RADNER

The television show "Laugh-In," from the late 1960's, was an important show for female comics in terms of the number of women who attained prominence through it. A second influential show was NBC's "Saturday Night Live," which enjoyed a long and successful run beginning in 1975. While the former concentrated on one-liners and short bits, "Saturday Night Live" dealt more in sketches and skits of a bizarre, weird, and occasionally raunchy nature. A highlight was the variety of strange characters portrayed by the show's regulars. The female comic who attained the greatest popularity on this program was Gilda Radner.

Born in 1946 and raised in an affluent suburb of Detroit, Michigan, Radner was marked by the show business industry from birth after her mother named her for the character played by Rita Hayworth in the 1946 film *Gilda*. Her father was involved in real estate and investments and was a very wealthy man.

Mr. Radner loved show business and had dreamed of being a song-and-dance man. Road show actors often stayed at a hotel he owned and he received complimentary tickets to their shows. He and Gilda regularly attended touring productions of Broadway shows that played Detroit. He died when Gilda was fourteen and left a large enough estate for her to become independently wealthy at the age of twenty-one.

Radner acknowledged the influence of his death on her future. Being very close to her father, she felt she might have simply married and settled down in Detroit to have children to please her father. She felt she never would have become as ambitious or driven, and realized that perhaps she became an entertainer because she wanted to be what her father loved. Her mother has been described as a frustrated ballet dancer and a beauty. Gilda, on the other hand, grew up overweight. She became the fat, funny, good-natured girl.

As a child she remembered putting on little skits and scenes to entertain her father and a family servant named Dibby who did a good deal of the work in raising Gilda. Her comic talents were not stifled at all by her family. A maternal grandmother and her father appreciated humor the most.

Since she was fat Gilda felt she would never be noticed on looks alone, so she opted for laughs. Making jokes and laughing about her own weight was a way of defending herself from unthinking remarks by others. She had always had such a fear of being the fool that she willingly played the fool.

It was a way of coping with life, but at that time Gilda never in her wildest dreams expected to make her living from it. For Joan Rivers the obese childhood was an invention, for Gilda Radner it was a painful reality. She attended public school until the fifth grade and then transferred to the Liggett School, an all-girl private institution where she completed her high school education. She left public school to avoid getting a teacher whom she heard was mean. During school she was "a cutup and silly" and became popular for that reason.

At the age of twelve she appeared in a school play for the first time and made enough of an impression that acting quickly became her major extracurricular activity. At eighteen she enrolled at the University of Michigan where she remained, off and on, for the next six years, majoring in drama. She left ultimately without getting a degree. During this period she held a number of odd jobs, including waitressing in a hamburger restaurant, clerking in a record store, and dusting china in a gift shop. Even though she was a drama student she didn't consider acting a viable profession, as she thought the idea of getting paid for "playing games" was too fantastic. She had started out with the idea of being a teacher for retarded children, but gave it up somewhere along the way.

Radner left the university in 1969 and moved to Toronto, Canada, with a man she intended to marry at the time. She played the role of a housewife for a time, taking arts and crafts courses and honing her domestic skills. She soon became bored with this and began hanging around a Toronto theater. One thing led to another, she got a job at the box office, and then went on to a few parts in plays. When she heard that a Toronto production of *Godspell,* the religious rock musical, was being cast, Gilda walked in cold off the street, auditioned, got the part, and stayed with it for a year.

From there she joined Toronto's Second City, an offshoot of the improvisational group based in Chicago and began her career in comedy. Through this group she met some of her future "Saturday Night Live" cohorts, including John Belushi and Dan Aykroyd. A Canadian television producer named Lorne Michaels frequently attended the shows. Michaels would later go on to mastermind the "Saturday Night Live" program.

At Belushi's invitation, Radner returned to the United States, where she became a player on the "National Lampoon Radio

Hour," a syndicated weekly program. She also had a one line part in the 1973 Jack Nicholson film *The Last Detail.* In 1974 she appeared on stage in the *National Lampoon Show,* an Off Broadway revue. She had already begun developing comic characters and on the Lampoon show she portrayed "Rhoda Tyler Moore," a blind girl trying to make it in New York. This included running with a cane full tilt into a wall.

The next year Michaels was putting together "Saturday Night Live" and when it came time to cast he hired Gilda first and without an audition. In what would turn out to be a vast understatement, she informed Michaels, "I don't do characters." Michaels would later say "she's right there between Charlie Chaplin and Lucy."

The one-and-a-half-hour show went on the air in October of 1975, broadcast live from New York three Saturdays a month. The cast was unsure of what to expect and were guaranteed only thirteen shows. As it turned out, the show was a smash from the start, especially among younger adults. At its peak it was attracting about ten million viewers. The show featured a group of comedians known as "The Not Ready for Prime Time Players" who did comedy, satire, and music. Each show featured a different star who was host for that week and around whom many of the skits revolved.

Besides Radner, the other charter members of the program were Belushi, Aykroyd, Chevy Chase, Jane Curtin, Laraine Newman, and Garrett Morris. In the early years of the program, Gilda preferred minor roles like Rosa the night cleaner who came on, got a laugh or two and then quickly exited. In theory the players were an egalitarian group, but it didn't work out that way in practice.

Chase was the star the first year. When he left at the end of the first season, Radner got a little more attention, but the major focus of the show switched to Belushi. At the start of the 1979-80 season four of the seven original members remained, the three women and Morris, a black. Curiously, there had been three white males on the show, all of whom had left to go on to try bigger and better things, with varying degrees of success. After that 1979-80 season, the show's fifth year, all of the original comedians left in a complete switch of cast.

During that last season Gilda was the acknowledged star of the program. Her wonderfully bizarre characters were one of the features of the show and almost as familiar to audiences as those of Lily Tomlin. One was Baba Wawa, a lisping takeoff of TV personality Barbara Walters. There was Rhonda Weiss, a gum crack-ing Jewish princess from Long Island; a punk rock masochistic singer named Candy Slice; and a re-creation of Lucille Ball's Lucy.

Radner also did Debbie Doody, Howdy's wife, and the sniveling teenaged nerd, Lisa Loopner. One of Gilda's regular bits on the show was portraying a hyperactive six-year-old, Judy Miller, outfitted in a Brownie uniform, absorbed in her bedroom in her own fantasy world. It was a regular feature on the show and was one of her more poignant characters. Gilda was a physical comedian and "very much in touch with her child self."

Another creation was the elderly and dotty news commentator Emily Litella, another in the line of malapropism deliverers. Litella would comment on items such as "Soviet Jewelry" and "Violins on Television." When informed of her errors, she would respond with the phrase "Never mind," a slogan that became famous among her fans. The Litella character came about one day when Radner and Jane Curtin were fooling around and was based on Dibby, the woman who had raised Radner.

Perhaps her most popular character was that of Roseanne Roseannadanna, the wisecracking and very gross news announcer. Whatever the topic under discussion, Roseanne always found a way to bring it around to facial sores, armpit hair, and other assorted bodily functions. The inspiration for the name came from one of Gilda's favorite songs, a pop tune titled "The Name Game," which had a refrain that went "Bannana-banna-bofanna." This character was developed to lampoon all the women then reporting the television news and who were coming across as: "We're women and we have credibility to report the news, we don't go number two, we don't fart—they're like this perfect. . . . And Roseanne, she's a pig."

Gilda identified with the Loopner character, finding parallels with her own adolescence as a dateless loser. She empathized less with Roseanne and has reported that people came up to her on the street and thought it funny to pick their nose in front of her. To which Radner indignantly said, "Roseanne never picks her nose—just talks about it."

The characters Radner has done have usually been a result of a collaborative effort. For the most part the writers have pushed her on from one character to another to keep her from getting too stale and typecast in one particular role.

Gilda developed the Baba Wawa character not by studying Walters herself but by asking other people what it was that she did. Gilda then focused on those traits in Walters that stood out for other people. Her characterization was not particularly nasty. In fact, one of the things that set her apart from Tomlin was her softer style. One critic who thought the show "might tip too far toward the mean and spacey," thought Gilda's "niceness" kept the show balanced. Said Radner of her approach to comedy: "I want people to like me." Compare this with Rivers, who expected and wanted a certain proportion of her audience to hate her.

Dedicated to the show, Radner worked virtually all day during the week rehearsing. She sometimes slept overnight at the studio to be handy in case one of the writers came up with a brainstorm in the night. All of this hard work paid off in 1978 when she won an Emmy for outstanding continuing performance by a supporting actress in music or variety.

Regarding herself as a "life comedienne," Radner commented, "My comedy is an observance of life. And so to start observing it too seriously would be the end of it." One thing she did take seriously, though, was the idea of losing her audience through boredom. Michaels once dubbed her "Kamikaze Radner" since she would go for the suicide attempt if she felt herself losing her audience.

In the summer of 1979 she appeared on Broadway in *Gilda Radner—Live From New York*. The show ran for a month and was largely unchanged from her television routines. Fans loved it and business was standing-room-only. The critics viewed it much more harshly, feeling she was beyond her depth away from the television screen and was less successful without the team humor. Nine people, including Radner, were credited with the writing. Warner Brothers released an album in the fall of that year and also released a film of that show in 1980, *Gilda Live*.

When she left the "Saturday Night Live" show, Gilda's popularity was such that NBC and ABC both offered her specials, variety shows, and her own series to entice her to stay in television. She turned down $850,000 to play the role of Olive in Robert Altman's *Popeye*. Eventually NBC signed her to a reported six-figure contract, which only stipulated that Gilda wouldn't sign with any other television network.

For Radner it was time to make a transition. She wanted to make the move from television comic to comedian in theater and films. She claimed the stage was her first love and appeared in summer stock in 1976. In 1980 she made a much-touted debut in a Broadway play, *Lunch Hour,* written by Jean Kerr and directed by Mike Nichols. Nichols wanted Radner for the play but Jean

Kerr was hesitant. Friends of the author couldn't believe that Kerr had written something suitable for Gilda: "They think of her as someone who does the kind of comedy where you have to blacken your teeth to be funny."

In that same year she appeared in her first featured film role, in Buck Henry's comedy *First Family*. Two years later she co-starred with future husband Gene Wilder in *Hanky Panky*. She had been nervous about getting into movies, feeling that she needed a live audience to work for.

Due to the physical nature of her comedy and the unusual characters, the charge of not being feminine has been levelled against Radner. She has responded to this in different ways. While she was with Second City a critic termed her "as funny as a female Jerry Lewis." Stung by this, she resolved to be more attractive.

On "Saturday Night Live" she was again labelled as "not primarily feminine." This time she said she was secure about her femininity and didn't worry about it: "But I know I've scared many men off because of humor. I'll be funny instead of feminine. You're not likely to see me sitting back at a party being pretty."

Radner noted that some male peers were hostile about her being open and funny. She attributed this to the power inherent in comedy and its resultant threat. This may be one of the reasons why such a large percentage of female comics, relative to men, successfully adopted child characters. Radner and Newman were once playing little girls in party dresses on the show and they asked, "When are they going to let us grow up?" Noted Radner of the child character she frequently used: "I have a feeling I'll get too old to play Judy Miller."

Gilda has been compared to a number of female comics who preceded her, including Gracie Allen, Beatrice Lillie, and ZaSu Pitts. She has also been ranked with Goldie Hawn and Lily Tomlin. Much of her appeal lay in her innocence and vulnerability. To reach the same level as Tomlin, however, Radner would have to develop her own independent material, something that wouldn't be easy because she realized, "I'm not a writer or a creator."

The fact that she has played so many different characters may be both an advantage and disadvantage for her future career. She had been able to avoid being typed as a specific kind of character the way Hawn was as a dumb blonde. Radner's own individuality had never really come through. This could lead to a more ready public acceptance in a greater variety of roles, since she doesn't have to fight off one particular stereotype.

The disadvantage lay in the very fact that she had no such ready identification to move to. Hawn may have been limited to dumb blonde types but she had been successful with them. Gilda had no such image to go along with. Not being a stand-up comic or writing most of her material made it unlikely that her career could focus on solo comedy work.

While she desired to make a transition away from television, it may be the medium that she was most suited to. Radner was aware of this, for she once said when asked about her future. "I guess it will come down to doing some kind of television. I grew up in front of a television, I guess I'll grow old inside of one."

In 1984 Gilda appeared in a small role in another Gene Wilder film, *The Woman in Red*. By that time she had altered her priorities again. Now she claimed she would do no more television and just do the occasional film. She then wanted to concentrate on writing, "short stories and poetry." Despite this she did co-star with Wilder and Dom DeLuise in the 1986 comedy *Haunted Honeymoon*.

ANDREA MARTIN

Second City in Chicago has been the training ground for top comediennes like Elaine May and Ann Meara. Its Canadian counterpart in Toronto has produced talents like Gilda Radner and Andrea Martin. The emphasis in these two companies on improvisation encouraged spontaneity, quick thinking, and originality.

Andrea Martin grew up in Portland, Maine. As the only Armenian in a Wasp community, Andrea always felt "a little odd." She had an early interest in acting and dance and liked to impersonate Sophie Tucker and Carol Burnett. Before joining Second City, she appeared on stage with roles in Noel Coward's *Private Lives*, starring Maggie Smith and Brian Bedford, *Godspell* with Gilda Radner, and *You're a Good Man, Charlie Brown*.

Martin heard that Second City was looking for female performers. She had just been in a revue called *What's a Nice Country*

Like You Doing in a State Like This and she enjoyed doing comedy.

In 1977 Second City in Toronto was televised on CBC and became a hit show, "SCTV." The half-hour comedy program was soon syndicated for U.S. audiences and was aired on 55 stations, including NBC. The irreverent show satirized television programming, lampooning everything from Carson to commercials.

Martin and Catherine O'Hara were the two female members of of a cast which included John Candy, Eugene Levy, Martin Short, Joe Flaherty, Rich Moranis and Dave Thomas (the latter two of Bob and Doug MacKenzie fame). The group wrote their own material.

Andrea Martin created a stock of bizarre characters that she would do during the entire run of the program. She was Pirini Scleroso, house-maid, and Libby Wolfson, the host of the "You're So Beautiful" show, who interviewed guests like Sue Bop(stein)-Simpson on the meaning of Hanukkah. The cool on-camera Wolfson was sometimes caught sniffing her armpits when she thought she was off the air.

Martin as Barbara Frump parodied the news show "The Journal." As psychiatrist Dr. Cheryl Kinsey, Martin played a sexual therapist who got a twitch every time she mentioned sex. In one piece she had Kinsey giving advice in a monotone on how to convincingly fake an orgasm by repeating: "Don't stop, lover, please don't stop. Oh, you're good, you're so good. Make me a woman, big boy." It was cut out of the U.S. syndication. As sex was an important element in Andrea's humor, television censorship was limiting for her.

Andrea performed the piece live on stage and felt that women were hesitant to applaud because they were with their husbands, and the subject wasn't one that was openly discussed.

One of Martin's best-known characters was station manager Edith Prickley. In her favorite outfit of fake leopard skin coat and hat, and rhinestone glasses, Prickley was described by one writer as "an amalgam of Rona Barrett, Joan of Arc, and Auntie Mame." Prickley once danced at Studio 54 with ex-Canadian prime minister Pierre Trudeau. "We're very much alike, Edith," Trudeau whispered. "Oh?" she replied. "Don't tell me you get cramps too?"

Martin has preferred revue or group comedy to stand-up. The SCTV ensemble was a close one, and Andrea married Bob Dolman a relative of Martin Short's. She has two children.

Martin also preferred a broader slapstick style of comedy, with plenty of props and costumes, to cerebral conceptual comedy. She claimed that she wasn't worried about looking homely or weird, although she didn't want to be typed in these roles. "I think it's important," she told *Close-Up* interviewer Tim Blanks, "for a woman in comedy to be feminine also. . . . I just played Sophia Loren for three commercial spots on SCTV. I didn't really look like her but I got a great sense of satisfaction that I could look really attractive going for her look and still make the commercials funny. Probably the most difficult thing for a woman in comedy to do is keep a level of femininity while she's being funny."

Martin felt that Second City hired her in the first place because she was funny but not an overbearing feminist, and thus unthreatening to men. Martin did not consider her humor political, and perhaps because of this she did not feel she had any problems as a woman in comedy.

She did comment, however, that since the majority of the writer-performers on SCTV were men, she had to sometimes write and perform scenes on her own that they couldn't relate to. For example, she did a spoof in which Edith Prickley cooked to the beat of a Rhythm-Ace, a device hooked up to organs.

For this reason she also found working with Catherine O'Hara most satisfactory. She explained to an interviewer: "The pieces I liked the most are the ones I did with her. I didn't have to fight to get something across. I don't like to admit that, because I'm really not a feminist. I very rarely laugh at other women comediennes."

Martin's defensiveness about feminism was also reflected in her material. In one scene with Catherine O'Hara she played an interviewer counselling a distraught newly divorced woman. At first she tried a pep talk saying that women could manage fine without men. Gradually her words lost fire and both women ended up crying for a man.

Yet Andrea has made an effort to do unconventional females. She had tried doing a lesbian sketch, but she felt it was not well received by audiences. She noted that people seemed to laugh easily at male homosexual characters, but she thought that perhaps lesbians were still too unfamiliar to most audiences.

She once did a screen test for an NBC sitcom in which she was to play a construction worker. Martin wanted to make the character tough and no-nonsense, but NBC wanted her to play the role with "breasts out."

With the demise of SCTV in 1983 Andrea was trying to decide how to develop her career. She believed it would be hard to maintain her characters because she wasn't interested in stand-up, while comedy-variety shows like Carol Burnett's were dying out. Whatever her future direction, it is to be hoped Andrea Martin will stay with comedy.

BETTE MIDLER

Dressed in the most outlandish clothing, she bounced, strutted, shimmied, and shook her way around the stage. This queen of camp did "trash with flash" and "sleaze with ease" and described herself as the "last of the truly tacky women." She was vulgar and outrageous. She was also a legend, self-styled as the Divine Miss M. She was of course, Bette Midler.

An enormous success on records, on tour, and in concert, she was a woman doing a parody of a woman doing a female impersonator. She has returned camp to women, good-naturedly spoofing other females.

Midler was one of many women comics who combined their humor with singing. Some of them drew a distinction between the two and did bits of comedy and bits of singing, with each segment separate. Others mixed the two together, in the tradition of Sophie Tucker. Midler chose the latter style. Clothing, gestures, and body language made her songs comical. She also threw in non-musical humor, often of the blue variety.

Around 1940 her house-painter father and mother migrated to Hawaii from Paterson, New Jersey, and a few years later, in about 1945, Bette was born in Honolulu. On the island her father worked as a painter for the U.S. Navy. Her mother was a movie fanatic and named all three of her daughters after movie stars. Bette was named after actress Bette Davis. Midler's mother pronounced the name "Bet" under the mistaken impression that that was how Davis said it, a pronunciation that has stuck.

Midler grew up in what she remembered as a slum near Pearl Harbor. Theirs was the only Jewish family around and the family was also the only white one in an all-Samoan neighborhood. In addition Bette grew up overweight and plain-looking. As a result she felt lonely and alienated and never had a sense of belonging. "That's why I went so far to make people laugh—to find some comfort, to be part of the group, and to be accepted." Throughout her stay in elementary and high school, she remembered herself as being "very funny."

Her upbringing was strict and she recalled lots of "angry bellowing" from her father. She was allowed to go to movies only if they were musicals, since her parents didn't want their daughter seeing "those things." She didn't swear until she was seventeen, since even uttering the word "darn" in her house could provoke a beating, and she never had boyfriends until later in high school. Her mother was happy when Bette eventually turned to entertaining as a career. Bette credited her mother with being a major influence, since she believed there wasn't anything you couldn't do just because you were a female.

Bette considered herself a rebel in the family and often found herself giving her father lip. She described herself then as less than outrageous, merely smartass. Her father wasn't happy when his daughter turned to show business. He has never gone to one of her performances, not willing to accept the sometimes lewd and raunchy Miss M. This was a source of pain for Midler.

She had turned her attention to performing at an early age and won a prize for singing the Christmas carol "Silent Night" in the first grade. Throughout her youth she continued to sing at local shows and parties. When she was twelve she attended her first live theater performance and was so impressed by what she saw that she decided to be an actress. By the time she had finished high school she had appeared in many amateur shows and speech festivals. She then enrolled in drama at the University of Hawaii but dropped out after one year. She worked at odd jobs for a year while trying to establish herself in a theatrical career. One of these was as a secretary at a radio station; another was in a pineapple factory where she separated the center slices for canning.

In 1965 she got her first acting job, with a bit part in the film *Hawaii*. When the crew traveled to Hollywood to finish shooting, Midler went along at a salary of $300 a week and $70 a day in expense money. Midler lived frugally and saved as much money as she could, so that six weeks later, when shooting was complete, she had saved enough to fly to New York City to try and break into show business. In the film *Hawaii* she was only on the screen for about seven seconds.

She stayed at the Broadway Central Hotel and once again held a series of odd jobs. She was a hatcheck girl, a typist at Columbia University, and worked for Stern's Department Store, where she sold gloves. Her career as an entertainer was limited to some minor acting, some children's theatre, and Catskill revues. She was briefly a go-go dancer at a Union City, New Jersey, bar. In 1966 she attended an open audition for the Broadway production of *Fiddler on the Roof* and landed a job in the chorus and as an understudy for the small part of Tzeitel. Within a few weeks the regular playing Tzeitel left and Bette played the role for the next three years.

A friend had a large collection of records, particularly blues, torch, and gospel by such singers as Aretha Franklin and Bessie Smith, and Midler spent a lot of time listening to and studying their styles. She then prepared some songs and, when the day's performance of *Fiddler* was over, would go to the Improvisation club.

A talent scout saw her act and signed her to an appearance on the David Frost show. This led to five more shots on the Frost show plus an appearance on the Merv Griffin show. However, Bette was then only a pale shadow of her soon to become outrageous self, and her career went nowhere. In 1969 she left *Fiddler*, feeling she was making no progress in theater. She was depressed enough to spend a year in psychoanalysis.

The rest of that year she concentrated on her singing and acting lessons. She got a part in the short-lived musical *Salvation*, which closed in April 1970. Midler then returned to working as a go-go dancer, this time at a Broadway bar. She next heard of a job coming up at the newly refurbished Continental Baths, a gay Turkish bathhouse in the basement of the Ansonia Hotel on Broadway. The owner decided to present entertainment on Friday and Saturday nights and was looking for a singer. Bette took the job, which paid $50 a night, and played to an audience of male homosexuals who were wearing bath towels.

It was at this unlikely source that the character of the Divine Miss M would emerge and rocket to superstar status, if not overnight, then within a couple of years. Something else which influenced her style was the Theater of the Ridiculous, which she had encountered for the first time when she came to New York. She thought them totally demented but admired their style and found them interesting physically. It inspired her to go for the garbage can clothes, the items that people threw out. Midler found value in the old clothes, the old style and the old music, stuff she had grown up with. These were all to become important elements in her act.

Until her booking at the Baths, her singing had been straight, very dramatic and serious. The Divine Miss M started out as a character to hide behind and have fun with, a gaudy and vulgar parody of a drag queen. For Midler, who was taught to be well bred and quiet, the character represented a complete antithesis to what she had been taught to believe. When she had been doing Miss M for a few years, Bette remarked, "She's an exaggeration of all the things I never thought I wanted to be. Though I tell you, since I've started doing her I've become much more like her than I ever thought was possible."

At the Continental Baths she found that the customers encouraged her outrageousness. "They gave me the confidence to be tacky, cheesy, to take risks. . . . They encouraged my spur-of-the-moment improvisations." The freakier she got the more the audience liked it. She also picked up the gay bathhouse argot and used homosexual in jokes. Midler was also encouraged to explore satire at the Baths, and she worked hard to get and hold the attention of the audience. "If I'd kept my distance, they'd have lost interest because there were too many other things going on in the building that were more fun."

She quickly became a hit at the Baths as word about Midler spread. Her growing reputation got her a guest spot on the Johnny Carson show. This led to many more appearances on the Carson show, and she almost became a regular over the following 18 months. She further honed her reputation for camp, since she didn't have all that much material. She began to resort to doing her fantasies of people like Betty Boop and the McGuire Sisters. With Carson's stamp of approval, her fame continued to grow. Starting in 1971 Midler gave concerts and did nightclub bookings around the country, to sold-out houses of enthusiastic fans.

In her act Midler hit the stage like a hurricane. She strutted, pranced, careened and tottered back and forth while waving her arms and popping her eyes. Her outfits were all bizarre. She wore toreador pants, satin and sequinned gowns from other eras, scarlet platform shoes, strapless tops, a black lace corset, Spring-o-lator shoes, and gold lamé pedal pushers. All this under a mound of frizzed-out orange hair. Her songs ranged from the 1920's to the 1960's, the latter being her favorite period. A few numbers were done straight but most were wild parody, glittery camp, and straight burlesque. One of her best known was a sendup of the Andrews Sisters' "Boogie Woogie Bugle Boy."

From the 1960's she did such tunes as "Do You Want to Dance" and "Leader of the Pack." She was backed by a three-member female, wonderfully named group, the Harlettes. While her show gave the impression of spontaneity it was carefully staged. Midler chose all her own material, which was arranged by Barry Manilow and delivered at a sound level said to be "about that of World War II."

In 1972 Midler acquired as manager one Aaron Russo, who was her lover for the first six months but her manager for the next seven years. He controlled and dominated Bette's career through that period. Her income that year was about a quarter of a million dollars, a figure she would quickly surpass in following years. In 1972 she released her first record album. It quickly went gold and was only the first of many she would release over the years. The next year she did a 32-city concert tour. Her original fans had all been New York City male homosexuals, yet she quickly was able to establish a national following of fans of all ages and sexes. She was riding high on a wave of a nostalgia craze which was sweeping the country.

Her appeal lay in her funkiness, her uniqueness, her humor and her bawdiness. Carson saw a special quality in her, an ability to grab the audience. He felt she had an empathy and rapport with the audience that was hard to duplicate, and equally hard to define. Others have felt that it was her vulnerability that has linked her to her audience, the same vulnerability and innocence found in Judy Garland or Janis Joplin. Her whole act was a contradiction. She gave a surface appearance of bad taste, sleaze, and inelegance, yet underneath it all was good taste and an almost innate elegance.

Midler grew up funny and witty, and until she began studying the Aretha Franklin-type records, she said, "I considered myself mainly a comedienne." She has retained comedy in her act.

When she wasn't singing, she was delivering light patter and jokes. Some of her jokes have been in the Lenny Bruce league, such as: "If Dick Nixon would only do to Pat what he's done to the country." Others have ranged from the limp-wristed variety to jokes about her often-commented-upon large bust ("Two reasons why I didn't become a ballerina") to campy introductions to her songs ("Here's another blasto from the pasto! You're gonna like this one 'cuz I shake my tits a lot!"). Her ability as a comic was clearly recognized by critics: "She has a gaiety and sweetness one seldom finds in a comic, man or woman." Another critic termed her an "expert comedienne." From the early 1970's onward she has employed gag writers.

Her 1973 tour culminated in New York at Broadway's Palace Theater, where she proceeded to break box-office records. She took a year off in 1974, pleading she was wrung out and in need of a rest. In 1975 she was back at the Palace Theater in a new revue, *Clams on the Half Shell*. This one smashed all-box office records again, including her own of 1973. For this revue her manager Russo brought in a director and mounted a visually extravagant production which had Midler being towed onstage at the start in a giant clam shell from which she emerged in the tattered clothing of a streetwalker.

She was also featured in the grip of a huge plastic King Kong atop the Empire State Building. She used other props such as massive jukeboxes, and had expanded her cultural range to parody such people as Mae West, Tiny Tim, Tina Turner, Bea Lillie, Don Rickles, Fanny Brice, and Martha Raye. As with all parodists, her attitude toward her material was ambiguous, a mixture of both love and hate. She reacted with sham incredulity to the amount of money people had paid to come and see her. She did Betsy Ross impressions while throwing in plenty of "dirty Sophie Tucker jokes." Applying a Falstaffian epigram to Gerald Ford, she cracked: "Not only is he dull himself, he is the cause of dullness in others."

Bette has taken her act to Europe and been just as successful there as at home. When she was playing the London Palladium in 1978, someone in the audience held up a sign saying, "We love your tits." Midler got carried away and exposed her breasts. She has flashed her audience at least twice. That time in London, Russo gave her a tremendous dressing down because of it. It was one of the last straws for Midler, who got rid of Russo the next year, after he had finished co-producing her first movie *The Rose*.

Russo had managed not only her professional life but her personal life as well. Midler's dependence can be seen in her relationship with him. The pair fought constantly and her year off in 1974 was actually due to her becoming professionally nonfunctional as a result of so many fights with Russo. She left for a period of some months before returning to his direction. The two of them fought openly and often, and friends of Midler hoped, for years, that she would get rid of him as her manager.

Russo's handling of her professional life was impeccable, however. Midler didn't appear in her first movie until 1979, but Russo had films in mind from the beginning. He booked her into the Palace Theater in 1973, at a time when no singers played there, because he felt a Broadway crowd meant a movie crowd and that's where he was steering her. "Movies are the art form of the day. To be a true legend, you can't do it just in music."

For her 1975 revue *Clams*, Russo made it visually extravagant to entice movie offers, and it worked. The offers began to roll in. Russo rejected many roles Midler was being considered for, including the Goldie Hawn part in *Foul Play*, the Talia Shire role in *Rocky*, and the Jessica Lang role in *King Kong*, as well as film biographies of Dorothy Parker and Sophie Tucker. Russo wanted a role that only Midler could play for her screen debut as a star.

When *The Rose* script came along, Russo accepted it and simply told Bette that this was the movie she was going to do. In the movie Midler played a self-destructive rock singer hooked on pills and booze, a story parallel to the life of the late Janis Joplin. There were parallels with Midler's own life as well, in particular the aspect of a dominant manager. Midler drew strong critical praise for her dramatic acting and received an Academy Award nomination as best actress. She also received $500,000 and a percentage of the profits for doing *The Rose*, an enormous sum for a first picture.

Russo laid a lot of guilt trips on Midler, such as paranoid bits about people out to get him. He claimed that Midler was all he had and that he was dying of leukemia. All were designed to keep Midler under his control. After *The Rose*, though, Midler finally got up the courage to get rid of him. In 1972 when she first became Russo's client she had told him she wanted to be a legend. And Russo had indeed accomplished that.

Her second movie was *Divine Madness*, which wasn't a movie at all but a filmed concert. Critics liked it but fans stayed away. In 1981 she starred in a filmed called *Jinxed*, which was poorly received on all counts. This marked one of the first major projects undertaken by Midler without Russo, and she admitted she was naive with respect to the business due to the sheltered life she had led under Russo's tutelege.

On the set of *Jinxed* Bette got a reputation for being difficult to work with. The director, Don Siegal, referred to her as "quite an unpleasant young lady." Her male co-star also badmouthed her and claimed he couldn't get through a love scene with her unless he thought of his dog. Bette claimed that she wanted to make the best possible movie. But the others weren't as motivated and came to resent her perfectionism.

Movie offers from Hollywood were scarce for several years. That may have been partly due to her attitude change. "When I was a newcomer, I laid back. Now that I have a little bit of knowledge, I kick ass."

Midler did concert tours in 1979 and 1982. The latter tour grossed $8 million. On stage she remained as wildly outrageous and vulgar as ever, still using outfits such as mermaid tails and parrot hats. She lampooned the British Royal Family and said the Queen was "the whitest woman in the world. She makes all the rest of us look like the Third World." Answering her own question about how Princess Anne would respond if asked her age, Midler pondered for awhile and then tapped out the number with her foot. She also laughs at herself with breast jokes.

Bette has been called ugly innumerable times, and the large size of her nose has also been pointed out repeatedly. She has said, "I hate it when they call me ugly, when they say I'm homely." Midler has considered getting her nose bobbed but had enough sense of self-worth not to do it. She has also been assertive enough to insist that while she may not have been conventionally attractive she was nevertheless sexy. In her act she told very dirty, and very funny, jokes in the guise of "Soph," an old woman who liked sex. In this persona many of her jokes touched on taboo topics such as crabs and menstruation, and attempted to give women power over sex.

Her act changed as she entered the 1980's, a time when she functioned as her own manager. She had moved a little more into making jokes, playing characters, and telling stories. The music portion, while still central, wasn't quite so predominant. She was developing new accents and characters, and the Divine Miss M, while still a big part of the show, was much less pivotal. This decreasing dependence on Miss M stems from her own philosophy that it was possible to end up living your life like your character would, and ultimately being destroyed by that character. "If you let your character define your personality instead of keeping your true self separate, your character will get you."

Midler has also successfully published two books, *A View from a Broad*, a comic look at taking her show on a world tour, and *The Saga of Baby Divine*, an illustrated pseudo-children's book. By 1983 her ninth record album had been released.

In real life Midler described herself as gentle and mild, referring to herself as a cynic and a tease. She was anarchistic on stage
but not in real life. Behind the façade of the Divine Miss M there
lurked a "bleak pessimist" who believed that life held more bad
times than good. Over the years she has gone through many
lovers and was not as eager to be "looked after" now by a man,
after her experience with Russo.

Her art and work were more important to her. Once asked if
her work suffered when there was no man in her life, Midler
replied, "No. Men suffer when there's work in my life." Midler
did eventually marry, however. In 1984 she wed performance
artist and commodities trader Martin Haselberg. Her off-stage
wardrobe was, of course, nowhere near as flamboyant as that of
Miss M. As she said, with her tongue in her cheek, "I wouldn't be
caught dead with a sequin on my body when I'm not working.
How tasteless!"

Midler described herself as "not stridently feminist." That
changed when she made *Jinxed*. Until then she had never considered her femininity an issue. She thought that if you went in
and said what you wanted, that would be that, provided you were
smart. "Well, that's not that. This last picture opened my eyes to
the world. I said to myself, I'm not the only woman who has gone
through this."

Back in 1978 when Russo still managed her, he had her future
planned for several years with world tours and a Broadway musical five years down the road. Since she moved out on her own, she
has seemed to be leaning toward a future involving more comedy.
Midler was interested in movies where she could do "a real
comedy where I get to faint and do pratfalls, fake swoons and
major mugging, because that always was my best thing." She got
her wish and appeared in two comedy movies in 1985–86, *Down
and Out in Beverly Hills* and *Ruthless People*.

She has gained enormous confidence in her comic talents. "I
think I'm hysterically funny," she stated. "For a long time I said,
'Oh, I'm no good. I'm just garbage—kick me, kick me. . . .' But
that's not so. I'm a terrific comedienne." She had always contributed comedy material to her shows but relied mainly on her gag
writers, not believing in her own ability to write stand-up
material. What gave her confidence was the writing of *A View
from a Broad*.

By 1984 Midler was leaning in the direction of stand-up
comedy for her future and soon released a comedy album. "I

wouldn't mind being a commentator, a stand-up comic like
Richie Pryor. He moves people socially. It's a challenge." Anybody who set out to become a legend, and achieved that goal in
less than a decade, is certainly equal to any challenge.

MADELINE KAHN

She started out in classical opera and ended up in a movie full of
belching, farting cowboys. The movie was Mel Brooks's *Blazing
Saddles* (1974), and Madeline Kahn played a dance-hall entertainer, Lili van Shtupp. Madeline got to sing in the movie but
her main contribution was comedy. She did a hilarious burlesque
of the Dietrich type femme fatale and was praised by critics as
"falling-down-on-the-floor funny."

Robert Berkvist of *The New York Times* described her role:
"Gartered, ruffled, a heaving sea of bosom and thigh, she sneers,
sulks, lisps, and pouts her audience into a state of frenzied lust.
Lili, Lili, Lili, they roar. Phooey, she yawns, go away. Later, in
her dressing room, she disarms the town's admiring sheriff by
accepting the gift of a single flower with the immortal words,
"Oh, one wed wose, how wovely."

Madeline Kahn took a circuitous route to comedy. She was
born in Boston in 1942. Her mother was interested in singing,
and her father was a dress manufacturer. Her parents divorced,
and her mother eventually remarried and moved the family to
New York.

Madeline's musical talents were encouraged, and as a child she
sang on radio's "Children's Hour." After high school Kahn won a
scholarship to Hofstra University on Long Island, and worked
towards a degree in speech therapy. When she auditioned for the
scholarship, one of her pieces was a monologue by Ruth Draper.
She also worked part-time as a singing waitress.

When Kahn graduated, she realized that teaching bored her,
and decided to try acting instead. Her first job was as a chorus
girl in the 1956 production of *Kiss Me, Kate*. During the next two
years she sang with the Green Mansions opera repertory company
in upstate New York.

Her comic debut on Broadway came when she performed in
Leonard Sillman's *New Faces of 1968*. Her song spoofs were noted

by critics, who called her "extremely funny." Kahn appeared in several other musicals, and worked in revues at New York's Upstairs at the Downstairs club, where Lily Tomlin was a fellow performer. Kahn also had exposure on television talk shows like Johnny Carson's and Merv Griffin's.

Madeline's range as an actress was demonstrated by her dramatic role in David Rabe's play *Boom Boom Room*. In 1973 it earned her a Tony nomination.

Kahn's talents as a comedienne were given full scope in the movies. Her first film *What's Up Doc?*, directed by Peter Bogdanovich in 1972, saw her in the part of Eunice Burns, a prim, whining fiancée of Howard Bannister (played by Ryan O'Neal). Madeline got raves from critics, which was quite a coup since the star of the film was Barbra Streisand. A reviewer for *Cue* wrote that she played her part with a "picture-stealing lunacy."

Kahn was seen in a few more films before she landed the role of Shtupp in *Blazing Saddles*. It won her an Oscar nomination for best supporting actress. It also endeared her to Mel Brooks and Gene Wilder.

Brooks hired her again for his 1974 comedy *Young Frankenstein*. Kahn played Elizabeth, the fiancée of Dr. Frankenstein. One of the most memorable scenes in the movie was when Elizabeth was raped by the monster, and burst into a sort of hysterical opera singing. The critic for *Cue* called Kahn "the ultimate comedienne," and Pauline Kael described her role as 'funny and enticing." Madeline later performed in Brooks's movie *High Anxiety* as well. And Brooks has remained one of her strongest supporters. "Madeline," he said, "would even be funny late at night in a closed Regal shoe store, singing and dancing in the aisles."

Gene Wilder offered Kahn a role in his 1975 farce *The Adventure of Sherlock Holmes's Smarter Brother*. Madeline again played a music hall entertainer, but continued to do well with this type of role. Richard Schickel of *Time* observed, "Kahn contributes another wonderful impersonation of a sex tease." She appeared in several other movies, including *Slapstick* with Jerry Lewis. Although they were not all well received by critics, Kahn usually was. *At Long Last Love*, directed in 1975 by Peter Bogdanovich, had reviewers praising Madeline for her "gift of satire," and for being "divinely funny."

Her experiences in film established Kahn as a comedienne. On stage she accepted more comedy roles, as in the 1977 production of *Marco Polo Sings a Solo*, at Manhattan's Public Theater. Jack Kroll of *Newsweek* felt that Madeline displayed "the sensual intelligence of the true comic actress."

But Kahn did not always have it easy. She had undergone analysis, and at the start of her career she was fired from a play. In 1978 she became ill during the Broadway run of *On The Twentieth Century* and was permanently replaced by her understudy.

Madeline has been described by Rex Reed as "the clown with the face of an angel," and though he risked sounding like a "male chauvinistic pig," he thought her a "dish."

But the "dish" believed that comedy had hurt her love life. In 1983 she told an interviewer for *People* magazine: "Men don't feel comfortable being romantic with a funny woman." Yet when asked by Michael Kearns of *Drama-Logue* in 1984 if it was important for her to be lovable, Madeline replied, "I don't think an actor should be afraid to be unlovable—particularly in comedy; you have to be willing to look like a fool. If lovable means never looking foolish, you're going to be restricted." Moreover, she stressed: "If I was required to give up my work for a relationship, that would mean I'd give up the relationship."

Kahn has commented on sexism in the movie industry. When she was interviewed in *Newsweek* in 1974 she complained, "When they want to focus on my breasts and I say no, they think I have a hangup. . . . If a scene isn't well written they'll drop your neckline to fill the void."

ABC television gave Madeline her own TV sitcom in 1983, "Oh, Madeline." Kahn played a wife and mother who was trying to keep her ten-year-old marriage from going stale. Kahn felt the character was "a little like me. She's curious. She doesn't want to die without having done certain things."

SUZANNE RAND

The team of Monteith and Rand quickly became the nation's biggest male/female comedy team in 1978. They were called the hottest pair to come along since Stiller and Meara and many comparisons were drawn between them and the team of Nichols and May, whose style they followed somewhat.

Suzanne Rand was raised in a suburb of Chicago and when young wanted to sing in cabarets. She fulfilled this ambition at the age of sixteen when she worked briefly as a torch singer in a Waukegan, Illinois, bar. She then majored in Theater at Stephens College in Missouri, aspiring to be an actress. Rand remembered herself as always being a cut-up as a child, and at college she was considered the funniest Juliet the school's drama department ever had. She had a tendency to turn tragedy into farce. She credited her father as being the major influence in developing her sense of humor. After college she spent some time with the Second City comedy group of Chicago, and then in 1972, at the age of twenty-three, she found herself a member of the Proposition Troupe, an improvisational group working out of Boston, Massachusetts. John Monteith had joined the group a little earlier that same year.

Each recognized their ability to make the other one laugh and thought they might be good together on stage. But nothing came of the idea for four years. In 1976 Rand got an offer to do an act at Cape Cod for the summer. She immediately recruited Monteith and the pair threw an act together in just three days. They repeated the act in 1977 and then made a New York City debut in early 1978 and swiftly established their reputation. They appeared in night clubs, Off Broadway, before President Carter at a gala Democratic Party fund raiser, on the Johnny Carson show, and, finally, on Broadway.

In the tradition of Nichols and May they appeared on stage without props, save for two chairs. A good deal of their act was improvised, and they created their own material. They didn't actually write their routine, preferring to tape it. As with all comedy teams their contrasting personalities tended to complement each other. Monteith was the low key, acerbic one, while Rand was demonstrative and outgoing. They appeared on stage in formal attire with Monteith in a suit and Rand in a dress. A lot of their material came from the drug culture. Relations between men and women was another major topic.

Most critics loved this highly verbal comedy team, and the only difference of opinion seemed to be whether they were best with their set routines or with their improvisational pieces. The team differed from their predecessors in having a certain off the wall kind of craziness. This opinion of their work was by no means unanimous. Some found their humor too weak and glib, their material too old and hokey. They were seen as clever people who could sometimes say clever things, but not as satirists. For these critics the comparison to Nichols and May was invalid. The earlier team were called razor sharp satirists while Monteith and Rand were judged to be people trying to be funny. One unimpressed critic went so far as to rename the pair No-Teeth and Bland.

Much of the criticism fell on the female half of the team. One critic said their work failed partly because Suzanne's technique was "so broad and heavy." A second critic called Rand the more gifted performer of the two, but he had a different complaint. He had decided on no logical basis, other than that Monteith seemed the "more cerebral" of the two, that he probably did the bulk of the writing.

For Rand, dressing up for her performance was a calculated and important aspect of her routine. It was in her interest to look her best. She wanted to create an image whereby the audience, seeing a "good-looking girl," would infer that the male half would do all the funny parts. She could then surprise the audience with the so-called contradiction of a sexy woman being funny. For Suzanne, female role models included Martha Raye, Eve Arden, and Lucille Ball. Ball in particular could be both wacky and pretty at the same time. Rand was flattered by the comparison to Nichols and May and acknowledged some similarities but felt there were differences in style. She claimed to avoid studying the performances of other comedians so as not to pick up any of their mannerisms. The exception was Gracie Allen, whom she idolized.

Suzanne Rand seemed confused about herself after two years of heady success. She felt the acting profession was one of the fairest around with virtually no sexism. She then admitted that one of the reasons the team was formed was that when Rand went around to auditions by herself she was always the "wrong type" and couldn't read for the parts she really wanted. Rand still harbored the desire to be a dramatic actress.

Oddly enough she didn't consider herself a stand-up comic because she worked with a partner. She felt one of the most frightening things in the world would be to stand up alone before an audience and tell jokes. Rand needed to bounce her lines off a straight man. Despite this she said she believed she could have made it in humor without Monteith.

After enjoying enormous popularity for a couple of years, the couple faded from the limelight almost as quickly as they had arrived. They continued to perform and tour through 1984 but with nowhere near their initial impact. The endless comparisons to Nichols and May perhaps set a standard for them that they couldn't attain. Their critics were partly right about the failures of their humor. Their material was too narrow and lacked a sharp edge. As they said of their routines, "we don't rip to shreds."

They also worked too hard at treating each other equally on stage. Most comedy teams or groups who have enjoyed success have done so by employing harder satire and/or dumping on each other, either in turn or always using the same victim. One usually played the dominant role and one the submissive. For Monteith and Rand the style may have led to overly bland material on which the audience quickly became satiated. The act lacked tension or excitement.

Some of this may have emanated from the apparent confusions in Rand's own mind over her place and role in comedy. She had the following comment to make about the team's material: "We don't believe in laying messages on the audience. We're real careful not to reinforce bad ideas or stereotypes, but we really don't try to teach the audience too much. Most of our jokes I consider victimless crimes in that we try not to demean or hurt a group or type. Sort of parody without pain."

MARILYN SOKOL

Marilyn Sokol was one of many of the new women comics who surfaced towards the end of the 1960's and into the 1970's. Many of them, including Sokol, were the products of improvisational groups and cabarets which had sprung up during this time. She also followed in the tradition of the singing comic.

Sokol mixed a little of everything into her act. She did straight stand-up comedy, sang serious ballads, and also did campy send-ups of songs in the style of Bette Midler. Raucous and unrestrained, she used plenty of facial expressions and has been called "rubber-faced." She became highly successful in the middle 1970's appearing on the Johnny Carson show and the Merv Griffin show, releasing a comedy album, doing television work, and appearing in films. She also played to standing-room only crowds with her comedy act in cities all across the country.

As a child her greatest ambition was to become a ballet dancer, but when she developed breasts as an adolescent, something ballet dancers usually don't do, she found her balance was lost and she gave up that ambition. She spent most of her childhood in the state of Maryland, moving there from the Bronx at the age of six. Her first two years in Maryland were spent in a small one-horse town that lacked amenities and was anti-Semitic. Sokol was a complete outcast and attributed the tragic bits in her act to the time spent in that town.

She was then taking ballet lessons and it was a method of protecting herself, since she didn't have to talk when she was dancing. Soon after graduating from New York University she went through the trauma of a marriage and quick divorce. Coming from a wealthy family she was able to persuade her parents to support her as she buried herself in singing, acting, and dancing lessons as a form of therapy.

In 1969 she was working as a storyteller for the Brooklyn Public Library when she got her first break, a part in the company of *Man of La Mancha*. From there she moved on to membership in three different groups which had formed in that era: the San Francisco Mime Troupe and the Open Theater and Ace Trucking Company, both of New York City. The last was an improvisational group.

She traced her comedy talents back to her family, in particular to her mother and sister. Her mother did a deadpan style of humor or farce around the house, often using kitchen items as props. Her sister was the family satirist and had promised herself to make at least one satirical or acerbic comment every day. Sokol remembered doing imitations as a child. By imitating her mother and sister she used humor to overcome her insecurities. Marilyn began to realize her own flair for comedy when she would audition for parts and people would laugh when she wasn't attempting to make them laugh. She then turned more and more to incorporating comedy into her act.

In the comedy portion of her act characters play an important role. Her best-known character was a nine-year-old girl named Rosarita Farkus who thrashed herself wildly around the stage while singing "Chicago" hopelessly off key. The character was audacious and precocious and contained traits Sokol felt she had in her as a child but never expressed. Sokol continued to work on developing new characters for her act, doing her own writing. The character of Farkus was invented while she was with the Ace Trucking Company. Just as quickly she could become an exaggerated Italian diva on stage destroying "Volare," or a manic Brooklyn rabbi doing a Top 40 radio show.

Other big topics in her material were dolls, babies, and pregnancy. She also did the street-wise woman. Her insecurities and fear of rejection from public exposure were largely eradicated through years of therapy, but a bit remained. Sokol thought this remnant of fear contributed to the raucous and endearing quality of her act.

She believed in dressing "elegantly" when she performed, to heighten the effect of a physical routine such as a pratfall. She had read that Charlie Chaplin gave the same advice once to Martha Raye. He had advised her to look gorgeous so that when she took a fall she would only have to trip a little bit. An elegant lady tripping was funnier than a slob falling down.

Sokol preferred doing character comedy to jokes and one-liners, since jokes tended to wear thin after a time. Characters could be intrinsically funny, lessening the need for gags. Of all the material she did, she had the least respect for her jokes, finding them the easiest thing to do. She used them only as a method of getting things rolling. Most of her material was derived by observing real-life situations. She didn't try out her act in clubs, but developed it instead in her living room before one or two people.

Like many of the new breed of female comics, she also used sexual material in her act. On the Johnny Carson show she once talked about her first "home run," a metaphor for the first time she had sex. Sokol was comfortable with this type of material since her mother's brand of humor at home often leaned to the bawdy and ribald. She avoided sexual humor that came from anger, however, preferring a posture of "innocence."

Combining humor and straight singing in her act allowed her to move people in the audience from laughter to seriousness without making any obvious transitions. And for her, this created a feeling of tremendous power. Perhaps, though, there was more to it than just that.

Her future desires seemed to lie in other areas and she only began to recognize herself as a comic years after the public had extended such recognition to her. Her use of singing in her act may have been a way of keeping alive her other showbiz aspirations. Perhaps at some level the role of comedian has always been a distant second or third choice for her. "My fondest wish right now is to do a play, to get back into live theater. I've missed it terribly. I started to do my act basically so that I would have more power to call shots, more autonomy. . . . Right now I would guess that people think of me more in terms of being a comedienne. And I think that I've begun to accept it and enjoy it because I know how hard it is to make people laugh."

ZORA RASMUSSEN

Zora Rasmussen was one of the current crop of comedians who combined singing with humor. *Vogue* has called her a "tall cuddly blonde," and *The Village Voice* has described her as a "gum-popping frizzy blonde." In the late 1970's she built up an enthusiastic cult following in New York City.

Considering herself unattractive as a teenager, Rasmussen eventually created a glamorous image. Thanks to contact lenses and a blond dye job she transformed herself from "cootie to covergirl." Her style of comedy was largely self-deprecatory, although Zora denied it.

She was born Kathy Rasmussen in Detroit, in the early 1950's, dropping Kathy for the more exotic Zora as a stage name. She remembered being funny in high school, which she attended in Detroit in the 1960's, simply because she wasn't cute. The first approval she got was for doing a pantomime in junior high, and with this confidence she determined to go into the theater. She continued to take part in school plays, mostly character roles, and then became a singer with a band called the Coty Combo. She appeared in eye-catching outfits, such as a formal gown, or tights, miniskirt and pilgrim shoes, doing songs like "Girl Talk" and Barbra Streisand's "Pe-e-eople."

Next stop was college, where she worked part-time manning a Good Humor ice cream truck and harboring a desire to be a singer. She was one of about 1,200 people who turned out for auditions for the Detroit company of the musical *Hair*. She made the final group of eleven from which eight were selected. However, she wasn't one of the eight. She had nerve, though, and kept calling the show until finally they took her on. She then moved to New York City to establish herself in show business. There she took on several odd jobs including singing waitress at "Once Upon a Stove" and a stint as a census enumerator— although Zora referred to it as a census fabricator since, according to her, she used to make up entire families, number of toilets, etc.

By 1977 Rasmussen was tiring of the endless rounds of auditions and not getting anywhere. She decided she needed a way of showcasing her talents and that year organized a five-woman comedy act called "Funny Ladies" (the name was later changed to "High Heeled Women"). She felt the idea was novel enough to get attention from club owners, and be effective as a showcase vehicle. The group did stand-up material and group sketches, such as the one in which Zora played Debbie Duzzit in "Date Night in Hawaii." The group didn't involve itself in any political topics because "people will think we're all dykes who want to destroy men and the family unit and start a revolution for equal bathrooms."

By the end of 1978 she was doing a solo act, and over the next couple of years built up a reputation with her act, billed as "Late Nite Madness," at New York clubs such as Reno Sweeney. Her act consisted of comedy interspersed with songs. The songs were mostly straight pieces done, as one reviewer said, "deeply schlocky." When it came to sentimentality she made Streisand "seem tastefully held back." Zora, referring to these two talents, said jokingly that she was "bi," that she wanted to do both. She admitted that it was hard "to integrate the music and comedy and make it work so you don't sound like a cheeseball." *The Village Voice* felt she had failed in this integration and considered Rasmussen to be a combination of Jerry Lewis and Dean Martin, her own straight person, when you wished Martin would quit the singing so Lewis could get on with the joking: "I wish the split between her comedy and her singing were less pronounced. . . . Zora's singing is not the same calibre as her comedy."

A lot of Rasmussen's humor dealt with what she called "cheese" things, which typified bland American culture such as shopping malls, teased hair and Tupperware. The term derived from the 1950's term "cheesey," used to refer to items like gold-flecked Formica. On stage she sometimes did semi-improvisation by stopping at some point and saying, " Where was I?" To which the audience would respond with a suggestion such as "waitressing." Zora would then improvise a bit such as: "I studied at Woolworth's. I took a six-week course in tuna fish and potato chip arrangement." One of her bits was to bring grape Kool-Aid on stage with her, the agent of the mass suicides in Jonestown, "just in case."

Much of her material revolved around how much of a loser she was as a teenager. "Honey, in high school, I was not cute. Ya know whaddimean? It was like I had a disease or something. People used to cross their fingers when I passed in the hall. I was a real cootie." To confirm this for her audience she then whipped out a large blowup of her high school yearbook photograph for all to see. Pointing to the glasses worn by this girl, she said, "I look like the back of a Plymouth." Her idea of oral sex "was talking about getting married." Speaking of her current sex life, she said, "My life is like Audrey Hepburn's in *The Nun's Story*. Where are the men in uniform nowadays?" Rather than considering her humor to be self-deprecatory, she regarded it as an example of the following philosophy: "Look at how I've come through, and we've all come through, and aren't we all better now?"

Rasmussen found getting started in comedy no harder for women than for men. In fact she thought it may have been a little easier for women since females were starting to find acceptance, audiences were curious to see them, and demand for them was high at the clubs. By the beginning of the 1980's, Zora was thinking of adding some sex gags to her act, which was new material for her. The first time she had sex, she said, she felt like Peggy Lee: "Is that all there is." She was also planning to try and develop character comedy to go with her jokes and monologues.

Zora's comedy came from her personal experiences. The self-deprecation was a mixture of insight and negative exaggeration. She did not downgrade her actual appearance, however. Regarding humor as sexy and armed with a belief that audiences wanted to look at somebody onstage who looked good, Zora pursued an image of glamour. "I want to get an image across. . . . A lot of comediennes play down their looks and become asexual. I want to have sex appeal." This image was not at odds, however, with the image of the physical comic Zora felt she was. While not broadly physical, she did make faces and flap her arms a lot, and she was singularly adept at making herself look cross-eyed.

She was also after respect and didn't want to be tagged as a dumb clown, or have to be always "on." "I'm not some kind of idiot. . . . My humor stems from intelligence. I don't want to always feel like I have to be the life of the party." Her act as a solo didn't get into any kind of feminist issues, for, as a reviewer once commented, "It figures that a woman who knows in her soul that contact lenses and hair dye changed her life is going to prefer facing a room full of Shriners to the stony-faced editors of *Ms.*"

ELAYNE BOOSLER

A twenty-one-year-old with a Farah Fawcett haircut and tan, Elyane Boosler worked as a waitress at New York's Improv. Born in 1953, the Jewish daughter of a Brooklyn tool-and-die manufacturer, she had no intention of becoming a comedienne. Before she knew it, however, she had progressed to introducing male comics and then to doing comedy herself. She eventually moved from the late night slots to prime time at the Improv, and worked campuses and small clubs like the Bottom Line.

As Boosler's career picked up she began opening acts for Helen Reddy, Ben Vereen, and Johnny Mathis. Reddy got her a spot on Carson's "Tonight Show." She moved to Hollywood because, as she said: "In New York they believe I'm in show business now because they can say, 'Fly her in from the Coast!'"

By 1976 comic Jimmy Walker had taken an interest in promoting Boosler's career. Calling her act "a little rough," Walker was convinced that she would be able to "iron it out." "Besides," he noted, "there's no way that being the best-looking female stand-up of all time is going to hurt her either."

Despite this sexist summation, Walker's faith in Boosler was not misplaced. Her material was making people laugh. Describing her home life, Boosler joked,: "My brother's gay. My parents don't mind as long as he marries a doctor." Claiming a close and sharing relationship with her mother, Elayne cracked, "When I got pregnant, my mother got nauseous." Boosler also joked a lot about men. She remembered one date with a foot fetishist. He asked her to have sex, so they went for a walk. She complained that men "want you to scream 'You're the best' while swearing you've never done this with anyone before." And as for the contraceptive sponge, it was "just a way of making sex seem more like doing the dishes." But Boosler wasn't disillusioned about romance: "Hookers! How do they do it? How could any woman sleep with a man without having a dinner and a movie first?"

Elayne's success did not bring immediate wealth. In 1975 she made $3,000 for her comedy work. Between gigs she lived on unemployment benefits and she worked the Improv for free. Only television spots and tonier clubs paid good money. Boosler was not dissatisfied, though. She was writing new jokes and getting inspiration from the likes of Rodney Dangerfield, who told her,

"Forget the bull, just work the material. Kiss it, punch it, lick it, but always work the material."

Elayne felt she was still developing a "comic identity" and had years ahead of her to establish herself. She even worried about the compromises of success, especially in television. She used phrases like "premature ejaculation" and other blue material in her act. "Who wants to work the material all these nights in search of an identity," she said, "and then get up in front of everyone and do 'white bread?'" Perhaps the reason Boosler still hadn't achieved widespread fame into the 1980's was because of her uncompromising stance.

Boosler's "good looks" have brought plenty of wisecracks from male audiences. She got heckled with lines like, "Hey, Elayne, wanna get laid?" or "You're pretty funny for a girl." When a heckler called "Take it off," Elayne replied, "I can't, I have a cold." Another male fan yelled, "Why don't you do a poster?" Countered Boosler, "I'm holding out for a stamp."

She told a *New York Times* interviewer in 1979 about the talk show host who asked her if she ever used "feminine wiles" in her act. "It's true," replied Boosler, "in the middle of a heavy political bit I get an urge to clean up the stage, to line the audience up in neat rows."

At first Elayne (who weighed 110 pounds) stayed away from diet jokes, but then decided that since male comics were using them, and since everyone related to them, she would use them as well: "I'm so compulsive about losing weight, I weigh myself after I cough." Boosler did try to avoid self-deprecatory jokes however.

As a female performer, Boosler was careful about sexism but not dogmatic. She told Mark Jacobson of *New York* magazine in 1976 that she could not use the stage as a forum to discuss women's issues. Commenting on feminists, Boosler said, "Talking about the things they want me to is just as bad as doing pots and pans. And it's not even as funny. They should wake up. I'm a woman and I'm up here trying to be a person, so what the hell do I have to talk about? I'm a woman who's a comic, not a woman's comic."

SANDRA BERNHARD

Sandra Bernhard was a young comedienne who spent five years doing stand-up in Los Angeles in clubs like the Comedy Store before she hit it big in the 1983 film *The King of Comedy*. In this movie directed by Martin Scorsese and starring Jerry Lewis, Bernhard played a lunatic rich girl obsessed with a TV talk show host played by Lewis.

Although 200 actresses auditioned for the part, Bernhard had that special manic quality required for the role. "I love getting crazy over and over," she said. At five feet ten and only 106 pounds, with thick lips and prominent nose, Bernhard had a face and body that could easily convey the offbeat. The movie role required her to be a sexual predator, and her way of throwing a kiss with her huge lips and menacing glare made her, as Scorsese said, "sexually threatening. It was a very subversive form of humor."

It was not only her physical appearance that landed Sandra the part, it was also her superb improvisations that impressed Scorsese. And Bernhard did prove to be brilliant in the film.

Sandra had a typical upper middle-class childhood. Born in 1955 to a proctologist father and artist mother, she grew up in Flint, Michigan, and Arizona. Set apart because of her unusual (though attractive) looks, Sandra decided she wanted to become an entertainer: "I did have a hang-up about my lips when I was growing up. The kids called them 'nigger lips' all the time. I didn't look like anybody else, and that scared people. I was stared at from the time I was able to remember. So I figured that I might as well make some money—if people want to stare at me, let them stare at me on the screen."

After high school, Bernhard spent a year in Israel working on a kibbutz. She then moved to Los Angeles to study voice. To support herself she worked as a manicurist-pedicurist at a posh Beverly Hills salon frequented by stars like Dyan Cannon. Her experience of "waiting on people's farshtunkener feet," as she called them, gave her plenty of material for her act. Her satires on fashion trends and commercials are done in the high-class drawl of the Beverly Hills princess. She'll pick a guy from the audience and in a breathy voice tell him she loves his sweat shirt and tennis shoes: "You're taking a fashion risk and I like that." Angered at the tyranny of clothing trends, she wanted to go around New York kicking the shoulder pads off Norma Kamali dresses.

Yet Bernhard perhaps relied too much on an easy gimmick. A large part of her act consisted of reading fashion ads straight from magazines in a voice which parodied the ice-cool culture of the ad world. "Mmmm. White rum and soda. Liza Minelli introduced me to it at an Andy Warhol party." And sometimes it was hard to separate Bernhard from the culture she was spoofing. Looking extremely stylish, Bernhard delivered a highly polished act.

Because it was hard to pin down just exactly what Sandra was trying to do, she sometimes alienated both male and female audiences. Sexuality was pivotal to her routine. She often fondled her breast while on stage and made lurid suggestions to men in the audience. Feminists felt she exploited her sexuality. Men found her overly aggressive. Never catering to the male ego, Bernhard made it clear that men were only good for one night stands and even those could be a bore: "There's a fine line between eroticism and nausea. When a man twists my breast nonstop for an hour like a computer game, I wanna throw up."

Bernhard was twenty when she performed for the first time. It was at "Ye Little Club" in Los Angeles. At first her act consisted mainly of Bette Midler imitations. Later she still relied heavily on impressions, but her repertoire expanded to include people like Burt Bacharach. Her bizarre introduction to the Bacharach numbers had her claiming to be Burt's girlfriend. She told the audiences that she had just moved in with him after murdering his wife.

Singing remained integral to her routine and she did some of the songs straight without any gags or impressions involved. This tended to make her act choppy, breaking the comic mood.

Like most newcomers, Sandra had a rough time to begin with. She once broke down and cried at the Improv. But she continued working. She appeared at the "Belly Room" at the Comedy Store, which was strictly for female comics. She got a few bit parts in films. Then *The King of Comedy* made her a success. She was just twenty-eight.

Critics have called Bernhard's brand of stand-up "uninhibited, original and radical." She uses her voice to convey humor rather than jokes. Her voice can be sultry but it often turns mocking or mean, as in her Marilyn Monroe routine. Bernhard sings "Happy Birthday to J.F.K." in the vulnerable Monroe voice, then becomes a high society phony: "Oh, Marilyn, we really love you." Sandra then explained that she thought they dug Marilyn up recently to see if she still looked good, and changing her tone to the society bitch again, she cooed: "Oh, Marilyn you look fabulous. Love your hair."

Nothing was sacred to Bernhard. She often made jokes at Jerry Lewis's expense. "I saw him kick one of those kids he was supposed to be helping." Her fantasy about President Ronald Reagan was to fuck him so long he'd die. Like Joan Rivers, Bernhard dropped names constantly, often doing unflattering impressions of those she mentioned. But she didn't spare herself, either. Aware of her own narcissism and arrogance, she joked, "I love sleeping on a full-length mirror."

Bernhard's career seemed to have a solid future. She has appeared on television's the "Tonight Show" with Johnny Carson and on David Letterman's "Late Night." As well as performing in Los Angeles, Bernhard has appeared at New York City's club "Catch a Rising Star." She has also made cross-country tours with her act. She now resides in New York.

Bernhard has described her nightclub act as "not just a stand-up routine. It's like a theater piece. I love live performing and I don't think I'll ever give it up. It's one of those few forms of performing where I can be myself and be totally honest, dealing with the moment, my emotions and the way I'm affecting the audience."

LIZ TORRES

Growing up Puerto Rican in the 1950's in the Hell's Kitchen district of New York City was no laughing matter. Torres's father died when she was fourteen and she shared a fifth floor walk-up with her mother.

But comedienne Torres was later able to joke about her neighborhood, and her experiences at Charles Evans Hughes High School where "girls would go into the washroom and disappear for three years." Though she laughingly complained about the "300-pound" dance teacher at Hughes, it was there that she became interested in dancing and drama.

At fifteen, Liz performed with a children's theater group and then won a scholarship to New York University's drama school.

She still had to earn part of the money to support herself, so the nineteen-year-old Torres took a job as a go-go dancer in 1967. Long working hours and full days at school proved too much to handle, and Liz dropped out of the university.

She took a singing and dancing job with "The Satans and Sinners Revue" and performed with them on the road and in Las Vegas. When the troupe went topless, Liz returned to New York.

Answering an ad for "freaks and weirdos," Liz got her first movie role in Peter Locke's film *You Gotta Walk It Like You Talk It or You'll Lose That Beat*. Though the movie fizzled, Locke and Torres became a hot item and moved in together.

Torres created a comedy act and began working clubs like New York's Improvisation, and eventually Studio One in Los Angeles. A *New York Times* reviewer, catching her act in 1971 at the Improvisation, called her performances "fresh" and "vital" and described her face as "mobile" and "expressive." He found her material uneven, however.

Liz also appeared in a couple of plays and by 1976 was starring in *The Ritz* on Broadway. She also had a few movie roles, such as in *Up the Down Staircase*.

In the 1970's Torres was hired for two television summer variety show. In 1972 she was seen on the "Melba Moore-Clifton Davis Show" and in 1975 on "Ben Vereen's Comin' at Ya." She was also invited on Johnny Carson's show, where her monologue received a standing ovation. Her takeoff of Maria Callas doing Janis Joplin's Greatest Hits was a huge success on the Dean Martin show.

Torres continued to work steadily in television. In 1976 she played Julie Erskine in the situation comedy "Phyllis." In 1976-1977 she played a Puerto Rican hospital worker, Teresa Betancourt, on "All in the Family." And in 1981 she was seen in "Checking In," yet another situation comedy.

In the meantime, she developed her nightclub act, a monologue of up to 40 minutes. Often dressed to the teeth, in white satin leotards, rhinestone belt and flowing scarf, the highly attractive Torres delved into her Latin background. She liked to contrast the poor neighborhoods of New York with the elite districts of Los Angeles. Paranoia in New York, she noted, "was tripping over a hostile transvestite hooker while someone's nudging a knife in your ribs." Paranoia in L.A. was "buying a half-million-dollar house and worrying that Alice Cooper might move in next door."

Moving into the character of a Puerto Rican maid, Cuca, Torres gossiped about everyone on the Beverly Hills/Bel-Air cleaning circuit, including the late Howard Hughes. Cuca claimed to be with a big agency in Los Angeles—not William Morris, though, more like Illegal Alien Domestics.

Torres joked about being named Puerto Rican Woman of the Year: "They didn't bother to give me an award. They just spray-painted my name on the Empire State Building." In another sketch as a loony Latin lady she spoofed Castro and Cuba by smoking a cigar and surrounding herself with two gun-toting bearded lady guerrillas.

Liz Torres was one of the few female performers who claimed she hadn't been troubled by sexism. "Being a girl," she told interviewer Viola Swisher, of *After Dark*, in 1977, "I have little trouble with hecklers, lots of sympathy from the audience. But other than the difference in heckling, forget sex discrimination in comedy. Either something is funny and people will laugh, or it's not and they won't. I like broad comedy, but I never deliberately make myself unattractive. I keep wanting to look gorgeous all the time."

MARSHA WARFIELD

Marsha Warfield has been one of the few black females who has been successful in comedy. Born in 1954 in Chicago's tough south side, Warfield never imagined she would grow up to be a comedienne. She worked as a telephone operator and then married the supervisor's son. She continued to work at clerical jobs but was bored with the nine-to-five routine. She decided on a whim to appear at a Chicago club, "The Pickle Barrel," which had an amateur night.

Her opening line was "I'm a virgin," because that was what new performers were called. She enjoyed performing so much that she split from her husband and moved to Los Angeles. She took a job with an answering service to support herself, and began appearing at the Comedy Store in the mid-1970's on their try-out nights. There she became so comfortable in front of an audience that she felt it was "like talking to friends in my living room."

In 1979 Warfield won the San Francisco International Stand-Up Comedy Competition. This was no small feat, as many top-rated comics such as Robin Williams have entered this competition in past years. Marsha then appeared on several television specials with Richard Pryor, Mac Davis, and Alan King. She also starred in "That Thing on ABC," a variety special. In 1982 she released her first album.

Warfield's material didn't have the depth or bite of Whoopi Goldberg's, which made Marsha a good candidate for television. Her jokes have been lightweight or downright corny: "What do restaurants do with frog arms?" or "Are there black people in Iowa? And if so, why?"

But she did try to convey the experiences of growing up female and included gags about sexual relationships and feminine hygiene products.

Warfield told *Ebony* in 1982 that as a black comedienne she had two strikes against her which made it all the more difficult to succeed. But she joked, "All you can do is try and not let it affect you. I don't let people *not* hire me because I'm Black and a woman."

WHOOPI GOLDBERG

Whoopi Goldberg called herself an actress and not a stand-up comic. She was hailed for her dramatic role in the movie *The Color Purple* (1985) and starred in a comedy film *Jumping Jack Flash* in 1986. But whatever label she chose for herself, audiences reacted to the humor in her pieces with laughs, just as they would for any comic.

Whoopi was born in Manhattan in 1950 and was raised by her mother, a Head Start teacher. Whoopi had an early interest in theater and appeared in children's plays at the Hudson Guild Theater. In the 1960's she gravitated towards the hippies. After a brief marriage, she moved to San Diego in 1974 with her daughter Alexandrea.

Goldberg was on welfare in between jobs such as bricklayer, bank teller, and beautician in a mortuary. On this last, Goldberg commented: "When you work in a beauty parlor, you can't talk back and you can't talk mean. But with dead people you can tell 'em how you really feel: 'I'm glad you're dead. I think you're a bitch.' You can grab their head and go, 'Hey come on. Sit up here. Let's try the Joan Crawford look on you. Nah, that doesn't work. Let's try Lucille Ball.'"

Goldberg joined the San Diego Repertory Theater and took on her stage name "Whoopi Goldberg" because it sounded interesting. She appeared in Brecht's *Mother Courage* and Marsha Norman's *Getting Out*. She then began to do comedy with an improvisational group called Spontaneous Combustion. Goldberg changed to comedy she said because as a black performer "I got tired of people in dinner theaters saying, 'We can't put you and a white guy together, because the folks from Texas can't handle it.'"

In 1981 she joined the avant-garde Blake Street Hawkeyes Theater in Berkeley. She fell in love with one of its founders, David Schein. With Schein's encouragement, Goldberg put together her own act, "The Spook Show," in which she played thirteen different characters. Critics raved about her performance. After touring Europe with Schein, Goldberg did a show in honor of Moms Mabley, which again was highly acclaimed by reviewers.

In 1984 she took her "Spook Show" to Manhattan's Dance Theater Workshop. Her sell-out shows were such a hit that Whoopi was written up in *Newsweek, Ms.*, and *People* magazines. Like Richard Pryor and Lily Tomlin, Goldberg played various characters in her hour-long act. Some of the characters, or "spooks," that she did included Fontaine, a dope fiend. He had a Ph.D. in literature but kept it low key: "I don't like to brag about it, 'cause I can't do jack with it." Sauntering around the stage, scratching his crotch, Fontaine took shots at every imaginable topic. He derided the defunct government CETA program as only good for "learning to part your hair," and described the movie *The Big Chill* as "a lot of motherfuckers sitting around crying about the sixties." Fontaine dismissed Mr. T. as "a guy with a Mohawk I'm supposed to relate to. The motherfucker is a throwback, man."

Fontaine launched into a discourse on his European trip and set the mood by singing "Around the world in eighty muh'fuckin' days." He became both the stewardess on the flight and the overcooked string bean served as part of the airline dinner. In Amsterdam he visited the house where Anne Frank was hidden. The audience tensed up, not seeing any possible joke here, but Fontaine brought it off by being emotional. As a character who would "just as soon kill someone" or "break a guy's legs," Fontaine was moved to tears by Frank's death at the hands of the Nazis: "It kicked my ass. I discovered what I didn't think I had: a heart."

When Whoopi did Fontaine for a student audience at Manhattan Community College she described a trip he took into the European Alps: "The last black person these folks seen was Hannibal." When the audience didn't laugh, Whoopi realized: "You don't know who Hannibal is! Is this a college? Check out the libraries, y'all."

Goldberg's teenage surfer girl character talked about her abortion. When a "mixture of Johnny Walker Red and jumping up and down fifty-six times" failed, she resorted to a coat hanger. After all, she said, "Like you can't go surfing with a baby on your back." When Goldberg performed this character in San Diego, right-to-lifers picketed her act.

One character that Whoopi did was a handicapped girl with a twisted body, head rolling to the side and distorted speech. When she was asked to go dancing, she declined: "This is not a disco body." Like Lily Tomlin, Whoopi has risked using a handicapped character and has done so without being offensive or patronizing.

Also like Tomlin, Whoopi created a character who was a child. Covering her corn-row hair style with a white skirt, Goldberg pretended she had long blond hair and said, "When I get big, I'm going to get on 'The Love Boat' but you have to have long blond hair. I'm going to be blue-eyed and white. I told my mother I didn't want to be black no more." The only problem remaining was how to get white, since "bathing in Clorox" didn't work.

Doing a spoof on a seventy-seven year old Las Vegas habitue, Inez Beaverman, Goldberg talked in a voice made husky by venereal disease and whiskey. Regretting Presidential candidate Jesse Jackson's use of the word "Hymietown," Inez shook her head: "He blew it, dolling. Jesse blew it. He blew it even more because he didn't cop to it. He tried to tippy-tip-tip around. What a shame. It was in the palm of his hand."

Goldberg's style of comedy attracted a broad-based audience. College kids, older folks, middle-class whites, and black people all turned out to see her. None of her shows were identical since Whoopi constantly interacted with her audiences and improvised on their reactions. *Newsweek* praised her characterizations, saying: "Her ability to completely disappear into a role, rather than superficially impersonate comic types, allows her to take some surprising risks."

In October 1984 Whoopi took her act to Broadway. Her show had been arranged by Mike Nichols, who respected her work and described her as "one part Elaine May, one part Groucho, one part Ruth Draper, one part Richard Pryor, and five parts never before seen."

Reviews of the show were generally favorable, although Frank Rich of *The New York Times* felt her sketches were weakened by "sentimental trick endings" and platitudes like "Take somebody by the hand and you are free." Concluded Rich: "Whoopi Goldberg's liberating spirit fills up the theater, even as her considerable comic promise is left waiting to be fully unlocked."

In a July 1984 article in *Vanity Fair*, Goldberg told interviewer Janet Coleman: "The avant-garde theater and the nightclub stage had been a haven, a sanctuary for expressing thoughts that could get you arrested or taken to Bellevue. . . . I want to do good work. I don't think I can compromise that and live. 'Cause if I have to shake my tits or play somebody's fucking maid for the rest of my life, it isn't worth it. My stuff, that's the one thing I know no amount of money can stop me from doin'. 'Cause that's the reason why I'm here on earth. I like to think that Moms and Lenny [Bruce] are leading me. Moms and Lenny are saying, 'Do it. It's going to piss a lot of people off.'"

ROBIN TYLER

Her mother, Tyler joked painfully, wrote her letters beginning "To Whom It May Concern." But Robin Tyler—lesbian, feminist and comic—earned a name for herself. Her radical comedy, political aggressiveness and controversial material has put her in a league with Lenny Bruce.

Tyler pulled no punches. She recognized humor as a weapon and referred to her bookings as war. "The comic's relationship to an audience," she said, "is an extraordinary power struggle. The conflict is usually subtle—the great comics manipulate us without our knowing it. At times, however, the battle is overt: some comics' best lines are devastating put-downs of hecklers. Regardless of how the campaign is waged, final victory comes when the comic has wrested, or the audience has relinquished, control."

Tyler has been known to use the overt method with hecklers. When a man in the front row put his foot on the stage, Robin jokingly asked him to remove it. He told her to fuck off. "Don't worry, darling," she hissed, "You can always be replaced by a Tampax."

Tyler credited lesbianism for her toughness. When she came
out, everyone asked her whether she was femme or butch. When
she heard that femmes were submissive and did the dishes and
housework, she opted for butch. Later she changed to a female-
identified woman. But her butch period gave her the drive to
compete in the male-dominated comedy business.

"I'm aggressive," she told an interviewer for *The Body Politic* in
1979. "We always talk about our right to be assertive. Assertion is
taking your own power, aggression is taking your power over others. I'm going to take power from the people who took power
from me. A comic must be aggressive with an audience. It's not
assertive, it's not sharing. Social satirists and people who deal with
political analysis have to be very strong. They're not just getting
up there and doing self-deprecating jokes."

Tyler learned to be strong as a teenager in Winnipeg when she
openly declared that she was gay. At twenty she moved to New
York City and worked as a singer in nightclubs. She then met
Patti Harrison, a $50,000-a-year model for Vogue and other high
fashion magazines. The pair teamed up as a comedy duo and at
first billed themselves under the unoffensive title "sisters"—Rachel
and Robin Tyler. They played Miami clubs and their material
was traditional woman's comedy. Gradually they became more
radical and began offending audiences.

They cut an album called "Try It You'll Like It." On the cover
was a picture of a man in an electric chair with dynamite wired to
it. Harrison and Tyler stood smiling behind him ready to blow
him up. The caption read "Male Chauvinism." They played San
Francisco's Playboy Club with the justification that they wanted to
perform in places where they could raise people's consciousness.
Suzanne Gordon, a reviewer for *Ms.* magazine, saw them perform
in 1973 at a San Francisco nightclub, "The Boardinghouse." She
was taken aback by their style. "Instead of being in possession of
the stage," wrote Gordon, "they were on the defense." She found
that their feminist material was not comic, but did admire their
humorous attacks on organized religion. Gordon was not comfortable with Harrison and Tyler's hostility, asking: "And doesn't feminism necessarily imply a new comedy, a comedy built not on
masculine put-downs, but on some common and ironic self-vision
that brings the audience along?"

But Tyler would make no apologies: "I think we musn't be
afraid of our own power. If my aggression is threatening to some
women—only some—then I feel I don't have to deal with my
aggression, they have to deal with their lack of it." She ended her

comedy album, "Always a Bridesmaid, Never a Groom," with the statement, "If I've offended any of you, you needed it." To the men in her audience she advised: "If anyone gets insecure, just do a crotch check. It's still there."

Harrison and Tyler worked cooperatively together for five years and cut two comedy albums. They mainly played the college circuit, but once bluffed their way into a USO tour of Vietnam. Their anti-war act was a first in front of American soldiers. They kissed on stage, and their material on poverty, racism, and sexism got them thrown out of the show.

During one of their performances a guy got up and started swearing at them. Thinking he was hitting them with the ultimate insult, he asked, "Are you a lesbian?" Responded Patti, "Are *you* the alternative?"

Harrison and Tyler opened their act by acknowledging audience applause with the line "Thanks for the clap. God knows as women we've had everything else." They asked the men in attendance if they liked makeup. The males applauded. "If you dig it, then why don't you wear it!" countered Harrison.

Complaining about male obsession with female tits and ass, Harrison challenged, "How would you guys like to go through life as nothing but cock and balls, cock and balls."

TYLER: There's all this preoccupation in this country with the size of women's breasts. So we finally figured it out, gang. Women do not have penis envy.

HARRISON: Men have mammary envy.

TYLER: That's because America is built on sucking. If you guys are going to judge us by the size of our breasts, we're gonna judge you by the size of your "wee-wee's."

HARRISON: And we know all men aren't created equal, don't we?

TYLER: Women have been discriminated against for centuries, and why?

HARRISON: Because we can't stand up to pee.

Joking about mindless television commercials, Tyler asked, "How many of you have time to go to your toilet bowl, lift up the lid, and talk to some dumb guy floatin' around in there?" Replied Harrison: "If I saw a guy floating in my toilet, *flush!*"

The comedy team was quick to pick up on sexism in advertising. They used the example of the "You've come a long way, baby, to get where you're going" ad. "Can you imagine," asked Harrison, "doing that to black people?"

"You've come a long way, Negro, To get where you're going today, You've got your own hair spray now, Negro, You've come a long, long way."

One of the ads they found most offensive was the airline's "Fly Me" commercials featuring pretty stewardesses. Joked Tyler, "How would men like it if a guy got up, dressed in a little blue pilot suit with a little white cap, and said, 'Hi, my name is Captain Jack, and I can get it up for you!'"

If Harrison could do her own version, it would be, "'Hi, my name is Helga. I'm with Trans Women's Liberation Airlines. You fly me and I'll kick your fucking ass!'" Tyler once cracked, "I would like to become president of a major TV network, and then I would ban all commercials that make women look like imbeciles—that would mean 24 hours of uninterrupted programming."

They would throw out lines like, "We happen to agree with the 'right-to-lifers' because if you don't agree with them . . . they'll kill you."

Despite the fact that they worked together successfully, Tyler eventually decided to strike out on her own. In an interview for *Lesbian Tide* in 1978 she explained: "In a comedy team you have to have difference. One plays stupid, one smart, one crazy, one sane. I played 'the kid' so I never really went on stage as Robin Tyler, as myself." As a solo performer, she noted, "I don't have to disguise my truth anymore."

And Robin's truth was razor sharp. This cost her some lucrative commercial bookings but as she told *Lesbian Tide*, "It would be easy to compromise. . . . But who cares? All money is to me is a tool to buy my freedom. If I can sustain myself and be successful doing what I want to do, saying what I want to say, what a great privilege that is!"

Still Tyler did appeal to certain audiences. She entertained at colleges, for women's groups, gay groups, and off-Off Broadway. She polished her act at L.A.'s Comedy Store.

Her stage persona was butch. She wore tuxedos, army shirts, and leather jackets, although she did tone this down for straight audiences.

Tyler's routine included a take-off on the birth of Jesus. Mary was the stereotypical Jewish mother. Arriving in Bethlehem with Joseph she *oy veyed* every time the donkey bounced her around. She nagged Joseph for bringing her to a dump like the stable, and proceeded to disinfect it with Lysol. She bellowed as she gave birth to Jesus and all in all made a mockery of the holy night. If the mother of God was not sacred, neither was her own. She once joked: "My mother said I drove her crazy. I did not drive my mother crazy. I flew her there. It was faster."

Other themes for Tyler were growing up Jewish, coming out as a lesbian, politics (Jimmy Carter was dumb enough to get born again and come back as himself) and macho men ("What are they playing with down there? Why don't they adjust it before they go out?"). She came out in favor of unionism, the elderly and minorities. Her symbol for the Democratic party was a classic: "I think," she said, "the Democratic emblem should be changed from a donkey to a prophylactic. It's perfect. It supports inflation, keeps production down, helps a bunch of pricks and gives a false sense of security when one is being screwed."

Tyler believed that every oppressed group like Jews or Blacks have had its share of comics ("I laugh that I may not weep"). Women and gays were now having their turn on stage. "Humor comes from pain," Tyler commented, but at first she didn't know how to make her anger funny. She learned not to be the brunt of jokes but to satirize an oppressive society. Tyler felt that comics like Joan Rivers and Phyllis Diller didn't have the support systems of women's groups that are available now, and so we can't blame them for using self-deprecating jokes. These women, she said, "did what they had to do. Since men controlled the media, they would only allow these women to be aggressive if they turned it on themselves."

As she admitted, Tyler herself started out in mainstream clubs with safe material and even appeared on ABC television in the Croft Comedy Hour. She was not happy as the show's "star" because she felt isolated and wasn't in control of her own product. With the coming of cable television, Tyler hoped there would be opportunities for more women producers and thus a potential medium for radical feminist comics.

When she went on the alternative circuit, Robin was free to make women the subjects, not the objects, of her humor. After all, as Tyler concluded: "They always said the women's movement had no sense of humor. Well, we do. It's just that we laugh when the joke's not on us."

Sources

Women and Humor

Allen, Robert Thomas. Women Have No Sense of Humor. *Maclean's*. 64:18+, June 1, 1951.

Allen, Robert Thomas. Women Have No Sense of Humor. *Reader's Digest*. 84:134-136, April 1964.

Austin, Mary. The Sense of Humor in Women. *New Republic*. 41:10-13, November 26, 1924.

Beatts, Anne. Can a Woman Get a Laugh and a Man Too? *Mademoiselle*. 81:140+, November 1975.

Burdette, Robert J. Have Women a Sense of Humor? *Harper's Bazar*. 36:597-98, July 1902.

Cantor, Joanne R. What Is Funny to Whom? The Role of Gender. *Journal of Communication*. 26:164-172, Summer 1976.

Coquelin, Constant. Have Women a Sense of Humor? *Harper's Bazar*. 34:67-69, Jan. 12, 1901.

Eimerl, Sarel. Can Women Be Funny? *Mademoiselle*. 56:150+, November 1962.

Fisher, John. *Funny Way to Be a Hero*. London: Frederick Muller, pp. 197-210, 1973.

Fisher, Seymour and Fisher, Rhoda L. *Pretend the World Is Funny and Forever*. Hillsdale, N.J., Lawrence Erlbaum Assoc., 1981.

Fury, Kathleen. Okay, Ladies, What's the Joke? *Redbook*. 155:163+, June 1980.

Janus, Samuel. Humor, Sex, and Power in American Society. *American Journal of Psychoanalysis*. 41(2):161-167, Summer 1981.

Levine, Joan B. The Feminine Routine. *Journal of Communication*. 26(3):173-175, Summer 1976.

Losco, Jean and Epstein, Seymour. Humor Preference as a Subtle Measure of Attitudes Toward the Same and the Opposite Sex. *Journal of Personality*. 43:32-34, June 1975.

Newell, Margaretta. Are Women Humorous? *Outlook and Independent*. 159:206+, October 14, 1931.

Thurber, James. They Don't Seem to Know It. *Maclean's*. 64:19+ June 1, 1951.

Trotter, Elizabeth Stanley. Humor with a Gender. *Atlantic Monthly*. 130:784-787, Dec. 1922.

Weisstein, Naomi. Why We Aren't Laughing Any More. *Ms*. 2:49+, May 1974.

Witty, Susan. The Laugh-Makers. *Psychology Today*. 17:22+, August 1983.

Aillman, Dolf and Stocking S. Holly. Putdown Humor. *Journal of Communication*. 26(3):164-172, Summer 1976.

1860 to 1919

Franklin, Joe. *Joe Franklin's Encyclopedia of Comedians*. Secaucus, N.J.: Citadel Press, 1979.

Fussell, Betty Harper. *Mabel*. New Haven: Ticknor & Fields, 1982.

Gilbert, Douglas. *American Vaudeville: Its Life and Times*. N.Y.: Whittlesey House, 1940.

Laurie, Joe Jr. *Vaudeville: From the Honky-Tonks to the Palace*. N.Y.: Henry Holt and Co., 1953.

McLean, Albert F. Jr. *American Vaudeville as Ritual*, Lexington, Kentucky: University of Kentucky Press, 1965.

Maltin, Leonard. *The Great Movie Comedians*. N.Y.: Crown Publishers, 1978.

Mordden, Ethan. *Movie Star: A Look at the Women Who Made Hollywood*. N.Y.: St. Martin's Press, 1983.

Samuels, Charles. *Once Upon a Stage*. N.Y.: Dodd, Mead & Co., 1974.

Slide, Anthony. *The Vaudevillians*. Westport, Conn.: Arlington House, 1981.

Smith, Bill. *The Vaudevillians*. N.Y.: Macmillian, 1976.

Staples, Shirley Louise. *From Barney's Courtship to Burns and Allen: Male-Female Comedy Teams in American Vaudeville, 1865-1932*. Ph.D. Thesis. Medford, Mass.: Tufts University, 1981.

Swortzell, Lowell. *Here Come the Clowns*. N.Y.: The Viking Press, 1978.

LOTTA CRABTREE

An Actress Who Gives Millions to Crippled Veterans. *Literary Digest*. 83:30-31, October 18, 1924.

Brown, Dee. *The Gentle Tamers: Women of the Old Wild West*. Lincoln, Neb.: University of Nebraska Press, 1958, pp. 14, 175-178.

Dempsey, David. *Triumphs and Trials of Lotta Crabtree*. N.Y.: Morrow, 1968.

An Irish Tribute to Lotta. *Living Age*. 323:399-400 November 15, 1924.

Liberty's Women. Springfield, Mass.: G & C Merriam, 1980, p. 83.

Lotta and the Soldiers. *Outlook*. 138:190, October 8, 1924.

Notable American Women. Cambridge, Mass.: Belknap Pr. of Harvard U. Pr., 1971.

Whitton, Mary Ormsbee. *These Were the Women, U.S.A. 1776-1860*. N.Y.: Hastings House, 1954, pp. 201-203.

MAY IRWIN

Cahn, William. *A Pictorial History of the Great Comedians*. N.Y.: Grosset & Dunlop, 1970.

A chat with May Irwin. *New York Times*. Dec. 25, 1898, p. 15.

Dictionary of American Biography. sup. 2 1958, pp. 335-337.

Irwin, May. I Want to Live to Be a Hundred. *Green Book Magazine*. 10:441+, Sept. 1913.

Irwin, May. My Views on that Ever-Interesting Topic—Women. *Green Book Magazine*. 8:1057+, Dec. 1912.

Liberty's Women. Springfield, Mass.: G & C Merriam, 1980, pp. 206-207.

McLean, Albert F. Jr. *American Vaudeville as Ritual*. Lexington, Kentucky: University of Kentucky Press, 1965, pp. 175-177.

May Irwin Forever. *New York Times*. April 13, 1917, p. 11.

May Irwin Dead. *New York Times*. Oct. 23, 1938, p. 41.

Notable American Women. Cambridge, Mass.:Belknap Pr. of Harvard University Pr., 1971, pp. 257-258.

Secretary of Laughter. *New York Times*. Oct. 24, 1938, p. 16.
Slide, Anthony. *The Vaudevillians*. Westport, Conn.: Arlington House. 1981.
Some of May Irwin's Ideas. *New York Times*. Nov. 19, 1899, p. 18.
A Stage Woman as a Cook. *New York Times*. Dec. 5, 1897, p. 14.
The Theatres. *New York Times* supplement. Jan. 17, 1897, p. 6.
Walsh, Jim. May Irwin. *Hobbies*. 68:35+ June 1963 & 32+ July 1963.
Williams, Wythe. Past Laughter. *Saturday Evening Post*. 203:42+, April 25, 1931.
Wilson Sees May Irwin. *New York Times*. Sept. 25, 1915, p. 11.
The Woman Who Dared. *Munsey's Magazine*. 22:590-592, Jan. 1900.

MARIE DRESSLER

Cahn, William. *A Pictorial History of the Great Comedians*. N.Y.: Grosset & Dunlop, 1970, pp. 118-122.
A Chat with Marie Dressler. *New York Times*. June 22, 1930, sec. 8. p. 2.
Dressler, Marie. *Life Story of an Ugly Duckling*. Boston: Little Brown, 1934.
For Hollywood to Ponder. *Commonweal*. 20:358, Aug. 10, 1934.
Kennedy, John B. Working Girl. *Collier's*. 86:16+, Nov. 1, 1930.
Liberty's Women. Springfield, Mass.: G & C Merriam, 1980, p. 108.
Maltin, Leonard. *The Great Movie Comedians*. N.Y.: Crown, 1978, pp. 90-101.
Marie Dressler Returns. *New York Times*. Nov. 28, 1923, p. 14.
Notable American Women. Cambridge, Mass.: Belknap Pr. of Harvard U. Pr., 1971, pp. 519-521.
Shipman, David. *The Great Movie Stars: The Golden Years*. London: Hamlyn, 1971, pp. 170-173.
Slide, Anthony. *The Vaudevillians*. Westport, Conn.: Arlington House, 1981, pp. 39-40.
They Stand Out From the Crowd. *Literary Digest*. 116:11, Oct. 7, 1933.
Tugboat Annie. *Time*. 22:23+, Aug. 7, 1933.
Turner, Zan. Marie Dressler. *Films in Review*. 26:419+, Aug. 1975.

TRIXIE FRIGANZA

Milestones. *Time*. 65:92, March 14, 1955.
Samuels, Charles. *Once Upon a Stage*. N.Y.: Dodd, Mead, 1974, pp. 111-112.
Slide, Anthony. *The Vaudevillians*. Westport, Conn.: Arlington House. 1981, pp. 60-61.
Trixie Friganza at Palace. *New York Times*. April 23, 1918, p. 11.
Trixie Friganza Is Dead at 84. *New York Times*. Feb. 28, 1955, p. 19.

IRENE FRANKLIN

Irene Franklin, 65, Dies in Englewood. *New York Times*. June 17, 1941, p. 21.
Samuels, Charles. *Once Upon a Stage*. N.Y.: Dodd, Mead, 1974, pp. 76-80.
Slide, Anthony. *The Vaudevillians*. Westport, Conn.: Arlington House 1981, pp. 57-58.
Stevens, O. Artist in Vaudeville. *Cosmopolitan*. 56:120-121, Dec. 1913.

ELSIE JANIS

Elsie Janis. *National Magazine*. 53:128, Sept. 1924.
Elsie Janis. *Green Book Magazine*. 14:716, Oct. 1915.
Elsie Janis Gives a Concert. *National Magazine*. 52:319, Dec. 1923.

Elsie Janis Is Dead in California. *New York Times*. Feb. 28, 1956, pp. 1, 25.

Elsie Janis Turns Back. *News-Week*. 8:26, July 18, 1936.

Gould, Jack. Elsie Janis Again Brightens Times Square. *New York Times*. Jan. 8, 1939, sec. 9, p. 3.

James, Edwin. L. Elsie Janis Wins Her Paris Audience. *New York Times*. May 14, 1921, p. 10.

Janis, Elsie, Is Imitation the Sincerest Flattery? *Saturday Evening Post*. 26:14+, Sept. 1925.

Janis, Elsie. The Story of My Life. *American Magazine*. 84:33-35+, Nov. 1917.

The Lady of a Million Laughs. *National Magazine*. 51:413-415, Feb. 1923.

Milestones. *Time*. 67:110, March 12, 1956.

Miss Elsie Janis Arrives in London. *New York Times*. Apr. 5, 1914, sec. 8, p. 6.

Orders from G.H.Q. *Time*. 28:37, July 20, 1936.

The Play. *New York Times*. Jan. 2, 1939, p. 28.

Radio. *News-Week*. 5:24 Jan. 12, 1935.

Samuels, Charles. *Once Upon A Stage*. N.Y.: Dodd, Mead & Co., 1974, pp. 67-73.

Slide, Anthony. *The Vaudevillians*. Westport Conn.: Arlington House, 1981, pp. 77-79.

Transition. *Newsweek*. 47:74, March 12, 1956.

The Ubiquitous Miss Janis. *New York Times*. Feb. 8, 1925, sec. 7, p. 1.

Woollcott, Alexander. The Uncanny Janis. *New York Times*. Jan. 17, 1922, p. 13.

NORA BAYES

After the Play. *New Republic*. 14:297, April 6, 1918.

Bayes, Nora. Why People Enjoy Crying in a Theater. *American Magazine*. 85:33-35, April 1918.

Liberty's Women. Springfield, Mass.: G & C Merriam Co., 1980, p. 25.

Nora Bayes Dies After Operation. *New York Times*. March 20, 1928, p. 27.

Notable American Women. Cambridge, Mass.: Belknap Pr. of Harvard U. Pr., 1971. pp. 116-117.

Samuels, Charles. *Once Upon a Stage*. N.Y.: Dodd, Mead & Co., 1974, pp. 80-88.

Slide, Anthony. *The Vaudevillians*. Westport, Conn.: Arlington House, 1981, pp. 6-7.

Sophie Tucker Wins Over Nora Bayes. *New York Times*. April 6, 1926, p. 26.

EVA TANGUAY

Eva Tanguay Dies. *New York Times*. Jan. 12, 1947, p. 59.

Green, Abel. *Show Biz: From Vaude to Video*. N.Y.: Henry Holt, 1951, pp. 28-9, 171-2.

Liberty's Women. Springfield, Mass.: G & C Merriam Co., 1980, p. 404.

McLean, Albert F. Jr. *American Vaudeville as Ritual*. Lexington, Kent.: Univ. of Kentucky Press, 1965, pp. 23, 61, 63.

Notable American Women. Cambridge, Mass.: Belknap Pr. of Harvard U. Pr., 1971, pp. 425-427.

Samuels, Charles. *Once Upon A Stage*. N.Y.: Dodd, Mead, 1974, pp. 54-66.

Slide, Anthony. *The Vaudevillians*. Westport, Conn.: Arlington House, 1981, pp. 146-8.

Tanguay Left No Will. *New York Times*. Jan. 24. 1947, p. 16.

SOPHIE TUCKER

Current Biography 1945, pp. 626+.

50 Years of Sophie. *Newsweek*. 42:80, Oct. 5, 1953.

Franklin, Joe. *Joe Franklin's Encyclopedia of Comedians*. Secaucus, N.J.: Citadel Pr., 1979, pp. 316-7.

Green, Abel. *Show Biz: From Vaude to Video*. N.Y.: Henry Holt, 1951, pp. 102-6.

I Love Them All. *Newsweek*. 67:91B, Feb. 21, 1966.

Milestone for a "Red-Hot Mama." *Theater Arts*. 37:12. Oct. 1953.

Millstream, Gilbert. First of the Red Hot Mamas. *New York Times Magazine*. Sept. 27, 1953, p. 19.

Miss Show Business. *Coronet*. 29:6 March 1951.

Notable American Women. Cambridge, Mass.: Belknap Pr. of Harvard U. Pr., 1971, pp. 699-700.

Red-Hot Sophie. *Newsweek*. 106:25, March 26, 1945.

Roberts, Katharine. Your Gal Sophie. *Collier's*. 101:26+, Feb. 19, 1938.

Samuels, Charles. *Once Upon A Stage*. N.Y.: Dodd, Mead, 1974, pp. 90-101.

Slide, Anthony. *The Vaudevillians*. Westport, Conn.: Arlington House, 1981, pp. 154-6.

Sophie Tucker Dies Here at 79. *New York Times*. Feb. 10, 1966, pp. 1&31.

Tucker, Sophie. *Some of These Days*. N.Y.: Doubleday, 1945.

BEATRICE HERFORD

Beatrice Herford, Monologuist, dies. *New York Times*. July 20, 1952, p. 52.

Draper, Ruth. *The Art of Ruth Draper*. London: Oxford U. Pr., 1960.

The Famous Beatrice Herford Monologues. *Ladies Home Journal*. 24:21, Oct. 1907.

The Famous Beatrice Herford Monologues. *Ladies Home Journal*. 24:15, Nov. 1907.

Herford. The Frivolous Side. *Harper's Magazine*. 124:317-20, Jan. 1912.

Hoyt, Eleanor. Beatrice Herford in Private Life. *Ladies Home Journal*. 23:35, May 1906.

Makes Vaudeville Debut. *New York Times*. Mar. 16, 1915, p. 11.

Miss Herford in Monologues. *New York Times*. Feb. 4, 1902, p. 6.

Miss Herford's Monologues. *New York Times*. Jan. 30, 1900, p. 7.

O'Hagan, Anne. The Art of Facial Expression. *Harper's Bazar*. 40:502+, June 1906.

Parker, Dorothy. A One-Woman Show. *Everybody's Magazine*. 44:34, March 1921.

Russell, Elizabeth H. The Home of Miss Beatrice Herford. *House Beautiful*. 39:6+, Dec. 1915.

Russell, Elizabeth H. Where Beatrice Herford Plays Store. *House Beautiful*. 42:12+, June 1917.

Second Thoughts on First Nights. *New York Times*. March 21, 1915, sec.7, p. 8.

Those Herford Monologues. *New York Times*. March 14, 1915, sec.7, p. 8.

RUTH DRAPER

Bellamy, Francis B. The Theatre. *Outlook and Independent*. 15:472, Mar. 20, 1929.

Ciardi, John. The Genius of Ruth Draper. *Saturday Review*. 44:90, Oct. 14, 1961.

Draper, Ruth. *The Art of Ruth Draper*. London: Oxford U. Pr., 1960.
Draper, Ruth. *The Letters of Ruth Draper, 1920-1956*. N.Y.: Charles Scribner, 1979.
Little Genius. *Time*. 63:52, Feb. 8, 1954.
Miss Ruth Draper. *New Republic*. 26:111, March 23, 1921.
National Cyclopaedia of American Biography. 45:292, 1962.
Notable American Women. Cambridge, Mass.: Belknap Pr. of Harvard U. Pr., 1971, pp. 699-700.
Origo, Iris. Ruth Draper. *Atlantic Monthly*. 202:56+, Oct. 1958.
Rosemary, That's for Ruth Draper. *New Yorker*. 29:64, Feb. 6, 1954.
Ruth Draper, *Commonweal*. 59:576, March 12, 1954.
Ruth Draper. *Catholic World*. 178:468-9, March 1954.
Ruth Draper. *Commonweal*. 23:524, March 6, 1936.
Ruth Draper-Dramatist. *Commonweal*. 11:283+, Jan. 8, 1930.
A Theater Rolled into One. *Literary Digest*. 100:23, Feb. 9, 1929.

MABEL NORMAND

Cahn, William. *A Pictorial History of the Great Comedians*. N.Y.: Grosset & Dunlop, 1970, pp. 98-100.
Franklin, Joe, *Joe Franklin's Encyclopedia of Comedians*. Secaucus, N.J.: Citadel Pr., 1979, pp. 253-254.
Fussell, Betty Harper. *Mabel*. New Haven: Ticknor & Fields, 1982.
Lahue, Kalton C. *Clown Princes and Court Jesters*. London: Thomas Yoseloff, 1970, pp. 258-266.
Lahue, Kalton. *World of Laughter*. Norman, Okla.: U. of Oklahoma Pr., 1966, pp. 71-87.
Liberty's Women. Springfield, Mass.: G & C Merriam, 1980, p. 305.
Mabel Normand, Film Star, Dead. *New York Times*. Feb 24, 1930, pp. 1,24.
Maltin, Leonard. *The Great Movie Comedians*. N.Y.: Crown Pub., 1978, pp. 12-21.
Marx, Arthur. *Goldwyn: A Biography of the Man behind the Myth*. N.Y.: W. W. Norton, 1976, pp. 82-111.
Normand, Stephen. Mabel Normand. *Films in Review*. 25:385-397, Aug/Sept. 1974
Notable American Women. Cambridge, Mass.: Belknap Pr. of Harvard U. Pr., 1971. pp. 635-637.
Ohio Bars Normand Films. *New York Times*. Jan. 10, 1924, p. 18.

LOUISE FAZENDA

Busby, Marquis You Don't Have to Be Beautiful. *Photoplay*. 37:47+, Jan. 1930.
Carr, Harry. Louise Gives a Party. *Motion Picture Classic*. 21:20+, April 1925.
Corliss, Allen. Fazenda—Comic Venus. *Photoplay*. *13:67+, April 1918.*
Crowther, Bosley, Louise Fazenda. *New York Times*. Jan. 30, 1938, sec. 10, p. 4.
Lahue, Kalton C. *Clown Princes and Court Jesters*. London: Thomas Yoseloff, 1970, pp. 147-155.
Louise Fazenda. *Films in Review*. 13:444-446, Aug/Sept. 1962.
Louise Fazenda Is Dead at 67. *New York Times*. April 18, 1962, p. 39.
Notes on New Pictures. *New York Times*. June 13, 1937, sec. 11, p. 4.
Obit. *Time*. 79:86, April 27, 1962.
Roberts Katharine. The Lady Can Take it. *Collier's*. 101:19, June 11, 1938.

Squier, Emma-Lindsay. And They Said She Couldn't Cook. *Photoplay.* 16:64+, Nov. 1919.

POLLY MORAN

Busby, Marquis. Three's a Crowd. *Photoplay.* 38:77+, June 1930.
Polly Moran, 66, Veteran of Films. *New York Times.* Jan. 26, 1952, p. 13.
Severance, Constance. Polly of the Laughs. *Photoplay.* 10:99+, Sept. 1916.
Spensley, Dorothy. Miss Moran, To You, Sir. *Motion Picture Classic.* 31:65, Aug. 1930.

The 1920's and 1930's

Dunning, John. *Tune In Yesterday.* Englewood Cliffs, N.J.: Prentice-Hall, 1976.
Harmon, Jim. *The Great Radio Comedians.* Garden City, N.Y.: Doubleday, 1970.
Menken, Harriet. Laughs from the Ladies. *Delineator.* 129:64-66 Aug. 1936.
Staples, Shirley Louise. *From Barney's Courtship to Burns and Allen: Male-Female Comedy Teams in American Vaudeville, 1865-1932.* Ph.D. Thesis. Medford, Mass.: Tufts University, 1981.
Wertheim, Arthur F. *Radio Comedy.* N.Y.: Oxford U. Press, 1979.

FANNY BRICE

Cahn, William. *A Pictorial History of the Great Comedians.* N.Y.: Grosset & Dunlop, 1970, pp. 66-68.
Cantor, Eddie. *Take My Life.* Garden City, N.Y.: Doubleday, 1957, pp. 42-50.
A Comedy Genius. *Literary Digest.* 117:20, June 2, 1934.
Current Biography 1946, pp. 73-75.
Debus, Allen. The Records of Fanny Brice. *Hobbies.* 61:34+, Mar. 1956.
Dunning, John. *Tune In Yesterday.* Englewood Cliffs, N.J.: Prentice-Hall, 1976. pp. 51-54, 216.
Grandmother Snooks. *Newsweek. 27:60, March 11, 1946.*
Harmon, Jim. *The Great Radio Comedians.* Garden City, N.Y.: Doubleday, 1970, pp. 18-22.
Katkov, Norman. *Fabulous Fanny.* N.Y.: Knopf, 1953.
Liberty's Women. Springfield, Mass.: G & C Merriam, 1980, pp. 51-52.
Notable American Women. Cambridge, Mass.: Belknap Pr. of Harvard U. Pr., 1971, pp. 107-108.
Slide, Anthony. *The Vaudevillians.* Westport, Conn.: Arlington House, 1981, pp. 15-17.
Sugrue, Thomas. Little Jumbo. *American Magazine.* 123:48+, Jan. 1937.
Swortzell, Lowell. *Here Come the Clowns.* N.Y.: Viking Pr., 1978, p. 150-151.
Wertheim, Arthur F. *Radio Comedy.* N.Y.: Oxford U. Press. 1979, pp. 368-376.

CHARLOTTE GREENWOOD

Charlotte Greenwood in Skit "Movieland." *New York Times.* June 28, 1927, p. 29.
Charlotte Greenwood, 87. *New York Times.* Feb. 14, 1978, p. 38.
Comediennes Furnish Lots of Fun at Palace. *New York Times.* June 21, 1927, p. 29.

Crichton, Kyle. Lady Longlegs. *Collier's.* 101:15+, Jan. 15, 1938.

Franklin, Joe. *Joe Franklin's Encyclopedia of Comedians.* Secaucus, N.J.: Citadel Press, 1979, pp. 152-154.

Long-Legged Letty. *Newsweek.* 10:24-25, Oct. 18, 1937.

Mullet, Mary B. A Tall, Thin, Awkward Girl Becomes a Broadway Star. *American Magazine.* 96:34+, Dec. 1923.

New Musical. *Newsweek.* 37:35, Jan. 1, 1951.

Norton, Elliot. Miss Greenwood Becomes a Goddess. *New York Times.* Dec. 17, 1950, sec. 2, pp. 3-4.

Slide, Anthony. *The Vaudevillians.* Westport, Conn.: Arlington House, 1981, pp. 63-64.

Splendid Vaudeville Bills. *New York Times.* March 9, 1926, p. 20.

BEATRICE LILLIE

Abramson, Martin. Queen Bea of Comedy. *Coronet.* 34:87-94, June 1953.

An Evening with Beatrice Lillie. *Newsweek.* 40:88, Oct. 13, 1952.

Bea Lillie. *Life.* 33:61+, Oct. 20, 1952.

Brown, John Mason. Queen Bea. *Saturday Review.* 35:26-27, Oct. 25, 1952.

Coward, Noel. An Old Friend Gives the Low-down on Lillie. *Life.* 56:129+, May 15, 1964.

Current Biography 1945, pp. 347-350.

Current Biography 1964, pp. 255-258.

Hayes, Richard. An Evening with Beatrice Lillie. *Commonweal.* 57:62+, Oct. 24, 1952.

Kolodin, Irvine. Queen Bea. *Saturday Review.* 39:47, Feb. 25, 1956.

Lillie, Beatrice. Every Other Inch a Lady. Garden City, N.Y.: Doubleday, 1972.

Marshall, Margaret, Beatrice Lillie. *Nation.* 175:365, Oct. 18, 1952.

Nathan, George Jean. Lillie the Lulu. *Newsweek.* 13:29, Jan. 30, 1939.

Old Favorite in Manhattan. *Time.* 60:57, Oct. 13, 1952.

Pearly Hoop of an Early Hoopster. *Life.* 45:18-19, Nov. 10, 1958.

Queen Bea, *Stereo Review,* 43:114, Sept. 1979.

Queen Bea Recaptures Broadway. *Literary Digest.* 120:18, Nov. 2, 1935.

Tynan, Kenneth. The Lady Is a Clown. *Holiday.* 20:96+, Sept. 1956.

Woolf, S.J. Beatrice Lillie's Recipe for Laughter. *New York Times Magazine.* Nov. 26, 1944, p. 13.

Young, Stark. Beatrice Lillie. *New Republic.* 50:169-170, March 30, 1927.

MOLLY PICON

Atkinson, Brooks. East Side Broadway. *New York Times.* Feb. 22, 1927, sec. 7, p. 1.

Barclay, Dorothy. Sweetheart of Second Avenue. *New York Times.* Nov. 13, 1949, sec. 2, p. 2.

Current Biography 1951, pp. 488-490.

Jules Bledsoe Makes Hit at the Palace. *New York Times.* July 1, 1929, p. 31.

Molly Picon. *New York Times.* Jan. 26, 1930, sec. 8, p. 4.

Picon, Molly. *Molly!* N.Y.: Simon & Schuster, 1980.

Schnack, William. Athos, Porthos and Miss Molly Picon. *New York Times.* Feb. 1, 1931, sec. 8, p. 2.

Slide, Anthony. *The Vaudevillians.* Westport, Conn.: Arlington House, 1981, p. 117.

GRACIE FIELDS

Caruso's Successor. *Time.* 31:22, Feb. 28, 1938.

Current Biography 1941, pp. 274-275.

Dolson, Hildegarde. Our Gracie. *Reader's Digest.* 42:22-26, April 1943.

Dunning, John. *Tune In Yesterday.* Englewood Cliffs, N.J.: Prentice-Hall, 1976, pp. 243-244.

Gracie Fields. *Life.* 13:124+, Dec. 21, 1942.

Grycie. *Time.* 40:59+, Nov. 9, 1942.

Heylbut, Rose. The Secret of Public Reaction. *Etude.* 61:100+, Feb. 1943.

Lancashire Lass. *Newsweek.* 20:80-81, Oct. 9, 1942.

Moules, Joan. *Our Gracie.* London: Robert Hall, 1983.

The Nightclub Beat. *Theatre Arts.* 26:797c, Dec. 1942.

Obit. *Newsweek.* 94:57, Oct. 8, 1979.

Obit. *Time.* 114:106, Oct. 8, 1979.

Our Gracie. *Time.* 50:52, Sept. 1, 1947.

Shipman, David. *The Great Movie Stars: The Golden Years.* London: Hamlyn, 1971, pp. 191-194.

Short, Ernest Henry. *Ring Up The Curtain.* Freeport, N.Y.: Books for Libraries Press, 1970, pp. 208-213.

The Star Can Act, Too. *Newsweek.* 51:62, March 31, 1958.

DUNCAN SISTERS

The Duncan Sisters. *New York Times.* Jan. 4, 1925, sec. 7, p. 1.

Duncan Sisters Give Travesty at Palace. *New York Times.* Nov. 15, 1927, p. 27.

Duncan Sisters Go into bankruptcy. *New York Times.* Dec. 8, 1931, p. 32.

Franklin, Joe. *Joe Franklin's Encyclopedia of Comedians.* Secaucus, N.J.: Citadel Press, 1979, pp. 118-120.

Lamparski, Richard. *Whatever Became of? . . . 3d ed.* N.Y.: Crown, 1970, pp. 158-159.

Mullett, Mary B. Two Girls Who Have Laughed Their Way to Fame. *American Magazine.* 100:19+, Aug. 1925.

Obit. *Time.* 74:98, sec. 14, 1959.

Slide, Anthony. *The Vaudevillians.* Westport, Conn.: Arlington House, 1981, pp. 40-2.

Walsh, Jim. The Duncan Sisters. *Hobbies.* 60:26+, Sept. 1955.

HELEN KANE

Esterow, Milton. Then and Now. *New York Times Magazine.* March 18, 1956, p. 49.

Franklin, Joe. *Joe Franklin's Encyclopedia of Comedians. Secaucus, N.J.: Citadel Press, 1979, pp. 178-179.*

Helen Kane Dead. *New York Times.* Sept. 27, 1966, p. 47.

Helen Kane Sings Baby Songs at Palace. *New York Times.* June 3, 1929, p. 27.

Lunacy Trio Stirs Hilarity at Palace. *New York Times.* Nov. 11, 1929, p. 20.

Obit. *Newsweek.* 68:78, Oct. 10, 1966.

Obit. *Time.* 88:114, Oct. 7, 1966.

Up from the Paramount. *New York Times.* Nov. 11, 1928, sec. 10, p. 2.

BELLE BARTH

Belle Barth Dead. *New York Times.* Feb. 16, 1971, p. 37.

Franklin, Joe. *Joe Franklin's Encyclopedia of Comedians.* Secaucus, N.J.: Citadel Press, 1979, p. 48.
Obit. *Time.* March 1, 1971, p. 62.

GRACIE ALLEN

Burns, George. Gracie Allen as I Know Her. *Independent Woman.* 19:198+, July 1940.
Burns, George. *I Love Her, That's Why.* N.Y.: Simon & Schuster, 1955.
Burns, George. *Living It Up.* N.Y.: G.P. Putnam's Sons, 1976.
Burns and Allen. *Newsweek.* 49:94, June 24, 1957.
Burns Without Allen. *Time.* 71:46, March 3, 1958.
Candidette. *Time.* 35:36, March 18, 1940.
Current Biography 1951, pp. 75-77.
Discreet Silence. *Time.* 32:21, Dec. 26, 1938.
Dumont, Lou. George Burns & Gracie Allen. *Hobbies.* 84:93+, Sept. 1979.
Dunning, John. *Tune In Yesterday.* Englewood Cliffs, N.J.: Prentice-Hall, 1976, pp. 102-105.
Films of Gracie Allen. *Films in Review.* 16:57, Jan. 1965.
Foster, Inez Whiteley. Gracie Isn't So Dumb Off the Air. *Independent Woman.* 26:292+, Oct. 1947.
Gracie Ends Act with George. *Life.* 45:87, Sept. 22, 1958.
Mitz, Rick. *The Great TV Sitcom Book.* N.Y.: Richard Marek, 1980, pp. 33-37.
Morris, Jane Kesner. Gracie Allen's Own Story. *Womans Home Companion.* 80:40+, March 1953.
Notable American Women: The Modern Period. Cambridge, Mass.: Belknap Pr. of Harvard U. Pr., 1980, pp. 13-14.
A Ray of Sunshine. *Newsweek.* 87:57, March 1, 1976.
Slide, Anthony. *The Vaudevillians.* Westport, Conn.: Arlington House, 1981, pp. 19-21.
Straight Man. *Time.* 42:58, Dec. 13, 1943.
Treadwell, Bill. *50 years of American Comedy.* N.Y.: Exposition Pr., 1951, pp. 149-50.
Wertheim, Arthur F. *Radio Comedy.* N.Y.: Oxford U. Pr., 1979, pp. 195-209.

JANE ACE

Aces Up. *Time.* 50:59-60, Sept. 8, 1947.
The Aces Move. *Time.* 40:90-91, Nov. 2, 1942.
Asy Eaces. *Newsweek.* 20:84-85, Nov. 2, 1942.
Beatty, Jerome. High, Low, Ace and Jane. *American Magazine.* 147:58+, Jan. 1949
Current Biography 1948, pp. 6-8.
Dunning, John. *Tune In Yesterday.* Englewood Cliffs, N.J.: Prentice-Hall, 1976, pp. 175-177.
Easier Aces. *Newsweek.* 31:51-52, Feb. 23, 1948.
Harmon, Jim. *The Great Radio Comedians.* Garden City, N.Y.: Doubleday, 1970, pp. 47-50.
Obit. *Newsweek.* 84:63, Nov. 25, 1974.
Obit. *Time.* 104:65, Nov. 25, 1974.
Wertheim, Arthur F. *Radio Comedy.* N.Y.: Oxford U. Pr., 1979, pp. 189-195.

GERTRUDE BERG

Again, Molly. *Newsweek.* 33:58, April 11, 1949.

Berg, Gertrude. *Molly and Me.* N.Y.: McGraw, 1961.

Birnie, William. Molly Goes Marching On. *American Magazine.* 132:24+, Nov. 1941.

Current Biography 1941, pp. 71-72.

Current Biography 1960, pp. 26-28.

Dunning, John. *Tune In Yesterday.* Englewood Cliffs, N.J.: Prentice-Hall, 1976, pp. 237-240, 294.

Freedman, Morris. The Real Molly Goldberg. *Commentary.* 21:359-364, April 1956.

Gertrude Berg. *New York Times.* Sept. 15, 1966, p. 43.

The Goldbergs. *Newsweek.* 31:75, March 8, 1948.

Harmon, Jim. *The Great Radio Comedians.* Garden City, N.Y.: Doubleday, 1970, pp. 59-63.

The Inescapable Goldbergs. *Time.* 37:55, June 23, 1941.

Liberty's Women. Springfield, Mass.: G & C Merriam, 1980, pp. 29-30.

Life With Molly. *Newsweek.* 33:58, April 11, 1949.

Long, S. Her Family Is Her Fortune. *American Magazine.* 154:108+, Dec. 1952.

Me and Molly. *Time.* 51:50, March 8, 1948.

Mitz, Rick. *The Great TV Sitcom Book.* N.Y.: Richard Marek, 1980, pp. 12-16.

Notable American Women: The Modern Period. Cambridge, Mass.: Belknap Pr. of Harvard U. Pr., 1980, pp. 73-74.

MINERVA PIOUS

Franklin, Joe. *Joe Franklin's Encyclopedia of Comedians.* Secaucus, N.J.: Citadel Press, 1979, p. 255.

Gibbings, D. Of Mrs. Nussbaum. *New York Times.* Oct. 28, 1945, sec. 2, p. 5.

Harmon, Jim. *The Great Radio Comedians.* Garden City, N.Y.: Doubleday, 1970, pp. 170-172.

Lamparski, Richard. *Whatever Became of. . . ? Second Series.* N.Y.: Crown, 1968, pp. 66-7.

Minerva Pious. *New York Times.* March 20, 1979, p. B19.

Wertheim, Arthur F. *Radio Comedy.* N.Y.: Oxford U. Press, 1979, pp. 339-40.

JUDY CANOVA

Crichton, Kyle. Hillbilly Judy. *Collier.* 109:17+, May 16, 1942.

Dunning, John. *Tune In Yesterday.* Englewood Cliffs, N.J.: Prentice-Hall, 1976. p. 336.

Judy Canova Dies. *New York Times.* Aug. 7, 1983, p. 32.

Judy Comes Down the Hill. *Newsweek.* 26:102, Dec. 17, 1945.

Lamparski, Richard. *Whatever Became of. . . ?* N.Y.: Crown, 1967, pp. 130-131.

Obit. *Newsweek.* 102:69, Aug. 22, 1983.

Parish, James Robert. *The Slapstick Queens.* London: Thomas Yoseloff, 1973, pp. 208-227.

MAE WEST

Adair, Gilbert Go West, Old Mae. *Film Comment.* 16:23-24, May/June 1980.

Blond, Buxom, Brazen. *Newsweek.* 33:73, Feb. 14, 1949.

Bretano, Lowell. Between Covers. *Forum and Century.* 93:97-99, Feb. 1935.

Brown, John Mason. Mae Pourquoi. *Saturday Review of Literature*. 32:50+, Oct. 8, 1949.

Catherine Was Great. *Theatre Arts*. 28:575-576, Oct. 1944.

Catherine Was Great. *Life*. 17:71+, Aug. 21, 1944.

Clarke, Gerald. At 84 Mae West Is Still Mae West. *Time*. 111:65-66, May 22, 1978.

Clarke, Gerald. She Was What She Was. *Time*. 116:80, Dec. 1, 1980.

Coffin, Tristam Potter. *The Female Hero in Folklore and Legend*. N.Y.: Seabury Press, 1975, pp. 167-177.

Condon, Frank. Come Up and Meet Mae West. *Colliers*. p. 26+, June 16, 1934.

Current Biography 1967, pp. 455-458.

Diamond Lil. *New Republic*. 55:145+, June 27, 1928.

Diamond Lil. *Commonweal*. 54:595-596, Sept. 28, 1951.

Eells, George. *Mae West*. N.Y.: William Morrow, 1982.

Franklin, Joe. *Joe Franklin's Encyclopedia of Comedians*. Secaucus, N.J.: Citadel Press, 1979, pp. 330-332.

Gibbs, Wolcott. Come Up and See Me Some Time. *New Yorker*. 24:38, Feb. 12, 1949.

Haddad, M. George. My Side. *Working Woman*. 4:88, Feb. 1979.

Hamilton, Jack. Raquel Welch, Mae West. *Look*. 34:46+, March 24, 1970.

Krutch, Joseph Wood. Furtherest West. *Nation*. 159:194, Aug. 12, 1944.

Krutch, Joseph Wood. In Defense of Mae West. *Nation*. 133:344, Sept. 30, 1931.

Lapham, Lewis. Let Me Tell You About Mae West. *Saturday Evening Post*. 237:76+, Nov. 14, 1964.

Lawrenson, Helen. Mirror, Mirror, on the Ceiling. *Esquire*. 68:72+, July 1967.

McCourt, James. Mae West. *Film Comment*. 17:16-17, Jan/Feb 1981.

Mae West. *National Review*. 32:1497, Dec. 12, 1980.

Mae West. *Life*. 26:105+, May 23, 1949.

Mae West Played Only One Great Role. *TV Guide*. *6:3+, May 1, 1982.*

Maltin, Leonard. *The Great Movie Comedians*. N.Y.: Crown, 1970, pp. 153-161.

Meryman, Richard. Mae West. *Life*. 66:60+, April 18, 1969.

The Peeled Grape. *Time*. 74:54, Sept. 28, 1959.

The Return of Mae West. *Newsweek*. 35:46, Jan. 16, 1950.

Roberts, Steven V. 76—And Still Diamond Lil. *New York Times Magazine*. Nov. 2, 1969, pp. 64+.

Shipman, David. *The Great Movie Stars: The Golden Years*. London: Hamlyn, 1971, pp. 557-561.

West, Mae. *Goodness Had Nothing to Do With It* Englewood Cliffs, N.J.: Prentice-Hall, 1959.

What Maisie Knows. *New Republic*. 111:219, Aug. 21, 1944.

Young, Stark. Angels and Ministers of Grace. *New Republic*. 77:73-75, Nov. 28, 1933.

Zinman, David. *50 Classic Motion Pictures*, N.Y.: Crown, 1970, pp. 3-5.

THELMA TODD

Franklin, Joe. *Joe Franklin's Encyclopedia of Comedians*. Secaucus, N.J.: Citadel Press, 1979, pp. 313-314.

Maltin, Leonard. *Great Movie Shorts*. N.Y.: Crown, 1972, pp. 85-91.

Thelma Todd. *Cinema Digest*. Sept. 19, 1932, p. 9.

Thelma Todd. *Films in Review*. 20:128, Feb. 1969.

Thelma Todd. *New York Times*. Dec. 17, 1935, pp. 1, 4.

ZASU PITTS

Crichton, Kyle. Mr. Woodall's Wife. *Colliers*. 97:26+, June 6, 1936.

Crisler, B.R. Random Notes on Pictures and Personalities. *New York Times*. Nov. 29, 1936, sec. 12, p. 5.

Franklin, Joe. *Joe Franklin's Encyclopedia of Comedians*. Secaucus, N.J.: Citadel Pr., 1979, p. 265.

Manning, Maybelle. A Cooking Fool Is ZaSu. *American Home*. 32:93-94, June 1944.

Miss Pitts Minus the Flutters. *New York Times*. Feb. 20, 1944, sec. 2, p. 1.

Notable American Women. Cambridge, Mass.: Belknap Pr. of Harvard U. Pr., 1971, pp. 547-548.

Obit. *Newsweek*. 61:63, June 17, 1963.

Obit. *Time*. 81:65, June 14, 1963.

Pitts, ZaSu. Recognition. *American Magazine*. 138:64, Dec. 1944.

Spensley, Dorothy. The Hands Speak. *Photoplay*. 30:46, Sept. 1926.

Who's Who on the Screen. *New York Times*. May 1, 1932, sec. 8, p. 4.

ZaSu Pitts. *New York Times*. June 8, 1963, p. 25.

PATSY KELLY

And Who Is Patsy Kelly? *New York Times*. Dec. 23, 1928, sec. 8, p. 4.

Crichton, Kyle. Haphazard Patsy. *Colliers*. 97:32+, April 18, 1936.

Crisler, B. R. Patsy Kelly. *New York Times*. June 30, 1937, sec. 10, p. 3.

Franklin, Joe. *Joe Franklin's Encyclopedia of Comedians*. Secaucus, N.J.: Citadel Pr., 1979, p. 187.

Greenbaum, Lucy. Of Bridget Veronica. *New York Times*. Aug. 27, 1944, sec. 2, p. 5.

Irish Eyes Are Smiling. *New York Times*. Oct. 23, 1932. sec. 9, p. 2.

Lamparski, Richard. *Whatever Became of. . . ?* N.Y.: Crown, 1967, pp. 104-105.

Lamparski, Richard. *Whatever Became of. . . ? Eighth Series*. N.Y.: Crown, 1982, pp. 154-155.

Maltin, Leonard. FFM Interviews Patsy Kelly. *Film Fan Monthly*. 117:3-14, Mar. 1971.

Patsy Kelly. *New York Times*. Sept. 26, 1981, p. 28.

Patsy Kelly. *Photoplay*. 49:80, March 1936.

Samuels, Charles. *Once Upon a Stage*. N.Y.: Dodd, Mead, 1974, pp. 181-183.

The 1940's and 1950's

Brooks, Tim. *Complete Directory to Prime Time Network TV Shows*. N.Y.: Ballantine Books, 1979.

Brown, Les. *Les Brown's Encyclopedia of Television*. N.Y.: Zoetrope, 1982.

Mitz, Rick. *The Great TV Sitcom Book*. N.Y.: Richard Marek, 1980.

Terrace, Vincent. *The Complete Encyclopedia of Television Programs, 1947-1979*. N.Y.: Barnes 1979.

CASS DALEY

Campbell, Kay. They Preferred Gaiety to Grandeur. *American Home*. 36:24, Nov. 1946.

Dunning, John. *Tune In Yesterday*. Englewood Cliffs, New Jersey: Prentice-Hall, 1976, pp. 210-211, 216.

Lamparski, Richard. *Whatever Became of. . . ? Fourth Series.* N.Y.: Crown, 1973, pp. 22-23.
Lamparski, Richard. *Whatever Became of. . . ? Eighth Series.* N.Y.: Crown, 1982, pp. 72-73.
Obit. *Newsweek.*. 85:51, April 7, 1975.
Parish, James Robert. *Hollywood Players: The Forties.* New Rochelle, N.Y.: Arlington House, 1976, pp. 170-175.
Speaking of Pictures. *Life.* 10:12-14, March 17, 1941.
Ugly Duckling. *Time.* 47:62, Jan. 28, 1946.

MINNIE PEARL

Cannon, Ophelia Colley. *Minnie Pearl, An Autobiography.* N.Y.: Simon & Schuster, 1980.
Eipper, Laura. Minnie Pearl. *Country Music.* 7:30-32, April 1979.
Thrasher, Sue. The Woman Behind Minnie Pearl. *Southern Exposure.* 2:32-40, Winter 1975.

ANNA RUSSELL

Anna Russell. *Musical Courier.* 152:18, Dec. 15, 1955.
Anna Russell and Her Little Show. *Theatre Arts.* 37:20, Nov. 1953.
Anna Russell's Little Show. *Commonweal.* 58:634, Oct. 2, 1953.
Bernheimer, Martin. A Qualified Goodby from Anna Russell. *Los Angeles Times.* Jan. 22, 1984, pp. 42+, Calendar section.
Comediva. *Time.* 84:50, July 17, 1964.
Craig, Mary. Anna Russell. *Musical Courier.* 158:7, Dec. 1958.
Craig, Mary. Musical Spoofing Raised to Art by Anna Russell. *Musical Courier.* 146:18, July 1952.
Current Biography 1954, pp. 549-551.
Foster, Joseph T. Anna Russell. *High Fidelity Magazine.* 3:55+, Nov/Dec. 1953.
Gibbs, Wolcott. Anna Russell. *New Yorker.* 29:69+, Sept. 19, 1953.
Introducing a Musical Satirist. *Music Clubs Magazine.* 31:7+, Jan. 1952.
Lyons, James. Musicians into Comedians. *Musical America.* 75:26+, Feb. 15, 1955.
Meadmore, W.S. Anna Russell. *Gramaphone.* 32:390+, Feb. 1955.
Rees, C.B. Anna Russell. *Musical Events.* 15:9+, Nov. 1960.
Russell, Anna. Hurricane Anna. *Musical Courier.* 152:8+, Nov. 1, 1955.
Wennerstein, Robert. Making the Suitable Noises. *Performing Arts.* 18:26+, Mar. 1984.
Whoop 'N' Holler Opera. *American Magazine.* 155:55, April 1953.

NANCY WALKER

Broadway Cheers New Comic Star. *Life,* 24:87, Feb. 23, 1948.
Brown, John Mason. Look Ma. *Saturday Review.* 31:26-27, Feb. 21, 1948.
Cadden, Vivian. The Women Who Help Us Laugh at Ourselves. *McCalls.* 103:102+, Oct. 1975.
Current Biography 1965, pp. 441-443.
Hayes, Richard. Nancy Walker. *Commonweal.* 63:543-4, Feb. 24, 1956.
Maney, Richard. Undefeated Walker. *New York Times.* April 4, 1948, sec. 2, p. 2.
Old Plays in Manhattan. *Time.* 67:34, Jan. 30, 1956.

Out of the Basket. *New Yorker*. 31:23-4, June 4, 1955.
Plutzik, Roberta. My Side. *Working Woman*. 5:114, Oct. 1980.
See, Carolyn. Rhoda's Mother Moves Out. *Ms*. 5:70+, Oct. 1976.
Shane, Ted. The Walker Brat. *Colliers*. 121:21+, May 1, 1948.
Walker, Nancy. Bring on the Comedians. *Theatre Arts*. 43:59-60, Oct. 1959.
Waters, Harry. Funny Lady. *Newsweek*. 86:57, Dec. 29, 1975.

CAROL CHANNING

Burns, George. *Living It Up*. N.Y.: G.P. Putnam's Sons, 1976, pp. 97-116.
Carol Channing on "Uniting People" Through Laughter. *U.S. News & World Report*. 86:56, Jan. 29, 1979.
Current Biography 1964, pp. 76-78.
Franklin, Joe. Joe Franklin's Encyclopedia of Comedians. Secaucus, N.J.: Citadel Press, 1979, p. 96.
Gentlemen Prefer blondes. *Life*. 27:68-71, Dec. 26, 1949.
Kaleidoscopic Carol. *Life*. 39:154-5, Nov. 28, 1955.
Keating, John. The Return of Lorelei Lee. *Colliers*. 125:30+, Jan. 7, 1950.
Millstein, Gilbert. Good-bye Lorelei, Hello, Dolly! *Saturday Evening Post*. 237:78-79, Feb. 22, 1964.
New Doll in Town. *Newsweek*. 66:74-5, Aug. 16, 1965.
The Wonderful Leveling Off. *Time*. 55:50-52, Jan. 9, 1950.

JUDY HOLLIDAY

Bird, Virginia. Hollywood's Blond Surprise. *Saturday Evening Post*. 228:26+, Dec. 31, 1955.
Born Recently. *Time*. 60:98, Oct. 6, 1952.
Born Yesterday. *Life*. 20:81+, Feb. 25, 1946.
Born Yesterday. *Newsweek*. 37:57, Jan. 1, 1951.
Bright Girl. *Newsweek*. 65:87, Jun 21, 1965.
Current Biography 1951, pp. 279-281.
Davis, Luther. It's a Living. *Colliers*. 117:15+, June 15, 1946.
Herrman, Helen Markel. Hey-Hey-Day of a "Dumb" Blonde. *New York Times Magazine*. March 4, 1951, p. 16.
Hine, Al. Three Smart Blondes. *Holiday*. 10:6+, Sept. 1951.
Israel, Lee. Judy Holliday. *Ms*. 5:72+, Dec. 1976.
Langner, Lawrence. A Whole Week of Hollidays. *Theatre Arts*. 41:27+, March 1957.
Notable American Women: The Modern Period. Cambridge, Mass.: Belknap Pr. of Harvard U. Pr., 1980, pp. 348-349.
Off on a Holliday. *Newsweek*. 40:38-39, Oct. 6, 1952.
Right Number. *Newsweek*. 55:92-93, June 27, 1960.
Sargeant, Winthrop. Judy Holliday. *Life*. 30:107+, April 2, 1951.

MARTHA RAYE

Allen, Steve. *More Funny People*. N.Y.: Stein and Day, 1982, p. 209+.
Byers, Margery. A New Old Face in 'No, No, Nanette.' *Life*. 73:77, Nov. 10, 1972.
Crichton, Kyle. Girl with a Voice. *Colliers*. 99:15+, May 1, 1937.
Current Biography 1963, pp. 356-357.
A Day's Work. *Time*. 63:70-1, March 1, 1954.

Kent, Leticia. A Mouthful from Martha. *New York Times.* Oct. 29, 1972, sec. 2, pp. 5+.

Muggs and Cupid Put the Bite on Martha in a Busy Week. *Life.* 36:133, May 3, 1954.

Parish, James Robert. *The Slapstick Queens.* London: Thomas Yoseloff, 1973, pp. 96-115.

Russell, Candice. Martha Troupes On. *Biography News.* 1:938, Aug. 1974.

Thomey, Tedd. *The Comedians.* N.Y.: Pyramid, 1970, pp. 176-190.

IMOGENE COCA

Back Together Again. *Newsweek.* 50:87, Aug. 5, 1957.

Burke, Tom. Imogene Coca Hits the Spot. *New York Magazine.* 11:46, March 13, 1978.

Caesar vs. Coca. *Newsweek.* 44:66, Oct. 11, 1954.

Coca, Imogene. How to be an Actress. *Coronet.* 37:50+, April 1955.

Coca, Imogene. I Married Somebody Else's Husband. *Colliers.* 129:22+, Feb. 23, 1952.

The Coca Question. *Newsweek.* 47:73, March 12, 1956.

Crichton, Kyle. Girl with a Funny Face. *Colliers.* 104:12+, Dec. 23, 1939.

Current Biography 1951, pp. 115-117.

Havemann, Ernest. Girl with a Rubber Face. *Life.* 30:53-6+, Feb. 8, 1951.

Lonely Saturday Nights. *Newsweek.* 43:83, Feb. 15, 1954.

Lords of Laughter. *Coronet.* 30:76+, Oct. 1951.

Return of a Talented Trio. *Coronet.* 43:18, April 1958.

Seldes, Gilbert. Comical Gentlewomen. *Saturday Review.* 36:37, May 2, 1953.

Sid and Imogene Go It Alone. *Life.* 37:57+, Oct. 18, 1954.

JOAN DAVIS

Co-op Joan. *Newsweek.* 30:58, Oct. 20, 1947.

Crichton, Kyle. Action. *Colliers.* 102:11+, Oct. 22, 1938.

Current Biography 1945, pp. 138-139.

Dunning, John. *Tune In Yesterday.* Englewood Cliffs, N.J.: Prentice-Hall, 1976, pp. 329-330.

Lucy's TV Sister. *Newsweek.* 40:63, Nov. 3, 1952.

Parish, James Robert. *The Slapstick Queens.* London: Thomas Yoseloff, 1973, pp. 152-174.

Radio Comedienne. *Life.* 19:93-96, Oct. 1, 1945.

LUCILLE BALL

Ager, Cecelia. Desilu, or from Gags to Riches. *New York Times Magazine.* April 20, 1958, p. 32+.

Andrews, Bart. *Loving Lucy.* N.Y.: St. Martin's, 1980.

Ask her Anything. *People.* 13:92+, Feb. 11, 1980.

Beauty into Buffoon. *Life.* 32:93+, Feb. 18, 1952.

Bell, Joseph N. Lucille Ball Remembers. *Good Housekeeping.* 183:118, Nov. 1976.

Berquist, Laura. Lucille Ball, the Star that Never Sets. *Look.* 35:54+, Sept. 7, 1971.

Birmingham, Frederic R. Everybody Loves Lucy. *Saturday Evening Post.* 244:60+, Winter 1972.

Birth of a Memo. *Time.* 61:50-51, Jan. 26, 1953.

Bowers, Ronald L. Lucille Ball. *Films in Review.* 22:321-342, June-July 1971.

Current Biography 1952, pp. 34-37.

Current Biography 1978, pp. 31-35.

Desilu Formula for Top TV. *Newsweek.* 41:56, Jan. 19, 1953.

Gould, Jack. Why Millions Love Lucy. *New York Times Magazine.* March 1, 1953, p. 16.

Grandpa's Girl. *Time.* 62:28, Sept. 21, 1953.

Harris, Eleanor. *The Real Story of Lucille Ball.* N.Y.: Farrar, Straus, 1954.

Hirschberg, Lynn. I Love Lucy. *Rolling Stone.* 398:25+, June 23, 1983.

Israel, Lee. Everybody Still Loves Lucy. *McCall's.* 100:72+, June 1973.

Johnson, Grady. What's the Secret of "I Love Lucy?" *Coronet.* 34:36-42, July 1953.

Krims, Milton. Mame. *Saturday Evening Post.* 246:36+, March 1974.

Lucille Ball. *New Republic.* 129:4, Sept. 28, 1953.

Martin, Pete. I Call on Lucy and Desi. *Saturday Evening Post.* 230:32+, May 31, 1958.

Millstein, Gilbert. Lucy Becomes President. *New York Times Magazine.* Dec. 9, 1962, pp. 36+.

Morella, Joe. *Lucy: the Bittersweet Life of Lucille Ball.* Secaucus N.J.: Lyle Stuart Inc., 1973.

My Favorite Redhead. *Newsweek.* 42:31, Sept. 21, 1953.

The New Tycoon. *Time.* 71:69-70, April 7, 1958.

Parish, James Robert. *The RKO Gals.* New Rochelle, N.Y.: Arlington House, 1974, pp. 393+.

Sassafrassa, the Queen. *Time.* 59:62+, May 26, 1952.

Sher, Jack. The Cuban and the Redhead. *American Magazine.* 154:26+, Sept. 1952.

Thomas, Bob. Lady Millionaire, Hollywood-style. *Good Housekeeping.* 166:50+, June 1968.

Thompson, Thomas. Lucy: Having a Ball at 62. *Ladies Home Journal.* 91:74+, Apr. 1974.

TV Team. *Newsweek.* 39:67, Feb. 18, 1952.

Unaverage Situation. *Time.* 59:73, Feb. 18, 1952.

Velocci, Tony. The Real Lucille Ball. *Nations Business.* 69:75-8, Oct. 1981.

Zolotow, Maurice. Lucille Ball: She Still Has the Comic Touch. *50 Plus.* 21:21+, March, 1981.

EVE ARDEN

"A" stands for Arden. *American Magazine.* 156:59, July 1953.

All About Eve. *New York Times.* Feb. 4, 1951, sec. 2, p. 5.

Best, Katharine. The Story of Even Arden. *McCalls.* 81:42+, Nov. 1953.

Carlile, Thomas. Eve Arden-Teachers' Pet. *Colliers.* 129:20+, Jan. 5, 1952.

Current Biography 1953, pp. 31-33.

Dunning, John. *Tune In Yesterday.* Englewood Cliffs, N.J.: Prentice-Hall, 1976, pp. 461-3.

Franklin, Joe. *Joe Franklin's Encyclopedia of Comedians.* Secaucus, N.J.: Citadel Press, 1979, p. 40.

Mitz, Rick. *The Great TV Sitcom Book.* N.Y.: Richard Marek, 1980, pp. 75-79.

No Competition. *Time.* 68:88+, Oct. 13, 1952.

Shipman, David. *The Great Movie Stars: The International Years.* N.Y.: A&W Visual Library, 1972, pp. 14-17.

MARIE WILSON

Crichton, Kyle. Oh, You Beautiful Blonde. *Colliers.* 123:28+, April 2, 1949.

Dizzy Blonde. *Time.* 50:96, Oct. 20, 1947.

Dunning, John. *Tune In Yesterday.* Englewood Cliffs, N.J.: Prentice-Hall, 1976, pp. 429-430.

Lamparski, Richard. *Whatever Became of. . . ? Third series.* N.Y.: Crown, 1973, pp. 72-3.

Marie Wilson. *Films in Review.* 24:125, Feb. 1973.

Marie Wilson. *New York Times.* Nov. 24, 1972, p. 40.

Marshall, Jim. Little Miss Innocent. *Colliers.* 117:16, Feb. 23, 1946.

Obit. *Newsweek.* 80:55, Dec. 4, 1972.

Obit. *Time.* 100:58, Dec. 4, 1972.

Whitney, Dwight. "My Friend Irma" Is Not So Dumb. *Coronet.* 29:58-62, Nov. 1950.

MOMS MABLEY

Behind the Laughter of Jackie (Moms) Mabley. *Ebony.* 17:88-91, Aug. 1962.

Current Biography 1975, pp. 261-264.

Fox, Ted. *Showtime at the Apollo.* N.Y.: Holt, Rinehart & Winstone, 1983, pp. 96-97.

Foxx, Redd. *The Redd Foxx Encyclopedia of Black Humor.* Pasadena, California: Ward Ritchie Press, 1977, pp. 113, 149, 222-24.

Jacobson, Mark. Amazing Moms. *New York Magazine.* 7:46+, Oct. 14, 1974.

Moms Mabley. *New York Times.* May 24, 1975, p. 26.

Moms Mabley. She Finally Makes the Movies. *Ebony.* 29:86+, April 1974.

Thomas, Barbara. Moms Mabley. *Biography News.* 1:1048, Sept. 1974.

JEAN CARROLL

Smith, Bill. *The Vaudevillians.* N.Y.: Macmillian, 1976, pp. 18-22, 252-259.

TV's Top Comediennes. *New York Times Magazine.* Dec. 27, 1953, p. 17.

KAYE BALLARD

Current Biography 1969, pp. 25-28.

Franklin, Joe. *Joe Franklin's Encyclopedia of Comedians.* Secaucus, N.J.: Citadel Press, 1979, pp. 46-48.

Reed, Rex. Two Hot Mamas in Hot Water. *New York Times.* Sept. 10, 1967, sec. 2, p. 33.

Tables for Two. *The New Yorker.* 33:46, Dec. 21, 1957.

Wilson, John S. Kaye Ballard Is "Home" for a While. *New York Times.* May 1, 1981, p. C12.

PAT CARROLL

Carroll, Pat. Re-creating Stein in Paris. *Horizon.* 23:38+, Nov. 1980.

Current Biography 1980, 35-38.

Kakutani, Michiko. Pat Carroll Pat Carroll Pat Carroll. *New York Times.* Aug. 1, 1979, sec. 3, p. 17.

ELAINE MAY

Baer, Betty. If Mike Can, Elaine May. *Look.* 34:M+, Feb. 10, 1970.

Behind the Lens. *Time.* 99:92, March 20, 1972.

Cotler, Gordon. For the Love of Mike—and Elaine. *New York Times Magazine.* May 24, 1959, pp. 71+.

Current Biography 1961, pp. 300-302.

Fresh Eggheads. *Time.* 71:53-4, June 2, 1958.

Fun with Human Foibles. *Life.* 49:65-6, Nov. 21, 1960.

New Recital on Broadway. *Time.* 76:73, Oct. 24, 1960.

Rice, Robert A. Tilted Insight. *New Yorker.* 37:47+, April 15, 1961.

Success Story. *Newsweek.* 51:64, Jan. 27, 1958.

Thompson, Thomas. Whatever Happened to Elaine May? *Life.* 63:54+, July 28, 1967.

TV Gets Laughs from its Griefs. *Life.* 48:106+, Feb. 15, 1960.

Two Characters in Search. *Time.* 76:61-2, Sept. 26, 1960.

The 1960's to the 1980's

Berger, Phil. The New Comediennes. *New York Times Magazine.* July 29, 1984, pp. 27+.

Bernikow, Louise. Women Comedians. *Mademoiselle.* 87:104-106, December, 1981.

Blakely, Mary Kay. Kate Clinton on the Feminist Comedy Circuit. *Ms.* 13:128, October, 1984.

Carr, Patrick. Comedy's Valley Forge. *New Times.* 10:40-41, January 9, 1978.

Cooper, Arthur. The New Stand-up Comics. *Newsweek.* 85:87-90, April 21, 1975.

Ferretti, Fred. Heard the One About the Female Comic? *New York Times.* March 2, 1981, p. A16.

Handy, Bruce. Funny Women. *Vogue.* 174:74, February 1984.

Hoffman, Jan. She Who Laughs Last. *Village Voice.* 26:1+, September 9-15, 1981.

Katz, Debra. Women Who Get the Last Laugh. *McCalls.* 110:62, March, 1983.

Klein, Julia. The New Stand-up Comics. *Ms.* 13:116+, October, 1984.

Klein, Stewart. The Queens of Comedy. *Harper's Bazaar.* 116:166+, August, 1983.

McGuigan, Cathleen and Huck, Janet. The New Queens of Comedy. *Newsweek.* 103:58-59, August 30, 1984.

Nietzke, Ann. Hostility on the Laugh Track. *Human Behavior.* 3:64-70, May 1974.

Prime Mime. *Playboy.* 29:93+, August 1982,

Quindlen, Anna. Women Comics Get the Last Laugh. *New York Times.* March 11, 1977, p. C12.

Shepherd, Richard F. "Last Stands Are Turning into New Lease on Life" *New York Times.* May 28, 1974, p. 41.

Stabiner, Karen. The Belly Room Presented Comediennes. *Mother Jones.* 4:45-49, July 1979.

Trillin, Calvin. Not Funny. *New Yorker.* 55:72-77, Jan. 7, 1980.

Wolmuth, Roger. Inside Comedy. *People.* 22:96+, August 13, 1984.

Young, Tracy. Comedy is the New Rock. *New Times.* 10:46-48, Jan. 9, 1978.

TOTIE FIELDS

Franklin, Joe. *Joe Franklin's Encyclopedia of Comedians.* Secaucus, N.J.: Citadel Press, 1979, pp. 129-130.

Fraser, C. Gerald. Totie Fields Dead. *New York Times.* August 3, 1978, p. B2.

The Happy Courage of Totie Fields, *Ladies Home Journal, 94:68+, May 1977.*

Higgins, Robert. Everyone's Favorite Size 44. *TV Guide.* 17:32-33, Jan. 4, 1969.

Lee, Shirley. Totie Fields: Everyone's Got to Cry. *Coronet.* 75:110-117, June 1977.

Lewis, Grover. Totie Fields Is Back on Her Foot Again, *New West.* 2:59-61, May 23, 1977.

Obit, *Newsweek.* 92:42, August 14, 1978.

Obit, *Time.* 112:74, August 14, 1978.

Taylor, Andy. I Didn't Lose My Talent. *People.* 7:28-29, March 21, 1977.

ANNE MEARA

Kanner, Bernice. Two for the Radio. *New York Magazine.* 16:16+, April 11, 1983.

Murphy, Mary. Meara Image. *TV Guide.* 4:2-5, March 15, 1980.

Phillips, B.J. Prime Time Comes of Age With Anne Meara. *Ms.* 4:62+, November 1975.

Richards, David. Stiller and Meara. *Biography News.* 2:201, Feb. 1975.

Waters, Harry F. Nun So Funny. *Newsweek.* 85:47-48, March 3, 1975.

CAROL BURNETT

Armstrong, Lois. Here Today, Gone to Maui. *People.* 17:86+, March 22, 1982.

Battelle, Phyllis. Carol Burnett. *Ladies Home Journal.* 100:26+, August 1983.

Birmingham, Frederic. A Carol Is a Song Is a Burnett. *Saturday Evening Post.* 248:54+, September 1976.

Boeth, Richard. On Stage: Carol Burnett. *Horizon.* 4:80, Sept., 1961.

Brookey, Harold. Why Is This Woman Funny? *Esquire.* 77:122+, June 1972.

Burnett, Carol. To Make Music in the Heart. *Good Housekeeping. 171:69+, Dec. 1970.*

Carol the Clown. *Time.* 79:56, June 22, 1962.

Current Biography 1962, pp. 64-66.

Downs, Joan. Here's to You, Mrs. Hamilton. *Life.* 70:92+, May 14, 1971.

Dworkin, Susan. Carol Burnett Getting On with It, *Ms.* 12:43+, Sept. 1983.

Ebert, Alan. Carol Burnett. *Ladies Home Journal.* 93:46+, Dec. 1976.

Garvin, Ann. Carol Burnett. *Good Housekeeping.* 151:34+, Nov. 1960.

Havemann, Ernest. The Only Girl Who Acts with her Back. *Life.* 54:84+, Feb. 22, 1963.

Hochstein, Rollie. The One Big Battle I Had to Win. *Good Housekeeping.* 156:87, May 1963.

Hoover, Eleanor. With a Long Postponed Trip to the Dentist. *People.* 20:75, July 4, 1983.

Horowitz, Susan. Carol Burnett Gets a Kick out of *Annie. American Film.* 7:46+, May 1982.

Janos, Leo. Funny Thing Happened. *McCall's.* 103:69+, June 1976.

Kroll, Jack. Altman's Wedding Day. *Newsweek.* 92:109, Sept. 25, 1978.

A Love Song to Mr. Dulles. *Life.* 43:99, Aug. 19, 1957.

Martin, Pete. Backstage with Carol Burnett. *Saturday Evening Post.* 235:36+, March 10, 1962.

Meryman, Richard. Carol Burnett's Own Story. *McCall's.* 105:126+, Feb. 1978.

Nichols, Mark. I.O.U. to Success. *Coronet.* 49:14, March 1961.

Nightingale, Suzan. She Chose to Make People Laugh. *TV Guide.* 6:17+, March, 13, 1982.

Scott, Vernon. As Life Unfolds Burnett's Just Having a Ball, *Vancouver Sun.* Jan. 12, 1984, p. D5.

Stewart-Gordon, James. The Human Cyclone Called Carol. *Reader's Digest.* 100:142-146, Feb. 1972.

Stuart, Neal G. The Life, Love and Laughter of Carol Burnett. *Ladies Home Journal.* 80:72+, April 1963.

Thompson, Thomas. The Unknown Carol Burnett. *Good Housekeeping.* 180:73+, Feb. 1975.

Waters, Harry F. TV: Laughing All the Way. *Newsweek.* 83:62+, Jan. 21, 1974.

Weller, Sheila. The Two Faces of Carol Burnett. *McCalls.* 109:54+, April 1982.

PHYLLIS DILLER

Blumenthal, Amy. Late Bloomer Phyllis a Funny Flower. *Vancouver Sun.* Oct. 10, 1984.

Current Biography 1967, pp. 98-100.

Collier, Denise. *Spare Ribs: Women in the Humor Biz.* N.Y.: St. Martin's Press, 1980, pp. 1-6.

Gardner, Paul. Is TV Ready for Phyllis Diller? *New York Times.* Dec. 13, 1964, p. 15.

Killer Diller, *Time.* 77:56+, March 24, 1961.

Klemesrud, Judy. A Centerfold for Laughing, Not Leering. *New York Times.* May 25, 1973, p. 41.

Nemy, Enid. People Think I Dress Funny, *New York Times.* Aug. 12, 1965, p. 17.

Parish, James Robert. *The Slapstick Queens.* London: Thomas Yoseloff, 1973, pp. 260-275.

"Phyllis Diller," *New York Times.* Aug. 27, 1976, p. 16.

Phyllis Diller Tells One About a Facelift—Hers. *Life.* 72:73, Feb. 11, 1972.

A Redbook Dialogue. *Redbook.* 129:58+, May 1967.

Reddy, John. TV's Killer Diller. *Reader's Digest.* 89:90-94, Nov. 1966.

Rubber-faced Comic. *Life.* 54:57-60, May 17, 1963.

Zolotow, Maurice. The Two Lives of Phyllis Diller. *50 Plus.* 19:12+, July 1979.

JOAN RIVERS

Adler, Jerry. Joan Rivers Gets Even with Laughs. *Newsweek.* 102:58+, Oct. 10, 1983.

Bell, Arthur. Bell Tells. *Village Voice.* 28:36, March 1, 1983.

Clarke, Gerald. Barbs for the Queen. *Time.* 121:85+, April 11, 1983.

Collier, Denise. *Spare Ribs: Women in the Humor Biz.* N.Y.: St. Martin's Press, 1980, pp. 6-11.

Collins, Nancy. Funniest Lady. *People.* 19:90+, April 25, 1983.

Current Biography 1970, pp. 352-354.

Dykk, Lloyd. A Vengeance on Bad Taste. *Vancouver Sun.* Dec. 11, 1983.

Gill, Brendan. Unhelpful Friends. *New Yorker.* 47:63, Jan. 8, 1972.

Hot Potato, *Time.* 88:61+, Oct. 21, 1966.

Israel, Lee. Joan Rivers and How She Got That Way. *Ms.* 13:108+, Oct. 1984.

Jahr, Cliff. No Kidding, Joan Rivers Is the Queen of Comedy. *Ladies Home Journal.* 100:86+, Nov. 1983.

Joan Rivers. *People.* 20:49, Jan. 2, 1984.

Keyes, John. Can She Talk? Are You Kidding. *TV Guide.* Oct. 27, 1984, pp. 2+.

MacVicar, Bill. She For Whom Nothing Is Sacred, *Globe and Mail.* Dec. 13, 1983, p. 16.

Manville, W.H. Who Are You, Joan? *Saturday Evening Post.* 240:67+, July 1, 1967.

Mee, Charles L. Jr. For Joan the Woe Must Go On. *New York Times Magazine.* Oct. 31, 1965, pp. 137+.

Meryman, Richard. Can We Talk. *McCalls.* 110:61, Sept. 1983.

Meryman, Richard. Directing Her First Movie. *People.* 9:44+, Jan. 9, 1978.

Movies. *Playboy.* 25:24+, May 1978.

Rampaging Rivers. *Newsweek.* 73:72, April 28, 1969.

Rivers, Joan. I'm Glad I'm a Middle-Aged Sex Object. *McCalls's.* 99:78+, Oct. 1971.

Thompson, Thomas. Why Are You Laughing Wilma? *Life.* 70:69+, Jan. 8, 1971.

20 Questions: Joan Rivers, *Playboy.* 28:149+, Aug. 1981.

Vile Bodies, *Village Voice.* 23:53, April 10, 1983.

Wolcott, James. I Know Why the Caged Bird Kvetches. *New York Magazine.* 16:51-52, Jan. 24, 1983.

GOLDIE HAWN

Ansen, David. The Great Goldie Rush. *Newsweek.* 97:52+, Jan. 12, 1981.

Armstrong, Lois. Off the Screen. *People.* 9:82+, March 6, 1978.

Burke, Tom. The Goldie Risk. *McCalls.* 97:81+, Oct. 1969.

Current Biography 1971, pp. 183-185.

Davis, Gwen. Goldie Hawn. *McCalls.* 164:62+, Oct. 1976.

Davis, Gwen. Why Goldie Hawn Is Smiling Again. *McCalls.* 105:28+, June 1978.

Fury, Kathleen D. All That Glitters Is Really Goldie. *Redbook.* 140:10+, Jan. 1973.

Goldie Hawn. *People.* 14:26-27, Dec. 29, 1980—Jan. 5, 1981.

Grobel, Lawrence. Playboy Interview: Goldie Hawn. *Playboy.* 32:71+, January, 1985.

Haddad-Garcia, George. My Side. *Working Woman.* 5:80, Aug. 1980.

Haddad-Garcia, George. Goldie Hawn Has the Last Laugh. *Saturday Evening Post.* 253:66+, May/June 1981.

Hammer, Joshua. Screen. *People.* 21:187+, May 7, 1984.

How Golden to Be Goldie, *Life.* 68:76-79, June 26, 1970.

Miller, Edwin. Pure Goldie. *Seventeen.* 40:180+, May 1981.

The Rabbit Bites and the Dogs Don't, *TV Guide.* 6:2+, May 8, 1982.

Robbins, Fred. The Darker Side of a Sunny Star." *McCalls.* 128:28+, April 1981.

Rollin, Betty. Goofy Little Goldie. *Look.* 33:75-76+, Dec. 2, 1969.

Ross, Shelly. Goldie Hawn. *McCalls.* 111:66+, Oct. 1983.

Thomson, David. Goldie Gets Serious. *Film Comment.* 18:49-55, Nov.-Dec. 1982.

White, Timothy. Private Goldie. *Rolling Stone.* March 5, 1981, pp. 18-21+.

Wilkie, Jane. Goldie Hawn. *Good Housekeeping.* 172:54-6+, May 1971.

Coombes, Al. Goldie Hawn's Heartbreak Choice. *Ladies Home Journal.* 99:22+, Jan. 1982.

Scott, Jay. Goldie Sinks to New Low. *Globe and Mail.* Dec. 24, 1984, p. 12.

RUTH BUZZI

Berkvist, Robert. No girl Wants to Schlump Forever. *New York Times*. April 13, 1969, sec. 2, p. 19.

Cooper, Cordell. Ruth Buzzi. *Coronet*. 15:16-23, Feb. 1977.

The Girls from L-I, *Newsweek*. 73:62, Jan. 27, 1969.

Whitney, Dwight. Life Has Not Been Kind to Gladys Ormphby. *TV Guide*. 17:14-17, Aug. 2, 1969.

Zolotow, Maurice. So She Put the African Violets in the Bathroom. *TV Guide*. *20:38+, June 3, 1972.*

LILY TOMLIN

Allen, Steve. *Funny People*. N.Y.: Stein and Day, 1981, pp. 271-280.

Bernikow, Louise. Excuse Me Do You Know Who Lily Tomlin Is? *Playboy*. 23:92+, July 1976.

Cohn, Ellen. Lily Tomlim. *New York Times Magazine*. June 6, 1976, pp. 39+.

Corliss, Richard. Sanforized. *Time*. 117:110, Feb. 23, 1981.

Current Biography 1973, pp. 415-417.

Davis, Sally Ogle. Why They Let the Travolta-Tomlin Turkey Out of the Bag, *Los Angeles*. 24:112+, Feb. 1979.

Earley, Sandra. Lily Tomlin. *People*. 6:24-25, Nov. 29, 1976.

Felton, David. Backstage with Lily Tomlin. *Rolling Stone*. April 7, 1977, pp. 11+.

The First Notebook in Lily Tomlin's Life. *Ms*. 5:51-52, Dec. 1976.

Hooked into Lily. *Time*. 100:62, Oct. 2, 1972.

Isler, Scott. Where Town Meets Country. *Crawdaddy*. Feb. 1978, p. 74.

Israel, Lee. Lily Tomlin. *Ms*. 2:46+, Jan. 1974.

Jahr, Cliff. What It was Like Making their Big Movie Together. *Glamour*. 79:136+, Feb. 1981.

Judge, Diane. Talking with Lily Tomlin. *Redbook*. 156:14+, Jan. 1981.

Kazan, Nick. Lily Tomlin Takes Her Chances. *Village Voice*. 20:88, Feb. 24, 1975.

Kroll, Jack. Funny Lady. *Newsweek*. 89:62-66, March 28, 1977.

Lily. *Time*. 109:68+, March 28, 1977.

Lily Tomlin. *People*. 8:60+, Dec. 26/Jan. 2, 1978.

Lily Tomlin: Appearing Nitely. *Stereo Review*. 40:120, Jan. 1978.

Lily Tomlin at the Circus. *New Yorker*. 47:33-34, April 10, 1971.

Michener, Charles. Lily's World. *Newsweek*. 79:91, April 17, 1972.

Robinson, Jill. A Bunch of Lily. *Vogue*. 167:148, June 1977.

Scott, Jay. All of Them. *Globe and Mail*. Sept. 8, 1984, p. E1.

Sragow, Michael. One True Vision, One Tired Joke. *Rolling Stone*. March 19, 1981, p. 45.

Stone, Elizabeth. Understanding Lily Tomlin. *Psychology Today*. 11:14+, July 1977.

Weiss, Paulette. Carly, Dolly, and Lily. *Stereo Review*. 39:54, August 1977.

Wetzsteon, Ross. Lily Tomlin: Funny You Don't Look Hostile. *Village Voice*. 22:71, April 4, 1977.

Young, Tracy. Lily Tomlin, Live, Knocks 'Em Dead. *Village Voice*. 20:129+, Nov. 3, 1975.

GILDA RADNER

Blount, Roy Jr. The Many Faces of Gilda. *Rolling Stone*. Nov. 2, 1978, p. 45.

Collier, Denise. *Spare Ribs: Women in the Humor Biz.* N.Y.: St. Martin's Press, 1980, pp. 130-140.

Current Biography 1980, pp. 327-329.

Gilda Radner: Live from New York, *New York Magazine.* 12:901, Aug. 27, 1979.

Gilda Radner Up to Her Old "Hanky Panky," *Rolling Stone.* June 24, 1982, p. 23.

Gilding the Lily, *Newsweek.* 94:68, Aug. 13, 1979.

Gill, Brendan. Gilda Radner. *New Yorker.* 55:62, Aug. 13, 1979.

Miller, Edwin. Gilda Update. *Seventeen.* 40:98-99+, Jan. 1981.

Orth, Maureen. Gilda on Broadway. *New York Magazine.* 12:54+, Aug. 6, 1979.

Radner, Gilda. Live! From Adolescence! *Crawdaddy.* March 1978, pp. 30+.

Rosen, Diane. My Side. *Working Woman.* 4:80, Jan. 1979.

Stone, Elizabeth. Gilda Radner. *New York Times Magazine.* Nov. 9, 1980, pp. 42-43+.

Vespa, Mary. Every Night Is Saturday Night. *People.* 12:69-70, Aug. 27, 1979.

Wolfson, Cynthia. Gilda Grows Up. *Globe and Mail.* July 28, 1984.

ANDREA MARTIN

Blanks, Tim. The Enigmatic Andrea Martin. *Closeup.* 2:47, 1983.

Brown, Ian. The Comic Triumph of SCTV. *Maclean's.* 95:28+, Dec. 27, 1982.

Collier, Denise. *Spare Ribs: Women in the Humor Biz.* N.Y.: St. Martin's Press, 1980, pp. 210-222.

20 Questions: SCTV. *Playboy.* 29:145+, May 1982.

Waters, Harry. Midnight Laughs in a New Key. *Newsweek.* 97:83-4, March 30, 1981.

BETTE MIDLER

Bette Midler. *Nation.* 220:605-606, May 17, 1975.

Bette's Back. *Newsweek.* 85:85, April 28, 1975.

Chambers, Andrea. Midler Has Been the Bette Noire of Showbiz. *People.* 20:115-118, Nov. 14, 1983.

Clarke, Gerald. Midler: "Make Me a Legend." *Time.* 114:69, Dec. 31, 1979.

Collins, Nancy. Bette Midler. *Rolling Stone.* Dec. 9, 1982, pp. 5+.

Current Biography 1973, pp. 294-296.

Graustark, Barbara. Talking with Bette Midler, *Redbook.* 159:6+, July 1982.

Hoge, Warren. Bette Midler Goes Hollywood. *New York Times Magazine.* Dec. 10, 1978, pp. 52+.

Merla, Patrick. The Merging of Pop and Rock. *Saturday Review of the Arts.* 1:54, Jan. 1973.

Michener, Charles. Bette Midler. *Newsweek.* 82:62+, Dec. 17, 1973.

Michener, Charles. The Divine Miss M. *Newsweek.* 79:76, May 22, 1972.

Poirier, Richard. Mass Appeal. *New Republic.* 173:25-28, Aug. 2&9, 1975.

Safran, Claire. Who Is Bette Midler? *Redbook.* 145:54+, Aug. 1975.

Screen. *People.* 13:52-55, Jan. 7, 1980.

Shalit, Gene. What's Happening. *Ladies Home Journal.* 97:30+, Feb. 1980.

A Star Is Reborn, *Maclean's.* 92:66-67, Nov. 19, 1975.

Steinem, Gloria. Our Best Bette. *Ms.* 12:41+, Dec. 1983.

Trash with Flash. *Time.* 102:62, Sept. 10, 1973.

Willis, Ellen. Believing Bette Midler Mostly. *New Yorker.* 49:61-62, Dec. 24, 1973.

MADELINE KAHN

Berkvist, Robert. "Woses Are Wed, Madeline's Wow," *New York Times*. March 24, 1974, sec. 2, p. 13.

Considine, Shaun. High Anxiety. *People*. 9:121-22, May 15, 1978.

Considine, Shaun. The Kaleidoscopic Madeline Kahn. *After Dark*. 6:32-35, July 1973.

Current Biography 1977, pp. 239-243.

Goldstein, Robert. Madeline Kahn of Manhattan. *People*. 20:61-62, July 25, 1983.

Kearns, Michael. Madeline Kahn Meets the Demands. *Drama-Logue*. April 12-18, 1984, p. 15.

Miller, Edwin. 3 Zings to Make a Zap. *Seventeen*. *R35:118+, Feb. 1976.*

Orth, Maureen. How to Succeed: Fail, Lose, Die. *Newsweek*. 83:50, March 4, 1974.

SUZANNE RAND

Clarke, Gerald. Telepathic Wit. *Time*. 112:65, Aug. 28, 1978.

Collier, Denise. *Spare Ribs: Women in the Humor Biz*. N.Y.: St. Martin's Press, 1980, p. 36-49.

Donovan, Mark. On Stage. *People*. 10:73-75, Oct. 23, 1978.

Gill, Brendan. Occasions for Laughter. *New Yorker*. 54:88, Jan. 15, 1979.

Holland, Jack. Monteith and Rand. *Drama-Logue*. May 10-16, 1984, p. 6.

Monteith and Rand. *New Republic*. 180:24-25, Jan. 27, 1979.

Schwartz, Tony. Fun Couple. *Newsweek*. 92:60, Aug. 28, 1978.

Simon, John. No Teeth and Bland. *New York Magazine*. 12:62, Jan. 22, 1979.

MARILYN SOKOL

Collier, Denise. *Spare Ribs: Women in the Humor Biz*. N.Y.: St. Martin's Press, 1980, pp. 104-114.

Stern, Ellen. Suddenly It's Sokol, *New York Magazine*. 10:88, Oct. 24, 1977.

Weller, Sheila. Can Marilyn Sokol Find Guilt without Sex. *Ms*. 7:31-33, Aug. 1978.

ZORA RASMUSSEN

Boyd, Blanche. Bi Bi Zora. *Village Voice*. 24:55, Jan. 1, 1979.

Collier, Denise. *Spare Ribs: Women in the Humor Biz*. N.Y.: St. Martin's Press, 1980, pp. 12-20.

Kushner, Trucia. Zora Says "Cheese." *New Times*. 10:44-45, Jan. 9, 1978.

Musto, Michael. Thus Spake Zora Rasmussen. *After Dark*. 11:42-43, Dec. 1978.

ELAYNE BOOSLER

Elayne Boosler: Stand-Up Comic. *Mademoiselle*. 82:183, Sept. 1976.

Jacobson, Mark. Funny Girl: New, Hot, Hip. *New York Magazine*. 9:32-36, March 22, 1976.

Quindlen, Anna. Elayne Boosler Cuts Up at Pace, *New York Times*. Oct. 12, 1979, sec. 3, p. 11.

SANDRA BERNHARD

Bacchus, Lee. Feverish Comedy. *Sun* (Vancouver). Feb. 28, 1984, p. B7.

Conway, James. It All Tastes So Good. *Sun* (Vancouver). Jan. 31, 1984, p. B10.

Hutchings, David. Ask No More for a Manicure by Sandra Bernhard. *People*. 20:49-50, March 7, 1983.

Reid, Michael D. Here Comes the Queen of Comedy. *Times-Colonist* (Victoria). Feb. 23, 1984, p. C8.

Stone, Laurie. Pretty Poison. *Village Voice*. 28:117, Oct. 18, 1983.

Wadler, Joyce. Hi, I'm Sandra Bernhard. *New York Magazine*. 16:36-39, Feb. 21, 1983.

LIZ TORRES

Freeman, Don. We Wanted a Funny, Tough, Strong-Minded, Independent, Contemporary Lady, *TV Guide*. 24:14+, April 3, 1976.

Swisher, Viola. the Latin Lunacy of Liz Torres. *After Dark*. 9:34-36, April 1977.

Weller, Sheila. Liz Torres. *Ms*. 6:29-31, Aug. 1977.

MARSHA WARFIELD

Marsha Warfield. *Ebony*. 37:40, June 1982.

Marsha Warfield. *People*. 13:108, March 3, 1980.

Who Will Succeed Moms Mabley as Top X-Rated Comedienne? *Jet*. 57:60-61, Nov. 15, 1979.

WHOOPI GOLDBERG

Coleman, Janet. Making Whoopi. *Vanity Fair*. 47:36+, July 1984.

Dworkin, Susan. Whoopi Goldberg. *Ms*. 20:12, May 1984.

Gussow, Mel. Whoopi as Actress, Clown and Social Critic. *New York Times*. Oct. 28, 1984, sec. 2, p. 5.

McGuigan, Cathleen. The Whoopi Goldberg Comedy Show. *Newsweek*. 103:63, March 5, 1984.

Nemy, Enid. Whoopi's Ready, but Is Broadway, *New York Times*. Oct. 21, 1984, sec. 2, pp. 1, 4.

Rich, Frank. "Stage: Whoopi Goldberg Opens," *New York Times*. Oct. 25, 1984, p. C17.

Whoopi Goldberg. *People*. 21:70, May 28, 1984.

ROBIN TYLER

Alverio, Anita D. Robin Tyler Turns Political Views into Laughs. *New Directions for Women*. 11:11, May 1982.

Edwards, Val. Robin Tyler. *Body Politics*. 56:21-23, Sept. 1979.

Gordon, Suzanne. The First Feminist Comedy Team. *Ms*. 1:26-27, March 1973.

Kaufman, Gloria (ed.) *Pulling Your Own Strings*. Bloomington: Indiana Univ. Press, 1980.

Koblin, Helen. Harrison and Tyler: Take Two. *Ms*. 2:116-117, Nov. 1973.

Lesh, Cheri. Robin Tyler. *Lesbian Tide*. 8:81, Sept. 1978.

Robin Tyler, *Lesbian Tide*. 8:8-9, Nov. 1978.

Robin Tyler, *Women's Press*. 11:14, May 1981.